The Experience of Human Communication

The Fairleigh Dickinson University Press Series in Communication Studies

General Editor: Gary Radford, Department of Communication Studies, Fairleigh Dickinson University, Madison, New Jersey.

The Fairleigh Dickinson University Press Series in Communication Studies publishes scholarly works in communication theory, practice, history, and culture.

Recent Publications in Communication Studies

Frank J. Macke, *The Experience of Human Communication* (2015)

Phil Rose, *Roger Waters and Pink Floyd* (2015)

Ronald C. Arnett and Pat Arneson (eds.), *Philosophy of Communication Ethics: Alterity and the Other* (2014)

Pat Arneson, *Communicative Engagement and Social Liberation: Justice Will Be Made* (2014)

Erik A. Garrett, *Why Do We Go to the Zoo?: Communication, Animals, and the Cultural-Historical Experience of Zoos* (2013)

Philip Dalton and Eric Kramer, *Coarseness in U.S. Public Communication* (2012)

Catherine Creede, Beth Fisher-Yoshida, and Placida Gallegos (eds.), *The Reflective, Facilitative, and Interpretive Practices of the Coordinated Management of Meaning* (2012)

Jolanta Aritz and Robyn C. Walker, *Discourse Perspectives on Organizational Communication* (2011)

S. Alyssa Groom and J. M. H. Fritz, *Communication Ethics and Crisis: Negotiating Differences in Public and Private Spheres* (2011)

R. C. MacDougall, *Digination: Identity, Organization, and Public Life* (2011)

Deborah Eicher-Catt and Isaac E. Catt (eds.), *Communicology: The New Science of Embodied Discourse* (2010)

Dan Cassino and Yesamin Besen-Cassino, *Consuming Politics: Jon Stewart, Branding, and the Youth Vote in America* (2009)

On the Web at http://www.fdu.edu/fdupress

The Experience of Human Communication

Body, Flesh, and Relationship

Frank J. Macke

FAIRLEIGH DICKINSON UNIVERSITY PRESS
Madison • Teaneck

Published by Fairleigh Dickinson University Press
Copublished by The Rowman & Littlefield Publishing Group, Inc.
4501 Forbes Boulevard, Suite 200, Lanham, Maryland 20706
www.rowman.com

Unit A, Whitacre Mews, 26-34 Stannary Street, London SE11 4AB

British Library Cataloguing in Publication Information Available

Library of Congress Cataloging-in-Publication Data

Macke, Frank J.
The experience of human communication : body, flesh, and relationship / Frank J. Macke.
pages cm. -- (The Fairleigh Dickinson University Press series in communication studies)
Includes bibliographical references and index.
ISBN 978-1-61147-548-7 (cloth : alk. paper) -- ISBN 978-1-61147-549-4 (electronic)
1. Communication. 2. Communication--Philosophy. 3. Interpersonal communication--Philosophy. I. Title.
P90.M136 2015
153.6--dc23
2014039995

∞™ The paper used in this publication meets the minimum requirements of American National Standard for Information Sciences Permanence of Paper for Printed Library Materials, ANSI/NISO Z39.48-1992.

Printed in the United States of America

I dedicate this book to Marian Zielinski, my one true love.

Contents

Acknowledgments ix

1 Introduction: The Experience of Human Communication as a Threshold of Relational Consciousness 1

2 Therapy, Vulnerability, and Feeling in the Interstices of Embodied Expression: An Explication of Human Communicative Experience 31

3 The Mirrored Body: Phenomenological Reflections on the Visual Experience of the Reflected Self 53

4 On Contact: The Phatic Function of Communication 71

5 Body, Liquidity, and Flesh: Bachelard, Merleau-Ponty, and the Elements of Interpersonal Communication 81

6 The Diabolical Parable and the Devil in Speech 103

7 Identity, Intimacy, and Eroticism: Deception, Sin, and the Existential Bargain of Adolescent Embodiment 119

8 An Archaeology of Gender Symbols and a Theory of Communication 139

9 The Flesh of Human Communicative Embodiment and the Game of Intimacy 167

10 The Dream and the Self: Consciousness, Identity, the Sign, and the Image 187

11 Conclusion: The Dawning of Communicology 207

References 225

Index 237

Acknowledgments

I want to acknowledge the encouragement I received from Gary Radford, the series editor at Fairleigh Dickinson University Press, whose enthusiasm and patience became so vitally important to me at various points in the completion of this manuscript. Everyone who worked and interacted with me, both at Fairleigh Dickenson University Press and at Rowman & Littlefield, has exhibited nothing but kindness, professionalism, and a clear dedication to literary excellence.

I owe a debt of gratitude to Mercer University's College of Liberal Arts in granting me the sabbatical time, release time, and professional support necessary to make this book a reality. The sabbatical time in 2005–2006 and 2013 made it possible for me to focus my creative energies on a level of writing and research I could never have otherwise undertaken. As well, the funds Mercer provided for professional indexing have helped to transform this text into a much higher quality and much more useful academic resource for both students and research scholars alike.

I also wish to acknowledge all of my teachers, colleagues, and friends in the International Communicology Institute. The Biennial Workshops and Symposia, started in the summer of 2000, have been a magnificent opportunity to launch new ideas, to refine works in progress, and to listen to brilliant minds addressing problematics in communication and culture, working with cutting edge theory grounded in Continental philosophy, phenomenology, existentialism, semiotics, and pragmatism. It is through these workshops and symposia that the intellectual history of Communicology, the human science of embodied discourse, has found its existential location and is philosophical voice.

I gratefully acknowledge the editor of *The American Journal of Semiotics* for granting permission to reprint the following articles: "An Archaeology of

Gender and a Theory of Communication." *The American Journal of Semiotics* 17 (No. 2, Summer 2001): 201–38. "A Semiotic Phenomenology of 'Contact': The Phatic Function of Body and Flesh in Jakobson's Model of Communication." *The American Journal of Semiotics* 27, 1–4 (2011): 81–94.

I also gratefully acknowledge Brill Publishing Group (Koninklijke Brill NV) and the editor of the *Journal of Phenomenological Psychology* for granting permission to reprint the following articles: "Seeing Oneself in the Mirror: Phenomenological Reflections on the Visual Experience of the Reflected Self." *Journal of Phenomenological Psychology* 36 (No. 1, 2005): 21–43. "Sexuality and Parrhesia in the Phenomenology of Psychological Development: The Flesh of Human Communicative Embodiment and the Game of Intimacy." *The Journal of Phenomenological Psychology* 38 (No. 2, 2007): 157–80.

Finally, I gratefully acknowledge the editor of *Philosophy Today* and DePaul University for granting permission to reprint the following article: "Body, Liquidity, and Flesh: Bachelard, Merleau-Ponty, and the Elements of Interpersonal Communication." *Philosophy Today* 51 (No. 4, 2007): pp. 401–15.

Chapter One

Introduction

The Experience of Human Communication as a Threshold of Relational Consciousness

THE PHILOSOPHICAL TASK OF COMMUNICOLOGY AND THE LIMITATIONS OF TWENTIETH CENTURY DISCIPLINARY WORK IN THE SOCIAL SCIENCES

It would, I think, be a fair statement that I entered the academic field of communication, speech, and rhetoric with a certain amount of skepticism. I did not take a course examining the theory of human communication until I was well into my doctoral program. Unlike a number of my colleagues who entered the field of communication as undergraduates (and who then began graduate studies with a strong sense of what the field of communication was "all about" and what sort of research best suited its scholarly and pedagogical missions), I chose political science as my major course of study. Even after several years of graduate study, I was not at all clear about what the parameters of all that is, or ought to be, included under the label "communicative experience."

I completed my doctoral studies at the time when the oldest and largest national academic organization of teachers and scholars in the areas of speech, rhetoric, and communication was debating the virtue of changing its name from the "Speech Communication Association" to the "National Communication Association." At the time, the terms of dispute concerned matters of semantic currency in research nomenclature—in fact, matters of professional conformity—rather than any sort of epistemological or ontological reflection on what *communication* means or why it is, in both its active and historical essence, a word better suited to its disciplinary work than "speech" or "rhetoric." That level of self-reflectiveness has not exactly been characteristic of the communication field, at least as reflected by the published writing in its leading journals over the last half-century (not to mention the textbooks written primarily for undergraduate students).

In this introduction, I seek, essentially, the answer to two closely related questions: First, what *is* communicative experience? And second: how do we know when we have communicated?—How do we know when communication has taken place? The long-standing truism emanated from Paul Watzlawick and the Palo Alto Group, that "we cannot *not* communicate" no longer works for communicology.[1] It has primarily functioned through the last decades as a postponement. By saying that *everything* that happens between persons, whether intentional or unintentional, conscious or unconscious—and at any distance—is a communicative experience, the concept of communication is not merely degraded, it is entirely devalued as a mode of human experience; it is reduced to its lowest common denominator in information theory, becoming no different from any act of animal/animated consciousness. I will attempt to move beyond the information-theoretic discourse of technocratic empiricism that, thus far, has created a century of confusion and misunderstanding of *both* the experience of culture and language *and* the processes of perception and consciousness.

I have long found it a source of bemusement that an academic field, during a century in which highly secular, intensely quantitative approaches to matters of mind and behavior have flourished in the social sciences (particularly in the United States), would so enthusiastically center its work on a word whose etymology and pattern of historical usage is saturated with spiritual, if not theological, symbolism. The word "communication" is, as a matter of history and etymology, more than just an accidental cousin with the word "communion." "Communication" signifies the unseen connection between persons. It is a connection sustained by feeling, memory, and tone, a connection that finds its resonance through its analogy to narrative forms coined via myth and dreamwork. The narrative forms are the forms of fiction. Bernard Stiegler, whose work I will draw from in chapter six, has remarked that "the power of saying *we* requires that I "fiction" a past that is not mine, and this allows me to fiction a future that I hope will belong to us. . . . This is nothing but a fiction. There is no infinite love—no *we* as the origin of an *I*—that is not a phantasm. But I repeat: without this fiction . . . the *we* is impossible."[2]

As such, the invisible, fictional *we* of communicative experience exists for us as an article of faith. It is solely an article of faith, no less than the primitive's totem or talisman, no less than the miracles recounted in scripture. In some cases, faith can and will be strong. We can see it in a mother's love for her infant child. We can see it the eyes of a couple on their wedding day. Nevertheless, a sudden faraway look in a lover's eye, brought on, possibly by any number of things, constitutes a seismic shift from the oceanic feelings of adoration and oneness that had seemed to be the defining emotion of a romantic coupling. Telling someone that he or she is a "soul mate" is absolutely and without question true—until it no longer is, until something changes.

Until it changes, we operate with energy derived from faith. We treat the relationship as though it is a fundamental reality in the life we have chosen to "flesh out." The familiar haunts of such relationships—not just of "soul-mate love," but of such a vast array of others: confidante, accomplice, economic partnership, or even enmity—are given in storylines, descriptive narrative accounts rendered in the phrasings of discourse most useful and familiar to the images of memories and projections. And, so, the quantitative social sciences, having enthusiastically adopted the term "communication" for the study of messages, outcomes, and influence, have spent the last several decades examining matters of myth, narrative, and faith in a context of, presumably, secular and "value-free" epistemology.

Now, I hold no brief whatsoever against either the concept or the applied theory of a value-free epistemology. The scientific enterprise, in whatever context it is undertaken, does not benefit from any level of outcome bias or axiological prejudice, even well-intended. But it becomes absurd to even begin to pretend that the study of "communication" can parallel the sort of theoretical and methodological neutrality that we have come to expect from the materialist natural sciences, particularly given that the subject matter entails value-saturated symbols of role embodiment and performance, roles that are deeply interlaced into cultural webs of romance and desire—desire both educated and shaded by tragedy, tragedy whose contours are continually redefined by changes in self, social order, and social possibility.

EMBODIMENT, RELATIONALITY, AND THE NARRATIVE OF SELF

Until the American embrace of Continental philosophy in general and existential phenomenology in particular in the 1960s, there had been only a limited range of insights into the concept of all that might be implied by "communicative experience" in the academic literature emerging from the relatively recent fields of speech, rhetoric, and communication studies. My doctoral program presented me with the opportunity to study with Richard Lanigan, whose first book, *Speaking and Semiology*,[3] constituted an extraordinarily important moment in the American embrace of existential phenomenology. Lanigan, in a deep and elegant study whose power still remains largely untapped by the field of "communication studies," enters into a rich dialogue with Merleau-Ponty's philosophical oeuvre to establish a discursive foundation for understanding communication as an existential condition of the lifeworld.

The communicative existence of the lifeworld is not reducible to intellectualism or rationalism. In many ways similar to John Dewey several decades before him, Merleau-Ponty approached the problem as a *psychological* matter.[4] Coupling insights from the psychoanalytic tradition with some of the recent discoveries in gestalt theory, Merleau-Ponty sought to ground the phenomenology of consciousness in the body—the body, with all of its aches and pains, with its dreams and illusions and hallucinations, with its struggles for development and competency in its early years and its loss of competency and fear of madness at the end. As such, the phenomenology of consciousness overwhelms the limits of rationalism and it does so because bodies are mortal and tragic, bodies are hormonal and sexual, bodies are situated in the world as creatures of consumption and survival.

Students of developmental psychology and theories of childhood learning are much more aware than their rationalist counterparts in philosophy and logic that the human being begins as an emotional creature. We exit the womb crying, helpless, and aching for human contact. Rationality comes later. Our earliest memories are images suffused with feelings, not narrative structures, and certainly not thoughts. We navigate our way through the challenges and struggles of family life by habituating narrative patterns prior to learning them and strategizing outcomes.

Religion has functioned, over the course of many centuries, as a mode of coordinating the mythic symbolism of life narratives. Narrative structure, religious or not, provides a means by which experience can occur in a time other than the chaotic micro-seconds unfolding before consciousness. The story arc can be no more than a speculation (and then a borrowed trope at that) but it enables experience to open itself up to a field of play, possibility, and intentionality. Without the speculated arc, without the fiction, we simply cannot anticipate what is likely to happen and what sort of choices we can consider for the comportment of our selves in the face of the next crisis, the next moment of uncoded and unplotted consciousness.

We think of many of our relationships as *covenants*. That is, we live as husbands, wives, parents, sons, daughters, with our expectations based upon experience and the various forms of culture. When we say that we are "in a relationship" with someone we are saying that we have come to habituate a covenant recognizable in our mutual experience. In a strict sense, we are, of course, always in "a relationship" with someone whose lifeworld crosses our own. What we seek, in any case, is a connection whose narrative pattern enables the possibility of new experience fostered, nonetheless, in a milieu of familiar action and generally recognizable roles. The connection between the selfhood of one person and the selfhood of another is what Merleau-Ponty means in his concept of "flesh," or chiasm.[5] It is through this intertwining that the self emerges.

George Herbert Mead maintains that the self is not a sustained moiety of consciousness.[6] That is, a human being does not "possess" a self as a matter of biology, genetic information, or even sustained psychological conditioning. For Mead, the construct that has come to be known as "personality" has a far greater permanence and stability than self (even though one's "personality" is a concept named by others, and is subject to impressions as well as differences in culture). The seeming stability of self, for Mead, is entirely a function of the stability of the social relations in which the person is enmeshed and intertwined. A person nested in a habitat of comfortable, enduring relations thus exhibits the characteristics of a secure, stable self. Likewise, it is by way of the forgetfulness that tends to coincide with the security of this habitat that the threads (braided into the momentary chiasma of selfhood) constituting the flesh of human relationship become less visible. The observer sees a body, and then comes to equate that body with its self. As such, the ostensible autonomy of the body seems to correspond with an ostensible secure and stable self; the active life of flesh becomes, in the forgetfulness of stable relations, nothing more than the outer layer of skin on the body.

It is the relationship, particularly the communicative relationship as covenant, that keeps the self from devolving into a nothingness. We recognize relationships because of their narrative foundation. Every covenant implies a story that serves it as probable context. The self, as we typically talk about it (and in such cases it is not uncommon to see it expressed with an uppercase "S"), is a wish made by subjective consciousness. When it is considered in the third person, as when we think about the selfhood of others, we conceptualize the presumed intentionality of the subject in terms of everything that we have chosen to observe about the subject's public comportment. It is this basic strategy of observation that comprises the concept of *ethos* as a mode of proof in Aristotle's *Rhetoric*. It does not matter that the conceptualization of intentionality is, from the start, epistemologically and ontologically impossible. We do it anyway. We do it in order to enter ourselves into relational connections that allow us to know where, at any moment, we "stand" and where we seem to be moving. And even though we have, at best, only an ambiguous (and partial) conceptualization of what any relational connection is, from moment to moment, we will enter into such partial and ambiguous relational conceptualizations with impossible conceptualizations of intentionality because it is, despite its impossibility, the only means by which the human soul is given life and meaning. The validation for any and all conceptualizations is emotional. Relational connectedness is, simultaneously, emotional connectedness, which then configures anxiety as a diagnostic index of insufficiently meaningful interpersonal and social bonds.

Again, the relationship is the *form* of human connection, and the form of a human relationship is narrative. Each pairing, association, link, affiliation, joint, coupling, social network connection is a token. More specifically, it is a portent. It literally foretells (por-tends) where the dramatic arc is intended. The relationship, as a form and as a token of a narrative/dramatic type, is not a static entity. Its architecture, as one might attempt to describe it, is that of a fluid set of scenes played out in human imagination. However, the scenes are not necessarily linear and coherent like structured memory or cinema. As the feeling of connection changes, the relationship changes and the scene changes with it. It is through the architecture of narrative—an architecture that is often liquid and surreal—that we live both with and through our beliefs.

The relational connections that attach us to the people in our lives help us answer the question of "who" we think we are at any given moment. The answer is only as stable as the connections that situate our place in the world: family, community, friends, leisure, work, school, and the multiple, churning positions of the other.

To speak of these connections as structures has been a substantial *tropic* error of the last century. "Structure" implies a persistence to form. The melting clocks of Dali's well-known painting have a form that, although signifying transition and impermanence, is likely to last through the duration of a sustained gaze; at most, they signify a structure capitulating to time. But the closest thing to "structure" in human relational connection is the pattern of repetition (itself a melting clock) in the comportment of the human beings entailed by social and cultural situations. These patterns emerge as "rules" in everyday interaction, some implicit and some explicit, some prescriptive and others simply descriptive. Sometimes we enter these patterns and they seem to be, without our presence, sufficiently formed on their own. Sometimes our entry enables a transformation, a correction, or, at least, a difference, in our comportment. When that occurs, it can be said that what we have entered is (after Foucault) a *dispositif.*[7] After Foucault, this moment in the hermeneutics of our subjectivity describes the communicative phenomena of freedom and power—and much richer answers to questions of identity and selfhood.

Some clocks melt more slowly than others. The family is the first that comes most fully to mind. The hands on the clock face of family are already softening and liquefying from the moment the infant becomes child and the child becomes adolescent. But the rules of family are like those of any grounded semiotic system. They are, as Julia Kristeva, has commented, a "logic that is within you, which you can domesticate but never dominate."[8]

The narrative conditions of human relationality may be as fleeting as a daydream. But they may also be grounded much more deeply. We are grounded in the trials of new experience and those vulnerable, ecstatic moments of survival. We are grounded in tears. We are grounded in all of the oceanic events of childhood. Such narratives can be (and most inevitably are) grounded in family. We are grounded in the pull of family attachments that, in their unique power, can be as dark as midnight and as light as noon. We are grounded in the experience of shared pain and loss. We would love to believe that we are grounded in faith and hope but we are, just the same, grounded in the imminence of total failure. We are grounded, in other words, in the *terms* of tragedy. (It is not that tragedy—understood, here, in terms intended to be consistent with both Nietzsche and classical philosophy—is not subject to interpretation; it is that there is a marked human tendency to know when our capacity for escape or fancy has been overwhelmed by a situation.) Success, however, is a relational condition that is significantly less grounded. The *terms* of success (or victory or good fortune or even wealth) are always subject to interpretation—so much so, it can be said, that many persons have little idea when they can feel satisfied, when to express gratitude, when enough is enough, or when to move on to another objective.

THE "TERM" AND THE WORD: COMMUNITAS, STRUCTURE, PHENOMENOLOGY, AND THE VANISHING POINT OF NARRATIVE

A communicative relationship, any communicative relationship, entails a set of terms. A "term" is a word that is used, upon agreement between parties, to express a *particular* idea. At the same time, the use of a term is a strategy of limiting the range and application of an expression. When the elements of habit combine to produce a discourse, terms of engagement and comportment begin to emerge. It is through these terms that we are able to act with increasingly less mindfulness—a lessening that can turn into forgetfulness if we are not careful. When one commits a transgression, the transgression is always a social matter. That is, the relational terms have been breached or defied or violated. Even the notion of a social contract, as enunciated by Locke, for example, entails a mutual stipulation and agreement on terms. Citizenship, however conceived, entails a strong grasp of the terms of humanity, power, and order (both implicit and explicit) within a social and cultural group. Terms change, of course. They can change overnight. But until they change, they signify what they have been anticipated to signify. They serve as the basis of discursive habit and social expectation.

It is when the *terms* of a relationship become simply *words* that the clock starts to melt. Words illuminate the theatres of imagination and then illustrate the geometry of ideas and concepts that configure action in the logic of expression. Terms, on the other hand, serve as the elements of a promise, and the notion of a promise implies the portent of human couplings and connections. Again, the relational token of human connection functions as a portent, and the pragmatic essence of a portent is a promise. A promise always entails the future performance of an act to satisfy the terms of a relationship that the *promiser* wants to inhabit. (The terms, of course, must be mutual.) The child promises to work harder in school not so much because of specific consequences but because of the implied terms of his family covenant. It is not the loss of a toy or a privilege, for example; it is the possible loss of everything associated with the habitus of the covenant that compels the promise—even if the promise is eventually broken.

It is the nature of phenomenological reflection to see the *terms* of any and all relationships—be they relationships between people, between people and objects, or between objects themselves—as the *words* (and then, as well, the signs and gaps) that constitute them. The semiology of the relationship is not displaced with another lexicon but is instead unclenched and unknotted within the expressive form of the signifiers constituting the terms. The semantic meaning of terms is opened up for inspection and interrogation. It is in this modality of thought that phenomenological reflection transforms the codes and images of "rationality" into the dreamwork of *illusio* and imagination. It entails not the destruction but the de-structuring of the language called into being by the terms of narrative habits structured into communal discourses.

Victor Turner's theory of "communitas" places the concept of the communal desire ("a bond uniting people over and above their formal bonds"[9]) in competition with (if not opposition to) the notion of structure. Turner writes:

> Briefly . . . the bonds of communitas are anti-structural in that they are undifferentiated, equalitarian, direct, nonrational (though not *ir*rational), I-Though or Essential We relationships, in Martin Buber's sense. Structure is all that holds people apart, defines their differences, and constrains their actions, including social structure in the British anthropological sense.[10]

As such, communitas (i.e., what Turner defines as an intense experience of community feeling) enables the participants *in phatic contact* to experience, and perhaps invent, new possibilities of selfhood. To be clear, the *term* (that is, the intertwined functions of *terminus ad quem* and *terminus a quo*[11]) is the discipline of consciousness—as the heart, it can be said, is the discipline of the soul.

Communitas, as Turner theorizes, enables at least a momentary release, a momentary suspension of that discipline. Experientially, it is an instance of the "free variation" implied by the phenomenological *epoché.* What we often feel inclined to refer to as "rationality" or "reason" or even "sense" is in reality a frame of consciousness *other* than the one we transcended in our survival of infancy and, importantly, which we experience again and again in the imaginaria of dreams. When we think of "reason" as our primary or natural state of consciousness we rupture the lived experience (*vécu*) of self and other. That experience is ruptured to the extent that the activity of desire is confounded by a dualism maintaining the existence of the perceptual object (regardless of whether it is a person, living thing, or inanimate entity) as a *ding-an-sich*—possessing meaning unto itself.

The notion that objects of perception exist meaningfully apart from human consciousness has been a premise of technocratic empiricism[12] for well over a century, as well as a theme of consumerist behavior in the sociology of modern materialism. So much of contemporary economic and psychological life flows with such seeming equability that it has become difficult, even in academic discourse, to question the extent to which the blind spots of object perception should be taken as common sense. But it is the recurring problematic experience of relational meaning that necessitates that the blind spots open themselves to exploration and assessment just as much as the presupposed content of the objects themselves.

The problematic experience of relational meaning is not just that "we do not see what we think we see" or "we see only what we want to see"—although those can, of course, serve to describe any number of perceptual ambiguities—but that the perceptual process is an envelopment, an enveloping activity, of embodied consciousness. It is not that we *enter into* an experience, it is that the experience has always already enveloped us; it has semiotically enveloped us in a scene of memory. The envelope is a semiotic mix of myth and poem, a mixture, an amalgam that is always in motion, a motion that is sometimes slight, subtle—and sometimes frenzied. The action, of course, is multiple and alive with simultaneity (as in James's well-phrased "blooming, buzzing confusion"[13]), but it is not remembered that way and, in the moment of meaningful object-perception, it is not experienced that way.

Experience, of course, varies. But to the extent it has unity, it is *I* who give it that unity. That is, time-consciousness, along with its contextualization in space-consciousness (and memory), is meaning, and meaning is a function of narrative. What I remember is history. What I perceive is history-in-the-making. The envelopment is, as Merleau-Ponty carefully argues, a matter of temporality.

> The present still holds in hand the immediate past, but without positing it as an object, and since the immediate past likewise retains the past that immediately preceded it, time gone by is entirely taken up and grasped in the present. The same goes for the imminent future that will itself have its own horizon of imminence. But with my immediate past I have also the horizon of the future that surrounded it; that is, I have my actual present seen as the future of that past. Along with the imminent future, I also have the horizon of the past that will surround it; that is, I have my actual present as the past of that future. Thus, thanks to the double horizon of retention and protention, my present can cease to be a present that is in fact about to be quickly carried off and de-

> stroyed by the flow of duration and can rather become a fixed and identifiable point in an objective time.[14]

The activity of desire motivating perception ("the imminent future that will itself have its own horizon of imminence") is the intentionality of embodiment. Past, present, and future are the elements of narrative structure. Visually, the present along with all of its implications offers a sort of map of the future (to wit: "the horizon of the future that surround[s] . . . my actual present [which will be] seen as the future of that past"). It is in this regard that *I* am time. *I am* history. (I am a clock, melting.)

But all of this is not simply a *mise-en-scène* for the experiential anticipation of a "horizon of the future." For this moment, any present moment, to *not* be "carried off and destroyed by the flow of duration" and to become, *instead*, a "fixed and identifiable point in an objective time" it must become an episode. In other words, the moment of my perceptual experience is enveloped by a dramatic arc just as it is described by an arc of intentionality.

The episode of perceptual memory is a bounded system of reflections and reversals that defines a particular relationship of subjectivity and objectivity, a relationship of self and other and same and different. The coherence of this system, however, is merely a supposition. The inability of a system's parts to add up to a sum that is rationally and objectively verifiable is not a failing of the system or its concept. The problem for the purely intellectualist analysis of any system is that the *telos* of the system is as much a necessary element of the system and its function as its boundaries or its other constituent parts—but the *telos* is in no way analogous to the elements of systemic *techne*. The *telos* of a system, as with the dynamics of a wish, must move across time. It must posit a concept of the system's existence at some point in the future. It is based upon a *want*, a *desire* that gains fulfillment in the imagined future—in other words, in *a time that has not happened*, the only existence of which is that of an image in consciousness.

The closure of a narrative is its thematic horizon, and the event of closure is not simply a matter of linear sequencing. The closure of a narrative is a mythic moment of resolution and redemption. The "reason" that a story ends as it does is a matter of emotional satisfaction—again a want, a desire—rather than being a function of abstract logic. The boundaries of the system of differences permitting the story to proceed as such also enable the moment of redemption to manifest in whatever form of meaning or satisfaction the storyteller wishes. Now, it goes without saying that storytelling is a communicative act. Its undertaking presupposes an interlocutor. The goal of a narrative is to produce a feeling of difference, or at least a different or differentiated feeling, and to generate a will to repeat its telling in whole or in part. Memory, at its fundamental core, is a repetition of signs and signatures. Quotation is an act of attraction and fondness as well as respect, and contributes powerfully to relations of intimacy.

Nonetheless, the resolution to a narrative is its vanishing point. It is a place in human imagination that follows from a set of events but whose meaning does not follow from the events in the formal logic of their sequencing. The last moment in a narrative is the point at which consciousness recapitulates and considers the episode thematically. The thematic phrasing renders the story possible, plausible, probable, and at the same time *satisfying*. There is nothing in the strategy or formula of a narrative that demands that its resolution function communicatively with a listener. It either does or it does not, in exactly the same way that something is funny, or not.

The role that I believe that I assume in my relationship with you is one that satisfies my sense of who we are together, whether as stranger, friend, enemy, or lover. It is in this context that Martin Buber's statement that "all actual life is encounter"[15] takes on particular significance. Our meaningful existence is recognized as an object of perception by others—that is, it is recognized in signs, in words, and in terms as an object of perception by others. It must not be forgotten that the "inter" of intersubjectivity entails the mutuality of our existence as perceptual objects for one another. We are each supporting characters in one another's dramas—even when we have not come to terms with one another. The intersubjectivity of perception is the mutuality and intercorporeality of our fictions. The *we* of me, the *we* of all of us, is the energy that engages the elements of memory.

TERMINUS, NARRATIVE, AND THE POWER OF FICTION: REFLECTIONS ON THE MONUMENT AND THE DOCUMENT

Contradictions in terms—or seeming contradictions—are often fully resolvable through the synthesis of lived experience (*vécu*). In other words, in the midst of ambiguities of all sorts—some surreal, some dangerously equivocal, some merely figurative—a moment of communicative experience can enable the world to suddenly make sense. "I speak, I lie," Foucault famously remarked at the beginning of his encomium to Blanchot.[16] And, along with Foucault, I speak, I lie, I fiction, I imagine, I project my soul into a future that can never happen as I picture it, and I experience an erotic truth when the self I release into the ether of the semiotic universe is returned to me as something strangely familiar—not the same, but familiar enough to keep going, to move on, and to do it again.

In his answer to the question "what is a person?" sociologist Christian Smith comments: "Communicating in relationships is not something that persons do for instrumental reasons after they are established as selves, but it is the very activity that helps to constitute persons as persons in the first place and is a central purpose of personal life. . . . Personal communication is not simply a means. It is also an end, insofar as persons are ends and communication constitutes persons."[17] Smith is not a phenomenologist and the broader implication of his observation does not exactly qualify as news to most philosophers of human communication, but there is, in his phrasing (couched as it is in a reflection on personhood), a sense of the ongoing process in the experience and realization of personhood. In particular, one gains a sense of the inherent instability of personhood. Personhood is not immediate and it is not reducible to any particular instantiation of the body. I come into being in every moment of interaction. I disappear in every moment of expression. We are each vanishing points in both the dramatic and intentional arcs of one another's lived experiences. We vanish in the moment of communication. We reappear at the moment the terms of relationship suggest themselves to us.

The appearance and disappearance of self is a sometimes-subtle (sometimes not), continuous, inexorable, yet compellingly powerful dynamic in the tragic view of human existence. It is not merely that human life is, in itself, finite, mortal, and fragile. It is that everything that constitutes meaning and significance for the understanding of human life, both in its broader conception and in its particular instances, is ephemeral and momentary. The occasional historical and epistemological conflation of the "document" and the "monument"—a theme taken up by both Cassirer and Foucault[18]—has, in its unraveling, proven to be a worthy investment of intellectual energy. What I find fascinating in this context, however, is the critical matter of what drives us and has long driven us to make and preserve "monuments" in the first place.

There is an over-determination of history in any monument. (This, I believe, offers at least the beginning of an account of the human will to "monumentalize.") At least in the context of its expression as an extension of authority in a dominant or official culture, the monument is an insistently intense and intentional statement of memory that, especially since the dawn of the industrial age, has been represented by signifiers of enormity (or power) and persistence.

The function of the document is that of a communicative, relational lesson. It is a text that instructs, and its movement is from one interlocutor to another, an author to a reader, a teacher to a student, a parent to a child, a friend to a friend.

The function of a monument is cultural—although, *more particularly*, it can be political, commercial, economic, aesthetic, psychological/emotional, or theological. It, too, is an instructive text. But its movement is projected across the time and space of everyday lived experience (*vécu*) and ordinary communicative encounters. When an iconic representation of a person appears as a sculpture of some sort or when her or his face appears on money, there is an unmistakable impression of the past that invests my experience of the moment with a sense of how my identity is to be measured. I am Frank Macke and I am simultaneously not Aristotle or George Washington or Queen Elizabeth—or you. Yet my identity is tested and reflected and measured in terms of narrative histories whose mythic imprints have lingered across generations and through the grain of my own biography. I grew up with stories of all sorts of monumental figures—some local, some familial, some national and international, some completely invented. Just like everyone else, I have built my life *in terms of* ego ideals. The monuments of culture defining and dominating the perceptual experiences of my life and times can, at times, become points of resistance, but they nevertheless function as the semiotic fabric—or at least threads—of a life lived with its own intentionality turned toward and always mindful of a horizon of genius, of great works, of nobility and sacrifices greater than my own.

The ideal egos and ego ideals of persons undergoing the processes of growth and development that define the passages from infancy to childhood to adolescence to adulthood are the monumental configurations of the selves negotiated in relational connections and interactions. Some of the monumental configurations are mythic and extend from themes and narratives generated through cultural institutions of all sorts. Others enter into the threads of biography and perceptual desire through the lived experience of encounter with others whose embodied fictions influence the terms and directions of our own. Sometimes these influences are subtle. Sometimes, such as when we are disciplined in the orders of our tribes and languages (by way of families and schools and the multiple voices of contemporary media), these influences can be overwhelming and impossible to resist.

In any case, it is not so much that our relationships change us as much as they define us. That is, they set the course of how encounters will commence and then, as the encounter progresses, the subtle shifts in roles combined with the expectation (or hope) in the performance of roles transform the manner in which we inhabit and embody all of the social dimensions of our psychological lives. The role is an assumption of a narrative trajectory and our perceptions of one another are projections based upon our interpretations of the possibilities at play in the course of our interactions. In short, relationships define us, but the definition process is ongoing and mobile.

The question, of course, is what we play for—what is meaningfully at stake—in the course of our interactional games. Much of human consciousness, both Eastern and Western, has brought us to the understanding that the hidden treasure of sacred communion (by which "sacred" should be interpreted in a broader phenomenological sense as "outside of everyday life") is the *lesson*, the *docere* (as Cicero would imply[19]), *viz.*, the *document*. But, at the same time, human consciousness venerates and celebrates marked signs of memory. We do so in the figure of ego identities that function as cultural icons: protagonists of all sorts, paragons of greatness, goodness, artistry, ingenuity, the redeemers, the redeemed—in other words, all of the *monumental* figures around whom stories of power and redemption are told. They exist alongside their shadow figures, their symbolic oppositions signified in cultural icons of shame. These monuments, in their variety and ubiquity, are essential to narratives of biography. They comprise the perceptual imagery of character as *ethos,* as well as *ethos* as character. It is distilled as the face and embodied visage of the other. When we remember, *what* it is that we remember is essentially monument, not document.

One does not interact with an anatomy—an abstracted body having no identity and consisting only of physiological information. The idea of communication presupposes the existence of the "person," and a person, a *persona*, a mask, is always-already a projection. The psychoanalyst Wilfred R. Bion considers the initial operations of projective identification in the child to be the first form of "thinking."[20] When people fall in love, what they fall in love with is a collaborative projection and the magnetic energies of a new horizon. Which is, of course, to say that what the person is in love with is something that has not happened, or has not happened yet—or, most likely, may never happen at all—and, with intense love, everything else seems reducible to some sort of symbolic distraction along the way to the next moment of intimacy or, perhaps, seems just a charade and falls away from consciousness. When we are alone we can, at times, entertain at least an illusion of control. But as we embody the lived experience (*vécu*) of our relationships with others, we surrender the horizons of perception again and again.

So much of what constitutes intense meaningfulness in our relational experiences in many ways amounts to a strong interest in what we think is going to happen next. Sometimes "what happens next" is a close or approximate analog to what had been visualized. Sometimes it entails certain scenic expectations—sometimes critical, sometimes peripheral—and sometimes what happens next is a complete surprise. But it can never be what we visualized for the simple reason that what we witness and partake of experience cannot be the same as what we author in imagination. We cannot be our own Prospero. This is why, well into the modern era, significant portions of humanity find themselves lost in myth and frayed narratives and praying helplessly to some sort of God or Prospero—something, anything to project an image of hopefulness across the ambiguous, if not mystified and disorienting, narrative horizons.

Of course, it is quite possible to move beyond the disappointment that inheres in the disjunction between anticipation and lived experience (*vécu*), or at least get beyond some (if not most) of it. Surrendering to the inherent surprise of lived experience—to the difference and discontinuity between what one visualizes and imagines in projection and perception on one hand

and, then, "what happens next" on the other—releases the *l'histoire* and meaning of selfhood into the fiction of its own boundaries. The loss of ego is survivable. It is difficult, especially in our current era, but it is survivable. Nonetheless, the ambiguity of ego along with the equivocality of its boundaries can be a source of tremendous anxiety, an anxiety experienced over against the fundamental anxiety of *Dasein*.

THE CRISIS OF SELFHOOD AND THE SATURATION OF NARRATIVE PROJECTIONS

The task of holding onto oneself, begun as we pass through the mirror stage in early childhood and continued in the formations of identity, often collapses into egocentricity, along with the attendant melancholy of whatever alienation and loneliness hastens the collapse. And then the melancholy makes it even harder, raising barriers between the imagination and its shifting horizons and distending the emotional space between persons still connected in relationship. The discipline of selfhood has no doubt transformed through an era in which narrative emplotments and projections and horizons have been continuously broadcast, repeated, and reinforced, and then overlaid and intertwined through a mass media culture of obsessive and compulsive storytelling.

A case could well be made that the emergence of "communication" as a subject of intellectual engagement and academic study has been motivated by a crisis of ego and selfhood generated by a continuous cycle of images, comparisons, and reflections that has managed to unmoor the subjective position of reflective consciousness from the period of the Enlightenment to the late modern period. The crisis obtains not so much because the position of the ego is "condemned to choose" its narrative framework of selfhood from an increasingly wide array of suggested possibilities but because it entails a matter of continuous comparison and measurement of self and identity over against the active memory of self just performed or recently rehearsed. The kaleidoscope of "selfhoods" and strategies of performance continuously threaten to cheapen the mode of subjectivity in which we *just* constituted the flesh of our relationship. Without a continuity of self-enacted and embodied through a sustained passage in one's life, relationships become vulnerable to strategy and manipulation or become secondary to transient urges and the seductions of confused and confusing images.

As such, the *instability* of self, along with an increasing *awareness* of the instability of self, has resulted in a concern for the *performance* of self and the *image* of self in psychological relationships. That, in so many words, can be taken as a summary of the academic field of communication studies (or communicology) insofar as an explanation might be given about the shift in broad public consciousness that has favored it as a problematic and thematic for research and which has also resulted in its popularity as a course of academic study unto itself. The academic study of human communication thrives in a cultural milieu in which the performance of selfhood in multiple, visible, discernable, identifiable contexts and games becomes a hallmark of social agency and psychological endurance. The late-modern "competent" communicator is, now, a person who exhibits a capacity to flow into and out of oneself as contexts, games, and situations demand.

It is not so much that the cultural climate favors egocentrism as some sort of philosophical preference as much as it has simply come to terms with the emotional labors of consciousness in a world saturated with the multiple and proliferating stories and ethics of characters and personalities, all seemingly full of meaning and purpose. Agency is no longer (if it ever was) a matter of pure competence; instead, it primarily entails a matter of comfort with the task of negotiating selfhood (rather than discovering or cultivating the historical character of selfhood) amidst the variables of discourse. As such, agency is as much a derivative of the therapeutic function of communication and culture as it is a function of intellectual and rational modalities of discipline—which is to say, in terms consistent with Jakobson, that the task of "holding onto oneself" increasingly entails placing a greater emphasis on the significance of *contact* than on matters of context, code, and message in the experience of human communication.[21]

The experience of human communication enables us to hang on to something real in the midst of all that is imagined, merely imagined, merely projected in the ghostly[22] realms of *eros* and *psyche*, of heart and soul. (This reality is grounded in the discovery of our native psychological institution, our heart and soul, in the *Dasein* of finite existence.) The soul does not aspire to be tethered to a dying body or dead corpus. That is why, even as infants, we ache for freedom. One of the ways of attaining it is to release the frustrated energies of subjectivity and ego into the flesh of a shared existence. We lose ourselves and find ourselves simultaneously. Sometimes we are braided in friendship, sometimes we are contracted—pulled and drawn and tightened and shrunk—together in pragmatic associations, and sometimes we melt into one another's dreams so richly and deeply that we no longer have any sense of boundary.

Another way of attaining freedom is to release ourselves from the modalities of connectedness in our patterns and habits of relations. Sometimes this release enables us to become members of different families, friendships, games, and social groups, or to transform our connectedness in our families, friendships, games, and social groups. Sometimes, although not often, the release is for its own sake—as a momentary sabbath from all that once connected and defined us. But ultimately it is a form of madness that seeks this release as a *style of being*, as a habituated personality for the expression of selfhood; it is, in short, to live as a consummate stranger. In the fullness of time, one's ego identity will become identifiable and either attachments will be made and care will be extended or the ego identity will be faced with the forces of correction and punishment. (Various modern forces now assimilate the stranger into the order of things.) As such, the pursuit of communicative experience has emerged as a *strategic* choice of a healthy individuated consciousness. Some will seek deeper contact than others, and are willingly transformed by the changes that ensue. It would be a fair thing to say that these moments of release and freedom that seem such primary elements to the essence of communicative experience are nurturing moments, moments that enable the systems of one's defining relationships of selfhood to become more healthy or robust. Nonetheless, even if the release and freedom are but momentary, the connectedness enables a recovery of self via the shared or braided or overlapping narratives that place our character into the foreground of other people's lives, *viz*., their projections, and their horizons of vision and hope.

It may very well be the case that the urgency to speak and interact is no different than it was in generations past, but the urge to *think about* the process of communication—and, in fact to use that word, *communication*, to describe the process of interaction—has come to be a defining feature of an overwhelming amount of intellectual work in the human sciences. Again, the language, in both academic and popular literature, goes well beyond the discourse of social theory as it has been served by the mathematical sciences. It fully crosses into the language of cultural and sacred traditions—of the eucharist and communion, of ritual, liminality, *mythos*, *ethos*, and communitas.

Needless to say, communication will, no doubt, continue to be discussed and even measured as a discrete (and, hence, digital) event. As well, such discursive treatment also fully describes the last half-century of psychology, wherein the domains of *psyche* and *geist* and spirit have been routinely discussed as quantifiable matters subject, as well, to a mechanical schema of process and activity. (Yet, despite all of the protests of the behaviorists and cognitive scientists, *psychoanalysis still thrives*, and still remains the fundamental discursive matrix of psychotherapeutic work.[23]) For the current and upcoming generations of academic communicologists, to pay scant attention to the symbolism inherent in the etymology of "communication" is to disregard the fundamental discursive matrix of how and what we experience through our relationships with one another or the way in which the semiotic and literary elements of culture enter into the phenomenology of mind. The insistence upon an information-theoretic model (or even, discursively, a motif) for the discussion of the psychological elements of human encounter and relationality (*both* emotional *and* rational) reduces the concept of "identity" to a categorical, type-token function of figural substitution.

THE TERMS OF SELF AND OTHER AND THE THRESHOLD OF COMMUNICATIVE EXPERIENCE

There may, perhaps, come a time in which neuroscience will yield a much clearer picture of how the brain functions as an organ of consciousness, although, at the current moment, there is—despite some overwhelming expressions of enthusiasm from various quarters—remarkably little evidence of progress in this regard. Alva Noë, reflecting on the fundamental limitation of neuroscience as a methodology of explanation, has commented that neuroscience "looks at events in the brains of individual people and can do no more than describe and analyze them."[24]

Noë concludes: "However surprising it may seem, the fact is we don't actually have a better understanding how the brain might produce consciousness than Descartes did of how the immaterial soul would accomplish this feat; after all, at the present time we lack even the rudimentary outlines of a neural theory of consciousness."[25] And as the absence of a neural or neurochemical theory of consciousness plainly announces itself to careful scholars of the human sciences—in much the same way as the absence of a phrenological or electro-colloidal theory of mind presented itself to nineteenth and early twentieth century psychologists—we confront the reality that technocratic empiricism has so strenuously sought to circumvent or perhaps permanently postpone for the last century, and that reality is revealed in the simple truth that a theory of consciousness is inextricable from a theory of language and culture, document and monument, and word and term.

It is a theory has been emerging since pre-Socratic philosophy. In many ways, the unity of the history of consciousness finds a more than satisfactory summation in the phaneroscopy of Peirce, the pragmatism of James and Dewey, and the phenomenological theory of Husserl, Heidegger, and Merleau-Ponty. The partitions between persons that produce genuine feelings of separation are elements of culture and language. The partitions are terminal points. It is commonplace to refer to these terminal points as "rules," as though there are principles that ground the flow of discourse toward certain themes and away from others—and, of course, in some cases we can articulate one or more principles for the order and flow of human interaction. But the vast majority of cases in which we find our experiences and ourselves distanced from the lives of others consist of partitions, discursive traffic signals, and caution signs that we heed as matters of habit and conformity. The principle underlying the rule is articulated later, if at all, and may well be a rationalization supplied to justify the choice to which one has found oneself already committed.

Erik Erikson famously remarked that the counterpart of intimacy is distance.[26] The distance we both find and further insinuate between one another—a distance that inhibits both meaningful expression and communicative experience—is a strategy and function of choice. We observe and assign terminal points and partitions of all sorts. The loss we may feel in the aftermath is a loss of language, of words we tell ourselves not to speak or seriously contemplate, of gestures and movements that we persist in keeping to ourselves. Much of the work that the heart does is repressive; that is, the personal discipline entailed in the control of our various impulses consists of sacrifices we make for others. (In the absence of our relations with others and the narratives that entail those relations, we would have little reason other than personal safety to not do what we feel inclined to do.) All of which is to say that the exercise of "self-control" and its attendant loneliness can lead to a kind of mourning, a kind of grief that finds its clearest analog in regret. Our dissatisfactions for the way things are and have been, with the way things seem to be going, even our nostalgia for times that seemed to slip through our fingers are translated as various aspects of wasted moments and wasted opportunities. We deny ourselves both first and second chances at interaction out of fears that are marked by remembered images and in projections of consequences we imagine will flow from what we say and do.

It is, of course, true that there are fundamental semiotic partitions between oneself and another that enable a necessary privacy for the quiet cultivation of a monadic illusion and projective image of ones future performances of selfhood—in other words, the role one desires to play in the enacted embodiment of ideal ego and ego ideal. Eva Simms has commented on the way in which the imaginative faculties and intellectual instruments of what we now generally term "the Enlightenment" produced new dimensions of interiority to the developmental lives and experiences of both children and adults. She writes:

> Most educated, literate adults today are completely unaware how profoundly literacy has altered and shaped the very structure of their lives and how much time they spend engaging a fictional world of ideas. Children do not participate in this world until they become literate and are educated, which means they only gradually absorb the symbolic universe the Western mind has created. . . . What we call the interiority of the self is actually the adults' continual immersion and exchange of ideas in the literate, textual symbolic order. Children have to be induced into this world . . . which in turn restructures their relationship with the social and sensuous world and produces educated, interiorized adult selves over the course of the long process of schooling.[27]

As such, these terminal partitions between monadic, imaginative selfhood and fully-fleshed, embodied relational connectedness provide a semiotic and pragmatic foundation for an understanding of communicative competence to be both a feature of normal, modern psychological life and an analytic foundation for a practical ethics of everyday, communicative competence.

As such, boundaries of personal being—selfhood, in other words—are terminological matters. "Doing things on one's own terms" has become a catchphrase of a strong, individualistic psychological constitution. Negotiating terms is basic to any sort of contractual relationship and collaborating on terms becomes essential for any sort of contracted or abstracted relationship to warm its temperature toward the various emotional thresholds of friendship. And in this same regard, "truth" functions as a terminological matter. In both the instance of "the lie," on one hand, and in the instance of *parrhesia* on the other, the problem is not so much with *telling* the truth, but in deciding what the truth is: how is the truth *to be phrased*? Not "any old word" (or even any *similar* word) will do in the expression of narratives critical to the moral/cultural life of interpersonal and group relations. In preliterate societies as well as in the modern social world, bad language—just as much as bad behavior—can result in various forms of ex-communication.

So much of life seems beyond words. But even in the emotional crucible of lived experience we eventually find ways to attribute narrative (and, hence, rational) language to the ineffable and elusive. Everything important to us has a way of, sooner or later, getting expressed, and those things that do not or cannot find expression become psychological shadows that haunt and trouble the "post-confessional" mind—that is, the form of subjective consciousness that has been granted, by way of cultural, terminal partitions, an interiority, an interior space of rumination and self-reflection. Simms notes that even after the Reformation and its ostensible resistance to the order of the confessional, "the impulse of the Reformation deepened the isolation of the penitent by removing even the connection of the 'church appointed judge.' Confession was now heard only by an invisible, interior God, and faith was a matter not of visible ritual gestures but of the 'inner man,' the inner self, an 'absolutely inner quality.'"[28] The haunting of mind thus occurs not as the persistence of an image or an impulse, or some sort of partial, perhaps psychologically undigested, sign or symbol, but the persistence of an *untold narrative*, a narrative given a general form by the terms of culture even before the traumatic memory or repressed episode is fully sorted out.

Sometimes it is a lack of faith in our own agency that causes us to turn away from some course of action. As well, fears, doubts, and failures in resolve guide us away from performances and expressions of selfhood as much as confidence and clarity of vision guide us toward them. Fear seems to always make us lose a little bit of ourselves, and it does so precisely because the archetypal symbolizations and imaginaria of our ego ideals demand fulfillments of choice and action in order to be sustained as energizing illusions and narrative horizons. When we do not act, when we do not follow through, we begin to feel our dreams pull away from us. Our idealizations of selfhood can indeed shift from the active and powerful to the passive, recessive, and submissive. In this lack of faith, we lose voice—at which point begin to we locate our remnants of hope in being "spoken for"; and the longer we go on without this sort of minimally redemptive soul advocacy, the more willing we find ourselves to be "spoken for" by voices whose advocacy bear increasingly less resemblance to the idealizations of self we once treasured as ego identities that seemed well within our grasp. Instead of holding onto ourselves, we mourn, or "feel sorry for" ourselves.

As well, we can find ourselves haunted (and, then, suffused with various combinations of guilt and shame, mourning and regret) even before we have done or said anything "wrong." Sometimes the terminological apparatus of a discourse as it operates not merely within a particular *dispositif* but within an episteme can function, effectively, as a prison or perhaps a chastity-belt for consciousness. The partitions that have produced the interiority of continuous self-reflection emerge, as Simms notes above, as features of the "literate, textual symbolic order." They are textual. Whether and, even, how they might be *terminal* is, however, open to question. Not only are they open to semiotic inquiry and interpretation (and as radical as we might wish), they exist in dialogue and in competition with *other* narratives and other textualities. When we are driving an automobile, we hope all of the other drivers treat the traffic signs and signals with the same seriousness as we do. This particular example is so clear in its aspects that it is commonly used in classrooms as an analogy to explain semiotic theory to students. For the philosopher of human communication, however, a particular difficulty of generalizability that quickly obtains is that so little of human psychological life compares to the sort of cooperation necessitated by preventing automobiles from crashing into each other.

THE THRESHOLD OF COMMUNICATION AS A PREFACE TO TRANSGRESSION AND AS A RECONCEPTUALIZATION OF ETHICS

Simply put, flesh is not traffic and the body is not a car. Although an important part of disciplinary work—be it raising a police force, raising children, building an organization, or even creating a new field of academic inquiry (like, say, communicology)—involves setting terms that are pragmatic, another important part entails the critical assessment of the terms that will need to be substituted or, at the very least, unwound, perhaps liquefied, and reinterpreted as signs. It is in this regard that the philosophical and human science questions of truth, power, freedom, and beauty are all intertwined. In both a cultural system and any particular discourse operating within that system, the terms that enable a statement to be appreciated, to be taken seriously, as truth ought to function harmoniously with the terms that empower persons to speak. Otherwise the discursive game becomes limited only to certain sorts of persons speaking certain ways at certain times.

The management of automobile traffic, on the other hand, is only concerned with preventing death and anguish. It has nothing to do with games and logics of truth or freedom, or even the enjoyment of the driver and the vehicle's occupants. It shares with all disciplinary operations a principal outline of what a participant is *supposed* to do and what she or he is *not supposed* to do. The key, I believe, is this: the *dispositif* of traffic management, traffic laws, and driver's education *exists entirely as a logic of repression.* As such traffic "crime" is quite similar to most other forms of crime in civic life, in that a set of terms designed to enhance public security has been violated by an observable behavior. This *logos* is not about transformations of consciousness, it is not about creative vision, it is not about anything other than a narrowly circumscribed set of outcomes.

"Ethical crimes" are different sorts of matters entirely. The terms of traffic effectively demand that automobile drivers be inhibited from communicating with one another. True, some may beep their horns and wave but even then such expressions can prove to be a source of distraction. Human communication, on the other hand, can be looked upon as discursive traffic only on the condition that we ignore the reality that crossing lines and loosening the hold of terms is vital for intimate experience. As I will point out in numerous places through this text, the work of Georges Bataille has become vital to my understanding of how human communication emerges as a matter of psychological lived experience.

In a passage that I cite in several of the chapters that will follow, Bataille offers a perspective on human communicative experience that is original, poetic, surprising, but manages to comport with the work I have braided together in the synthesis of communicology I find myself advocating at this stage in my work as a scholar. Bataille writes: "*Thus 'communication,' without which nothing exists for us, is guaranteed by crime. 'Communication' is love, and love taints those whom it unites*" [emphasis in original].[29] Moreover, the spectre of danger, inherent in the terminal partitions demanded from the enforcement of criminal law for the purposes of public safety, undergoes a mythic reversal when we address the flow of communicative experience, as Bataille continues: "A fundamental principle is expressed as follows: 'Communication cannot proceed from one full and intact individual to another. It requires individuals whose separate existence in themselves is risked, placed at the limit of death and nothingness; the moral summit is the moment of risk taking, it is a being suspended in the beyond of oneself, at the limit of nothingness."[30]

There is an intense irony that the experience of human communication should exist in the context of a disciplinary psychological development that demands that we respond, at least reflectively, to the icons, indices, and symbols signifying taboo. Human communicative experience, in this regard, is marked psychologically as a kind of threshold, a preface, to transgression. (It is in this context that we can see the problematic and thematic of Foucault's well-known homage to Bataille in a somewhat broader perspective.[31]) Certain *dispositifs* exist to keep us safe. Certain others exist to help us become stronger, more capable, perhaps extraordinary exemplars of human citizenship in a community that is and always has been continuously changing, continuously growing (both in terms of size and complexity), and continuously perplexed by the fact of its own existence as such. This is why repressive regimes always fail as forms of human governance. They substitute the concern for safety and security for the will to power. The will to power, however, is impossible to extinguish by the terminological exercise of the rules of the game.

Repression, broadly conceived, does have a place in human affairs. The control of impulsive behavior is the essence of etiquette and human civility, and the elimination of order, rule, and injunction in human affairs offers nothing meaningful in terms of "freedom." However, in *Twilight of the Idols*, Nietzsche comments: "Freedom is the will to be responsible for ourselves. It is to preserve the distance which separates us from other men."[32] The study of communicative experience, particularly as it has been contemplated from the emergent field of communicology, is about precisely this sort of responsibility. Consistent with Nietzsche's notion of the "revaluation of all values," communicology will take on the phenomenological task of reconsidering all of what constitutes *ethos* and will be ultimately faced with the task of reconceptualizing the terms of all of that which constitutes "the ethical" in human relationships and human expression.

Allowing our epistemology to hide behind the premises of technocratic empiricism is not merely to postpone this responsibility, it is to shrug it off entirely. It is to say, in effect, "communicative experience—that is, *other* than that which is proscribed by information theory—*does not exist.*" It is to prefer the answers that appear as if they will come from neuroscience, even if they never arrive, as they most certainly will not. But if we let ourselves study communicative experience, if we let ourselves study it closely and carefully, we will take on the question of ethics and we will take on the still unfinished tasks of psychology—fascinating and important tasks that were initiated by Wundt in his formulations of *Volkerpsychologie*, tasks that were initiated by Peirce, James, Dewey, and Mead in their attempt to move the work of philosophy to the newly formed human sciences, and tasks that were initiated by Husserl and Merleau-Ponty regarding perception, expression, and consciousness. We will consider, yet again, the role of anxiety in human embodiment, the experience of ecstasy (*ek-stasis*) as a defining and transformational moment of power and fear, along with the concept of freedom as it relates to beauty, freedom, and meaningfulness. There's quite a bit of work to be done. And, right now, for me, this is the only science that matters.

THE BOOK AND ITS CHAPTERS

I sincerely hope that what I am offering is a pioneering study that advances the *raison d'être* of communicology while at the same time offering scholars of the human sciences a new way of thinking about embodiment and relational experience. The foregoing discussion set out to address the broad definitional question implied by the title. That is, I suggested a foundation for how one might explicate the parameters of communicative experience. Again, human consciousness, human expression (which takes so many forms, depending upon who is paying attention, what she or he is paying attention to, and why), and human information exchange does not necessarily imply that communication has occurred. In this regard, the iconic prison warden in the acclaimed film *Cool Hand Luke* was quite correct when he asserted that "what we've got here is failure to communicate." Sometimes communication simply does not happen. What I am endeavoring to show is *how* it happens when it happens as well as what elements are critical to its occurrence. A critical premise (and recurring theme) of this book concerns a central phenomenological understanding that consciousness of one's Self *and* one's body is only possible through human relationship. As such, the chapters of this book take on themes of embodiment and relational connectedness as they concern matters of how each contextualizes the other.

The rest of the book is laid out in ten chapters. The first chapter is titled: "Therapy, Vulnerability, and Feeling in the Interstices of Embodied Expression: An Explication of Human Communicative Experience." It offers a phenomenological explication of Jurgen Reusch and Gregory Bateson's concept of the four levels of communicative experience. I begin by considering both the title and the principal argument of Martha Nussbaum's book, *The Therapy of Desire*, in terms of how therapeutic experience might be understood in the context of Heidegger and Merleau-Ponty. Given that it sets forth some critical terms for understanding the concept of body and flesh through the experience of expression and meaning, this chapter becomes be a useful way to begin the text.

The next chapter concerns consciousness, embodiment, and self-reflection. In many ways it takes up the problematic of Narcissus' fate. It is titled: "The Mirrored Body: Phenomenological Reflections on the Visual Experience of the Reflected Self." The pivot point of the chapter concerns a passage in Merleau-Ponty's well-known essay, "Eye and Mind," in which he writes: "A Cartesian does not see *himself* in the mirror; he sees a dummy, an "outside," which, he has every reason to believe, other people see in the very same way but which, no more for himself than for others, is not a body in the flesh." And, so, this chapter raises the question of what one sees when looks at oneself in the mirror. As well, the now-common assumption that we have arrived at a postmodern condition of experience, knowledge, and interpretation comes into question when we consider the possibility that the human sciences have not sufficiently embraced a post-Cartesian perspective on mind, body, self, and vision. The chapter closes with a reflection on the contact of the self and the other in vision. Simply, the self and the other are not "signs" that are "read" in the context of a perceptual field. Rather, the interpersonal world embodied through the vital flesh of self in communion with other is reflected to the eye only if the observer cares to take note, to imaginatively flesh out the world embodied in the moment of a thoughtful glance.

The fourth chapter is a reflection on Jakobson's model of communication, with particular emphasis on his notion of "contact," which he designates as the phatic function of human interaction. As such, this chapter is titled: "On Contact: The Phatic Function of Communication." In this chapter I observe that the notion of "contact" between persons entailed by an instance of communication has, generally, been presupposed by most theoretical efforts at demarcating, illustrating, or symbolizing the eidetic elements of human transaction. This presupposition tends to operate on the unstated premise that communication occurs "within" a space, a space that is populated by (at least) two separate bodies able to identify and acknowledge one another as addresser and addressee. The phenomenological nature of contact is rarely opened up for examination. The purpose of this chapter is, thus, to question the nature of contact, to problematize the notion of space as energized, embodied, and constituted through a moment of communication.

Following upon the theme of "contact," communication, and flesh, I open up a deeper discussion in the subsequent chapter, titled: "Body, Liquidity, and Flesh: Bachelard, Merleau-Ponty, and the Elements of Interpersonal Communication." In this chapter I examine reflective consciousness in search of a genuinely "post-Cartesian" experience of spirit and substance, a challenge that I do not think has been sufficiently taken on by the human sciences. Phenomenology awakened modernity to the possibility of reason grounded in the experience of a vital, fleshly consciousness. Yet, for all of the discourse on the body as a site of power, "the body" still seems too often discussed as an organic autonomy, as a meaty tissue enclosing a shell of subjectivity. Gaston Bachelard's reflections on air, water, and dreams can, I think, offer a unique possibility for awakening postmodern and post-Cartesian consciousness to a new encounter with a semiotic phenomenology of the body and flesh. *Chiasm*, for Merleau-Ponty, is an interlacing of a being with, potentially, all other beings. Flesh cannot, thus, be encountered as a familiar "thing." It is continually in process, continually alive and dying, constituted of flows and vapors, presenting itself to everyday perception as an illusion of substance and a deception of material stability. Flesh might, I suggest, best be understood as an *intersubjective plasma*, as a complex of fluid elements that are just as capable of hardness as they are of liquidity. "Assets" of memory and experience become "liquid" in moments of communicative intimacy. As such, I consider the body *not* as a medium of communication but as communication itself, as communication entered and exited by way of liquidity and crystallization.

In chapter six, I examine the semiotic and linguistic grounding of the act of human expression. It is titled: "The Diabolical Parable and the Devil in Speech." In this chapter, I engage in a close reading of the concepts that inhere in a term absolutely vital to semiotic and phenomenological inquiry regarding the event of human communication: *parole*. The concept of *parole* is the French word for the standard English "speech." Yet the concept of *parole* has a much richer etymological history than that of "speech." The connection of *parole* to the word "parable" potentially situates the derivation of this concept of speaking to both poiesis and theology. But there is more. This chapter thus provides a careful examination of the "diabolic" and the "parabolic" in human expression. My objective is to consider the nature of "evil" as it is manifest in the "diabolical" praxis of *parole*/parable. The word "evil" and the word "devil" bear only a slight historical relationship to one another. Yet based on a similarity of spelling and an ostensible compatibility of meaning, the two terms have nevertheless become deeply interrelated in the patois of modern discourse. That is, the figure of the "devil" (e.g., Satan) has been taken as a signifier of "evil," a word which only until recently has come to mean "extreme moral wickedness." The word "evil" denotes (from its literal origins), simply, "uppity." As such, a "devil," serving as a figure of evil, potentially represents an entire spectrum of conceit, including, perchance, pride, arrogance, narcissism, immodesty, and unpleasant disposition. Following a theme resonating throughout Nietzsche's *Also Sprach Zarathustra*, I argue that the necessity of human communication thus entails a synthesis of "evil" with "parable." Which is to say that I maintain that rhetorical expression is a function of mastery and parabolic expression. I further argue that parole necessarily entails elements of imagination. As such, human communication will emerge as a function of transgression rather than—as it is commonly presupposed—a function of consensus and unanimity.

Following upon the theme of embodiment as meaningful expression (wherein meaningfulness is simultaneous with the crossing of boundaries), chapter seven takes up the problematic of human psychological development and the experiential interstice occupying the space between good and evil. It is titled: "Identity, Intimacy, and Eroticism: Deception, Sin, and the Existential Bargain of Adolescent Embodiment." The fundamental question of this chapter concerns the themes of adolescence, ecstasy, and change. This passage is never simple and is fraught with tension and radical boundary questions. The passage from the communicative *ek-stasis* experienced by a "parent's child" into the *ek-stasis* experienced by a being, in these new moments, principally "marked-by-others" (and without a rehearsed and inhabited adult subjectivity), is a passage *away* from the familiar temple of family order—and *toward* the uncertain sketch of an ideal ego insufficiently reflected in the narrative orbit of lived experience. Adolescence is a period marked by a desire to keep secrets. The embodied consciousness of the pubescent being entails a new world of interlinkages and interlacings and it employs its expressive/perceptive agency as best it can in the domain of a new concept of human possibility—"suspended in the beyond of oneself," as Bataille phrases it, "at the limit of nothingness." Yet, in the context of the world of its family and familiars, the ecstasy of adolescent embodiment is, literally, a sin and a crime.

Bataille, following Nietzsche's concept of a philosophy beyond good and evil, asserts that "since 'communication' can't take place without wounding or tainting our humanity, 'communication' itself is guilty." My argument is that, for Bataille, the experience of communication is the experience of *flesh* in all of its complex denotations, what Merleau-Ponty terms *chiasm*. Simply, to communicate, to experience communion, is to experience one's sovereign existence *and* its negation simultaneously. In this essay I closely follow Bataille's concept of communication as a way of investigating the transgression and crime of intimate experience, an experience that can only commence with the sin of the flesh. Bataille marks the experience of communion as something distinctly spiritual, not as the sacred, but as a means of access to the sacred. I further suggest that Bataille's approach to experience, communion, and communication (at once fully counterintuitive to a modernized Western consciousness, and a "shameless" apposition to the tone of American "family values") finds rich illustration in Hermann Hesse's *Demian,* and offers a new conception for therapeutic transformation—what Foucault terms the "art" of living.

In chapter eight, I take up the concept of gender as grounded in the phenomenology of communicative experience. It is titled: "An Archaeology of Gender Symbols and a Theory of Communication." To communicate is, paraphrasing Bataille, to lose oneself into a nothingness. But it is a darkness from which one exits, and in this reemergence into one's patterns of memory, a transformation of one's body becomes perceptible. In examining the movement along this arc, I examine the concept of transformation as a matter of gender. Carl Jung's concepts of *anima, animus*, and "animosity" offer tremendous promise in the description and explication of the space of this creative moment. My thesis here emerges as a semiotic phenomenology of the mythic archetypes of the institutes (*in-stasis*) of memory. This chapter seeks to develop a theory of communication that articulates the event—and not merely the eventuality—of memory's death and transformation in its digression from its grid of inhabited space. What I shall attempt to offer is a discourse that articulates the quality of "life beyond the limit"—the quality of the space of embodiment that is unraveled and liberated in the *ek-stasis* (viz., the death and forgetting) of consciousness within its recollected and inhabited identity.

Chapter nine involves an exploration of communicative intimacy which, I argue, is entirely the province of dyadic (or *inter*personal) communication). It is titled: "The Flesh of Human Communicative Embodiment and the Game of Intimacy." In the three published volumes of his *History of Sexuality,* Foucault reflects on themes of anxiety situated in the Christian doctrine of the flesh that led to a pastoral ministry establishing the rules of a general social economy—rules that enabled, over time, a discourse on the flesh that took thrift, prudence, modesty, and suspicion as essential ethical premises in the emerging "art of the self." Rather than sensing flesh as a charged, motile potentiality of attachment and intimacy, it came to be seen as skin—as the limit of a sovereign body, embedding guilt and shame into the texture of its expression. As such, this chapter pursues the psychological and communication problematic of intimacy as a critical and developmental experience of the flesh. Foucault's concept of self-care and *parrhesia*, Merleau-Ponty's concept of flesh and embodiment, and Bataille's concept of glory and eroticism contribute to a phenomenology of human development that seeks to articulate an idea of a self differentiated from the unspoken binds of familial anxiety and emotionality.

In chapter ten, I consider the experience of reverie and dreaming in the emergence of personal identity and narrative consciousness. The focus of this chapter, titled "The Dream and the Self: Consciousness, Identity, the Sign, and the Image," turns on our deep experience of the *image*—with particular reference to the image of what Erik Erikson terms "identity." I contend that the conjunction of semiotic scholarship with the human sciences' assimilation of phenomenology and psychoanalytic theory has thus far been unable to render a sufficiently lucid explication of the experiential differences of the *image* and the *sign*. As such, this chapter explicates these experiential differences, and does so in terms of what seems the inherent nature of image (or *imago*) to the development and unfolding of the self. Unlike the "sign," the image/*imago* is always in motion. When it is still, it enters the play of a conscious grammar. Following the work of Bachelard, Binswanger, Foucault, Merleau-Ponty, and Lacan (as well as Erikson), I initiate a discourse regarding the tension between the conscious grammar of interpretation and the unconscious work of dreams and their elusive images.

Finally, in chapter eleven, which I have titled "The Dawning of Communicology," I conclude the text by opening a discussion of what I envision as a possible future for the human science of Communicology.

NOTES

1. See Watzlawick, *Pragmatics of Human Communication*. Regarding the insufficiency of the notion that "we cannot *not* communicate," see especially Eicher-Catt and Catt, *Communicology*.
2. Stiegler, *Acting Out*.
3. Lanigan, *Speaking & Semiology*.
4. For a thorough discussion of Dewey's strategy to push turn-of-the-century philosophical work toward the project of psychological investigation, see Thomas Alexander, *John Dewey's Theory of Art*. Alexander also provides an extensive discussion of a theoretical parallelism between the work of Dewey and Merleau-Ponty.
5. Although this is a point that should flows from any broad, basic understanding of Merleau-Ponty's work, an excellent source for see how the concept is explicated can be found in Evans and Lawlor's edited work, *Chiasms*.
6. See Mead, *Selected Writings*, 142–49.
7. See Foucault, *Power/Knowledge*, 194–228.
8. Kristeva, *In the Beginning*, 55.
9. Turner, *Dramas, Fields*, 46.
10. Turner, *Dramas, Fields*, 46–47.
11. This distinction is Husserlian, and it is proven to be a valuable means of explicating the concept of *epoché*. This particular elucidation of the concept of time in narrative/conceptual perception emerges from the work of Dorian Cairns, a key Husserl interpreter. See Cairns, *The Philosophy of Edmund Husserl*, 215–30.
12. I distinguish technocratic empiricism from empiricism broadly considered to the extent that phenomenology is hardly opposed to the fundamental premises of empiricism. For an interesting discussion of Husserl's phenomenology in the context of radical empiricism (such as that proposed by Peirce and James), see Vanatta, "Radical Empiricism and Husserlian Metaphysics," pp. 17–36. My use of the term technocratic empiricism entails not simply a reference to the positivist legacy as exercised by behavioral psychology but to the mindset of applied science whose preoccupations with quantitative measurement have regularly come to exceed the demands of social theorists of all stripes. Simply, it has come to be expected that scientific reason must be quantifiable, even when the participants in academic discourse are not asking those sorts of questions.
13. See James, *Principles of Psychology*.
14. Merleau-Ponty, *Phenomenology of Perception*, 71–72.
15. Buber, *I and Thou*, p. 67.
16. Foucault, *Thought From the Outside*.
17. Smith, *What is a Person*? 72–73.
18. See Cassirer, *The Logic of the Cultural Sciences*, and Foucault, *Archaeology of Knowledge*.
19. See Cicero, *On the Orator*.
20. Bion, *Learning from Experience*, 31. See also Kristeva, *Melanie Klein*, 178–80.
21. It is not at all clear when, or even how, the transition occurred, but Martha Nussbaum makes a clear case that the therapeutic dimension of rhetoric and dialogue in the classical age (and for Plato, in particular) is a dimension of message and code—that is, in the sense that matters of text and mind fundamentally eclipse matters of emotion and embodiment. See Nussbaum, *Therapy of Desire*.
22. My use of the word "ghostly" in this context is meant to invoke the concept of *Geist*, which is the German equivalent of "mind" or "spirit."
23. See Safran, *Psychoanalysis and Psychoanalytic Therapies*. See especially Safran, *Negotiating the Therapeutic Alliance: A Relational Treatment Guide*.
24. Noë, "Art and the Limits of Neuroscience." *New York Times*, 4 December 2011: The Stone (Opinion).
25. Noë, "Art and the Limits of Neuroscience." The conclusion Noë draws here is further elaborated in his text, *Out of Our Heads*: *Why You Are Not Your Brain and Other Lessons From The Biology of Consciousness*.

26. See Erikson, *Childhood and Society*, 264.

27. Simms, *The Child in the World*, 219.

28. Simms, p. 201. Simms draws reference to the works of van den Berg (*The Changing Nature of Man*, 225–30) and Illich (*Gender*, 150-55).

29. Bataille, *On Nietzsche*, 18.

30. Bataille, *On Nietzsche,* 18–19.

31. See Foucault, "A Preface to Transgression."

32. Nietzsche, *Twilight of the Idols*, 71.

Chapter Two

Therapy, Vulnerability, and Feeling in the Interstices of Embodied Expression

An Explication of Human Communicative Experience

THE DISCOURSE OF MODERNITY AND THE CONCEPT OF *GEISTLICHE* THERAPEUTIC EXPERIENCE

The modern intellectual world has had, for a number of years, a difficult time with the concept of psychological therapy.[1] It is not that the ever-evolving clinical practice and medical industry of psychological therapy has fallen in any significant way. It is quite the contrary: according to a recent and thorough report of the U.S. Department of Health and Human Services, from 1993 to 2003 American mental health providers saw a roughly 60 percent increase in the rate of persons electing to employ mental health services.[2] The difficulty happens to be one more of impression and phrasing. It began a century ago, as the new field of psychology was finding its place in American academic and intellectual life. At the turn of the century "the treatment of persons with mental illnesses was not even remotely considered as one possible function of a psychologist. That was regarded as the province of medical practitioners, who in the first place were not scientists and who in the second place were not doing too well at it."[3] Eric Caplan's history of psychotherapy takes note of a comment by Boston neurologist Richard Cabot in 1908: "Psychotherapy is a most terrifying word, but we are forced to use it because there is no other which serves to distinguish us from the Christian Scientists, the New Thought people, the faith healers, and the thousand and one other schools which have in common the disregard for medical science and the accumulated knowledge of the past."[4] Caplan maintains that "winning professional support for psychotherapy would require a long and arduous battle. American physicians who promoted the clinical use of mental therapeutics confronted substantial opposition—particularly from the ranks of their professional colleagues."[5]

This diffidence has carried over into matters of academic discourse and curriculum. Among the vast majority of psychology departments in American colleges and universities, the notion of psychological therapy has essentially become dissociated from pedagogical and research curricula. Kurt Danziger has noted that "the Western cultural roots of Cartesian psychology are glaringly obvious, yet its preconceptions are so deeply enmeshed with the procedural norms of traditional scientific psychology that alternative approaches have long been subject to disciplinary marginalization."[6] As a consequence, students interested in becoming counselors and clinicians find themselves having to enroll in schools of education or social work, particularly in pursuing graduate-level work, in order to locate the most direct conduit to professional certification and practice as therapists. Danziger likewise maintains that matters pertaining to the history of psychoanalysis and depth psychology are increasingly treated within academic departments of psychology as a series of awkward questions that the field of study would just as soon avoid.[7]

At the same time, the intellectual response to the growth of psychological therapy outside of the field of psychology, psychiatry, and medicine has not been altogether positive—or even tolerant. Sociologist Eva Illouz writes: "The very seductiveness of consumption and therapeutic self-absorption marks the decline of any serious opposition to society and the general cultural exhaustion of Western civilization. . . . In calling on us to withdraw into ourselves, the therapeutic persuasion has made us abandon the great realms of citizenship and politics . . . because it has emptied the self of its communal and political content, replacing this content with a narcissistic self-concern."[8] Illouz's perspective, though strident, is not altogether uncommon. Illouz insists that her position is sympathetic with that of Foucault. Though I strongly disagree both with her characterization of Foucault and with her description of therapeutic practice, I think it is well worth noting that there has long been a body of resistance to the concept of *Geistliche* development and transformation whether guided by a therapist or via some comportment of "self-help." Typically, this position—most commonly taken by politically conservative writers—gains whatever persuasive force it attains by romanticizing the concepts of Self and agency and then mystifying the process of experience and metamorphosis to the point that even historically significant strategies of teaching and learning are to be held with some measure of doubt. Some things simply cannot be taught in school, it might be said—or perhaps it is that these experiences of enlightenment can only come through the suffering that is life itself. Or perhaps: if there were a formula for overcoming naiveté, then all would be wise. As such, any guide toward *Geistliche* transformation would only cheapen the experience, would it not?

THERAPY AND PHILOSOPHY

My ambition in this chapter stems from a fascination with an aspect of human experience that can, I believe, best be labeled as *therapeutic*. The difficulty over the course of the last century with the concept of therapeutic technique or the various therapeutic professions has to do with the emergence of methods—and the concept that such methods could be said to have any legitimacy at all—for the elucidation of mental and emotional states.[9] Irrespective of whether or not a doctor or therapist or teacher or clergy could effectively change such mental and emotional states, the mere possibility that such states might be knowable or subject to diagnosis immediately suggests a *topos* of resistance or dissent. More than just a *medicalization of madness*, as Foucault so famously phrased it a half-century ago, what emerges is a type of medicalization of mind. A therapist, whether licensed or not—perhaps surreptitiously, perhaps empowered through a school system or government agency—enters into a rational game with a "client" on the premise that he or she knows what the client is thinking and how the client came to think those thoughts. This basic relationship becomes, essentially, the foundation for Foucault's *Collége de France* lectures on "psychiatric power."[10]

Now, on one hand, it does not much matter that either the elucidation of mental and emotional states or the strategy deployed for doing so is correct or incorrect, accurate or inaccurate. More than the thoughts or emotional states themselves, it is the simple matter that *a process* has been deployed for psychological—*Geistliche*—analysis. When a family member or intimate associate makes such a comment about our intentions or our emotional states, we regard the comment as a product of *l'histoire*, understood in this context as relational lived-experience. Lived experience of my bodily habits, my modes of expression, the surplus value of my relational being which I freely offer to everyone within the orbit of my life—all of this has figured into my consciousness of how we all talk about one another, and I have been aware of it (just like everyone else) since early childhood. We *can* insist that a given comment is mistaken on the basis that the person speaking it does not *really* or *truly* know us. But we also know that when a comment is accurate, its truth is a consequence of an unambiguous perception derived from a careful observation of how we have acted in our relational lives. This is the psychological hold that family and intimate friendships will always have on us. It is the recursive *pharmakon* of intimacy alongside our canny suspicion of knowing outsiders.

But on the other hand, it indeed *can* matter greatly that the elucidation of mental and emotional states as well as the strategy deployed for doing so *is* correct. The doctor or teacher or cleric (or some symbolic conjunction or imaginative combination of more than one of the above) can perform a therapeutic function when he or she is capable of telling the truth about our inner lives. This species of magic that such a master performs is no mean trick. In fact, the word "magic" is nothing more than an illustrative noun taken from a word of Persian origin, borrowed in Latin as "magus" (or as the plural, "magi"). The Latin "magus" gives us the word magister, or as we know it in contemporary English: "master." The magic of the master is magisterial. Historically it has always functioned as a sign of both power (as *pouvoir*) and knowledge (as *savoir.*) In looking after our bodies, we seek out the best available care for our medical needs. The magic of medical masters in any age and in any part of the world defines the strategy of somatic diagnosis and therapeutic treatment.

When we each cultivate our selfhood, we seek out other sorts of masters, and do so ultimately to a point that we will embody these forms of mastery and gestures of magic for our own rehearsals and expressions of being. And in this regard, mastery functions not simply as "expression" or "performance," it becomes the modality of consciousness itself. At a primitive level, experimentation and play enable a phenomenon of self-mastery, as when a child tests his or her own strength or dexterity or plays with an unfamiliar object. But to the extent we seek both pleasure and significance in the multiple dimensions of our social being, the learned consciousness embodied by anyone who can surpass our powers at whatever it is we care to do becomes the elementary basis for culture itself.

Stewart Justman remarks that "the idea of therapy traces back . . . to Plato. According to Plato, philosophy itself is the corrective or cure—the *therapeia*—of human ignorance and confusion."[11] Now, I as well affirm the notion that there *can be* a therapeutic quality to intellectual work: as culture, as cultivation and development, as problem diagnosis and problem resolution, and, in fact as healing. This therapeutic quality, which can be identified in numerous ways, often goes unrecognized in modern life, particularly as the neurotic, yet commonplace, drive to think with greater speed, alacrity, and efficiency, continues to commodify the task of thinking as a modality of "mental labor" subject to measures of aptitude and constancy. The therapeutic quality of which I am speaking is situated in the *chiasm* of body and self, in the *chiasm* of the relations of *parole, langue, langage, discours*; in short, it is situated in the flesh of thought. In his lectures on the "Hermeneutics of the Subject," Foucault concentrates his attention on a particular aspect of care and self-care, which he locates in the Greek notion of *epimeleia heatou.* He writes:

> For "take care of" Epicurus employs the verb *therapeuein*, which has several meanings: *therapeuein* refers to medical care (a kind of therapy for the soul which we know was important for the Epicureans), but *therapeuein* is also provided by a servant to his master. You know also that *therapeuein* is related to the duties of worship, to the statutory regular worship rendered to a deity or divine power.[12]

It is essential to the phenomenology of language and communication that the other is always present in signs and that, moreover, there is no element of language that is not haunted by the *l'histoire* of bodies—of generations, of *bios*, *thanatos*, *eros*, of sex, struggle, anxiety, of birth and the fragility and contingency of life, and the tonality of laughter and tears. The history of the word "therapy" reminds us that therapy and therapeutics entail a kind of "ministry." The Greek *théraps* refers to a servant, as Foucault points out, but this also refers to the kind of service conducted by way of a minister or an attendant or perhaps an intimate friend. More to the point, *therapeutikós* refers to the *tékhne* not merely of "healing," but of healing through the presence of an other's care—through the subjection of one body to another.

In a text promisingly titled *The Therapy of Desire*,[13] Martha Nussbaum offers a contextualization of what she takes to be the therapeutic function of philosophical thought. She ties the purpose of classical philosophy to the concrete reality of human suffering, employing a vision of human compassion that, nobly enough, seems to extend beyond the subjective position of the thinker. Nussbaum, a resolute neo-Aristotelian rationalist, reads the classical tradition as a therapy of good arguments, the implicit desire of which is to cure the social and political world of its bad ideas and logical failings. Yet her sense of caring in its "desire" to perform acts of "goodness" very much manages to ignore the embodied experience of the philosopher.[14] It is certainly well-meaning, at least in a liberal-political sense, but it is, at the same time, an abstract medical prescription for a symbolic—perhaps imaginary, perhaps entirely fictitious—body from a doctor who need not have a body of his or her own.

Interestingly, an important element of the classical tradition about which Nussbaum seems to be the least curious in a book dedicated to the therapeutic function of classical philosophy (and to which, at points, she expresses a certain measure of impatience[15]) is the school of philosophy generally attributed to Pyrrho of Elis (circa 360–275 bc), a modality of thinking in which radical, antidogmatic skepticism is taken, for all intents and purposes, as an end in itself. Pyrrhonian skepticism, as explicated by Sextus Empiricus, pursued its reflective method to lead the thinker to a state of *ataraxia*, or "unperturbedness." The state of *ataraxia* is not one of bliss, and certainly not nirvana. Neither is it a function of *pathos* or the passions. Sextus Empiricus writes:

> Skepticism is an ability, or mental attitude, which opposes appearances to judgments in any way whatsoever, with the result that, owing to the equipollence of the objects and the reasons thus opposed, we are brought firstly to a state of mental suspense and next to a state of "unperturbedness" or quietude. . . . "Suspense" is a state of mental rest owing to which we neither deny nor affirm anything. "Quietude" is an untroubled and tranquil condition of the soul.[16]

Sextus makes clear that the rigorous skeptic is not "*wholly* untroubled."[17] Moreover, he asserts that the skeptic "is troubled by things unavoidable; for we grant that he is cold at times and thirsty, and suffers various affections of that kind."[18] Yet the skeptic possesses a distinct advantage in such cases. By not committing to a belief that any of what befalls her or him is "naturally" or essentially evil, the skeptic manages to escape with less discomfort than the ordinary philosopher, and with considerably less psychological misery and emotional strain than the nonthinker.

Scottish philosopher Bob Plant has observed that "therapeutic objectives governed a number of ancient philosophies, but none more so than Pyrrhonian scepticism. For the Pyrrhonist, it is the human tendency toward belief (that is, belief *per se*) that requires philosophical treatment. Only by eliminating our ontological, epistemic and normative commitments can we attain an 'untroubled and tranquil condition of [the] soul' or *ataraxia*."[19] Again, the state of *ataraxia* is not one of pleasure (*plaisir*), but I would strongly argue that it is not only *therapeutic* but that it is likewise descriptive of a necessary *Geistliche* transformation. Irrespective of how it might eventually be classified in any larger scheme (regardless of whether it should be), it entails an embodied perceptual difference. As such, *ataraxia* comports with a phenomenological sense of ecstasy as, perhaps, the necessary shadow of *ek-stasis*. It is descriptive of any embodied sense that the boundaries of vision have changed and that the terms of the changes have suddenly enabled a set of signs to express ones range of movement within this new visual field.[20]

The "equipollence of objects and reasons" reads as an odd term of art, even for contemporary treatments of Hellenistic philosophy. Yet it refers, simply enough, to equality in power, force, and significance of any two interpretations and, hence, of any two arguments made about an object or circumstance observed by two persons. Conventional reason, both classical and modern, would accord a presumption to the more probable and/or commonplace of interpretations, which would also seem to make for some highly frustrating philosophical and pedagogical work for dialecticians and theorists accustomed to work with presumptions and probabilities, especially those rendered axiomatic by the methods of normal science. Pyrrhonian skepticism, on the other hand, would not permit any such presumption.

Especially given the dialogic nature of its praxis, equipollence is in fact fully analogous with the neutralizing of presumption that enables a psychotherapist to engage in dialogue with any patient of any sort, which is particularly important when communicating with a tensely guarded bipolar patient or paranoid schizophrenic. When the patient is convinced the therapist is harboring judgment, the dialogue cannot proceed. There is conversation, perhaps, but no dialogue. When the Pyrrhonian interlocutor has fully adopted this stance in relation to the world of phenomena and perception, she or he has positioned her or his communicative body toward listening and dialogue. As such, equipollence is as much a position of ecological respect as it is a critical stance of the skeptical thinker, functioning reflexively like the terms "apposition" and "opposition" in Roman Jakobson's phenomenology of language[21] and Richard Lanigan's semiotic phenomenology of communication.[22] In *The Logic of the Cultural Sciences* Ernst Cassirer notes: "what we must make clear is that skepticism also has its rightful claim. . . . It is better to renounce knowledge than to be blind to a problem because we have contented ourselves with a pseudo solution."[23]

Nonetheless, the method of equipollence, as with the phenomenological *epoché*, does not in fact entail a renunciation of knowledge. Certainly thought and dialogue will encounter frustration with regard to the presumptive existence of the ostensibly concrete "things" whose persistence comes to define the perceptual *habitus* of discourse. But such frustrations are synonymous with what Merleau-Ponty identifies as *écart* and dehiscence[24] encompassed by the birth and life of any new field of vision. Along these lines, opening and sustaining an epistemological dialogue that questions the presuppositions of the external physical world seems curiously well placed in these times. One hardly needs to invoke the rhetoric of Baudrillard to build a credible case that the perceptual world defining the late-modern experience of society, community, and politics has become a play of light and shadow. This argument has, in fact, become commonplace among media scholars as well as the standard complement of social theorists and philosophers. Yet Baudrillard's critique[25] is significant precisely because it advances theoretical discourse regarding media, reality, perception, and experience fully beyond the Platonist's and the rationalist's reduction of the simulacrum problematic as being essentially a failure of knowledge and ethics. It has become impossible to address such a thing as a social reality without recognizing that what we have come to take as "knowledge" about others of all sorts is mediated not only through filters of language, culture, and political-economy but through weird, kaleidoscopic prisms of instantaneous electronic journalism and opinion-spreading, explosive and repeated audiovisual distractions, along with cybernetic viruses and virtual cancers infecting databases and rapidly corroding accumulated wisdom. We address the voice and experience the flesh of the other in a technological milieu of attention-deficit disorder. We now come to terms with the other in a time of terror.

ENNUI AND EMBODIMENT

Nonetheless, in having said all this, it is important I make clear that this chapter should not be read as a call for Pyrrhonian skepticism to emerge as the most recent philosophy *du jour*. Moreover, what I am envisioning is not meant to comport with any historical and/or anthropological sense of how the skeptics (or stoics or epicureans) truly performed their thought at the time that they inhabited the Earth. Walter Benjamin, in his comments on Baudelaire, famously remarked on the extent to which the ache of boredom "tirelessly generates antiquity" and that boredom "lays down centuries between the present moment and the one just lived."[26] In other words, a certain preoccupation with the distant past emanates from a peculiar dissatisfaction with the present. In any case, it should be clear enough that Foucault's desire to reassess the disciplinary motifs of Hellenism is neither meant to pursue history for its own sake nor is it intended as a gesture toward curing what ails the modern project. (I am unconvinced, however, that the same can be said of Nussbaum's recovery of stoicism.)

And despite the discourse on Pyrrhonian method specified by Sextus, a case for radical skepticism's sufficiency as a human science has hardly been made. Simply, we are not *without* knowledge. We *know* that there is an other and that this other is both in possession of and possessed by a body of some sort. What we do not know is how this "other body" functions and how it senses—how it perceives and expresses sense. We can only wonder what good it serves and, if we are given to care, what it feels. And in this regard we have, no doubt, undergone a loss of a *common* sense. What is it that we love when we say that we love an other? How can we love that which seems so mysteriously ensconced within the simulacrum, within the body-outline of the other? What does the saying of love mean? Is there really an exchange of feelings, or is it just an exchange of sayings? What more can we know?

What I wish to take from the method of radical skepticism are two basic things: the concept of *ataraxia*—particularly as it is interpreted by Sextus Empiricus—and the postulate of communicative equipollence. In many ways radical skepticism's concept of *ataraxia* anticipates the existentialist's encounter with the emotional reality of *ennui*. One's experience of *ennui* is not the end-point of radical reflection. Instead, it holds the possibility of the beginning of a full encounter with one's world. It is my argument that this therapy emerges from what Merleau-Ponty terms the *dehiscence*—from the splitting-open, the fission—of an embodied consciousness of a world that, in effect, throws the "embodiment" out of its house, half-dressed and out of its mind, out of its shell, and into another world.[27] New consciousness emerges from new feelings and sensations. And so, among the possibilities of this or any other discovery, we are able to discover that we are *not yet dead*. Our personal body is revealed to us as though for the first time and we become questionable to ourselves at the very moment we discover ourselves.

Here, the "I" of me and the "me" of me are no longer in geosynchronous orbit but I still recognize them both. To the extent the experience is jarring for the self, the range of new vision has not as yet fully and actually occurred. What is jarring is the intuited sense of its possibility—that in fact the water really could break and we would, in fact, have to enter a new world. What is jarring is the anticipation of change; and what is also jarring is the anticipation of loss. The psychology of terror clings to the anticipation of what *may* eventually happen. The dehiscence, the splitting open, is, if I let myself feel it, an ecstasy, an *ek-stasis*. The body's coming-into-being is its coming-into-being for me. It is at this moment that I can, to paraphrase Whitman, sing my body electric. Because I am not dead yet, I am—in the expression of the "me" that is now me—very much alive. The song of my body, the rhythm of my heart, the rhyme of my thought is only therapeutic if I am sufficiently aware that I am alive.

The application of philosophical work to the transformation of consciousness and Self, what Foucault, after Pierre Hadot, termed *epimeleia heatou* (and Hadot himself called "philosophy as a way of life"[28]) is undertaken as a therapy of vital experience. Samuel Beckett's *Waiting for Godot* is built on this vulnerable foundation, this narrative foundation of vulnerability. All too many of us, and all too often, all too often, are not dead yet and we do not fully know it. As with Vladimir and Estragon, dehiscences of mind and body may well have come and gone, yet we stand in wait for the seemingly important one that may well happen, and perhaps (hopefully) sometime soon. Until then, we are as good as dead (or, at least, little better than dead)—dead to one another but, most critically, dead to ourselves. Benjamin writes: "We are bored when we don't know what we are waiting for. That we do know, or think we know, is nearly always the expression of our superficiality or inattention."[29] *Ennui* is hardly a pleasant feeling, but it is a feeling. If one can appreciate this anxiety for what it is, one can see that it is a sign of life, perhaps the most basic sign of life opening itself to reading and interpretation—it is the remainder of life after one has taken worried account of all that can fall away. *Ennui* and "annoy" share the same Latin root form, *in odio*, which does not really signify boredom at all. *In odio* denotes "in hatred." To feel *ennui* is to sense the odiousness of what one's world has become. And thus the experience of *ataraxia*, I suggest, is what remains of *ennui* once we let go of the anger.

In an extended commentary on the work of Walter Benjamin, Carlo Salzani addresses the discomfort of *ennui* (or spleen) by referencing a passage from Georg Simmel: "Benjamin's generation was strongly influenced by the analysis of metropolitan life made by Georg Simmel. 'The psychological basis of the metropolitan type of individuality,' he wrote in 'The Metropolis and Mental Life,' 'consists in the *intensification of nervous stimulation* which results from the swift and uninterrupted change of outer and inner stimuli."[30] Salzani continues: "In Benjamin's reading of Baudelaire, spleen is ambiguously related to, and at times confused with, *ennui*: 'One of the central motifs of this poetry,' Benjamin quotes from François Porché, 'is, in effect, boredom in the fog, ennui and indiscriminate haze. . . . In a word, it is spleen.' Benjamin simply follows a fashion in the Baudelairean critique which treats spleen and *ennui* as synonyms: both are characterized by 'dull, glib sadness,' 'weariness' [*Müdigkeit*], and 'naked terror' [*nackten Schreckens*]."[31]

Now, what we see in contemporary times is that the experience of the therapeutic moment has all too often come to be associated with a vacation from the sort of disciplinarity that Foucault, in the *Hermeneutics of Subjectivity*, terms the *askesis* of self-care—visually summarized in alluring images of the beach, a cold drink, a warm bath, stolen moments, tax havens from the wages of mental labor. (Even Siddhartha's river in Hesse's novel can, to an impatient reader, present itself as such.[32]) But there is a basic difference between pleasure and therapy. When *ataraxia* is taken as interchangeable with pleasure, it becomes a means of psychological and emotional avoidance. The life of an embodied mind becomes caught in suspended animation. The therapy of entertainment is sought by a body whose suffering is primarily experienced as fear, a fear of an anguish that one is convinced lies in waiting. It is the sign of flesh being consumed by its own life. Salzani comments: "This overstimulation and the consequent defensive strategy of the conscience produce what Benjamin calls the "atrophy of experience" [*Verkümmerung der Erfahrung*]."[33]

THE COMMUNICOLOGY OF *GEIST*

In *Was Heisst Denken?* Heidegger makes the claim that "science does not think" and, a bit later, that "only when a person speaks does that person think—not the other way around, as meta-physics still believes."[34] For Heidegger, a thinker experiences the calling of thought toward itself, from its inception in mind to its expression in signs, and the thinker becomes the medium of this transformation and coil. So, the other is present in thinking. Thought is present, in fact *comes to presence*, in speaking. The other is *called* in speech. Speech "thinks" the other. And, as such, it can likewise be said that otherness comes into being—is *conceived*—in the expression of the self. Here, one might suggest that ordinary metaphysics finds itself tongue-tied at precisely the same moment in which it attempts to speak itself with its object.

Heidegger's reflections in the first chapters of *Was Heisst Denken?* reveal his fondness for a particular passage from Hölderlin. He returns to it over and again. I think it captures the "therapy problematic" as I have sketched it thus far: "We are a sign that is not read,/We feel no pain, we almost have/Lost our tongue in foreign lands."[35] The skeptic's postulate of equipollence is critical to this process. In my view, the phenomenological turn that must occur for a therapy of desire to begin is one of spirit—in other words: *ataraxia* entails a psychological, a *Geistliche*, shift. It is a turn that must transpire (i.e., *trans-spire*, literally, to spirit across) in noetic space, which is to say it is not *entirely* a temporal matter even though it is otherwise principally a matter of eidetic experience. In describing a movement of consciousness across a gap, a flow of energy across a synapse, we must allow sufficient space for the play of semiotic motion. It goes beyond the notion of simply "one thing, stretched." For Lacan, the imaginary order enables an intrapersonal, intrasubjective account of the delicate noetic relations of "I" and "me."[36] Within this order, subjectively reflected images are multidimensional. They are multidimensional and they have texture. Anything that is ambiguous cannot be accounted for by one measure, one percept alone. Attempting to do so turns them into "signs that are not read."

The difficulty of temporality in this regard is that in speaking of things whose lives are, as Heidegger would have it, "thought-provoking," we must refrain from the tendency to let language exist for thought as a merely verbal event. We must not let our language lay flat. Spirit, first, requires a live body to receive it, to breathe it in. All too often we English speakers have let the word that the German language comfortably is spoken as *Geist* be translated as "mind" or "intelligence" and, in the forgetfulness of our rationality and the deflation of our spirit, have permitted our intelligence of life and experience to lay flat. To lose "our tongue in foreign lands"—to dwell poetically in language—necessitates that we let our selves be haunted by the world, and in turn to haunt as we are haunted, to trouble, to disturb, to stir up the elements.

Equipollence, which I am inclined (at least for the purpose of this essay) to blur with the broader gesture of phenomenological reduction, describes an ecological stance of thought. It is the stance of thought that enables the ethic of *Geist*, its *habitus* and dwelling, to be addressed intrapersonally (noetically) and semiotically without resorting to the often-arbitrary presumptions (or occasionally hair-splitting dogmas) of ordinary consciousness. The therapy of desire requires intellectual room to turn around and a level playing-field. Simply, communicative ecology is both a spatial and a temporal matter.

Jurgen Ruesch and Gregory Bateson describe the motility of spirit in the dialogue of mind as a form of communication. They refer to it as "in*tra*personal communication," and they entail its operation within a systems framework of cybernetics and the nascent communication theories of clinical psychology and applied psychoanalysis. Their groundbreaking and influential 1951 work bearing the still-intriguing title, *Communication: The Social Matrix of Psychiatry*, identifies four modalities, four networks, four levels, four economies of human interaction.[37] These modalities are designated not by convention but by inexorability. They are as close to a *natural* order of relationship, transformation, and information transfer as the general academic field of communicology is going to come for a very long time. The in*tra*-personal modality of communication is an ecology inasmuch as it entails a reflective (and recursive) dialogue of mind. The intrapersonal modality of communication is intended to capture the essence of what others have been inclined to call, for various purposes and at various times: thought, intuition, cognition, reflection, meditation, imagining, and dreaming.

Against the traditions of classical and Cartesian thought that would consider the proper function of mind as a repression of the body, Merleau-Ponty considers mind (or *Geist*/spirit) and thought to be a "sublimation of the flesh."[38] He maintains: "Thought is a relationship with oneself and the world as well as a relationship with the other. . . . [I]f we make the thought appear upon an infrastructure of vision, this is only in virtue of the uncontested evidence that one must see or feel in some way in order to think, that every thought known to us occurs to a flesh."[39] Merleau-Ponty stresses that "the passage to intersubjectivity is contradictory only with regard to an insufficient reduction."[40] In other words, the dialogic character of thinking situated within the context of our perception and experience is only possible if we can accept the world and all of its spontaneity as it is. Such was the challenge of equipollence in antiquity, and such is the challenge of phenomenological reduction today.

The word "sceptic," traced back to antiquity, did not originally denote "doubt" but, instead, implied "one who looks, considers, observes."[41] Barnhart's research takes note that the connotation of "skeptic" as "one who has a doubting attitude" is first recorded in English in 1615.[42] So, after two millennia, doubt is what we have added; neurosis is what we bring to it now. The psychological doubt of neurosis diminishes consciousness. It postpones *ataraxia* inasmuch as it disables equipollence. It disables capacities for opening up, and exploring *through the opening* the new and unfamiliar language of the newly visible, or of the visible suddenly cast in different light. Anxiety is the source of tension, a stretching of consciousness across space and time in anticipation of a new beginning. Anxiety is not *ennui*. Anxiety is not *ennui* because it is much more complex. It is felt in that which aches to be born and, as well, it is in anxiety that we may feel inhibited or bewildered at the moment of dehiscence.

SYSTEMIC DIFFERENCES AND THE EXPERIENTIAL SPACE OF THE COMMUNICATIVE BODY

For Ruesch and Bateson, the other three modalities of human communication are *social*. That is, they imply the communicative presence of an embodied otherness. Nonetheless, all four modalities of human communication contribute significantly to the experience of what can, I think, rightly be called "institutions" of experience and consciousness—at least in a general sense. The nature of an institution is inescapably a structural matter. Though institutions are sites of transformation, in precisely the sense of dehiscence, catharsis, perception, and *ataraxia* that I have suggested thus far, they are describable in terms of a rudimentary regularity of relations that has enabled insights from psychoanalysis and systems theory (two human science disciplines often charged with the crime of "structuralism") to blend with the general project of existential phenomenology.

The *ataraxia* of a communicative relationship is enabled in the gestalt of the dehiscence of open, dialogic exchange. Verbal performance is always of secondary importance—not unimportant, certainly, but secondary to the event of an "opening-up" that is no way attributable to the contribution of one speaker or another. In Merleau-Ponty's elegant phrasing: "to the extent that what I say has meaning, I am a different 'other' for myself when I am speaking; and to the extent that I understand, I no longer know who is speaking and who is listening."[43] Dialogic transaction is not to be grasped as a consequence of either choice or linear sequence; one is mistaken to privilege the syntagmatic axis of language over the paradigmatic axis, or vice versa—or even to recognize their functions as separate from one another. Nonetheless, human relations do not occur in a context of "no context." And to the extent communicative transaction is virtually interchangeable with the concept of systemic or organismic transformation, an institute (or an institution, broadly conceived), I will contend, is the house of that transformation. Another way of phrasing this is to suggest that the idea of an institution is the necessary systemic economy that serves to contextualize the experience of system ecology.

The word "institution" is instructive in this regard. The Latin word *institutio* is derived from the Greek *in-stasis*. *In-stasis*, phenomenologically considered by way of a basic tableau of dialogue and recognition, can be taken as a companion term to the Heideggerian concept of *ek-stasis*. If so, *in-stasis* would describe the discursive (i.e., relational or interstitial) conditions that enable or empower an ecstatic transformation of bodily being.[44] When we speak of something on the order of, say, "institutional decline" we are, then, emphasizing particular qualities of specific instances of institution rather than expressing the notion that historical institutions of sociality and communication are moving toward extinction. (This is a distinction that is understood by the human sciences, but typically neglected by journalism.)

For Ruesch and Bateson, the recurrent structures of human communicative experience are: first, in*tra*personal communication; secondly, in*ter*personal communication (that is, communication limited to two persons); third, group communication (that is, communication between "one and many"—however, the arithmetic principle that differentiates a group network from an interpersonal network is the simple presence of more than two persons; *viz.*, when a third person enters into a conversation, it is no longer interpersonal). Finally, there is the cultural network of communication, which Ruesch and Bateson describe as "many-to-many," or "inter-group" communication. In cultural communication, people are understood principally by their roles and social functions rather than their individual names. They are understood through the semiotic/symbolic filter of their social affiliations. We have all too frequently, out of discursive habit, come to interpret the network of cultural communication as being *the* principle domain of institutional power and knowledge when, in fact, the cultural network is limited in its capabilities to certain types of information and certain exercises of power. Given its structure, a culture has only so much power at any given moment as the groups who constitute its networks permit it to have. The same can be said for the power of an individual or group.

Instances of institution are everywhere around us and across the span of history, and they can, of course, be specified, differentiated, and categorized to an infinite degree. This, as far as I know, has never been at issue. At least in terms of lived human interaction, what matters is that we have, by virtue of our mortality and our thrownness, a finite range of institutional experience. Our stock of memory is not inexhaustible; we can only live "so long." The structure of an interpersonal dyad reveals to each of us a limited and definable spectrum of possibilities for what an episode of interaction might mean, and how its narrative elements combine to give us a sense of how the relationship might be classified as an event, and how the event, in turn, may be assessed in terms of its quality.

INTERPERSONAL AND GROUP COMMUNICATIVE EXPERIENCES: THE FAMILY PROBLEMATIC

The interpersonal dyad is the principal communicative modality by which we experience intimacy. It may be said that intimacy is the intentionality of dialogue. Yet intimacy itself is irrelevant to any sort of outcome that may be achieved through mutual understanding, semiotic clarity, or even insight. And that is because intimacy is not an end state; it is instead a continuous process, a continuous dehiscence and "opening up" (*écart*), a horizon of new beginnings. Here, the later writing of Husserl proves instructive: "the flesh is also uniquely constituted in that it is, so to speak, half constituted as a thing and yet not experienceable for itself in a motion of a thing."[45] In essence, the conscious body is flesh—that is, it is palpable, tangible life—for the simple reason that is not finished yet, not dead yet, still hungry, still thirsty, still inquisitive, still shopping, still looking around. It is on the basis of how we experience intimacy that that we establish terms for what constitutes friendship. As with marriage, there are cultural expectations and group norms for the parameters of what "ought," for any given person, to be considered a good and valuable friendship. These norms are anything but stable rule systems and, unlike, marriage, are not subject to schemes of codification that engender much in the way of intercultural or inter-group meaning.

On the other hand, rituals of friendship, though they are different across societies and cultures, can easily be recognized as one enters into different domains of communicative practice. That is, we can observe and understand the intentionality of people being friendly without understanding much else of a language or discourse system. We may not understand specific rituals of friendship, but we can understand the human desire for intimacy and how the flesh of communication seeks to deliver itself to this inner directed process. The notion of friendship does not, in itself, denote anything but a broad range of intimacies. It may either lack or possess vehemence; it may either lack or possess abandon. It may or may not be erotic—or, for that matter, sexual. Because of its range of experiential potentialities it possesses a necessary but not sufficient relationship to the cultural practice of marriage. "It is obvious," Georg Simmel writes, "that the intimacy of the dyad is closely tied up with its sociological specialty, not to form a unit transcending the two members."[46] And that, I would argue, is because with marriage or other forms of other-conscious symbolisms, we proceed to invite interlopers of all sorts into the fabric of the dyad. The greater the extent of the invitation (whether conscious or unconscious, intentional or unintentional) the greater will be the inhibition to experience intimacy within the exclusivity of the dyad. Simply, it is hard to experience, express, and exchange romantic feelings in a house full of relatives.

Group communication can be seen as a broader systemic context for intimate, dyadic processes, family systems, and subsystems. As well, it can be understood as a network for formal, public, non-intimate discussion, deliberation, learning, and decision-making. An organization or government of persons with at least one significant common interest would, thus, fit the domain of group communication. (As well, three or more people headed out for an evening's entertainment would also fit the domain of group communication.) Modern government's commitment to practical and rational legitimation in the creation and execution of public policy is premised on an Enlightenment model of freedom and a Classical model of citizenship. To the extent that intimate and informal elements of group communication filter into the processes of the formal, public, non-intimate group network, we witness an analog of what Jürgen Habermas has come to describe as "legitimation crisis."[47]

Allow me to illustrate. Our first and most profound group experience is the family. Now the family system as experienced by the child is decidedly *not* based upon an Enlightenment model of freedom and a Classical model of citizenship—and this reality obtains regardless of whether the family system is communicatively healthy or pathological. The family system, in this regard, functions as a group network of communicative relations but meets the primary pragmatic conditions for what Michel Foucault terms a *dispositif*, or disciplinary apparatus. Regardless of whether the pedagogy of authority is taught to the child elegantly or abusively, and regardless of whether the transmitted authority is that of a long-standing family tradition or simply the vehemence of the controlling parental psychology, the child learns the value of a conservative acquiescence in the authority of governmental will. In saying this, I am merely describing the inexorable realities of the child's entrance into the nurturing, pedagogical world of parental *eros*. A family is an inescapable fact of human reality. There is, simply, no functional alternative for the raising of children.

The functional subsystems of the family network—that is, the marital system, the parental system, the mother-infant system, the sibling system, the grandparental system, the aunt/uncle system—are built upon exercises of dyadic intimacy. Through these subsystems, each family member potentially experiences moments of ecstatic individuation. He or she is presented the opportunity to feel an exclusive relationship with another family member, to share secrets, to receive messages of evaluation or affirmation, to safely interrogate one's identity, to be given an opportunity to privately express needs and to be intimately understood. As children we learn to experience dialogic intimacy in the context of intrusions and jealousies. We learn the power of secrets at the same time as we learn the fragility of trust and confidence, and we learn this even if we are without siblings. It is here, in these moments and through these habituated experiences, that we learn to address our hungers for intimacy through interpersonal networks other than the mystified capacities of a caring parent to make things all better.

Our experiences within the hierarchy of family intimacy and family disciplinarity, thus, significantly participate in the shaping of our orientations toward interpersonal communication habits on one hand, and formal group decision-making rituals on the other. But the interdependence and interpenetration of these networks and of the institutional choices implied therein does not stop there. Each family is enveloped by culture and sees itself as either challenging or reifying cultural traditions. The embodied choices and expressive activity of a family, both centrifugally and centripetally, are historically situated within a general social and political economy. Which is also to say that a family's discursive matrix may well be extraordinarily imaginative or pathologically bizarre, but the family, ultimately speaks its version of a national language and its symbolic comportment accords, in some fashion or another, with the recognizable psychological flux of its time and place. Moreover, patterns and flows of language, rhetorics, rationalities, and rationalizations are experienced and reexperienced by the family, collectively and individually, and its surrounding social networks. Concern about social position and cultural value commonly seeps into the smallest details of everyday life—how long to cut a child's hair, how often to change sheets or mow the lawn, how the family members choose to converse at the dinner table,

Just as important as a family's participation, whether strategically, resistively, quiescently, or unconsciously, in the cultural milieu of its principal social networks is the modality of in*tra*personal reflection and the embodied disciplinary *habitus* of thinking. What I am getting at here is not what is meant by such terms as "self-talk" or "intra-psychic" processes. If Heidegger has taught us anything it is that thinking is not a discourse event—and its domain is hardly exhausted by the field of cognitive science. For we are ultimately within the domain of thought when we find ourselves addressing the world that seems, even still, to be trapped inside the organic tissue of our flesh. It is within the domain of thought that we, at times, seek therapeutic treatment for the somatic effects, often severe in their debilitation, that coincide with our stressed habituation of neurotic anxiety. When we speak of our feelings we speak of something that remains just out of the reach of rational consciousness—which is to say that when we speak of our feelings we are speaking of our flesh in its carnal dialect. Our feelings are the only voice we have to experience of our flesh. Pain, laughter, even dizziness, is the *Ursprache* of *Dasein*. It is not a language, it is only voice, or, rather, it is the simultaneity of voice-in-speech. It could be said in the same breath that all doctors minister to the mind and that all doctors minister to the body. Existentially there is no difference.

The experience of *ataraxia*, thus, is not a therapy of desire if, by those terms, one is referring to a pedagogy of right thinking, of learning to want the right things for the right reasons. And yet, this is precisely the therapy of desire that Martha Nussbaum prescribes in her text. It is said that shame is the feeling one experiences when one senses that the other is about to behold the truth of what has been hidden behind the curtain. The therapy of philosophical reflection may have elements of what, in a bold poetic sense, may be termed "interior design," but is not about home decoration. Given that we are all composed of flesh, and that flesh communicates, at least in part, by way of a visible skin (a skin to which we customarily add clothing) we all are hiding something. What we hide behind the curtain is the motility of psyche, and the motility of psyche, Merleau-Ponty makes clear, is what defines the flesh of our communicative realities. Getting one's house in order is a blood matter. What is behind the curtain is not merely in the language of our thought, but in our interpersonal affairs, our families, and our social groups. We attempt to obstruct lines of vision from the drama of what shames us but our ongoing drama nevertheless remains out there for everyone to see. We are shamed by its visibility. The curtain, it turns out, is really for our own eyes.

THE CULTURAL INSTITUTION OF THE FAMILY AND THE *IN-STASIS* OF COMMUNICATIVE AGENCY

Culturally and historically, we have come to experience the essential reality that we are active, infused members of a communicative group before we come to experience meaningful dyadic interaction.[48] Intimate interpersonal communication thus does not come naturally to us as we live through the entrenched *habitus* of family systems. Working from the existentialist premise that "autonomous self-acceptance develops from the courageous exploration of self-doubts," David Schnarch contends that "many couples who complain of a lack of intimacy are actually intolerant of the intense awareness of self and other created by the recognition of existing in two separate but congruent realities."[49] He then concludes: "The capacity for intimacy is directly linked to the ability to tolerate existential loneliness and the relativity of one's perceptions. Differentiation is what permits an individual to participate in a system—whether a marriage, a family, or a society—without being captured by it."[50]

Nonetheless, we begin the spiritual journey of our subjective lives as "captives" of a *dispositif.* The move toward consciousness is an engagement with the intersubjectivity of our expressive and perceptive embodiment, but it is a movement that is without grace if we cannot address the enmeshment and embeddedness of our subjective consciousness *in* our families of origin. No matter how great one's commitment to an emancipatory philosophy, without experiencing the dehiscence of one's perceptual consciousness out of the emotional boundaries of the family unit—out of the nuclear *gemeinschaft* of love and knowledge that functions as all one knows of self and identity through childhood—one cannot quite live through the phenomenology of intersubjectivity.

This is also to say that if the disciplinary consciousness of one's family of origin is not transcended through new experience and through willing engagement in other fields of disciplinary choice, one does not fully engage in interpersonal communication.

On this point I want to be as clear as possible: it is not the family of origin that is ever "at fault." Nor can the *institution* of the family, particularly as it has progressed and adapted, be blamed for one's failures in intimacy. To live one's thinking, as Heidegger might have it, or to experience the therapy of desire, accepting *ataraxia* as both condition and consequence of an engaged dialogue with the world, one ought not attempt to reinvent the systems by which childhood is experienced. In other words, uniquely damaging instances of family dysfunction are the product of individual choices, not the fault of a repression inherent in the simple fact that parents possess the power to enforce rules of order on their offspring.

What remains problematic is the condition of self-renunciation to which we grow all too familiar in our childhood experience of family *logos*. Foucault has identified this difficulty as one coincident with "the tradition of Christian morality which makes self-renunciation the condition for salvation."[51] While I cannot disagree with Foucault's hypothesis, it also seems that there is a pattern, *seemingly* entrenched in the history of families and the subdued discourse of children's experience in the West, of self-renunciation that arises from being nurtured and instructed by adults. Simply, developing the capacity to recognize, elaborate, and respect one's own psychological boundaries comes slowly to children in even the most enlightened family systems.

A sense of agency gradually emerges both from the process of language acquisition and from the process of psychosocial development. The parental system can initiate the process of individuated agency, but it cannot complete it. Only the adolescent can recognize and grasp the dream of his or her own exit. The exit is slow, bewildering, complicated, and is never complete—and the more deeply enmeshed the system of family relations, the greater the likelihood that the dream will be deferred. Murray Bowen conceptualizes the family as an "emotional unit," a network of interlocking relationships anchored in subjective processes of anxiety management as well as task-oriented system maintenance. In this regard, it is not merely that children enter a world whose rules they cannot choose, it is that they enter into the unfinished intergenerational emotional work of their parents.[52] And these same parents whose, perhaps, deeply unsatisfying experiences of interpersonal intimacy compound the psychological demands placed upon the family network, are the child's existential exemplars of how interpersonal communication is to emerge in dialogic encounter.

Foucault observes that the classical injunction "know thyself" has eclipsed the ancient Greek concept of "taking care of oneself." He asserts that knowing oneself, in other words, taking a concerned, ascetic account of what one does and how one acts, was grasped as the purest "way to self-renunciation," and that we "find it difficult to base rigorous morality and austere principles on the precept that we should give ourselves more care than anything else in the world."[53] Now, the economy of pleasure that describes the day-to-day affairs of people anxiously seeking therapeutic release from the work and pressure of a fearful and increasingly inhospitable world would seem to contradict the premise of self-renunciation. But it does not.

And it is here that Heidegger's concept of thinking, Merleau-Ponty's concept of flesh, and Foucault's concept of "self care" begin to overlap in important ways. The problem that has emerged is one of guilt. For the unreflective and undifferentiated person, instances of interpersonal communication are always haunted by familial presences, introjections, symbolisms, and undigested, perhaps surreal myths and lessons from a childhood whose memories linger in irregular and inconsistent ways. We hunger for a meaningful intimacy but, simultaneously, we are deeply afraid of it. To speak openly, Foucault maintains, has become one and the same as to confess the shame of one's flesh. And so we follow social tendencies to ritualize interpersonal situations around tightly mannered premises so that the bare minimum is ever spoken, or we ritualize interactions of love and care, desire and vulnerability around *carneval* excesses in which speech flows generously but without a "thoughtful" will.

The body of thought, the care of the self, in short, the ministry of therapy, all begin from the notion that the flesh is anything but a source of shame. Giving ourselves more care than anything else in the world is what leads us to draw the curtains wide and let the energy, the light of our desire become the "show" of our life. It is Foucault's general admonition that, in the intimate pursuit of our selves, we ought not be concerned with our lives as things whose natures can be known. Intimate contact, fleshly contact, is a commitment to the problematic of living carefully, of living as best we can. The longer we spend in the emotional haunts of the family's symbolic matrix, the less clearly we will be able to visualize freedom in accidental moments of dehiscence.[54]

As a child, I was not sure if I really owned my body. I saw myself as indisputably belonging to my family, and they, in a way, to me. Irrespective of whether or not I felt loved (which, of course, I most often did), I could certainly feel that I was a preoccupation and, often, a problem to be addressed. In wanting to be a comfort and not a problem, I was like all children. For a very long time I saw my freedom as inseparable from my family's degree of concern about me, which, I now know is as commonplace as it is dispiriting.

David Michael Levin writes that "there is an ideal which is implicit in the body of radically reflective experience: an ideal I would describe in terms of its 'spirituality.' Merleau-Ponty's notion of 'flesh' moves us very much closer to an understanding of the body's 'participation' in this spiritual dimension of existence."[55] The spiritual dimension—again, the *Geistliche* dimension—does not so much entail an "inward turn" as much as it entails a turn toward the invisible, toward the other side of the body. Merleau-Ponty notes that "a philosophy of the flesh is the condition without which psychoanalysis remains anthropology."[56] Anthropology, in the sense implied by Merleau-Ponty, is a precategorized analysis of what one has come to observe, however carefully; it is a not-fully-engaged description. It also is not fully a *participation* in the field of that which can reverse the eye of the observer back upon herself. The philosophy of the flesh entails a ministry, an engagement with "the sensible being . . . that feels itself in me."[57] It emphasizes the consubstantiality and recursivity of all therapeutic encounters. It requires that the "minister" or "magister" of whatever sort, be able to let loose of her or his body—to cross over, to interlace, to experience the ataraxia, if not the ecstasy, of flesh yet again.

NOTES

1. Now, let me say at the beginning that a word so common to contemporary life as "psychology" will need to be used with a certain caution. The concept of "psyche" that is implicated in virtually all uses of the word, whether academic, naive or even historical, is profoundly equivocal. The standard academic usage refers to a research, medical, and educational discipline for the study of the mind, but even then the divisions between the cognitivists, the behaviorists, the clinicians, the neuroscientists, the Freudians, the neo- and post-Freudians, the Jungians, and so forth, render disciplinary definitions more problematic than helpful. And then aside from academic usage, everyday usage struggles with the persistent semantic exoticism of the word "psyche." It can mean brain, mind, soul, spirit, consciousness, thought, emotion, reason, and intention, it can mean these notions separately, in combination, or all at once.
2. Mark, Levit, Coffey and others, *National Expenditures for Mental Health Services and Substance Abuse Treatment 1993–2003.*
3. Reisman, *A History of Clinical Psychology*, 47.
4. Caplan, *Mind Games: American Culture and the Birth of Psychotherapy*, 4.
5. Caplan, 4–5.
6. Danziger, "Comment," 271.
7. Kurt Danziger, *Naming the Mind.*
8. Illouz, *Saving the Modern Soul,* 2.
9. Foucault, *The History of Madness*, 449–54.
10. Foucault, *Psychiatric Power.*
11. Justman, *The Psychological Mystique,* 1.
12. Foucault, *Hermeneutics of the Subject,* 8–9.
13. Nussbaum, *The Therapy of Desire.*
14. Jack Abecassis, "The Fragility of Philosophy: Passions, Ancient and Modern," 918–42.
15. Nussbaum, 312–15.
16. Sextus Empiricus, *Outlines of Pyrrhonism*, I: 8–10.
17. Sextus Empiricus, I: 29.
18. Sextus Empiricus, I: 29.
19. Plant, "Perhaps: Jacques Derrida and Pyrrhonian Scepticism,"137.
20. I would also maintain that a fair reading of Pyrrhonian skepticism could locate the trajectory of its essential method well within the orbits of contemporary semiotics, phenomenology, and grounded postmodern reflection—which is also to say: communicological.
21. See Holenstein, *Roman Jakobson's Approach to Language.*
22. See Lanigan, *The Human Science of Communicology.*
23. Cassirer, *The Logic of the Cultural Sciences,* 100.
24. See Merleau-Ponty, *The Visible and the Invisible.*
25. See especially Baudrillard, *Simulations.*
26. Benjamin, *The Writer of Modern Life,* 139.

27. Merleau-Ponty, *The Visible and the Invisible*, 146.
28. Hadot, "Forms of Life and Forms of Discourse in Ancient Philosophy," 483–505.
29. Benjamin, *The Arcades Project*, 105.
30. Salzani, "The Atrophy of Experience: Walter Benjamin and Boredom," 131.
31. Salzani, "The Atrophy of Experience: Walter Benjamin and Boredom," 137.
32. See Hesse, *Siddartha.*
33. Salzani, "The Atrophy of Experience: Walter Benjamin and Boredom," 137.
34. Heidegger, *Was Heisst Denken?* 8, 16.
35. Hoelderlin, cited by Heidegger in *Was Heisst Denken?*, p. 18.
36. Lacan, *The Language of the Self*, 174–75.
37. Ruesch and Bateson, *Communication.*
38. Merleau-Ponty, *The Visible and the Invisible*, 145.
39. Merleau-Ponty, *The Visible and the Invisible*, 145–46.
40. Merleau-Ponty, *The Visible and the Invisible*, 172.
41. Onions, *Oxford Dictionary of English Etymology*, 796.
42. Barnhart, ed., *The Concise Dictionary of Etymology*, 723.
43. Merleau-Ponty, *Signs*, 97.
44. See Macke, "Quintilian's *Institutio Oratoria* and Postmodern Pedagogy," 192–93.
45. Husserl, *Husserl at the Limits of Phenomenology*, 151.
46. Simmel, *The Sociology of Georg Simmel*, 127.
47. See Habermas, *Legitimation Crisis*.
48. The lone exception might seem to be the case of the mother who raises her one and only child in the absence of any everyday assistance from and interaction with others, a circumstance that cultures across the globe have never embraced, and which does not mark any identifiable social trend. But even in this case, the presence of the absent father will become a matter of growing awareness for the child. His existence is certainly a source of consciousness for the mother, even if she would rather forget.
49. Schnarch, *Constructing the Sexual Crucible*, 112–13.
50. Schnarch, 114.
51. Foucault, "Technologies of the Self," 22.
52. See Kerr and Bowen, *Family Evaluation.*
53. Foucault, "Technologies of the Self," 22.
54. See Sennett, *Respect in a World of Inequality*, 170.
55. Levin, *The Body's Recollection of Being*, 68.
56. Merleau-Ponty, *The Visible and the Invisible*, 267.
57. Merleau-Ponty, *The Visible and the Invisible*, 255. See also Dillon, "Merleau-Ponty and the Reversibility Thesis," 86.

Chapter Three

The Mirrored Body

Phenomenological Reflections on the Visual Experience of the Reflected Self

INTRODUCTION: THE CARTESIAN IN THE MIRROR

In an essay titled "*L'Oeil et l'esprit*" completed in the summer of 1960, Merleau-Ponty studies the aesthetic domain of painting with a greater clarity and a greater depth than in any of his previous or subsequent works, which, given his abiding interest in the work of Cézanne throughout his intellectual life, is saying quite a lot. In this essay, subsequently published in English as "Eye and Mind," Merleau-Ponty offers a sustained gaze into the unique human possibility of inventing expressive visual objects that are more than forms, more than structures, more than geometric configurations of the physical life world. The more closely one reads "Eye and Mind," the more one begins to undergo the stirring awareness that it is about considerably more than painting.

There is one particular sentence in "Eye and Mind" that continues to resonate with me more deeply and more fundamentally than any statement Merleau-Ponty makes throughout his later work. About one-third of the way into this essay, he writes: "A Cartesian does not see *himself* in the mirror; he sees a dummy, an 'outside,' which, he has every reason to believe, other people see in the very same way but which, no more for himself than for others, is not a body in the flesh."[1] This statement never ceases to amuse me, and for a variety of reasons. Not only is the statement a remarkably efficient condensation of the problem of dualism inherent in the semiological practices of modern empiricism, but it also succeeds in situating the dualist error squarely in front of itself—and for all observant eyes to see. What *does* a

Cartesian see when she or he looks in a mirror? For that matter, how, for a Cartesian, is "self" revealed to itself? As I consider this question and its implications, I am left, finally, to consider: what do *I* see when *I* look in the mirror? To what extent is what *I* see "me"? To what extent does my visual encounter with my body reveal the subjectivity that *sees*?

Martin Dillon has maintained that "solipsism is inherent to Cartesian thought."[2] As such, one might be inclined to ask: is vision an operation of the exquisite machinery of my consciousness that privileges "only me" to see the world and its objects as figures and backgrounds of my experience? Or is vision, in its irreducibility to an object of analysis, simply to be taken as yet another demonstration of the innate and self-evident truth of reason, of the divine light implanted in us all? These are questions I will not tackle as specific matters at this moment inasmuch as they are, in the broader gesture of their articulation, so richly symbolic of a philosophical discourse embedded in the episteme from which Descartes was himself attempting to escape through the adventure of his own thought. (It hardly need be said that Descartes' vision was not, simply, to catalog the received ideas of his world.) Yet, as Merleau-Ponty argued throughout his intellectual life, Descartes was, despite his genius, bound to fail in his attempt to situate the existential ground of the cogito within an imagined reflective mechanism of the embodied mind. His recourse to solipsism addressed the initial *phenomenal* matter of that which appears to consciousness, but it failed to see the *phenomenological* event of communication: that mind is transformed by encounter with instances of itself—that, in effect, all consciousness (and all experience) is relational.

Merleau-Ponty wrote "Eye and Mind" during the composition of both *Signs* and *The Visible and the Invisible*. Galen Johnson observes that it was "chronologically and intellectually interlaced" with both of these works, and indeed one finds critical themes from both of them fully circulating through the language and argumentation of "Eye and Mind."[3] The theme of "intertwining"—what Merleau-Ponty conceptualized as *chiasm* (or "flesh")—is itself intertwined and interlaced in the language of "Eye and Mind" at the very same moment the essay articulates its position on the intertwining of inner and outer, of flesh as "an 'element' of Being."[4] For acolytes of Merleau-Ponty's developing thought, the discourse on "flesh" at that unique epistemic moment was beginning to feel its own flesh; the corpus of Merleau-Ponty's works, already vital, had the uncanny pleasure of sensing its reach and feeling its body beyond its immediate grasp.

EXPERIENCE, SIGN, PERCEPTION, AND BODY IN THE LATE WORK OF MERLEAU-PONTY

In the course of his extended commentary on *The Visible and the Invisible*, Douglas Low has remarked that "Eye and Mind" was Merleau-Ponty's "most complete professional statement of his continually developing 'later' philosophy."[5] Sartre famously commented that it "says it all providing one can decipher it"[6]—to which Low adds: "By carefully reading this work along with the rest of Merleau-Ponty's later texts, the keys to this deciphering are beginning to be placed in our hands."[7]

Now, the purpose of my essay is not to speak historically or even epistemologically about the significance of "Eye and Mind," nor is it to place its discursive achievements within any sort of scheme or matrix of Merleau-Ponty's overarching philosophical projects. A number of works, impressive in their ambition and exploration, have already succeeded in doing so.[8] These works have been dedicated to the sort of exegetical commentary that might see Merleau-Ponty's later works as having arrived at a "new ontology"[9]—at a place where philosophical work can begin again.

Importantly, however, the issue for me is not whether a careful reading of Merleau-Ponty could produce the "deciphering" to which Sartre refers. Simply, there is nothing to gain by treating a philosopher's work as a sort of rebus, or even as a surrealist game that can, through an antic of thought, be decoded and mastered like any other. Vincent Descombes has remarked, "The pursuit of truth that has the character of absolute certainty marks the inauguration of modern philosophy."[10] I have long taken Merleau-Ponty's thought as, among other things, an attempt to overcome the false parameters of a modernist philosophy of language, a philosophy which holds that the elements of thought and expression remain, in their instrumentality, distinct from that which is intended, expressed, and perceived. In its function, that which we have come to call, generally, "language" (*langage*) sustains a *quality* of transcendence, but its existence is not merely transcendent, nor is it that of a transcendent structure. Merleau-Ponty, like Foucault, can rightly be said to doubt the concept of language (both *langue* and *langage*) as a domain unto itself. And I think Merleau-Ponty would agree with Foucault's broader argument, expressed through the first several chapters of *The Archaeology of Knowledge* (1972), that the enunciative capacity of a sign bears a fundamental indifference to the surface-perception of a thing that can be (and often is) taken as a sign. In these times, it seems the former remains the work of a phenomenology of communication and language, and the latter has become the property of what is now called "cultural studies."[11]

The "new ontology" implied by Merleau-Ponty's concept of flesh and vision entails a move toward a new horizon of experience and thought and into a different matrix of expression and phenomena, a matrix of expression outside of modernist ambitions. Here, Merleau-Ponty serves as the exemplar for my own endeavors; to wit, I find that genuine intellectual work begins when one finds oneself speaking with trepidation rather than with certitude.

For me, the impression that comes ever more sharply into focus with each reading of "Eye and Mind" is that the rationalist associations and equations seemingly embedded in the practice of "thinking" *with* "writing" have been built upon a motile and shifting ground. Rather than serving as a "foundation" (as the term is typically understood) for knowing and sensing, the rationalist assumptions embedded in our habits of visualizing the world arise from the kinetic flesh of bodies of all sorts and then fall back again upon a surface of consciousness that cannot remain the same. The process of reflection, after all, should not entail presuppositions of unfathomable interiorities and inscrutable meanings. Simply, reflection describes the encounter of kinetic surfaces, one with another, one touching another, one energized by the other.

The tain of a mirror, it should be noted, is not such a surface. For vision, the tain is but a nothingness, neither here nor there in the proprioception of seeing, existing only as reflectional relay—no more real than the surface of the water that tempts Narcissus. The mirror as a reflective instrument of everyday vanity or self examination, as a looking-glass placed at eye-level on the walls of homes or in the hands of someone momentarily concerned with his or her facial appearance, after all, is a relatively modern device.[12] Its technology enters into the lived-experience of everyday practical consciousness at roughly the same time as Descartes—which is why a theory of seeing, such as he attempts to articulate in the *Dioptrics*,[13] seems such a pivotal moment in the development of a philosophy of mind which sought to be coterminous with a philosophy of being.

Image perception matters to phenomenology because the perceiver and the perceived are both moving through time and space, going, embarking, departing, turning and returning, going again, even in sleep. Moreover, there is far more activity in the perception of the surfaces of things than is given in even the most careful reading of Descartes' *Dioptrics.* Simply, any surface, kinetic or not, reflective or not, is subject to a contest of projections, any one of which might prove satisfactory as a context for perception and interpretation. It entails a level of ambiguity unbearable even to a philosophy of ambiguity, a fact that arises inasmuch as we now live in a world with a rapidly multiplying number of contexts. The same cannot be said for the enunciative power of the sign. To conflate a reflective or even shiny surface with an enunciative sign is to confuse a fragment of a memory with a useful element of meaning. My position here accords with that taken by Dillon in his phenomenological critique of poststructuralism titled *Semiological Reductionism.*[14] In fact, many of the positions taken by Dillon against deconstruction are amplifications of forceful positions articulated by Foucault himself.[15] Basically, not everything that glimmers and draws our attention is a sign. Language is not a "surface phenomenon."

To identify a percept of any sort as some sort of intentional agent of signification is to operate on the premise that something meaningful must be going on somewhere of which, we can only assume, the percept must be playing an active part. Such a premise, no doubt, can find its adherents in an era pulsing with electronic messages, as well as relays and returns of those same messages. But Foucault limits his concern for expressive signs to what emerges from an enunciative field; his method offers us a means by which we can grasp the communicative power of situated and embodied *statements* (i.e., discursive formations or "speech acts"). The "person" I see in the mirror is a sign; it functions, if I so allow, as a sign of "me," but also as a sign of many other things. The reflective surface *may* be a sign, but it does not operate as one if my proprioceptive focus remains on the object in the mirror. This, no doubt, is also one of those elemental truths that "painters have always known": to entail a reflective surface in a painting, one must illustrate that which has been reflected. To signify the reflective surface *itself* by way of the brush and palette is, literally, to paint nothing at all.

In *The Dioptrics*, Descartes does not operate from a footing that enables this level of complexity. He is concerned with the seeing of *things*. The visual problematic of the reflective surface, simply, does not come up. Nor is Descartes concerned with signs and the expressive capacity of that which is addressed in the reach of the optical organ. The Cartesian body can understand the mechanics of its sensory apparatus, but it does not *yet* see itself seeing. For Merleau-Ponty, "the enigma is that my body simultaneously sees and is seen . . . it touches itself touching; it is visible and sensitive for itself."[16] Now, the Descartes to whom Merleau-Ponty is responding is not the Descartes of seventeenth-century Paris. He is responding to a system of thought that, simply put, continues to make phenomenology necessary. As such, it might best be said that Cartesian thinking describes the episteme from which phenomenology seeks to escape.

REFLECTIONS AND ECHOES OF DESCARTES IN TWENTIETH CENTURY CULTURE AND THOUGHT

Merleau-Ponty notes that Cartesians hold to "a naïve idea of a primordial world anterior to human fabrication"[17]—a point of view that I will argue fully raises the question of whether Merleau-Ponty's notion of the flesh can be grasped by the discourses of modern thought. Admittedly, my approach here will be much more genealogical than it will be straightforwardly phenomenological. In short, I think it is worth considering that, despite the expanding influence of Merleau-Ponty's thought at, roughly, the time during which

"Eye and Mind" was composed that Merleau-Ponty still *appeared* to be grappling with Cartesian dualism. Now, in saying this, I am not saying that Merleau-Ponty's choice to once again situate and unpack the Cartesian fallacy is mistaken or even peculiar. Instead, what I am pointing out is that, given the detailed and exhaustive critique of Cartesian rationalism in *The Phenomenology of Perception*,[18] yet another offensive *seemingly* aimed at the foolishness of dualism seems, at least on the surface, to be quite unnecessary. Simply, Merleau-Ponty's work had found itself at the center of French intellectual life, and he had already convincingly made his case.

Now, one might be inclined to see this choice as a matter of unavoidable intellectual-historical context. That is, one could posit that Merleau-Ponty merely inherited his fascination with Descartes from Husserl and the half-century of phenomenological writing that preceded his own work. As such, according to this formulation, to continuously interrogate Cartesian rationality is to do what a good phenomenologist does. I raise this point not simply to eliminate from consideration obvious and laughable failures of explanation but to highlight something significant about Merleau-Ponty's later work. It should not take much convincing for one to conclude that Merleau-Ponty's continued interrogation of Descartes was intentional and strategic—more specifically, that he could not comfortably develop his theme of the flesh, of chiasm, of intertwining and the reversibility of perception without paying particular attention to subtle nuances of Cartesian thinking with regard to the various *techné* of visual representation and the metaphysics of visual experience. Perhaps more importantly, the particular sentence from "Eye and Mind" that initiates my own curiosity here demonstrates the power of Merleau-Ponty's strategy of contextualizing the dualist problem as being, in the final analysis, one of *vision*. Not only is this fully apparent when one pays close attention to the language and logic of "Eye and Mind," but when one looks closely at the strategy and composition of *The Visible and the Invisible* one begins to gain a sense of how imbedded the Cartesian tradition of thinking about reflection and perception is in the habits and practices of "seeing" itself.

Thinkers of all stripes now regard solipsism as a philosophical mistake. Interestingly, instances of solipsistic thought are no longer purely philosophical matters; more to the point, they have been, through the last few decades, unproblematically and commonly medicalized as symptoms of delusion in psychopathology. Yet an inescapable fact is that recourses to solipsism are still not at all unusual patterns of reason in contemporary social life. An all-too-common first instinct is to assume insanity if someone perceives something that others cannot. Even while renouncing something along the lines of a philosophical doctrine of solipsism, one still reinforces its foundations by asserting, directly or indirectly, that my visible flesh marks the limit of my consciousness, or that my body marks the limit of my autonomous being (serving, additionally, as the container for my conscious mind).

The concept of "the flesh" that Merleau-Ponty develops both in "Eye and Mind" and in *The Visible and the Invisible* is a much richer, much more poetic and adventurous explication of the concept of embodied experience and the lived-body of perception and expression that he introduces in *The Phenomenology of Perception.* And without having to psychologize or historicize his intentions, we can comfortably say that Merleau-Ponty makes this case because, simply, it was always already there in the gesture of his thought. The intentionality of his writing in these later works is revealed as a matter of phenomenological depth: he is, ironically, *fleshing out* a concept of the body with a *language* of flesh and depth, touch and palpability, of chiasm and carnality that had not yet fully appeared in his discussion of gesture, sexuality, and motility in lived-body experience.

Moreover, it can be said that in perfecting his concept of embodiment he substantiates and embeds his reply to the institution of Cartesian thought in general and to the habits of modern consciousness in particular. In *The Prose of the World,* Merleau-Ponty observes:

> The transformations in Descartes's philosophy are famous. We explain him by the standards of our own understanding in the same way that modern painting classifies El Greco or Tintoretto. Before us, Spinoza, Malebranche, and Leibniz, as is well known, each in his own way put in the accents, altered the relations between "foreground" and "background," and defended his own Descartes. . . . Descartes is one of those institutions which are outlined in the history of ideas before they appear in person, as the sun can be seen before it suddenly unveils a renewed landscape.[19]

The echoes of Descartes that Merleau-Ponty hears incite the *parole parlée* of his own experience of chiasm and flesh. But it is not the voice of Descartes who made the pilgrimage to Notre-Dame-de-Lorette that he hears, but the echoes of his own time, the echoes of his own world, in essence, the echoes present and resonant in the *parole parlante* of his own body.

Descombes offers a fascinating narrative of "the generation of 'the three Hs'"(namely, Hegel, Husserl, and Heidegger) whose work during the early decades of the twentieth century was the primary source of influence for European postwar intellectuals.[20] Descombes emphasizes that this generation was led, in many respects, by Alexandre Kojève by way of a highly influential course on Hegel and phenomenology that he taught "at the Ecole Pratique des Haute Etudes, beginning in 1933 and lasting until 1939."[21]

Three of the students in this course, whose enrollment included numerous influential figures in European arts and letters, were Lacan, Sartre, and Merleau-Ponty. From Descombes' perspective, it was these three thinkers more than any others who were to become the standard bearers for the "generation of the three Hs." But this is not to say (despite, generally speaking, a fairly strong mutual regard for one another's work through the first half of the century) that the primary epistemological judgments of these three intellectuals could be seen as broadly overlapping, particularly on the matter of Descartes. Descombes remarks that Sartre's doctrine of humanism, assembled and articulated around the time of the publication of *Being and Nothingness*, was in many ways nothing more than an inverted Cartesian theology, placing "man" at the center of creation instead of the figure of "god."[22]

But for Merleau-Ponty, a series of much more complex matters pertaining to Descartes was "there" at the beginning. In *The Structure of Behavior* he is compelled to respond at length to both a Cartesian and a pseudo-Cartesian notion of perception.[23] From the start, it could be said that Merleau-Ponty sought to understand the modern objectivist problem in the context of the authorial origin of modern philosophical discourse. Yet, the working notes from *The Visible and the Invisible* reveal that his preoccupation with the Cartesian problematic was not without appropriate intellectual respect. He writes: "The Cartesian idea of the human body as human *non-closed*, open inasmuch as governed by thought—is perhaps the most profound idea of the union of the soul and the body . . . human only by reaching completion in a view of itself which is thought . . ."[24] The matter of Descartes, for Merleau-Ponty, is not that he "got things wrong" but that he seemed headed through a doorway that phenomenology itself needed to enter.

In the final years of his lectures to the *Collége de France*, Merleau-Ponty devoted a series of courses to the concept of nature. Commenting on Husserl, Descartes, and the "Copernican view of the universe," he remarks in 1960 that "Through meditation we must again learn of a mode of being whose conception he [Copernican man] has lost, the being of the 'ground' (*Boden*), and of the Earth first of all. . . "[25] Gary Madison comments at this juncture: "It is precisely this primordial mode of being that is *forgotten* ('forgetfulness of the Earth') as we progressively adopt 'the Copernican constitution of the world' whereby we leave behind our starting point, forget our terrestrial roots and 'come to consider the world as a pure object on an infinite reflection before which there are only interchangeable objects.' This forgetfulness of the originating, of the *arché*, reaches its completion in the Cartesian view of the world and in the classical sciences of nature."[26]

So, in his comment that "a Cartesian does not see *himself* in the mirror" it can well be said that Merleau-Ponty is not referring to a particular class of specific individuals who subscribe to the discourse and logic of Rene Descartes but to an ever-growing tendency in modern thought, to a forgetfulness of being that is, at once, a forgetfulness that belongs to the *habitus* of rationality. Merleau-Ponty is committed to a *meditation* on our modalities of being and sensing and perceiving, a meditation that, aside from a relatively small cadre of acolytes still dedicated to his thought, seems to have barely evolved at all since his untimely passing, a meditation that can accept neither solipsism nor the objectivist illusion as its fundamental starting point.

Four decades have passed since the publication of Merleau-Ponty's last principal works. Given the contributions of phenomenological thought to the growth of hermeneutics, critical theory, ethnography, and postmodern/poststructural modalities of thought, one might well be inclined to draw the conclusion that Merleau-Ponty's concept of the body has become a matter of second nature to inquiry in the human sciences. In a number of important ways, Merleau-Ponty's seminal contributions *are* presupposed in the work of Bourdieu, Foucault, Guattari, Deleuze, Lyotard, and Kristeva. As well, Bataille's theory of eroticism and Merleau-Ponty's concept of embodiment are remarkably similar in a number of respects despite the fact that there was no direct dialogue between them or between their works.

Yet to listen closely to the discourse on the problem of "the body" that has emerged as a central feature of cultural theory, cultural criticism, and cultural studies,[27] one might be inclined to think that Merleau-Ponty was but a minor footnote, if that, to a phenomenological movement that died in Europe shortly after World War II and which never really gained much of a methodological foothold in the English-speaking world.

As I write these words, several of Merleau-Ponty's primary texts are no longer in print in North America. Despite the popularity of "critical" and qualitative approaches to the human sciences, existential phenomenology (as such) is no longer "fashionable" as either a methodology or as a course of study in graduate programs. The sudden popularity of "cultural studies" is not to blame, for it is only a symptom of an embedded consciousness that Merleau-Ponty had fully anticipated in the composition of his later works. The modern social sciences, from the Vienna Circle, to behaviorism, to the powerful emergence of cognitive science, have rarely paid close attention to the insights of Continental thought. And now the postmodern wave of theorizing and polemicizing the problematics of nature, culture, and society has, in its own forgetfulness of being, forgotten the phenomenology of lived-body experience. As such, it has forgotten its epistemological *Grund*—and, at least from the standpoint of sales and marketing, it seems to have forgotten Merleau-Ponty. Postmodern and poststructural writing, in its quest to situate and find its own body in the mirror, cannot see the genealogy of its body; it cannot see its historical Self. The claim to a post-*modernism*, thus, is not necessarily an affirmation of a post-*Cartesianism*.

And so, as I now see it, the questions that arise from Merleau-Ponty's infamous remark are much more general, much broader than those which previously came to mind. Perhaps all too many of us are Cartesians. Perhaps we are and do not know it. Perhaps we are and simply do not care. As such, what is it that "we" see when *we* look into the mirror? What is the flesh that we behold? To what extent is our self-reflection at all possible?

THE MIRROR *AND* THE FLESH/ *MY MIRROR* AND *MY FLESH*

I can still fully recall standing in front of the bathroom mirror in my early-to-mid-teens. My parents' house had just one bathroom, so any time given to matters of personal vanity was at a premium. At the age of fourteen, I took all of the time I could. As an anxious kid, I had more than my fair share of facial blemishes, and I took inventory of them at every opportunity, if only to gain a kind of psychological foothold, if not a psychological control, over my capacity to anticipate their configuration on my chin, cheeks, and forehead. By studying my face, I attempted to gain some sort of insight about how I might be perceived by my classmates. I would liberally apply Clearasil to the blemishes to see if by slathering on the pinkish-tan (that is, "flesh-toned") ointment I could perceive them with less clarity—or, perhaps, not see them at all. At first, only a bleary-eyed squint would make this remotely possible. But then as I let my eyes focus, I saw the topography of my complexion in its full reality. The inflamed bumps on my face were, with the cosmetic ointment, less inflamed, but they also did not participate in the tonality and coloring of my fleshly facial skin. After wiping off some but not all of the Clearasil, I would then render a judgment about my readiness to venture out. I had no faith whatsoever in the ointment to offer any sort of medical relief for the blemishes. Essentially, I took it to be a cosmetic, a conclusion that I quietly kept to myself. Washed and scrubbed, sore and inflamed, the blemishes seemed to dry up and disappear with greater efficiency, but I was not at all comfortable with even the idea of entering the unpitying milieu of my high school with a face that felt as though it could glow in the dark.

The kinetic sculpture of my face—itself, of course, nothing more than a "surface matter"—was an exasperating reality to the fourteen-year-old version of my Self, a Self who longed for the sanctuary of a stable personal appearance, of a face I no longer had to discipline like an unruly child, of a face that I no longer had to track like wild game. What I wished for was a face that, with its order and predictability, would no longer be visible to me, a face I really did not have to notice. What I wanted, if only for a day, was a face I *could not see* when I *looked* into the *mirror*.

Richard Lanigan has commented [28] on several occasions that undergraduate students seem no longer to "have" bodies when they take their seats in university classrooms. I have taken this to mean that the convenience of the bodies that brought them to class—that enable them to function in the disciplinary modalities of hanging out, in the visualizing and performing of Spring Break, bodies that continually debut for one another—become considerably less convenient, less fitting in the disciplinary modality of the classroom. Within minutes these bodies cannot find a comfortable position; they seem reluctant to express themselves, not only toward the expression of a sincere and original thought but to simply raise a question or to ask their teachers or classmates to repeat a valuable point that they may not have fully heard.

The level of comfort or discomfort in "student bodies," regardless of whether such bodies are the students in my classrooms, my own body as a student in classrooms years ago, or my teenaged memory of my self, standing before the mirror, is a function of desire. We embody a consciousness of judgment that witnesses our reflected body-image or body-space as a ratio of reflected presence to reflected vision. We take note of a process in the very place of our observation. We take note that we are not *where* we want to be, that we have a vision of ourselves some place else, at some other time, in a different body state and with a different body-image. We see our embodied body-*image* as Linneaus saw the insect *imago* years before—as that to which we are ever-developing and evolving toward. The image is never, itself, "real." Perhaps it is but a *telos*. In any case, it is a portal that, if entered, leads us to yet another story of our lives.

It can be said, although in a somewhat limited way, that my body is but a technique of my species-being–that I embody the world in a certain way and with a particular style that expressively places what I do and how I accomplish what I do alongside the accomplishments of all others. It can even be said that when I see the "humanity" of animals in the comportment of their bodies I am making this same sort of comparative assessment. In this regard, the manner in which the activity of desire functions, whether it be in a disciplinary or punitive fashion, will depend entirely upon whether my comparative assessments of body-image and body-technique are *o*ppositional or *a*ppositional. An oppositional comparative assessment will place the visible signatures of myself in contest with all that I take as "not-self." In this framework, I inhabit an economy of signs that reveals various forms of what I, then, take as levels of value in various styles of expression and being. An *a*ppositional comparative assessment will enable the possibility of an ecology of desire, a desire in which I anticipate and accommodate the likelihood of change in my sense of my own body image along with the depth of my embodied life world—for Merleau-Ponty, literally, the flesh of my Being—that substantiates and grounds my embodied desire and makes my body-image meaningful for me. Apposition and opposition, ecology and economy are not either-or choices but are instead necessary elements for an embodied system of choice and action.

Right about the time when I turned thirty years of age—although I am sure that this economy of observation had begun to develop in my mid-twenties—I started to acknowledge a constancy in my self-perception. Like the central character in the film *Groundhog Day*, I could take note of no fundamental or meaningful changes in the surface of my flesh. Certainly, weight would come and weight would go, but I began to see less and less of myself when I set to the morning tasks of preparing my body for a day outside the second skin of my home.

The more comfortable I became in the routine tasks of my "body-image preparation" the farther removed I was finding myself from an active memory of boyhood body-image perception and the quiet (and occasionally not-so-quiet) terror of finding my Self in the mirror each morning. As well, the *habitus* of my established body-image experience made it difficult, if not troubling, to envision the progression of facial and fleshly changes that would inevitably come to Being were I fortunate to live long enough—to see my sixtieth year, my seventieth year, my eightieth year.

The habituation of my Self as a kind of expressive envelope—as a social sign, in effect, as a dummy, as an outside—made it increasingly possible for me to intellectualize, rationalize, and presuppose my organic existence and the ecology of my flesh. Having become an established body-image, I took liberties with matters of self-care and self-discipline. Simply, if a vehicle starts properly and gets us where we want to go, we feel less of a need to look under the hood. The more established and unsurprising I found my Self to be—in other words, the more I had become an enveloped establishment—the more I began to treat myself like my automobile. Dings and rust spots were attended to only if immediately noticeable, and even then the matter of attention was largely a function of insurance coverage. My mechanic, like my physician, saw me as lazy and bereft of common sense—and with insufficient technical knowledge to confidently tend to matters of routine maintenance.

Having so established my Self, I separated my ghost from my machine and allowed the ghost to transcend the banal, mindless technicalities of engine maintenance. I did not look into the mirror to see a Self, to be surprised by myself, or even to take note of the subtle patterns and changes in the chiasm of my overall facial expression (or its motility) to gain a sense of the Self I had become.

Instead, I looked into the mirror and I saw my car. Merleau-Ponty reminds us that the Cartesian's "'image' in the mirror is an effect of the mechanics of things. If he recognizes himself in it, if he thinks it 'looks' like him, it is his thought that weaves this connection. The mirror image is nothing that belongs to him."[29] For a meaningful post-Cartesian, post-Copernican and post-modern movement to have occurred in the domain of the intellectual culture that Merleau-Ponty so exquisitely and creatively touched, the meditation on embodied knowledge, embodied sense, and embodied Being should have been able to facilitate a perception of self in the experience of visible reflection. Now, "body" is not the same thing as "body-image," as "Self" is not "self-perception." But to follow Merleau-Ponty's critique carefully, one should be able to see *something* meaningful of oneself when one looks at the reflection of one's body.

My body—*any* body—is not a fully established empirical fact. It is always in composition and decomposition. My envelope, my skin, is a sign of me and the complex sign-system that I embody. My vision of this sign is both index and icon, signal and symbol. I bear the relationship to my "I think" as I live the event of "*I am*" and *re-member* the body of my assembled world.

SELF AND BODY, BODY AND OTHER: "REFLECTIONS" ON THE EVENT OF COMMUNICATION AND THE PHENOMENON OF INTERPERSONAL CONTACT

To see one's Self is to make meaningful and substantial contact with the ecstasy and tragedy of one's fleshly being. In the closing notes to *The Visible and the Invisible* Merleau-Ponty writes that "The flesh is a mirror phenomenon and the mirror is an extension of my relation with my body. [The] mirror [is] a realization of the *Bild* [or culture] of the thing."[30] In other words the mirror reminds me that there is *at least* one other feature, one other aspect to my body. At least. At the very least. The post-Cartesian meditation begins with an affirmation of my constitution of the event of the other side. When a banner or flag is flipped over, we recognize its other side as necessary to the dimensionality of its being, of its-being-at-all. But we can quickly become enervated if it is not turned right-side out again. A flag flown upside down is a sign of distress or at least some sort of negation of "patriotic mind."

The mirror reflection of my body image is to display the aspect or "side" of my flesh that I am looking for. If I cannot locate it, then I have lost a sense of my Self. On a good day, I am likely to be satisfied with any image that appears to me. On such a day I benefit from a lack of certitude: simply, it is unclear to me what I am looking for. I take that which is reflected and accept it as my foundation for embodiment. On such a day, not only do I accept myself as I am, but—more importantly—I accept the phenomenal *context* in which this perceptual *contact* is made. On such a day I can feel, both consciously and unconsciously, the *ek-sistence* of my body as the irreducible condition on which all of my subsequent identifications will be made.

In an important Nietzschean sense, all of our lives are tragedies. We are born. We die. In between we experience unfulfilled desires, heartache, and loss. We get hurt and angry precisely as we induce hurt and anger. We taste cynicism and *ressentiment* and spit it back into the world. The joyous laughter that punctuates and diacritically underscores the events of meaning and discovery that reveal for us the evanescent light of our identities—that offer us the hope of an answer to a question that we *may* eventually learn how to ask—is our embodied experience of the desired face unveiled, of the flag finally flown as we would have preferred it from the start.

The tragedy of Narcissus is not that he saw his reflection, or that he saw it in the water, nor even that he, miserable, weary, and languid, let himself die. Again, we are all going to die, and we are most fortunate when we have some sort of control over which activity becomes the one of our final consumption. So in a sense Narcissus got what he wanted—and far be it from me to formulate a moral argument against his context of choice. No, Narcissus needed to experience himself in the mirroring surface of the water. What I take as phenomenally "tragic" is that he died alone, lost in a delusion of autoerotic semiosis, and—given the common misapprehension of this myth in Western culture—existentially *misunderstood*. Narcissus, like all living beings, has a right to enjoy himself. He even has a right to be wrong and to be depressed. That he is still employed as an instrument of moral argument for having committed these unforgivable sins does not speak well for the West. Inasmuch as he had life, he always already had the "whole world" in his flesh. What is particularly tragic is that he reduced the meaning of the visible, sensible world to what he let himself believe was *the sign* of his body.

Along similar lines, this, I think, is the basic accusation Merleau-Ponty levels against the "Cartesians" in "Eye and Mind": that being who looks at its reflected image is not a mere sign any more than the reflected vision, captured by light and captivating to the observer, is itself merely a sign. One may inscribe the carnal tissue of one's flesh with scars or tattoos, but flesh is itself neither text nor sign. Quite simply, there is no fault in wondering or imagining what others see when we look at ourselves in a mirror, when we apprehend our body image, when we imaginatively inhabit the shape and drift of our flesh as well as the shape we are in. I accept that what I see in the mirror is my Self, and its truth is affirmed by the simple fact that I, like Narcissus, feel for what I am seeing; I care about this vision, my vision. It is this sort of mindfulness that makes a vision visible.

I would even go so far as to say that such wonderment is the foundation for our *deepest* contact with the Other. Such wonderment is not narcissism. It is imaginative interpersonal regard—the fleshing-out of our relationships in fragments of reverie, the creative possibility of the styles in which I can and might take shape before *your* very eyes. It is here, in this moment, that I let you into my life. It is here that, for the first time and through the skin of my flesh (perhaps even the skin of my teeth), I let *you* see *me*. And I do this because I intend to return to you. I intend to return to you in some shape or other, hopefully (and perhaps), some time, some place soon. Hopefully, in the flesh.

It is *you* who always hold the key that will unlock the door to the *imaginary* recognition of myself (i.e., *symbolic* and *real*). Joël Dor, in his recent commentary on Lacan, posits that, for the young child, "the experience of the mirror stage is prior to the advent of the body schema."[31] In more explicitly Lacanian terms, my recognition, my *re-cognition*, of my body image as it is reflected back to me at the points in my life of which I care to take notice, is the legacy of my communion with others. I see what others have seen in me. I see "me"; I see myself. I find possibilities of being through aspects of my body that have come to life in the perceptions of others. So beheld, I am held, holding onto the memory of having been reflected, reflecting on the power and life I embody in your eyes, the vision of myself I gain not from mere reflection but from the unanticipated light of your eyes. Lacan writes: "the important point is that this form situates the agency of the ego, before its social determination, in a fictional direction, which will always remain irreducible for the individual alone."[32]

For Lacan, the mirror is both vehicle and metaphor for our originary points of contact with our exterior reality, an exterior reality that will surprise us and renew us as we search, throughout our lives, for the existential code, experienced in dehiscence, that keeps our fiction together, together and moving on, moving and going—the code that directs us away from the predicament of Vladimir ("Didi") and Estragon ("Gogo") in *Waiting for Godot.*[33] I am reminded of the familiar refrains through Act I and Act II: "Nothing to be done" . . . "Let's go" . . . "I can't go on like this" . . . "Let's go"—with the play closing upon the stage directions: "*They do not move.*" Whether we like it or not, we are always somewhere, and the simple fact of our birth reminds us that we are inescapably linked to others, the phenomenal reality that burrows underneath Descartes' (or anyone's) encounter with the "fact" of radical doubt. Neither the mirror nor the schema of that which is reflected back to the eye is, itself, anything. It is because the act of perception is itself accomplished by a body in motion, by a body *going*—going on, going someplace, in search of some time, in search of revelation, a revelation of that which has been forgotten—that the reflection is at all possible as a source of meaning.

Merleau-Ponty assures us that the Cartesian, rational and cerebral, "can believe that the existing world is not visible, that the only light is the light of the mind."[34] The Cartesian attempts a fiction, positing that there is no depth, no thickness to the world. Depth, for Merleau-Ponty, is not nothing. It is, instead, "my participation in a Being without restriction, a participation primarily in the being of space beyond every [particular] point of view."[35] It is the life that comes to Didi and Gogo while they wait, on the false hope of a vulnerable fiction, for something "else." It is the life that we brush off when we are holding out for something more certain.

In Jakobson's model of human communication, the "phatic function" describes the recognition and maintenance of "contact" between the addresser (self) and the addressee (other).[36] In most typical explications of this model, the phatic function is deemphasized in the narrative explication of communicative functions in the order of their importance. In most typical explications, the discursive dimensions of "context" and "message," because of their immediacy to the codified world of the lexical and linguistic, receive the greater degree of analytical attention.[37] The phatic dimension is either taken for granted—as if to say "ah, but of course there must be contact for communication to take place"—or described, merely, as a system of gesture (vocalic and physical) signaling, say, understanding and desire for the continuity of dialogue: "ah, yes . . . I see . . . Uh huh . . . Please continue . . . Yes, do go on."

However, Greimas and Courtés, in their highly praised and important compendium, *Semiotics and Language,*[38] choose to be *a*typical in *their* reading of the phatic function. They draw attention to the fact that for Malinowski, the word "phatic" was initially operationalized within the term "phatic *communion*."[39] They write: "In his eyes the communication of information, such as it takes place during verbal exchanges between human beings, is secondary to the desire to establish and maintain intersubjective solidarity and, more generally, social cohesion. This solidarity and cohesion are the foundation for phatic communion, thanks to which one can 'speak of nothing and everything.'"[40] Communication is, thus, a derivative of this embodied, fleshly *mutuality* of phatic communion. And, if we are listening, communication—lived, embodied, poetic, unanticipated, while at the same time strategic and willful—is the experience of depth. It is the experience of bread and wine, flesh and blood, soul and spirit. It is the energy of the flesh that thinks and the body that moves.

As such, the self in the mirror, the *persona* in the mirror, the body-image, my *imago* (if *you* will), is a reflected trope—a turn, a movement—of my flesh. It is not a snapshot of identity, but is instead kinetic and motile. If I look closely what I see is a body with, at least, an interior and an exterior, a tragic body, a body of works, a psychological entity whose flesh cannot, by itself, fully explain what compels it to laugh, to think, to reflect, to change, to go, to go on. And, indeed, I must go on. Merleau-Ponty has discovered the radical element of my ambition: "Consciousness is in the first place not a matter of 'I think that' but of 'I can'"[41]—and, again, later: "it is a question of a power—of an I can."[42] I *can*. I can go on. *We* must go on, for *I* can and must go on. Let's go.

NOTES

1. Merleau-Ponty, "Eye and Mind," 170.
2. Dillon, *Merleau-Ponty's Ontology*, 113.
3. Johnson, "Ontology and Painting: Eye and Mind," 37.
4. Merleau-Ponty, *The Visible and the Invisible,* 139.
5. Low, *Merleau-Ponty's Last Vision,* 56.
6. Sartre, *Situations*, 321.
7. Low, *Merleau-Ponty's Last Vision,* 56.

8. See Madison, *The Phenomenology of Merleau-Ponty*; Dillon, *Merleau-Ponty's Ontology*; Evans & Lawlor, *Chiasms*.
9. Dillon, *Merleau-Ponty's Ontology*, 6.
10. Descombes, *Modern French Philosophy*, 1.
11. See Schwartz, "Everyman an *Übermensch*: The Culture of Cultural Studies."
12. See Melchior-Bonnet, *The Mirror: A History*.
13. Descartes, "The Dioptrics."
14. Dillon, *Semiological Reductionism*.
15. Foucault, "My Body, this Paper, this Fire."
16. Merleau-Ponty, "Eye and Mind," 162.
17. Merleau-Ponty, *Nature*, 15.
18. Merleau-Ponty, *The Phenomenology of Perception*.
19. Merleau-Ponty, *The Prose of the World*, 91–92.
20. See Descombes, *Modern French Philosophy*.
21. Descombes, *Modern French Philosophy*, 10.
22. Descombes, *Modern French Philosophy*, 29–30.
23. See Merleau-Ponty, *The Structure of Behavior*.
24. Merleau-Ponty, *The Visible and the Invisible*, 234.
25. Merleau-Ponty, *Themes from the Lectures*, 121–22.
26. Madison, *The Phenomenology of Merleau-Ponty*, 213.
27. See Schwartz, "Everyman an *Übermensch*: The Culture of Cultural Studies."
28. Lanigan's work is grounded in Merleau-Ponty. For a representative summary of his most recent theoretical writing, see Lanigan, *The Human Science of Communicology*. This comment was first noted during the First Biennial Meeting of the International Communicology Institute, Southern Illinois University, Carbondale, IL, July 2000. For Lanigan's fullest explication of Merleau-Ponty's philosophy of expressive embodiment, see also Lanigan, *Speaking and Semiology*.
29. Merleau-Ponty, "Eye and Mind," 170.
30. Merleau-Ponty, *The Visible and the Invisible*, 255.
31. Dor, *Introduction to the Reading of Lacan*, 97.
32. Lacan, "The Mirror Stage as Formative of the Function of the I," 2.
33. Beckett, *Waiting for Godot*.
34. Merleau-Ponty, "Eye and Mind," 186.
35. Merleau-Ponty, "Eye and Mind," 173.
36. Jakobson, "Linguistics and Communication Theory," 75–77.
37. In the overwhelming majority of texts on communication theory, the Jakobsonian notion of "contact" is rarely, if ever, mentioned. One will find quite a bit of attention paid to the idea of "context," suggesting that the phatic domain of communication is itself subsumed by the notion of context. I would go so far as to say that the interpretation of the "communication event" by the majority of leading scholars in the field of communication theory has, for the last half-century, been framed in terms of linguistic and cognitive assumptions. As such, students of human communication theory come to understand the moment of human communication as a discourse event—or, more specifically, as a discourse event whose semiotic boundaries and functions are essentially mental, rational, and codifiable.
38. Greimas and Courtés, *Semiotics and Language*, 1982.
39. Malinowski, "The Problem of Meaning in Primitive Languages."
40. Greimas & Courtés, *Semiotics and Language*, 231.
41. Merleau-Ponty, *Phenomenology of Perception*, 137.
42. Merleau-Ponty, *The Visible and the Invisible*, 225.

Chapter Four

On Contact

The Phatic Function of Communication

THE PRESUPPOSITION OF CONTACT

The notion of "contact" between persons entailed by an instance of communication has generally been *presupposed* by most theoretical efforts at demarcating, illustrating, or symbolizing the eidetic elements of human transaction. That is, it has been presupposed rather than being explored or investigated. The common presupposition of "contact" between participants in communication tends to operate on the unstated premise that communication occurs "within" a space, a space that is populated by (at least) two *separate* bodies able to identify and acknowledge one another as addressers and addressees.

The phenomenological nature of human contact is rarely questioned. The purpose of this chapter is thus to question the nature of contact, to problematize the notion of space as energized, embodied, and constituted through a moment of communication. After working through various aspects of Merleau-Ponty's phenomenology of the body and Foucault's theory of discourse, I will then examine the phatic function—understood as the syntagmatic relation of contact— in Jakobson's communication model. I will then consider the concept of *phatic communion,* as explicated by Malinowski,[1] against a backdrop of what might best be termed a "philosophy of the flesh."

THE BODY PROBLEMATIC AND INTERSUBJECTIVITY: THE PRESENT DISJUNCTION BETWEEN MERLEAU-PONTY'S PHENOMENOLOGY AND POSTMODERN CULTURAL THEORY

When I find myself, from time to time, perusing the ever-expanding literature on language, culture, and postmodern social theory I have begun to feel that there has become *almost* too much talk of "bodies." The current embrace of "the body" in the humanities scholarship of the English-speaking world began roughly three decades ago as an extension of Foucault's thinking on madness, medicine, power, and sexuality. Foucault's was certainly not the first set of texts entailing the body as both topic and boundary condition but, upon its initial translation into English in the 1970s, his critique of totalizing and repressive institutions began to insinuate itself fully into the discourse of social theory—becoming, in many ways, the doctrinal centerpiece of critical reflection on matters of repression, exclusion, alterity, and silence.[2] The field of cultural studies, still emergent and still struggling to situate a coherent theoretical and empistemological ground for its work, did not emerge as an academic entity until after Foucault's 1984 passing.[3] When it did begin to mark its presence in academic circles, discourse about the body became principally concerned with the exercise of strategies, regimes, and technologies of biopower.

By the early 1990s a new sort of "repressive hypothesis" had begun to emerge with regard to the problematic of the body and power, and a philosophically skewed reflection of Foucault's rhetoric quickly became the *lingua franca* of cultural studies and American postmodernism.[4] Expressive transgression became, at times, the principal ostensive objective of writing directed at repressive, silencing, marginalizing institutions.[5] This, of course, is exactly the opposite of what Foucault was getting at in his critique of the juridico-discursive model of power and revolutionary theory.[6]

Transgression is only liberatory within a certain context, a simple truth that even the historians of Sade can fully appreciate. It is an assertion of what one psychologically must believe is "self" against a discursive order that, when embodied and enacted in its usual way, would seem to limit the contextual range of satisfying interactions with other meaningful selves. For the repressive hypothesis to perform its work (as a species of *ressentiment*) the institution and its discursive order must, then, emerge as "other," enabling transgression (or "resistance") to become the expressive and productive extension of the revolutionary attitude. Bodies, as such, are seen to transgress the boundaries of other bodies, reinforcing a persistent crypto-Cartesian premise that we are each sovereign in the lodging of our skin.

Biopower, however, is only a description of a set of *historical* practices. Dreyfus and Rabinow maintain that biopower is the set of historical practices "which produces the human objects systematized by structuralism and the human subjects explicated by hermeneutics."[7] Ultimately, this is why Foucault shifts his thinking away from the limiting and contextualizing instincts of modern humanism (in both its romantic and Marxist variants) and toward a notion of disciplinary power enabling new forms of subjectivity.

Now, "the body" is certainly not irrelevant to a study of power, meaning, and culture. It may well be the single most important concept for the work of the human sciences in the current millennium. My primary concern is to avoid what I take to be a key error common to both the quantitative and qualitative social sciences. This error concerns the notion of mind, body, and intersubjectivity. Prior to the field of psychology's current preoccupation with brain, neuro-chemistry, and cognition, it had for some time been reasonably comfortable with the idea of "mind" as a historical—and trans-historical—medium of conceptual and eidetic agency. The brain was understood as the primary organ of thought, but thought itself, according to the general tradition of German Idealism, was situated outside of flesh, transcending flesh, situated in what even Dilthey was to term "objective spirit."[8]

It was, generally speaking, here, on this broad plateau of thought, that the nineteenth-century philosophy of science, in the guise of logical empiricism, took its so-called "linguistic turn" toward logic, grammar, semantics, and the methods of scientific analysis. Ironically, it was on this plane of thought that the philosophy of mind turned toward psychologism. Julian Roberts notes that in Husserl's thinking, "John Stuart Mill . . . stands for the doctrine that logic is a part of psychology."[9] As an offshoot of the positivistic movement in scientific thought, psychologism, as Husserl perceived it, "contends that logic is the technical part of psychology, it is the 'craft' of which psychology is the science."[10]

At this point, the metaphysical intersubjectivity of mind sustained its unity and explanatory power in what remained of Idealism. Now, having shifted its own focus toward the epistemological sanctuary seemingly inherent in the intersubjectively valid conditions of reason, language, and scientific inference, positivism saw itself as enabled to turn "mind" away from spirit. And inasmuch as the *Geist* of classical metaphysics had no place in the emerging sciences of mind, positivism turned its focus again outward, away from the traditional problematics of consciousness and toward the order and comportment of the material world. I offer this brief, admittedly cursory, review of the last century or so of thinking on the subject of mind, body, and intersubjectivity principally to assert the following: that the notion of intersubjectivity—its history, its plausibility, as well as its possibility—is anything but foreign to western philosophy but has been, nonetheless, confined to the activity of mind. It was not until Merleau-Ponty that the concept of an embodied intersubjectivity, an intersubjectivity of experience and flesh, had been explored in any systematic way.

Merleau-Ponty's phenomenology established a fundamental break from the transcendental *logos* of idealism and the externalizing tendencies of positivism.[11] It not only put the body back into play as a medium of consciousness and perception but succeeded in problematizing the concept of "body" itself—its psychological being, its ground of reason, and, importantly, its limits and boundary conditions. It is this latter lesson that seems to have been forgotten as the human sciences shifted into their postmodern phase of cultural critique. In its most commonplace contemporary usage intersubjectivity presupposes a notion of subjectivity that is bounded by an individuated consciousness. In this view my subjectivity maintains its experiential unity as the domain of my personal memories, my private thoughts, and my creative intentions. As such, the experience of intersubjectivity "simply" entails the interpenetration of these separate subjectivities, understood and experienced by each interpersonal subject as a bounded and personal consciousness. Language, having been sufficiently problematized by decades of critique from numerous academic circles, is no longer taken as the repository for "objective spirit."[12] For the strains of idealism that still circulate among philosophers of mind, body, and culture, *Geist* (to the extent such a thing can still be productively spoken about) resides in *communication*—that is, in relational connections, in the communion of perceptions, in the kinesis of what language *does* in whatever manner it happens to be invoked.

The academic tradition that even now goes by the name of "psychology" set reason against the body and took up the matter of desire as a creature of "context." Merleau-Ponty's *Phenomenology of Perception* carefully set the issue of desire aside and resituated the cogito of perception in the embodied flesh of what Heidegger and Nietzsche saw as our vulnerable, urgent, and tragic being.[13] If I may be so bold, "context" is not a term that Merleau-Ponty would have been inclined to use to address either the soul or *Geist* of embodiment. As Martin Dillon puts it: "In the *Phenomenology of Perception*, Merleau-Ponty undertakes the task of incarnating consciousness and putting it back into the world."[14] As such, the life of consciousness is not separate from what I live. Dillon makes this point even more emphatically:

> The soul, now as consciousness, became first *causa sui* and then cause of the world: a thing necessarily apart from all things. Nietzsche, Heidegger, Sartre: the defilers of the soul. The cause of itself and all things fell from grace and back into the world where it appeared as the cause of nothing, itself nothing, still not a thing. Merleau-Ponty inherited the soul as Being and as Nothingness and set out alone to do what none before him—or since him—could think to do: first he made the soul a thing, a body, and then he incarnated all things into Flesh. His successors have yet to appear. Those who follow him in time are still resisting incarnation: they are still trying to make the Flesh become word; they are still seeking to obtain release from the world by transforming it and themselves into a text. The text is the latest in the vicissitudes of *Geist*.[15]

The rhetoric of Dillon's position may seem, perhaps, disconcertingly blunt, but his point is one with which I am in full agreement. The terms "text" and "context" even when used in an insistently, if not rigorously, "nonpositivistic" sense threaten to shift the notion of embodiment *back* toward the dualisms of individuated being, of mind and body, of consciousness and world that were actively in play before the advent of Husserl's phenomenology. Merleau-Ponty's thought took the human sciences across a great distance. It is not clear to me that there are many people now keeping up.

CONTACT AND FLESH

The *flesh* of the phenomenological body is inconceivable without *contact*. Without contact, it is inconceivable and it is, in turn, incapable of conception. It is without life and, even worse, it is meaningless. Embodied contact is what enables an observer of human interaction to interpret communicative exchanges from the standpoint of discursive and historical context. The moment of cultural postmodernity, if one can speak intelligibly of such a thing, may well have been that point at which we became aware of the possibility that there might be nothing of meaning and experience outside of discourse. Dillon himself warns of a "postmodern dualism of language and its other."[16] His argument continues: "Language is a gift into which we have always already fallen unawares. Postmodernism [is] . . . at best a benign jolt that would waken us and bid us stare into the mouth of this gift. . . . One way not to see the world is to read it as a text; the world as text has been lived by somebody else first."[17] As such, context is a critical instrument of the *interpretation* of perception and expression. It is not perception itself, nor is it the necessary and sufficient ground of meaning and interpretation. The limit of context as an instrument of knowing and interpretation is consciousness. The limit of consciousness, I will argue, is situated within the domain of *contact*.

In an explication of Jakobson's model of communication,[18] Richard Lanigan identifies contact as the fifth of six critical terms that describe, in turn, six elemental functions in a meaningful event of human relationship.[19] Jakobson does not place the terms "contact" and "context" into any sort of opposition. They are situated in a vertical relationship, along with the terms "message" and "code." The relationship between these terms is appositional and paradigmatic. Along a horizontal axis are the terms "addresser" and "addressee." Addresser and addressee are not articulated as oppositional or appositional terms. Their positionality is given not on an axis of metaphor but on an axis of metonymy inasmuch as they occur in a sequential diachronic relationship. As such, they are, by function and by definition, combinatory.

The element of contact performs what Jakobson, after Malinowski, terms a *phatic* function.[20] Jakobson describes the phatic function as "the first verbal function acquired by infants; they are prone to communicate before being able to send or receive informative communication."[21] In the terminology of infant and child psychological development, the process that Jakobson describing here is known as "attachment." Now, Jakobson does not systematically pursue the notion of psychological attachment in his address of childhood language acquisition. As a matter of fact, the explication of the communication event in virtually all academic writing, whether modeled upon Jakobson's terminology or an alternative theoretical approach, has tended to focus on human communication principally as an *adult* experience. For each and every one of us, however, these habits begin long before we are cognizant. The attachment we seek from birth is a fleshly attachment; it is an attachment to the other by way of flesh.

Margaret Mahler has theorized that up until the first year or so of life, infants do not seem to have a full awareness that they and their mothers are separate beings.[22] Merleau-Ponty's concept of flesh seems particularly well-suited to an explication of Mahler's hypothesis.[23] This first experience of contact is a syncretism more than it seems a chiasm—that is, a criss-crossing and interlacing of the perceiver with the perceived. It is, to paraphrase the singer Paul Simon, the lived experience of "the mother and child reunion." According to decades of research on attachment theory, it is from a secure base of attachment that the child, the becoming-person, the emergent personality can successfully undergo a process of psychological differentiation and individuation.[24] The separation does not come easily, according to Mahler, and it is facilitated by the child's dependence upon a transitional object—typically described in the literature of child development as, say, a security blanket, perhaps a special toy or stuffed animal. In any case, it is something the child takes to bed with him or her. Over time, the material transitional object becomes discarded for an eidetic substitute. Whereas the material thing had been animated as an extension of the child's secure basis of attachment, perceptions of the world itself become animated as a feature of the child's developing imagination.

In any case, this profoundly communicative event entails a foundational experience of chiasm. Insight into this communicative event entails a philosophy of the flesh. Douglas Low maintains that Merleau-Ponty's later phenomenology emerges as "a philosophy of chiasm, of *Ineinander*, of flowing into one another of subject and object, of self and other, of language and meaning."[25] A philosophy of the flesh is not, expressly, an inquiry into the matter of skin upon skin—of the hairs, or cilia, aspiring from skin brushing upon one another. A philosophy of the flesh is an engagement with human engagement. It is an inquiry into human inquiring.

Simply, we are not nor are we ever complete unto ourselves. Perhaps "our" greatest interpersonal myth is the notion that my skin marks the limit of my flesh and that my flesh marks the limit of my body. Quite to the contrary, I will die if there is not breathable air in this room—air, spirit, organic spirit that is not yet an element of my body. Atoms conjoin with other atoms to form molecules. I do not breathe pure oxygen. I breathe combinations: breathable combinations. At my birth, there was, first, liquid and then there was air. There was air, and then there was milk. Now, milk is an extraordinary "combination." It is the organic depth of human contact. It is the river of nativity flowing from the mother to her child. Enclosed within its whiteness is everything we need in order to survive those difficult hours of transition.

Perhaps our greatest *existential* myth is that we are thrown: simply, we are *not* thrown. We are *led* and then *caught*. Upon our birth there is no "thud." Instead, there are hands. Gaston Bachelard comments directly to this point. "Before the human being is 'cast into the world,' as claimed by certain nasty metaphysics, he is laid in the cradle of the house."[26] The so-called "existential beginning" is, for Bachelard, a "secondary metaphysics." "It passes over the preliminaries when being is well-being, when the human being is deposited in a 'being-well. . . .'"[27]

In a richly poetic essay on the theme of mother, milk, and flesh, Eva-Maria Simms writes that prior to our ruminations on being thrown, our being is "housed in the circle of a maternal space."[28] Our lives begin in this intimacy. After Bachelard, Simms remarks: "the work that remains still undone is an understanding of human existence prior to the upright posture, and as beginning and arising out of a primal housed-ness and well-being."[29] This work, thus, embraces the transitional objects as well as the transitional-object-spaces of the home world. For Foucault, this work entailed the appreciation and study of discourse and *dispositif.*[30] For me, this is the task of the philosophy and phenomenology of the flesh.

In many ways, the flesh is sufficiently implied and implicated in Jakobson's model of communication. And importantly, it is not my argument here that the communicative element of "contact" reign supreme over the element of "context." My point of view is motivated by my recognition that the human sciences have listed in the direction of contextual explanation for their perceptions, perceptions that, in turn, have emerged from epistemic patterns of various idealisms and utilitarianisms. The hermeneutics of desire do not begin necessarily from the reality that desire cleaves inherently to historical games of interpretation.

CONCLUSION: THE INCIDENTAL ACCIDENT OF FLESHLY COMMUNION

Again, according to Jakobson, the phatic function describes the recognition and maintenance of "contact" between the addresser and the addressee. My argument, to be clear, is that context is neither logically prior to nor logically instantiated by the notion of contact. The notion of phatic communication as supportive or "merely" supportive of contextually prior and purposive messages in human communication is the primary error that my argument seeks to address. Do we hold one another in order to dance? Or, do we dance simply for the joy of holding one another? *Both* the dance *and* the holding are important. More important is that the discourse of the dance entails the flesh of holding *and* that the flesh of holding must entail a discourse, an intentionality, a home, a pattern, a matrix: a circle of being.

Phatic communion is not merely supportive communication; it is the *genealogical*, fundamental, and existential ground of the communication event. Context, on the other hand, is the semiotic (or hermeneutic) and *archaeological* ground of communication. Where message and code are, as Lanigan explicates, matters of space-binding and time-binding (respectively) contact and context are matters (respectively) of birth, infancy, and mortality, on one hand, and development and discipline on the other.

Malinowski himself refers to phatic communion as "a type of speech in which ties of union are created by a mere exchange of words."[31] Further, he contends: "language does not function here as a means of transmission of thought."[32] As such, Malinowski is circumscribing a matter of great epistemological significance. The phatic function, the element of contact, he argues, is *outside* the realm of cognition and of thought. More specifically, the phatic function, the element of contact, describes the fundamental limit of cognitive science. Leonard Lawler has skillfully revealed some major epistemological shortcomings in the field of cognitive science, precisely the sorts of limitations considered by psychoanalysts and Continental philosophers for some time.[33] Malinowski's formulation demonstrates the same sort of deficiency. The description of phatic communion wonderfully illustrates the rupture of the intentional/thetic communicative "message" and "code" from the experiential meaning of the communicative event. The field of psychology, now dominated by the epistemic hold of cognitive science, has found itself bewildered and tongue-tied, practically all but speechless, on the subject matter of human intimacy.[34] Nonetheless, major depressive disorder, which is the most widespread and fastest growing physiological and psychological condition in the developed world[35] is in its essence an *intimacy problematic.*[36] The depressive withdraws from the world. One cannot think one's way out of a depression. One cannot think one's way into an intimate contact with others. Simply put, intimacy is far less a modality of context than it is a matter of contact.

In a wild sense of Peirce's notion of abduction, one cannot abduct another without "laying hands" on them. "Laying hands" can imply theft. It can imply discovery—particularly as one says: "I've looked all over for that book but I have not laid my hands on it." Laying hands implies healing.

Originally a doctor, a physician, was a layer of hands. Laying hands is also erotic—in ways, of course, far too numerous to mention. To lay hands, to give a hand, to lend a hand is to help, to lead, to instruct. To lay hands is to give of oneself in a fundamental way. The experienced truth of intimacy is a "gift" in the truest sense. In German, the word "gift"—a lexeme having the same etymology as the English word of the same spelling—means "poison." I am immediately led to think of the gift of the "poisoned" apple. I am thinking, as well, of the gifts given that we do not want or that we did not ask for. And I am thinking of the ennui that inescapably attends the receipt of our greatest wish and out heart's desire.

Practicing psychoanalysts are absolutely right when they teach their patients that intimacy entails great courage.[37] Though it may seem to be premised upon an attachment to the familiar—to the familiar person who speaks a warming discourse—it is in fact a release, or in Merleau-Ponty's language, a "dehiscence."[38] Intimacy is a release into the wild of the seemingly familiar. True, intimacy is premised upon a secure base of attachment. Yet it is an exploration and an adventure into the ambiguous and rarely seen contours of flesh. It is, in a sense, all of the possibilities of mystery and excitement that lie at the threshold of an ostensibly chaste kiss.

In *Respect in a World of Inequality*, Richard Sennett remarks that "Adam Smith famously defined sympathy as often falsely imagining the pain of another as one's own."[39] It can, then, perhaps be said that intimacy works analogously—as the false imagining of another person's communicative desire. Sennett continues: "In time the confusion between self and other came to seem to me a vital clue in understanding what oils the gears of mutual self respect. It begins as a mistake."[40]

It is a mistake, in other words, from the standpoint of a given hermeneutics—suggesting, at various points in time, a comedy of contexts. Is the emperor wearing clothes or isn't he? Is he appropriately dressed? Can an emperor never be naked? Michaelangelo's David is naked. Can he not be my emperor if I should choose him to be? Or shall we put it in the vocabulary of Levi-Strauss: Is this food cooked? Or is it raw? Again, it begins as a mistake. A mistake, after all, is an accident, and an accident, like its semantic cousin "incident," is literally something that "befalls." Both deriving from the Latin *cadere*, they signify the falling-ness of our communion and our communication. The communicative event is an incidence of our flesh, an accident of our crossed paths that befalls us. We fall, and then perhaps we catch one another.

Again, it begins as an accident. "By making Adam Smith's 'error' of mutual identification and so of sympathy, we overcome differences which stand in the way of working together."[41] Our flesh thinks with a different logic. Perhaps it might even be better to assert that contact speaks its own logic of context. It is a logic of attachment, of signs and symbols in transition, of things that are not what they seem, of subjects and objects unaware of their limits. Context may well reveal a critical logic of a communication episode. Contact, understood from a philosophy of the flesh, reveals the logic of the necessary mistake—the chance, the error, the crossing-up, the incident, and the possibility—that gave birth to it.

NOTES

1. Malinowski, "The Problem of Meaning in Primitive Languages."
2. See Turner, *The Body and Society*. See also Hepworth, Turner, and Featherstone, *The Body: Social Process and Cultural Theory*.
3. See Schwartz, "Everyman an *Übermensch*." See also Elliott, "What Was Cultural Studies?"
4. See Schwartz, "Everyman an *Übermensch*." See also Storey, "There's No Success Like Failure."
5. See Jacoby, *The End of Utopia*.
6. Foucault, *Discipline and Punish*.
7. Dreyfus and Rabinow, *Michel Foucault: Beyond Structuralism and Hermeneutics*, 103
8. Schmidt, *History and Structure*, 12–15. See also Bubner, *Modern German Philosophy*.
9. Roberts, *Logic of Reflection*, 159–60.
10. Roberts, *Logic of Reflection*, 159–60.
11. See Madison, *The Phenomenology of Merleau-Ponty*.
12. See Schmidt, *History and Structure*. See also Roberts, *Nothing but History*.
13. Merleau-Ponty, *Phenomenology of Perception*.
14. Dillon, *Merleau-Ponty's Ontology*, 102.
15. Dillon, *Merleau-Ponty's Ontology*, 101.
16. Dillon, *Semiological Reductionism*, 102.
17. Dillon, *Semiological Reductionism*, 103–04.
18. Jakobson, "Linguistics and Communication Theory."
19. Lanigan, "The Self in Semiotic Phenomenology."
20. See Malinowski, "The Problem of Meaning in Primitive Languages."
21. Jakobson, "Linguistics and Communication Theory," 75.
22. See Mahler, Pine, and Bergman, *The Psychological Birth of the Human Infant*.
23. See Merleau-Ponty, *The Visible and the Invisible*.
24. See Fonagy, *Attachment Theory and Psychoanalysis*.
25. Low, *Merleau-Ponty's Last Vision*, 104.
26. Bachelard, *The Poetics of Space*, 7.
27. Bachelard, *The Poetics of Space*, 7.
28. Simms, "Milk and Flesh," 23.
29. Simms, "Milk and Flesh," 23.
30. See Foucault, "Technologies of the Self."
31. Malinowski, "The Problem of Meaning in Primitive Languages," 315.
32. Malinowski, "The Problem of Meaning in Primitive Languages," 315.
33. Lawler, "Becoming an Auto-affection." See also Descombes, *The Mind's Provisions*.
34. Schnarch, *Constructing the Sexual Crucible*, 89–144.
35. NIMH, *Depression*.
36. See Kristeva, *Black Sun*.
37. See Schnarch, *Constructing the Sexual Crucible*.
38. Merleau-Ponty, *The Visible and the Invisible*, 146.
39. Sennett, *Respect in a World of Inequality*, 44.
40. Ibid.
41. Ibid.

Chapter Five

Body, Liquidity, and Flesh

Bachelard, Merleau-Ponty, and the Elements of Interpersonal Communication

THE "BODY THEMATIC" AS PROBLEMATIC

The theme of "embodiment" has emerged over the last two decades as a highly prominent topic in the human sciences. Much of this discourse has been developed from the work of Foucault, some of it is derived from Merleau-Ponty, and other points of view have contributed by way of anthropology, feminism, and psychoanalysis. Though this discourse has energized contemporary discussions of power and agency, there is a difficulty that this thinking must eventually encounter as it addresses the experience of embodiment as an intersubjective encounter with its own otherness. More specifically, Merleau-Ponty's phenomenology, as it unfolds in *The Visible and the Invisible* challenges reflective consciousness to open itself up to a genuinely "post-Cartesian" experience of spirit and substance.[1] It is not at all clear to me that the post-Cartesian challenge has been sufficiently taken on by the human sciences.

Phenomenology awakened the modern mind to the possibility of embodied subjectivity, of reason grounded in the experience of a vital, fleshly consciousness. Yet, for all of the discourse generated on the body as a site of power and contest, the concept of the body still seems too often discussed as a creature of organic autonomy, as a soft, at times bony, tissue that encloses a shell of subjective experience and existence. It is my belief that an attentive reading of Bachelard's reflections on air, water, and dreams can offer a unique possibility for revisiting the thought of Merleau-Ponty—of awakening postmodern and post-Cartesian consciousness to a much richer encounter with the phenomenology of the body and the experience of the flesh.

Merleau-Ponty defines "flesh" as *chiasm*, as an interlacing of a being with, potentially, all other beings. As a complex tissue *of* experience and *in* experience, flesh cannot, thus, be encountered as a familiar "thing." It is continually in process, continually alive and dying, made up of flows and vapors, presenting itself to everyday perception as an illusion of substance and a deception of material stability. I will argue that flesh might best be understood as an *intersubjective plasma*, as a complex of fluid elements that are just as capable of hardness as they are of liquidity. "Assets" of memory and experience become "liquid" in moments of communicative intimacy and psychological transformation. As such, this essay will consider the concept of the body *not* as a medium of communication but as communication itself, as communication entered and exited by way of liquidity and crystallization.

THE CONDITIONS OF EMBODIMENT

What is my body?—*this* body that writes and speaks *these* words? Is it merely a bio-mechanical thing? My eyes that gaze upon my arms, my legs, my face in the mirror: they too are *of* this body, this body upon which they are focused like cameras. That which gains the attention from the modern psychiatrist and neuroscientist—in other words, my brain—still, through their investigations, earns the full academic credit for thinking about this body, my body. Yet it too is entirely *of* this body. This place of thought, where Descartes once began, is also the place of feeling and sensation. I am conscious of my body and its parts. And by way of my body and its thinking and reflective properties, I am also conscious of being conscious—as I am also aware of what coming-to-consciousness feels like, especially of moving from sleep to awakening, or of being jarred to attention from reverie.

Conscious of my body, conscious of my consciousness, and of even my capacity for self, I remain somewhat baffled—especially in this context—about the comfortable certainty exhibited currently across academic fields that my *mind* is *embodied.*[2] There is still so much to be discovered regarding the limits and conditions for both my body and this entity that has been named "mind." In German, the preferred term for "mind" is *Geist*, which is customarily translated as "spirit" (or its Anglo-Germanic cognate equivalent "ghost"). Yet Anglo-American thinkers have instead long gravitated toward the word "mind." Our science seems so much more comfortable with it. While spirit refers, etymologically speaking, to something a body *does*—that is, "to breathe"—mind, etymologically, refers, simply, to "mental activity." The name "mind," thus, is not even referential; it resists the essential task of metaphor: it resists being seen in terms of something other. Nevertheless, my mind is not a closed, containable, "embodiable" system any more than my body is reducible to my skin, organs, teeth, and bones.

Somehow I cannot escape the possibility of thinking that the existence of "mind" (especially in its Anglophone semantic incarnation) is merely a wish that Western consciousness has been making with its heart since the age of Descartes and Spinoza. It relieves the body of so much responsibility. The body, with its carnality, with its need for food and water, with its urinary and bowel activity, with its hormones, with its reproductive urges and orgasms, with its burps and farts, its aching feet and its need for sleep—how can it maintain accountability for serious *mental* activity? But a half a millennium after Descartes, psychiatry and neuroscience, just as much as cultural studies, seem poised to implicate the body yet again.[3]

The brain is the organ of consciousness, feeling, and all other mental activities, we are told, with all sorts of scientific evidence to locate consciousness, yet again, in an organ of the body. According to Anthony Damasio, interpreting Spinoza, the brain is a body part and the mind is a refined, internal element of that body part.[4] In the breath of this one idea, contemporary psychiatry and neuroscience have returned to the work of seventeenth century anatomists. Though it has come as a consequence of the anatomizing of moods and anxieties, the many people who have witnessed the benefits of contemporary psychopharmacology are no less grateful for the elevated focus on brain activity in psychiatry and neuroscience. Nevertheless, regardless of that which can be said with conviction (if not certainty) about mind, spirit, or ghost, the discourse of the scientific and medical community has taken physical ownership of all of it and has placed its narrative under the same sort of analysis applied to the study of the spinal cord or the optic nerve.

A full and satisfactory concept of the body, however—regardless of the mind and its imaginative breath, breadth, and energy—remains, at least in terms of modernity, an *empirical* chimera. Does my body include the oxygen I am about to inhale and, on the same token, should I include the air I am about to exhale? What about my hair, some of which is certain to be washed down the drain with tomorrow morning's shower? What about the water I know I am going to need for my system's continued health? I know that I am going to need it a week, a month, perhaps, if I am still blessed with life, a year, a decade from now? I know that I shall consume it. It must be a part of me. But where should I draw the line? Is the water, now flowing into the reservoir, already a relevant feature of my body?

The mind is not a thing, consciousness is not a thing, and, importantly, the body is not a thing. Or, if we must insist that it does indeed possess sufficient qualities of thingness and that it exists as a recognizable entity in time and space, we must at least admit that the body is not a bounded entity, that its existence has meaning precisely to the extent that it transforms and projects itself through time and space. It is not enough to say that my body exists as a biological thing, as a carbon-based life form, that it has a life and a half-life. It must also be said that my body is not an autonomous thing. It is *entirely* contingent, and I am (living through my body *as* myself), as well, entirely contingent. Not only is my body contingent upon the well-being of other bodies (not to mention the bodies from which it was conceived and the female body from which it was given birth), it is contingent on the earth. It is contingent on all elements of what philosophers and scientists have long chosen to call "nature": earth, wind, fire and water.

ELEMENTS OF EXISTENTIAL EMBODIMENT: NATURE AND FLESH

It is certainly not my intent, through this discourse, to simply reinvent the work of Merleau-Ponty, particularly his revolutionary explication of corporeality as the ground of perception, consciousness, and thought. *The Phenomenology of Perception* succeeded in closing the book, so to speak, on the dialectic of body and mind that served as the fundamental metaphysical puzzle of the second millennium. As well, the Platonist's "heaven" of ideas, having survived the Christian era in the West, becomes, with Merleau-Ponty, contextualized as a function of embodied consciousness, along with Descartes *cogito*. My intent is to join with Merleau-Ponty's thinking with regard to the *flesh* of this body, of my body—that is, its thickness and texture, its intensity and expression.

In *The Visible and the Invisible* Merleau-Ponty writes of "the emergence of the flesh as expression,"[5] enabling dialogue, perhaps intimacy with things and others in particular habits and modalities. The point where I feel most fully connected with Merleau-Ponty's discourse can be found in the following passage:

> We understand then why we see the things themselves, in their places, where they are, according to their being which is indeed more than their being-perceived—and why at the same time we are separated from them by all of the thickness of the look and of the body; it is that *this distance is not the contrary of this proximity*, it is deeply consonant with it, it is synonymous with it. It is that the thickness of the flesh and the thing is constitutive for the thing of its visibility as for the seer of his [or her] corporeity; it is not an obstacle between them, *it is their means of communication*. [emphasis mine][6]

In this critical passage, Merleau-Ponty addresses the event of communication and proximity as a matter of thickness, perhaps viscosity. He continues: "The *thickness of the body*, far from rivaling that of the world, is on the contrary *the sole means I have to go unto the heart of things*, by making myself a world, and by *making them flesh*" [emphasis mine].[7]

To reiterate what I am finding as the critical feature of this passage through conjunction and emphasis: "the *thickness* of the flesh and the thing . . . *is* their *means* of *communication*." For Richard Lanigan, an American Merleau-Ponty scholar whose work is fundamental to a phenomenological philosophy of semiotics and human communication, *The Phenomenology of Perception* was absolutely essential to the emergence of a theory of existential communication.[8] On the other hand, what Merleau-Ponty undertakes in *The Visible and the Invisible* is to give this theory *substance*—that is, to explicate not merely a dialogue between things and bodies in their givenness (their proximity, their correspondence, or their narrative coextension), but a *communion*: a relationship of gravity and of density and, hence, an opportunity for intimacy and mutual transformation.

In this discourse that I am presenting here, written with my body, murmured silently, and now spoken out loud, the communion I seek is with my patient listeners. I am, with and through my body-experience, speaking outside my body, speaking both *to* and *with* your body. The thickness that I present, my gravity and density, is not a superficial matter, nor is it merely a matter of the language that I speak or the existential distances and barriers that separate you from me. It is precisely my thickness, my density as you perceive it, that serves as the source of your curiosity. It is everything about this moment that serves as a source of amusement, fascination, or frustration. It is everything that is, at this moment and through the arteries of perception, not yet known. It is what remains to be seen, the not as yet visible.

Merleau-Ponty rightly cautions that his use of the word "flesh" ought not be taken in its customary literal sense. And so, in this regard, it ought to be fairly obvious that one should not interpret a philosophy of the flesh to mean, as so many Anglophone speakers might be inclined to think, a philosophy of human skin or, worse, of naked (and naughty) human skin. On this very point, Véronique Fóti remarks that Merleau-Ponty's use of the word "flesh" has "fostered either a certain literalization and Dionysian license, or else consignment to obscurity."[9] This is to imply that rather than evoking an erotics of intellectual depth, adventure, and, in this context, pleasure, the notion of flesh since its articulation in *The Visible and the Invisible* has provoked a callow, perhaps fetishistic discourse regarding sex and power, desire and satisfaction, sensuousness and fantasy, obscenity and victimage.

What I have found notable, however, is that this sort of discourse has arisen more from the cultural turn toward "the body"—ironically, a turn taken, for the most part, with but scant reference to Merleau-Ponty—than from any invocation of a philosophy of the flesh. The turn has indeed been significant, emerging perhaps as the most prominent focus of Anglophone "cultural studies," and it has been taken largely through various ideological interpretations and political applications of Foucault. It seems at least plausible that the turn in this direction was inevitable, that the politics of social theory was bound and determined to arrive at the most personal levels of expressive engagement, resistance, liberation, and self-identity. It may even be said that this turn, earnestly and openly beginning in many ways with the investigations of Freud, was not only inevitable but that it was going to happen despite Merleau-Ponty's admonitions—that it was, in effect, going to happen over Merleau-Ponty's dead body.

A query into sexuality is not simply a matter of prurient probing but a style of searching for truth. Moreover, as Foucault has famously professed, this particular search for truth has been ongoing since antiquity and has been largely governed in the West, at least up to this point, by the various ruptured narratives of Christianity. And especially through its most recent incarnation it has been very much a search for a particular kind of truth: the truth of human subjectivity. In his introduction to the published memoirs of Herculine Barbin, Foucault plainly articulates the nature of this ongoing hermeneutics of the sovereign (yet anatomically categorical) sexual body in the voice of the modern inquisitor:

> Wake up, young people, from your illusory pleasures; strip off your disguises, and recall that every one of you has a sex, a true sex. And then, we must also admit that it is in the area of sex that we must search for the most secret and profound truths about the individual, that it is there that we can best discover what he is and what determines him. And if it was believed that it was necessary to hide sexual matters because they were shameful, we now know that it is sex itself which hides the most secret parts of the individual: the structure of his fantasies, the roots of his ego, the forms of his relationship to reality. At the bottom of sex, there is truth.[10]

Along these same lines, the most important thing I have come to conclude from the last several decades of postmodern thinking on biopower, sexualized bodies, and ideologies of resistance is that the hermeneutics of subjectivity as a search for truth from within the narrative of the body's sexual experience can only arrive at an intellectual cul-de-sac when it jettisons, along the way, the phenomenology of intersubjectivity. It is precisely at this juncture that Merleau-Ponty's dead body must breathe again. And it is precisely here that I seek to reawaken its flesh, and in turn my flesh, to an elemental phenomenology of embodiment on the other side of Foucault.

What can also be said about the hermeneutics of the subject is that, despite its infinite regress and its occasional participation in rhetorics of *ressentiment*, it nonetheless demonstrates a yearning for depth in the invisible and anxious domains of human expressive contact. Recent family-systems oriented applications of psychoanalytic theory been inclined to argue that this particular hunger for insight is at once a yearning for depth by way of intimacy.[11] It is in this light that I can fully sense what Merleau-Ponty means when he maintains that "[a] philosophy of the flesh is the condition without which psychoanalysis will remain anthropology."[12] A philosophy of the flesh is not merely a philosophy of human communication, it is a phenomenology, perhaps a theology, of *communion*. The blind psychoanalytic impulse that Foucault parodies is not in error because it is psychoanalytic or even psychiatric, but because it cannot grasp that its object of analysis is poetry and not prose. To reiterate Merleau-Ponty's own words once again: "the *thickness* of the flesh and the thing . . . *is* their *means* of *communication*."[13] It is the thickness, the density, the interconnectedness, the complexity that gestures beneath the thin pellicle of what is known that draws us in—that begins to give a voice to our anxieties about all that we do not know, all that remains just beyond our grasp and cannot yet believe.

BACHELARD, FOUCAULT, AND MERLEAU-PONTY

"The flesh is not matter," Merleau-Ponty writes, "[it] is not mind, [it] is not substance. To designate it, we should need the old term 'element' in the sense it was used to speak of water, air, earth, and fire . . . The flesh is in this sense an element of Being."[14] In this passage, Merleau-Ponty invites a discourse to situate itself within the inarticulate interstices of what might well be called a scientific and philosophical stammer. This discourse itself might well be called a dreamwork of human elemental being—not a scientific reverie necessarily, but, perhaps, a reverie upon the poetic interlacings of how the language of nature is brought to bear on the matter of human experience.

It is at this very crossing point that work of Gaston Bachelard arrives ready-to-hand. I can say with complete conviction that no twentieth-century thinker, certainly not a philosopher of science, can come close to the capacity of Bachelard to offer a discursive entryway into the phenomenology of flesh. Bachelard's intellectual legacy is an admixture of insights from the natural sciences, phenomenology, psychoanalysis, and literary theory. Although he did not set out to accomplish this set of tasks as a carefully outlined program, Bachelard took up the matter of the four elements of nature as a lifelong intellectual pursuit. He was part of a distinguished Parisian intellectual group during the pre- and post-World War II period, having submitted his doctoral thesis to the University of Paris in 1927. Foucault has remarked that Bachelard, with Georges Canguilhem, fell onto one side of a dichotomy in mid-century French philosophy, a split that drew attention to a dividing line that separated "a philosophy of experience, of meaning, of the subject, and a philosophy of knowledge, of rationality and of the concept."[15] On the other side of the divide was Sartre and Merleau-Ponty.[16]

It was not that Merleau-Ponty and Bachelard were working at cross-purposes, it was that for much of his career Merleau-Ponty's perspective on human experience was part of a new Hegelian consciousness (centered on experience, the dialectic of history, and to unseen patterns of unfolding historical events) initiated by Kojève during the mid 1930s, while Bachelard's intellectual development was far less concerned with the political-historical sweep of the existentialist movement and focused much more closely on epistemology, the history of concepts, and the history of science. Sartre, by the 1950s, was very much at the furthest end of this continuum, especially after his break from Merleau-Ponty, which is also to say that Merleau-Ponty was himself moving away from, if not abandoning, the anthropological and political fixations of his earlier intellectual development.

In Merleau-Ponty's lectures at *the Collège de France*, he time and again took up the question of "nature" and began a move toward the development of his thinking that resulted in *The Visible and the Invisible*. In these now published lecture notes, there are important references to Bachelard—not many, but some—that demonstrate an accord with Bachelard on the articulation of scientific voice. From the outset, Merleau-Ponty maintains that nature cannot be conceived as "the idea of an entirely exterior being, made of exterior parts, exterior to man, and to itself, as a pure object."[17] By the close of the lectures, in 1960, he clearly envisions the being of the human, body and flesh, as situated in between nature and *logos*, necessitating a scientific discourse sufficient to articulate the quality of this enmeshment.

At the time Foucault completed his doctoral thesis under Canguilhem (a version of which is published as *Madness and Civilization*), Foucault's intellectual sympathies had grown much closer to the work of Bachelard. David Macey (1993: 69) comments: "For Foucault, Bachelard goes some way towards capturing the lived reality of the imagination. . . "[18] Moreover, for Foucault, "[t]here were two Gaston Bachelards. The Bachelard who theorized epistemological breaks and whose work, like that of Canguilhem, had such an impact on Foucault's vision of the history of the sciences, was also the author of quasi-psychoanalytic studies of the imagination. Foucault admired this Bachelard too, and saw him as an author who had unleashed a surprising dimension of epistemology."[19]

Now that much of the dust has settled on the various ruptures of twentieth-century Continental thought, from Husserl's crisis of the European sciences to the twilight of modern anthropological "man," reading Bachelard and Merleau-Ponty side by side should, by now, seem wholly unproblematic. To the extent that Merleau-Ponty invites his readers to interrogate the existential *nature* of flesh, how it is experienced, how it summons and energizes perception, how it makes visible the imaginary of transformative experience, I find it incumbent upon my own development as theorist of communication to feel to the poetic pulse of flesh. It is through the anima and animus of flesh that we touch and are touched. I seek to understand how such a quality as *thickness* mediates and enables *communicative encounter*.

Thickness implies a texture as well as a complexity, a density, an opaqueness. Thickness serves the architect and builder as both a strength and a reinforcement. As well, it implies an intensity, as one might observe in a word or phrase thickly underlined on the page. But these are all semiotic modalities of encoding and decoding information. Communication and information are wholly distinct elements of semiotic moments. Information is that which is transmitted. Greimas and Courtés define information as "any element that can be expressed with the aid of a code."[20] Communication, on the other hand, necessarily *entails* information but it is not reducible to the code or even to what might be interpreted as the psychological intentionality of the code. Communication entails a transformation in the system function of an organism. However it cannot be sufficiently grasped as an essentially quantitative or digital phenomenon. Deleuze and Guattari note, after Nietzsche and Merleau-Ponty: "things are interactions, *bodies* are communications."[21]

To my mind the fullest articulation of the experience of human communication has been offered by Georges Bataille. Bataille follows both Nietzsche and French Hegelianism into the depth of human connectedness. I cited Bataille's definition of communicative experience in chapter 1. It is, I believe, important at this juncture to cite it again: "'Communication' only takes place *between two people who risk themselves*, each lacerated and suspended, perched atop a common nothingness."[22] The system transformation that is necessarily implied in this consequence of interaction is described as follows: *"Thus 'communication,' without which nothing exists for us, is guaranteed by crime. 'Communication' is love, and love taints those whom it unites"* (emphasis in original).[23] A few paragraphs later, Bataille concludes: "A fundamental principle is expressed as follows: 'Communication cannot proceed from one full and intact individual to another. It requires individuals whose separate existence in themselves is risked, placed at the limit of death and nothingness; the moral summit is the moment of risk taking, it is a being suspended in the beyond of oneself, at the limit of nothingness."[24]

In more concretely Merleau-Pontyan terms, Bataille contends that communication violates the everyday presupposition of the visible, that we are in fact separate subjectively-conscious beings. Bataille's assertion that "love taints and unites" articulates the interactional reality of flesh. When we experience love, we become energized with a consciousness that we are interlinked and intertwined, enmeshed, webbed, and consubstantiated and at an overpoweringly fundamental level. We are constituted of the same energy, the same elements, the same *Grund*—and the fact of our speech and the simultaneous consciousness of a world made manifest in the semiotic constitution of our minds brings us to the threshold of a new vision. Something is conceived and born between us. This something is not seen with our eyes, but in the ecstasy, the *ek-stasis*, of this moment everything that is addressed in our eyes affirms the substance of being. And then, over time, we can, through consciousness and memory, take account of its thickness and viscosity.

The essence of *eros* resides, I fully believe, in the charged, electric currency and vital flow of intimate communication. Maurice Merleau-Ponty's well-known aphorism on intersubjectivity articulates the dimensions of this experience: "To the extent that what I say has meaning, I am a different 'other' for myself when I am speaking; and to the extent that I understand, I no longer know who is speaking and who is listening."[25] As such, the experience of *eros* is lived as a vanishing point for ego. In authentic communication, one forgets who one is; the inhibitions that serve as boundary markers for what shall constitute the self's concept of intimacy lose their active presence. We give up control and let the event define itself. It is in this light that I see *both* eroticism and communication entailing what we live as the core of our "genetic" experimentation—which, I would argue, is what accounts for the pleasure of the polymorphous power that circulates through us when we first take the risk to hold hands with a person who at that very moment sufficiently fulfills our love-object fantasies. In such moments we become real to ourselves for the first time. Human erotic contact is no longer at that point a mere abstraction—a story we read about, a movie that we may wish to emulate. We do not hold it in memory. To the contrary, *it holds us*, and holds us passionately and meaningfully with thick muscled arms, by way of our embodied memory of this experience.

So much of our psychological existence is carried out as a struggle between our separateness and our mutuality, our individual genius and the fundamental contingency of human consciousness. We present ourselves to the world of our social existence as solids. We tan, tone, tint, bejewel, even tattoo the contours of our flesh to symbolically mark our faith, a faith that is often fragile, in the quietly aging truth of our individual, embodied identities. What Calvin Schrag (1991) identifies as the "space of intersubjectivity"[26]—the experiential interstice of psychological ambiguity for the mind still wrestling with Descartes—is the flesh. It is the flesh, subdued in the pedagogy of Western consciousness, taught to speak in a voice and gesture of self-sufficiency. Strength is not merely thickness, this voice speaks, it is solidity and hardness. A mature person, ultimately, cannot be thin-skinned. From Aristotle's *Rhetoric* onward we have found ourselves the pupils of a pedagogy for the discipline of a mind increasingly impervious to the appeals of *pathos*. After all, it is the emotion that honors the fallacy, is it not? It may well be said that *logos* has long been a fetish for a cultural consciousness quietly committed to a certain type of rigidity. The stoic silence of numbers and neutral nomenclature is the authorized, schoolbook language of elements and motion, and the voices that inquire into the nature of beings and objects must be taught to ask questions that are legitimately answerable.

Bachelard comments: "The eye itself, pure vision, becomes tired of looking at solids. It needs to dream of deforming."[27] Which, for me, is to say that that the character of mind, the experience of time, and the movement of an object in space (which may well be the only way that the experience of space truly "matters") is one of fluidity. A being disengages from fixity and recenters itself, redefining if not reenchanting everything that circulates about it. Systemically and organismically, this is not a matter of impulse but a critical sign of life.

It is flow and fluidity that satisfies the existential measure of interaction, and it is liquidity that offers a semiotic feature of communication having occurred, or on its way. This feature resides within the context of another dynamic, a dynamic that Bachelard describes: "Hard and soft are the primary qualifiers of the *resistance* of matter, the initial *dynamic existence of the resistant world*."[28] It is uncertain what so many communication theorists specifically have in mind when they reaffirm the famous axiom that a "person cannot not communicate,"[29] for it is only true in a limited way. Human beings are strikingly resistant to communication. We transfer and project information everywhere we can. The cell phone has become an appendage of the anatomical body. Our communicative actions are a feature of our desires for social recognition and relational control. Information of a certain type flows our way and we soften. But information flows against us or perhaps misses us entirely and we find ourselves hardening.

Yet there is, for me, no convincing pattern of signs to suggest that the flood of information technology has enhanced our emotional connectedness to others. Information technology expands, but so does the sophistication of military technology. The flow of people through technologized urban centers and traditional Western cities creates bottlenecks in our time because of an anxious awareness and vicious talk about the everpresence of foreigners, strangers contaminating the social body, outsiders who do not belong, with whom a vocal plurality resists communication. Contemporary terrorism is, without doubt, a grossly violent assault on flows and interactional patterns; it kills people and makes others move in different ways. It hardens societies. The current war on terror is in its essence turning out to be a war on fluidity itself. It affirms and rigidifies all hardness.

Transformative intimacy, which is certainly inclusive of the notion of erotic intimacy, entails a softening of substances as well as surfaces. A softening is not the same thing as a weakening. Solidity and hardness have their purpose, but they are not necessary or sufficient features of strength. Liquidity is necessary for mixture. The syntagmatic axis of language is referenced by Jakobson as an axis of combination. On this axis, signs are linked in space, and they are linked in flow. It is a habit of mind to address a sign as an object, as a thing. In its thingness, we reason with it as a bounded entity. We treat it as though it has solidity, as though a sudden ambiguity or morphing would constitute a crime against rational thought. On the syntagmatic axis of language, signs mix and flow. They liquefy in thought and expression. Bachelard maintains that "murmuring waters teach birds and men to sing, speak, recount . . .there is, in short, a continuity between the speech of water and the speech of man. . . . [O]rganically, human language has a liquid quality, a flow in its overall effect, water in its consonants . . . this liquidity causes a special psychic excitement that, in itself, evokes images of water."[30]

Perceptual unity entails an intimate relationship between the objects held within the gaze of the perceiver. Reminiscent of the melting clocks in Dali's paintings, the objects transform into retinal images that, like the signs and images of any language, flow together without marked boundaries of differentiation. For one another, we are each signs. Our relations can be discussed as a kind of grammar. In neurotic anxiety, we can feel held in place by this grammar. We are, in this instance, signs that are far too carefully read, defined by others, unable to go with the flow, unable to mix, unable to find our element. Socially, we harden. We congeal. Bachelard underscores the significance of this phenomenon for communication: ". . . I cannot emphasize too much how important the experience of fluidity and pliability is to an understanding of the psychology of the creative unconscious."[31] Schnarch's important work on intimacy and eros reminds us that intimacy is not a commitment to a certain place at a certain time. Syntagmatically or paradigmatically, it is not a "death sentence." Instead it is a commitment to the process of transformation. More than that, intimacy defines the process of change in interpersonal communication systems.[32]

In a transformation of self, flesh becomes real while remaining obvious only to memory and the imagination. For Merleau-Ponty, this was embodied subjectivity giving itself over to presence—that is to say, the present moment, the present self, the presence of things, new experience happening now. He writes in "Eye and Mind" that a painting constituted a "second-order" visibility.[33] It is not "the image of an image" but constitutes "the visible itself which is seeing itself in the vision of the painter, and afterwards, in that of the spectator."[34] As such, the "first-order" visible does not consist of the external reality of the so-called things themselves but, just the opposite, consists instead of an awakening inside of my being, as Merleau-Ponty writes: "Since things and my body are made of the same stuff, vision must somehow take place in them; their manifest visibility must be repeated in the body by a secret visibility. 'Nature is on the inside,' says Cezanne. Quality, light, color, depth, which are there before us, are there only because they awaken an echo in our body and because the body welcomes them."[35] And within this welcoming body, it might be argued, there is not simply a softness but a liquidity—a liquid center, if you will. Here, Bachelard's comments on dreaming prove useful: "There is still water at the bottom of all memory. And in the universe, still water is a mass of tranquility, a mass of immobility. In the still waters, the world rests."[36]

In an intimate flow of liquidity, I would argue, the world comes alive. Hardware becomes entirely dependent upon software. Liquidity becomes both message and medium simultaneously, and we no longer know who is speaking and who is listening. Bachelard speaks again: "If the reader can be convinced that there is, under the superficial imagery of water, a series of progressively deeper and more tenacious images, he will soon develop a feeling for this penetration in his own contemplations . . . He will recognize in water, in its substance, *a type of intimacy* that is very different from those suggested by the depths of fire or rock."[37] When one is immersed in water, the liquid medium becomes as much a nothingness as the air that occupies the ostensibly unoccupied space in everyday object perception. But it is through the wind of speech that the seemingly separate objects at different positions in the geometry of my gaze become fully interconnected. The fluidity of language serves as the enabling condition of the vowel and voice of that which is spoken. The elements of our being are the *Grund* of all being, and these elements are always in motion.

What I have thus far argued is not fully sufficient, at least in terms of what I had intended, to make clear how the thickness of the flesh and of the body gets us to "the heart of things." Speaking from the standpoint of systems psychotherapy, Schnarch maintains that the normal pattern of communication in human relationships entails a resistance to intimacy.[38] Intimacy in human relationships entails nurturing that which is born between us. It is not merely a matter of "closeness," nor is it the feeling of fusion that occurs to lovers overwhelmed with sudden raptures of desire and infatuation. To nurture that which is born between us is to live through it—at a minimum to acknowledge that this vitality exists and that it holds the potential to engage us further into the flow of being and into the otherness of our inhabited world. To nurture that which is born between us is to speak and perceive differently.

None of what I have come to grasp through Merleau-Ponty and Bachelard suggests that this potentiality is reducible to a strategy of language. There is nothing abstract about flesh and so, there is nothing that can be articulated ideologically or structurally that entails a route to the secret residing in the visible habits of embodied subjectivity. Martin Dillon makes this point quite straightforwardly: "Merleau-Ponty . . . set out alone to do what none before him—or since him—could think to do: first he made the soul a thing, a body, and then he incarnated all things into Flesh."[39] Articulating Merleau-Ponty's concept of flesh in terms of Bachelard's poetics of elemental being is to express a potentiality. Foucault identifies the nature of this task explicitly in terms of Bachelard's work: "For Bachelard, studying the concept of fluidity does not, for example, imply studying the equations of fluid mechanics. . . . It means something very different. It also means showing all that fluid can be, all it represents in people's imagination, in the imagination of the masses."[40]

INTERPERSONAL COMMUNICATION AND THE MOISTURE OF INTIMACY

I am told that at an earlier time in the American Southeast it was not altogether unexpected during a moment of rising temperature or tension (perhaps erotic, perhaps merely anxious), to hear a Southern woman speak of getting "the vapors." Perhaps this is a mere fiction of Southern talk, perhaps it is mere legend sustained by the ghosts of Stephen Foster and Tennessee Williams, and perhaps not. In either case the metaphor is perfect. A diminishment of the capacity of cool reason correlates with the increasing presence of steam and moisture. Along similar lines, I have heard it spoken on a number of occasions that Southern women do not perspire—instead, they "glisten." Glistening moisture, vapors emanating not merely from flesh but as flesh: liquidity surfaces as the sign of a communion beyond the control of conscious intentionality. *Humid* and *humor* possess the same linguistic root. A sense of humor is a sense of flow, and by extension this momentary semantic phenomenology leads us to conclude that both currency and curricula are humorous affairs. We have a capacity to elementally experience liquidity. We can experience liquidity as a textural modality of our flow through the continuum of our intersubjectivity. Liquidity as tears, liquidity as sweat, liquidity as salivation, liquidity as sexual arousal—flesh not simply as a medium of liquidity *but as liquidity itself.* What I am seeking to explicate here is that our intimate and interpersonal communication is damp, if not wet, in its essence. A chaste kiss is a dry kiss, and though it succeeds in communicating something, it is barely memorable. In the clinches and in one another's clutches, we moisten.

Vision is itself awash in liquidity. Ocular vision occurs through a process of light filtered through the aqueous humor of the eye. Tears wash dust and other obstructing, potentially irritating, particles from the cornea. The lubricating effect of moisture is essential to the essential dynamic of an *Augenblick*; that is, the eyelids must be able to glide over the cornea to enable the moment of vision to occur within the field of an undifferentiated gaze. *Der Augenblick*, the transformative moment of vision, depicted as it was initially via Luther, and then Kierkegaard and Heidegger,[41] is what enables us to see that Being's oceanic repose has a shoreline and, again, that all habitable space is surrounded by water. A moment's vision is possible to the extent that the vital and fundamental punctuation serving as the enabling condition *for a sign to emerge as such* (namely, the mere blink of an eye) is only possible by the liquid element of lubrication. That which becomes visible is named and numbered among other signs. Gary Madison's reading of *The Visible and the Invisible* makes this point quite clearly:

> As soon as one takes notice of the existence of this "extraordinary overlapping" between vision and the visible in the body itself one must say that it recognizes in what it sees the "other side" of its visionary powers. Precisely because the body which sees is itself a thing, a visible, because it is "a thing among things," it must be said that in the body *it is the visible which sees itself* and that the body and the world are thus "made of the same stuff.""[42]

Liquidity enables the "blink," and the blink differentiates intentional consciousness, making possible the image, the sign, and the visible world—all of which come to being as objects set apart from the oceanic and inarticulable.

In cold weather, as well as during periods of anxiety, our skin tightens and our mouths dry. Of course, "skin" is not what Merleau-Ponty means by flesh, but skin is also more than merely a sign or entailment of flesh. It is the outward marker of my organic and organismic presence; it is the water's edge of my intending consciousness—not the limit of its reach but, to the contrary, the symbol of its potential for isolation. In cold weather we can see our breath—which is to say that we can, during such moments, visually isolate the vapor that has *always* been present with each exhale. Intimate talk may warm us and perhaps burn, but it arrives with a quotient of moisture.

Communicative expression that inhibits or limits the reach of trust essential to the experience of intimate exchange is, thus, "dry." It can be a dry but "cool" exchange (perhaps social pleasantries or business transactions) or a "cold" exchange (distancing, aloof, bitter, disdainful), or even a hot exchange (perhaps angry, fierce, severe). In any case, the dryness either instills or perpetuates a separateness, perhaps a splitting, of my embodied position from what I take to be your positioned, projected and intentional consciousness.

The rupture in our posed and presupposed separateness occurs from novel perception. Again, the *Augenblick*, the moment of discovery, dissolves the presupposed limit condition. The liquidity of tears enables the eyelids to blink and a long look is punctuated. It can possibly be said that the visible emerges as a sight for sore eyes. With a flux of intimate exchange now possible, our mutuality is enabled as a current, and I am drawn outside of what I thought to be Self. The flesh of the body given life between my listener and me—hopefully between you and me—is composed of all four elements. And the tissue that makes up the nerves, the fat, the sinew, the muscle and bone of my biological anatomy is an explication of earth, wind, fire, and water. Humors flow through me. Or perhaps it might better be phrased that the thawed, saturated, and liquid element of flesh humors me. It moves the projection of my awareness and carries me right along, carrying me to the relative stillness of pooled waters, or perhaps carrying me into the eye of its storms. Blood flows through me and expresses the pulse of my anxious heart as it nourishes the tissues and matter of my working systems. It is a barely contained fluidity that will flow from lacerated tissue until clotting, coagulation, and thickening get this flow back within the anatomical order of things. All organic ruptures are by nature temporary; organisms adapt and then settle.

Medical science does not agree on a specific percentage, but the consensus that has emerged is that 50-65 percent of the adult human anatomical body is composed of water.[43] It is generally agreed that babies have the most, being born at around 75 to 80 percent. The human brain, it is generally agreed, is composed of approximately 70 percent water and the lungs are nearly 90 percent water. What can be immediately summarized is that we are more liquid at birth than as we mature. (By about one year of age, the proportion of water drops down to about 65 percent.) There is a wonderful irony in that the organic entity that Western culture has come to associate with dry reason is far more liquid than the body taken as a whole. And for me, it is not the least bit surprising that the organic entity that is essential to the "hot air" of verbal communication is by far and away the body's most liquid asset.

THE MEDIUM OF COMMUNICATIVE EMBODIMENT

There is both an economy and an ecology to the communion of verbal communication. Assets that we may have insisted are wholly personal are released into a flow of culture, of time and space, of context and contact. Having held them behind a thickness of opaque textures, they are now released into the plasma of an intermingled consciousness. The flow of my life out from my private accounts, expressed through my anatomy and into the world of others, the flow of your life into the sensitive, sensual domain of my fragile reality—this flow enables human culture to be understood as a congress of pooled assets, and it is the essential liquidity of the concept of "body" and the oceanic tide of what we still nervously refer to as "soul." This flow enables the potentiality of lingering images and impressions, glistening memories, foggy recollections, cloudy, perhaps dark and ominous storms of agony and paralyzing dread.

The opening of *my* world to the currency of that which is both elemental and extraordinary about *you* is the source of the communicative moment in which subjectivity can become witness and apprentice to a vital and powerful flesh, a flesh that now exceeds and informs the "individuality" that Western consciousness still seeks as the narrative illusion of our lives. The opening of my world, however, is not and cannot be a permanently sustained condition of flesh. My argument is that flesh, as with the anatomical body, is more liquid than solid—not that liquidity ought be taken as the absolute condition of flesh. The possession of assets is the skeleton and sinew of subjectivity; we cannot both exist as beings on one the one hand and give everything away on the other. The possession of assets held in common trust is the fundamental architectural condition of intersubjectivity. But the private confidence of that which can only belong to one person at a time, and which makes name (identity) and character so psychologically and culturally vital, is also that which makes such an event as an *inter*subjective experience possible. There can be no pleasure and no *ek-stasis* in intimate communication if we have no experience of consciousness outside it. Yet once the notion of liquidity is held in the imagination as the substantive attribute of flesh in the body's intimate communication with other bodies, we gain a clearer sense of what Merleau-Ponty was seeking in a philosophy of *chiasm*.

The "humorous" element of flesh that I have endeavored to explicate in this essay is, ultimately, the medium of the fundamental transformation of consciousness that surfaces and comes to pass from intimate communicative contact. Please allow me to linger on this thought a bit longer: the *humorous*, namely, the *liquid* element of earthly being is the principal medium of the *communicative* body. Now of course the body must dwell in all four of the primary elements: earth, wind, fire, *and* water. And, as well, flesh is derived from all four elements. Or to return to Merleau-Ponty's reflection that "[t]o designate it [i.e., flesh], we should need the old term 'element'" and that "[t]he flesh is . . . an element of Being,"[44] it may perhaps best be said that talk of flesh resists the sort of technical specificity that characterizes modern scientific prose. In the domain of Bachelardian poetics, talk of the elements sustains the reversibilities, contradictions, overlaps and interconnections in what can be read as a four-term semiotic square of scientifically symbolic (yet psychologically quite real) elements that emerged from archaic scientific discourse. And in the discursive context in which we are presently imagining the communicative body, it can be claimed that communication has been experienced as a drift into new consciousness—or, in other words, that consciousness takes note of an elemental feeling that something is different.

In this regard, philosophical reflection emphasizing aspects of communicology and psychoanalysis can venture where technical scientific discourse cannot. Bachelard notes: "Dreams, even more than clear ideas and conscious images, are dependent on the four fundamental elements."[45] Alchemy is possible in poetics. Not only is it possible, it happens all the time. In the flow of poetic humors, we can be amused by the expression of an idea both true and false, both imaginatively viable and scientifically impossible—a tennis-playing jellyfish, a pat of butter writing detective novels. As I take it, Merleau-Ponty's phenomenology seeks to understand the flesh as, itself, such an alchemy. Flesh, like mud or plasma or steam or modeling clay, is not describable as solid matter. Though bones and teeth exhibit none of the viscosity of skin and organic tissue, they are as much entailed (and given meaning) by the currency and flow of fleshly activity as the air we breathe and the fire that warms us and lights our visible world.

Understanding the activity of flesh in, with, and amid the communicative body animates thought about the body's regard for its own life. In communicative exchanges that liquefy and soften, moisten, perhaps saturate, quench, lubricate, marinate, bathe, shower, immerse, or flood, the fixed connection between ego and belief can begin to dissolve, enabling the consciousness to entertain images and thoughts of all sorts. What seemed foolish impulses and dumb ideas just moments before can be entertained in the humors of a consciousness suddenly beside itself. It is by way of a liquid medium that the concept of influence (in-*fluence*) can be more clearly understood for what it is and how it works. Liquidity is a medium of currents and waves. Liquids can gel, dry out, and harden. They can evaporate from the heat and freeze in the cold. But their presence changes things. As Bachelard maintains: "One cannot bathe in the same river twice because already, in his [or her] inmost recesses, the human being shares the destiny of flowing water. Water is truly the transitory element. It is the essential ontological metamorphosis between fire and earth. A being dedicated to water is a being in flux."[46]

CONCLUSION: THE DREAM OF MIND AND THE COURSE OF FLESH

Thus far, the post-Cartesian discourse of body and spirit sought by Merleau-Ponty (not just in *The Visible and the Invisible* but throughout his life and works) has not, for the most part, been very well served by the building interest in "embodiment," particularly as it has manifested in cultural studies and cognitive science. For a genuinely post-Cartesian discourse to emerge, a critical mass of human scientists will need to be roused from the notion that "the body" is something contained within the outer epidermal layer of the skin. As such, assertions that "mind" is embodied, assertions that on the surface might seem "phenomenological" to a reader insufficiently literate in Continental philosophy, can only further perpetuate the positivist/behaviorist assumption that "mind" (fully entailing spirit, subjectivity, consciousness, and will) is somehow, somewhere, housed in organic tissue (probably the brain) belonging to an individual. Not only will consciousness remain a cosmic (and in many ways, *comic*) mystery to any scientific or philosophical enterprise committed to such assumptions, but the limit conditions for what constitutes "body" will continue to pass without careful scrutiny. Living bodies are never finished in their development and adaptive changes, and must actively draw upon the earth's resources to sustain themselves. But this is not to say that we are, in our essence, "consuming beings," actively eating and drinking and taking and using for the survival of our consumptive species.

Human life is so clearly not restricted to material forms of desire and survival for its own sake. We are creatures who dream and imagine, yet reason carefully with one another, often arguing over details, definitions, and inaccuracies. We crave novelty, change, and laughter, yet we fear madness (especially our own) and will choose stability and security during periods of anxiety and uncertainty. Decades of psychoanalytic and psychiatric research in attachment theory have produced convincing evidence that we enter the world with as strong an appetite for communication and contact as we have for any and all other forms of sustenance.[47] Our childhoods are spent gaining approval and validation from the very same parental authority from whom we will later seek to detach, and which we might later become. Just as our bodies are never sufficient unto themselves, our Selves are never independent of their families, cultural origins, communicative contexts, other selves with whom we come into contact, or other selves whose being remains foreign to us. As such, the notion of an "individuated Self" becomes, for me, as phenomenologically difficult as the notion of an embodied mind.

Commenting on the shapelessness of contemporary life, Zygmunt Bauman has employed the metaphor of "liquidity" as a means to critique habits and patterns of modern social interaction.[48] On first blush, it might appear that his thesis runs contrary to the one I have argued here. But Bauman's position is in fact remarkably compatible with the theme of liquidity as elemental to communicative experience. His critical position concerns sedimentation, memory, and community rather than the experience of flesh and the transformation of consciousness in interpersonal communication. Bauman's perspective is significant because we can only live "in the moment" for so long. Moments are significant inasmuch as they are *ek-static*. The fiction of "extending" such a moment (which Bauman sees as the myth of modern *techné*) has the effect of washing the ecstasy of such moments beyond the reach of cultural perception. My argument is that without a consciousness of flesh, reflection on the body and its experience is condemned to a thinking about objects: limited objects, objects whose subjectivity may well be the subject of fanciful speculation (in literature, the arts) but whose activity and pragmatics are reducible to all that can be objectively recorded about their survival and their biological species-being.

In the context of a discussion about Damasio's thinking on mind, brain, and body, Ian Hacking insightfully observes that "Descartes, Leibniz, and Hume 'de-anthropomorphized' *conatus* and causation,"[49] which is to say that the last four centuries of the Western scientific narrative of embodiment has taken the human experience—namely, language, culture, history, and the complexity of desire—out of the "meaning of life." In this context, it may well be said that Merleau-Ponty's philosophy of the flesh begins as a conscientious effort to *re*-anthropomorphize *conatus* and causation. Hacking suggests that the internalist, mind-in-the-brain movement afoot in psychology, psychiatry, and neuroscience (of which Damasio's work has emerged, of late, as a highly prominent exponent) is an attempt to by-pass, if not eliminate, the significance of subjective experience. As he phrases it: "The concept of the mind as a complex piece of metabolism seems to have mislaid the 'I.'"[50]

So, for Hacking, the issue of the embodiment of consciousness as it surfaces in the context of neuroscience suggests the problematic of "'I' and mind," whereas for Merleau-Ponty the problematic emerged as one of "eye and mind." For a philosophy of the flesh, as I have attempted to explicate it here, there is no elemental difference. Merleau-Ponty maintains: "Thought is a relationship with oneself and with the world as well as with the other; hence it is established in the three dimensions at the same time. And it must be brought to appear directly in the infrastructure of vision."[51] It is not simply enough to say that the body is *involved* in thought, it is that the body *is* thought. Madison, in a close reading of a closing fragment of *The Visible and the Invisible*, makes the case quite directly: "'States of consciousness' and 'acts of consciousness' and all of the rest of the positivist 'bric-à-brac,' Merleau-Ponty says, are '*differentiations* of one sole and *massive* adhesion to Being which is the flesh.'"[52] Madison continues: "'I' am there precisely when the flesh of the world prepares in itself a 'hollow,' an 'interior.'[53]

Rather than a positing consciousness as a succession of ideas, William James proposed the concept of a "stream of thought"—an idea that slipped into the discourse of psychology and psychiatry over a century ago and which is essentially taken as a given in all aspects of contemporary clinical work. Streams of thought, streams of consciousness, the liquidity of mind, the flow of spirit all participate in the particular energy that serves as the life of flesh. It cannot say precisely where it is because it has no certain empirical location. In Richard Lanigan's important explication of Foucault's theory and methodology in the case of Herculine Barbin, the tragic nineteenth-century French hermaphrodite,[54] he concludes his monograph with the observation that in the authentic speech of a person whose mortal embodiment functioned as a repudiation of the context and code of cultural discourse, "somebody is nowhere."[55] In an important way what the inconvenient fact of Barbin's life demonstrates is that in the ecstatic discovery of the *flesh*, some *body* is always already nowhere. It is "nowhere" for the same reason that we cannot step in the same river twice. What we find on any map is the trace of the river's movement: the geographical interstice marked by primordial geological formations and sedimentary deposits of earth, the banks that enable us to engineer bridges to cross over a flow that might engulf us if we are not sufficiently amphibious, if we are not powerful and attentive. The liquidity of flesh is experienced through its flow. No one gets to keep it. We can only feel its current and let it speak through us. And perhaps at some point neuroscientific speculation may come to realize that the power of a river's current cannot be sufficiently experienced by studying the chemical composition of its banks.

NOTES

1. Merleau-Ponty, *The Visible and the Invisible.*

2. In cognitive science, there are two highly prominent works featuring this concept. The first is Lakoff and Johnson, *Philosophy in the Flesh.* The second is Varela, Thompson, and Rosch, *The Embodied Mind.* Both texts exhibit diffidence, if not resistance, to the theory and method of phenomenology. Varela, Thompson, and Rosch make reference to Merleau-Ponty's work, but draw a clear line separating their intellectual commitments from Merleau-Ponty's explication of intersubjective experience and the *corps propre*. In cultural studies, prominent and influential works—most notably Turner, *The Body and Society* and Shilling, *The Body and Social Theory*—feature discourse about the body principally addressing matters of textuality and the exercise of strategies, regimes, and technologies of biopower. Matters of "mind," "spirit," or "consciousness" are deferred back to modernist assumptions, exhibiting no philosophical commitment to the notion that "flesh" might be something other than "skin."

3. For a comprehensive summary of key aspects of this emerging movement in neuroscience and psychiatry, see Kandel, *Psychiatry, Psychoanalysis, and the New Biology Of Mind* and Kandel, *In Search of Memory: The Emergence of a New Science of Mind.* See also Ledoux, *Synaptic Self.*

4. See Damasio, *The Feeling of What Happens*; *Descartes' Error*; and *Looking for Spinoza.*

5. Merleau-Ponty, *Visible*, 145.

6. Merleau-Ponty, *Visible*, 135.

7. Merleau-Ponty, *Visible*, 135.

8. Lanigan, *Speaking and Semiology.*

9. Fóti, *Vision's Invisibles,* 69.

10. Foucault, *Herculine Barbin,* x–xi.

11. See Bowen, *Family Therapy in Clinical Practice*; Kerr and Bowen, *Family Evaluation*; and Kerr, "Chrionic Anxiety and Defining a Self," 35–58.

12. Merleau-Ponty, *Visible*, 267.

13. Merleau-Ponty, *Visible*, 135.

14. Merleau-Ponty, *Visible*, 139–40.

15. Foucault, "Introduction," 8.

16. Foucault, "Introduction," 8.

17. Merleau-Ponty, *Nature*, 8.

18. Macey, *The Lives of Michel Foucault*, 69.

19. Macey, 69.

20. Greimas and Courtés, *Semiotics and Language,* 156.

21. Deleuze and Guattari, *What is Philosophy?* 123.

22. Bataille, *On Nietzsche*, 20–21.

23. Bataille, *On Neitzsche*, 18.

24. Bataille, *On Neitzsche*, 18–19.

25. Merleau-Ponty, *Signs*, 97.

26. See Schrag, *Communicative Praxis.*

27. Bachelard, *Water and Dreams:* 106.

28. Bachelard, *Earth and Reveries of Will,* 13.

29. This axiom has become entrenched in the discourse of the academic field of communication studies since the 1960s. Its most prominent initial publication appeared in Watzlawick, Beavin, and Jackson, *Pragmatics of Human Communication.* Since then, it has been reiterated in virtually every college textbook on communication theory and praxis.

30. Bachelard, *Water*, 15.
31. Bachelard, *Water*, 13.
32. See Schnarch, *Constructing the Sexual Crucible.*
33. Merleau-Ponty, "Eye and Mind," 164.
34. Madison, *The Phenomenology of Merleau-Ponty,* 100.
35. Merleau-Ponty, "Eye and Mind," 164.
36. Bachelard, *The Poetics of Reverie*, 196.
37. Bachelard, *Water*, p. 6.
38. Schnarch, pp. 103–25.
39. Dillon, *Merleau-Ponty's Ontology*, 101.
40. Foucault, "*Gaston Bachelard, le philsophe et son ombre: piéger sa proper culture*," 16.
41. See Dreyfus, *Being-in-the-World,* 321–22.
42. Madison, *Merleau-Ponty,* p. 98.
43. See generally Ball, *Life's Matrix*. See also Chumlea, Guo, Zeller, Reo, and Siervogel, "Total body water data for white adults 18 to 64 years of age," 244–52. See also Askew, "Water," 98–108.
44. Merleau-Ponty, *Visible*, 139–40.
45. Bachelard, *Water*, p. 4.
46. Bachelard, *Water*, p. 6.
47. See Bowlby, *The Making and Breaking of Affectional Bonds*; Bowlby, *A Secure Base*; and Sroufe, *Emotional Development.*
48. See Bauman, *Liquid Modernity*; Bauman, *Liquid Life*; and Bauman, *Liquid Love.*
49. Hacking, "Minding the Brain," 35–36.
50. Hacking, 36.
51. Merleau-Ponty, *Visible,* 145.
52. Madison, 238.
53. Madison, 238.
54. See Foucault, *Herculine Barbin.*
55. Lanigan, *Human Science of Communicology,* 113.

Chapter Six

The Diabolical Parable and the Devil in Speech

PAROLE AND SPEECH

In this chapter I will engage in a close reading of the concepts inherent to a term absolutely vital to semiotic and phenomenological inquiry regarding the event of human communication: *parole*. The operation of *parole* as the French word for the standard English "speech" is the customary reading of *parole*'s function in semiotic and phenomenological approaches to the study of language. Yet the concept of *parole* has a much richer etymological history than that of "speech," whose origins are tied to, merely, an onomatopoetic purpose—"suggesting," according to lexicographer John Ayto, "that the English word's use for 'utter, say' arose via an earlier 'crackle, prattle, babble chatter."[1] *Parole*, on the other hand, shares the same origin as both "parable," "problem," and "symbol." Robert Claiborne observes that "from the same source is the Latin, *parabolare*, 'to talk' (? "throw forth" words), whence the 'parliament' and 'parlor' where different kinds of talking take place."[2] The connection of *parole* to the word "parable" potentially situates the derivation of this concept of speaking to both *poiesis* and theology. But there is more. Claiborne continues: "A related Greek word, *diábolos*, to slander (? "throw dirt on"), was used to mistranslate Hebrew 'Satan' as 'slanderer' (actually it = enemy), whence (via Latin) 'devil' and 'diabolic.'"[3]

Following Foucault's general method of genealogical inquiry, I will attempt to radically consider the complex relations (namely, the *le même et l'autre*) of the "diabolic" and the "parabolic" in human speech.[4] My objective is to discuss the nature of "evil" as it is manifest in the "diabolical" praxis of *parole*/parable. The word "evil" and the word "devil" bear only a slight historical relationship to one another. Yet based on a similarity of spelling and an ostensible compatibility of meaning, the two terms have nevertheless become deeply interrelated in the *patois* of modern discourse. That is, the figure of the "devil" (e.g., satan) has been taken as a signifier of "evil," a word which only until recently has come to mean "extreme moral wickedness."[5]

The word "evil" denotes (from its literal origins), simply, "uppity."[6] As such, a "devil," serving as a figure of evil, potentially represents an entire spectrum of conceit, including, perchance, pride, arrogance, narcissism, immodesty, and unpleasant disposition. Following a theme resonating throughout Nietzsche's *Also Sprach Zarathustra,* I will argue that the necessity of human communication thus entails a synthesis of "evil" with "parable." Which is to say that I will maintain that rhetoric is a function of *mastery* and *parabolic* expression. I will further argue that *parole* necessarily entails elements of devilish imagination. As such, human communication will emerge as a function of transgression rather than—as it is commonly presupposed—a function of consensus and unanimity.

THE EXCESSES OF EVIL

The modern world has come to know and understand evil with remarkable proficiency—that is, insofar as evil, from its ancient origins in the notion of inflated self-worth to its modern sense of wickedness, continues to be defined and understood as a form of extreme behavior. Another way of phrasing this observation is to claim that apart from the modern world's capacity to recognize the works of evil only *after* they have occurred, the capacity to recognize evil in advance of its occurrence is to postulate its form as immoderate, if not distended. We are concertedly and unequivocally horrified by the killing fields of Cambodia, the Nazi death camps, the gross, nihilistic violence of modern ideological and religious terrorists—but, at the same time, we know that the concept of evil is in no way reducible to such extreme cases.

In much the same manner that the world of public health cannot "tolerate" cancer, AIDS, and the numerous types of environmental pollution, the enlightened modern world has also come to abhor racism, sexism, terrorism, and colonialism. These latter forms of intolerance signify a rupture in the course of the Western mind; that is, they have served as a shock to certain dead levels of historical abstraction that had impeded the progress and flow of reason, dialectic, rhetoric, and communication. Intolerable deeds are, thus, inseparable from categories of intolerance, leading one to wonder whether, in any instance of unreasonable violence, what we hate more is the deed or the category from which it seems derived.

Random, *anomic* violence is not computable in the modern Western mind. True, the specific victim of violence will probably never know, comprehend, or in any way identify his or her killer with his or her specific intentions. But the cultural world that expresses its horror toward the killing cannot escape viewing this act as a *performance* of some sort. In this limited context, violent manifestations of evil are "always" staged acts, with intentionality (if not articulate motive), drama, catharsis, heroism, victimage, and redemption. Freud's aphorism that "there are no accidents" seems far less an invention of his own mind than it is a reflection of a radical investment of history with a transcendent law of communication—if you will, a Judeo-Christian communication imperative. Physical violence, it may be said, communicates inartistically, if not badly. Yet, it does, nevertheless, *seem* to communicate.

The great difficulty in all of this is that a common discourse concerning good and evil has been formed on the basis of public (and publicized) "newsworthy" events, a discourse that succeeds only in dissimulating the concepts of evil, otherness, alterity, difference, incommensurablity, the alien, and the shadow. Now, I am not suggesting that a discussion of evil can be shepherded toward a rational foundation such that its true specimens can be recognized and named once and for all. But, at the same time, I will contend that any discourse on evil that attempts to break free of dominant ethical presuppositions will need at the very least to question the authority of what appears to be the current universal assumption that *communication*, as an interpersonal *performance activity*, is the desirable end state—*viz*., the teleology—of human relations.

In *The Transparency of Evil*, Jean Baudrillard speaks of a sort of "communication utopia" concocted, over time, by the Western mind.[7] In this utopia, the human mind, as the captain of its body, is motivated toward an understanding of the Other. The mind, then, "embodies" Otherness as "difference." Not, mind you, as *this*-Other, or as *an*-Other, but as nothing more than a difference, a difference from itself, a difference from the same.

The moral problem of the modern Western mind is not in language (either as *langue* or as *langage*). It is not in the ostensible dynamics of *le meme et l'autre*. It is not in the grammar of pronouns and prepositions. The architecture of language, whether as mirror, as opposition, as apposition, or as delay, is merely a symptom of the desire of the human institution of which language is a function. The moral problem of language is that language is a communication medium whose existence must, with each generation, be institutionalized and then reinstitutionalized. Language "is," and even were Chomsky correct that language's potential is always "in us," the existence of language (*langage*) presupposes the existence of social, speakable languages (*langue*)—and in any given case, such language must always be learned and subject to continual praxis. Which is to say that the moral problem of language is that language has no morality in itself. Its soul, like the soul of any machine, is in us. It is, thus, not subject to a law of communication. What *is* subject to the law of communication is the institution of speaking (as *parole*). So it is in the institution of speaking (*parole*), I will contend, that one can locate the moral problem of the Western mind.

THE HIDDEN SPEECH OF THE PARABOLA

One way of apprehending *parole* is to see it as the ghost of algebra. To wit: the parabola that is plotted on a two-dimensional graph is never to be found on what we see as the plotted graph. The modern intellectual works that so far have come to define the phenomenology of language, the body, and the social world have tried to get at this essential truth for well over a century (especially, in many ways, beginning with Peirce): this notion that speech is phenomenally different than speaking, that written work is phenomenally different than writing. The clearest articulation of it with regard to speech (*parole*) itself is to be found in Merleau-Ponty, who distinguished *parole parlée* (speech spoken) from *parole parlante* (speech speaking).[8] *Parole parlante*—understood from a more decisive semiotic vantage point as a "parabola-'parabol-ing'" (or a parabolic-arc-in-motion)—is precisely the "arc-'type'" that cannot be found on the math student's graph paper. The spoken word, "speech spoken" (Merleau-Ponty's *parole parlée*), is the only map that we "have" of *parole*.

As we well know, students often tire of their assigned algebra problems—because, perhaps, for all of their work calculating and plotting the points described by an algebraic function, all they have left at the end of the day are pieces of paper with arcs penciled on them. It is the case that the spirit of these algebraic functions finds its home in the flight itself, in the motion of objects thrown, moving, from one place to another.

The flight of human spirit is, literally, the flight of air (namely, the air that resides in our bodies and which is expelled in the exhale of our "expression" [from the Latin *ex*/"out" + *premere*/ "push"]). And the flight of air is, literally, the energy of speech: *parole*. The arc of an expression, any expression, is the spirit that is cast from the body of a speaking subject to the body of a listener, literally energizing the space between them, giving life to this space, embodying this space, extending one's body to the reach of another. The word "parabola," like it its first cousin "parable," is a descendent of the Greek *para-bállein*. The lexical unit *bállein*, from which the modern "ballet" and "ballistics" are derived, literally means "throwing," or "to throw"—revealing the inevitable root metaphor of a body, simply, throwing-its-Self, in the thrownness-of-itself, whose movement constitutes a dance in the flight of itself.

The function of the Greek lexical unit *para* is somewhat more ambiguous. *Para* seems to function as a preposition, typically referring to placement or position: viz., "beside," "beyond," "contrary to."[9] So, it can be said that *para-ballein* describes a "pro-ject" (Latin, literally a "forward throwing"), a projection, a flight of intentionality, an arc whose reality is unmappable, but which is nevertheless known to us as the map of the parabolic arc. And the flight of air, of spirit, projected through human oral expression is the parabolic arc of parole. It is the ghost of human communication: the revenant of embodied intersubjectivity.

Now, the ghost of human communication is not communication itself. Communication, it may be said, is the mathematical function that the parabola describes. It is both pattern and matrix, both strategy and site, both expression and perception. And it also should go without saying that communication, like mathematics, exists only theoretically. Though a love letter may, even upon continual readings (and through time), produce feelings of warmth and excitement, neither the letter, the language in which it was written, the ink that was committed to the paper, nor the feelings themselves constitute communication. And neither are they rhetoric or *parole*. A ball in flight is nothing more than what it is: a round object set in motion. Likewise the flight itself is of no matter, no substance. And what is said of an object's flight, its dance, its movement, from here to there can also be said about a community, a city, a friendship, a corporation, a university, or a mathematical set. We are tempted to address them as empirical, substantive things, but their existence is for us merely eidetic, merely theoretical.

And for each of these entities to exist in any *meaningful* way, they must first be haunted. In this way, communication has all of the substance of a memory. The haunts of memory are nothing if not haunted. Memory, like mind and consciousness, consists only of the energy that circulates through it. Shards, threads, impressions of images, like the long-forgotten-about contents of a junk-drawer containing buttons, dead batteries, paper clips, old coupons, ticket stubs—none of these elements has any value save the speech that dances between them and is thrown from them. The pieces of mind and memory are all "arc"ed together as we hear them speak silently to us, and their orbits are reflexively changed the very moment we project them, in *parole*, to others.

The "law of communication" that serves as the implied target of Baudrillard's critique, a critique of what he perceives as an increasingly prophylactic culture (viz., a culture of safe sex that in turn prefigures an emergent cultural aesthetics of anodyne, antiseptic and prudent *eros*), is not a critique of communication *per se*, or of the importance of communication in addressing the human condition. In many ways Baudrillard's critique offers a logical extension of Merleau-Ponty's critical explication of *parole parlante* and *parole parlée* in the *Phenomenology of Perception*. Communication, understood as the invented and remaindered body arising from a *maieutic* moment in which speech spoke and continues speaking, cannot be mapped, it is not a thing, and, as such, it cannot be cited as a *telos*. Baudrillard's concern is that the modern world's contemporary preoccupation with "communication" appears naively intended to transform Otherness (the foreign and the strange)—which is an essential, exotic, and exorbitant element in the consciousness of experience—into a rational function of difference. He asks, "Do we now ever describe a mad person as 'mad'? As a matter of fact, we are so terrified of Evil, so greedy for euphemisms to denote the Other, misfortune, or other irreducibles, that we no longer even refer to a cripple as such."[10] Later he adds: "We already know to what dangerous extremities we are led by prophylaxis in every sphere: social, medical, economic, or political . . . an endemic terror may well be instituted that is every way as dangerous as the epidemic threat of catastrophe."[11]

In the process of naming the alien and familiarizing it with its "given" space, *parole* is subject to a new set of conditions. Baudrillard contends that "Communication in not a matter of speaking but of making people speak . . . these are operations, not actions."[12] His concept of the law of communication understood as a regulative ethics identifies a problematic in that it insinuates, into the unknowable futures of unplanned interactions, an economic theory of intentionality and utility—in short, a transactional model of the will or spirit. To wit, speech, when it is recognized as "communicative," is to occur within ethical and practical orbits of communication—orbits, parabolic arcs, that are designated prior to the path of an object thrown. He argues that

> These days even wanting is mediated by models of the will, by forms of making people want something—by persuasion or dissuasion. Even if such categories as wishing, being able, believing, knowing, acting, desiring and enjoying still retain some meaning, they have all been monopolized, as it were, by a simple auxiliary mode. . . . There is to be no knowledge save that which results from having (people) know. No speaking save that which results from having (people) speak.[13]

As such, instead of foreigners in one another's worlds, we are each guests. If we regulate our interactions accordingly, then we get each other to speak; we are, then, "communicating." Baudrillard thus satirically concludes: "I am your guest, you are my guest—we exchange pleasure as a part of a performative interactivity. Anyone who seeks gratification without communication is a pig."[14] It is Baudrillard's position that the whitewash of operational modalities implied in the "law of communication" is not nearly so portentous as the logic of identity coded into a distinction-based or "difference"-based perspective on culture. To this end, he cites the example of racism: "Racism does not exist so long as the other remains Other, so long as the Stranger remains foreign. It comes into existence when the other becomes merely different—that is to say, dangerously similar."[15] The rational, scientific regulation of *parole* on the topic of race cannot eliminate the fear, in fact the terror, felt by people about others who look and behave in a manner of radical difference—about others with whom there seems no immediate promise of communication. "Wherever exchange is impossible," Baudrillard writes, "what we encounter is terror. Any radical otherness at all is the epicenter of a terror: the terror that such otherness holds, by virtue of its very existence, for the normal world. And the terror that this world exercises upon that otherness in order to annihilate it."[16] Baudrillard is then left to this judgment regarding the example he has illustrated: "[I]f racism in its viral, imminent, current and definitive form proves anything, it is that there is no such thing as the proper use of difference."[17]

The function of *parole* in the context of any sort of law of communication, that is, any sort of contract, any sort of expectation (namely, a communication ethics[18])—modernist, classical, or otherwise—is performative. Which is to say that in this context human expression is "assessed." We give ourselves the option to choose it. We also assume the option to name it, which is, at once, to limit it, to cease full participation in it. We put faith in the contexts of discourse so that the discourse itself is relieved of the existential phenomenology of discursive experience. We respect, in functional contexts, the law of communication so as to relieve us of the possibility of communication. In the typical culture of commercial transactions, the drama of emotional risk and metaphysical disorder that characterize the experience of interpersonal communication is carefully and minimally staged so as not to disrupt the process of buying and selling. A good waiter, for example, is one who learns to refrain from certain comments regarding the patron's menu choice, eating habits, and so forth. Along these very lines, Greimas and Courtés have operationalized their understanding of communication ethics in terms of "deontic modalities." They note that "the term deontology is used to designate the system of rules for conduct that one is supposed to follow in the practice of a profession or an activity. This is also called professional ethics."[19] But the matter exceeds the domain of economic necessity and functionality when we can begin to take notice of an ethical imperative emerging as a mythic subtext to the universal matrix of communicative possibility.

SEMIOTIC VIOLENCE AND THE IRRELEVANCE OF EVIL

The concept of evil has become a discursive reflection, in fact a pervasive cognitive synonym, for the concept of violence. The examples I cited earlier each remind us of a tragic violence—of pain and suffering and death forced upon the bodies of helpless and innocent persons. War itself is always a violence. It resists violence by deploying counterviolence. And all of this leads us, characteristically, to associate the notion of violence with the color of blood. When such a pervasive—and intensely pervasive—connotation of the word "violence" is semantically conjoined with nonfleshly, nonphysical conceptions of "body" and "embodiment" to yield such terms as "semiotic-violence," "emotional-violence," or "rhetorical-violence" we still see red. And in this capacity, someone guilty of violent speech (*parole parlée*) has engaged in an act of terror that, connotatively, places him in culturally synchronous orbit with Sade, Hitler, Timothy McVeigh, and Osama bin Laden.

It goes without saying that the "law of communication" seeks to limit, if not exterminate, the possibilities of semiotic violence. As a rational objective of certain pedagogical and institutional policies, along with the political discourse that soon becomes indistinguishable from such policies themselves, the idea of limiting semiotic violence now finds itself functioning as a moral condition of communication ethics.

But the moral strength of this ethical stance immediately finds itself somewhat neutralized when one takes the time to carefully examine what the term "violence" means. There's nothing in the etymology of the word to necessarily suggest blood, suffering, or death. Joseph Ayto reasons that the term "was derived from the [Latin] noun *vís* 'force, energy' (whose accusative form *vim* is probably the source of English 'vim')."[20] Claiborne refers to the Proto-Indo-European (P-I-E) root form *weih* (itself meaning, simply, "force") to draw the conclusion that violence literally signifies "to use force on."[21] Now it is clear that "violence" has come to mean the same thing as brutality and savagery. But the point where the energetic, perhaps passionate, perhaps vehement, perhaps fiery and forceful expression of one's will passes into an objectively perceptible moment of inhumane cruelty is not at all clear. As with the popular (yet, alas, inapt) contemporary dialogue on the nature of evil, we find ourselves here discussing situations ex post facto with the heavy handed authority of a priori moral presuppositions.

When we see the tragedy of lost life and innocent blood, we presuppose the activity of violence. An accident of force, although often deadly, is merely a collision; sometimes it is simply a bump. An exchange of force, also potentially deadly, may be called a fight, perhaps a battle, perhaps a war. Sometimes one side ends up "violated" far more extensively than the other side is "violated," and when that is the case, we are almost correct in saying the side with the lower percentage of casualties is "more" violent than the other. But to infer, even on the basis of blood and suffering, that one side was more evil than the other is to make a gross categorical error of logic. A battlefield full of casualties is not necessarily a sign of violated innocence and, likewise, an absence of passion and vehemence in the expression of one's will is not necessarily a sign of virtue. The eventual symbols of "victory" and "honor" are derived, over an expanse of time, from the application of cultural premises and historical knowledge. Which is to say that the movement of culture, the dance of culture, elects to celebrate and mourn the bodies whose expenditure affirms the culture's inner logic. But on the same token, Afghanistan's (or Serbia's or Iraq's) children have not been cultured toward a "proper" appreciation of American imperialism and, likewise, the family of the Unabomber (Ted Kaczynski) will fight to prevent his execution. The movement—the energy, the force—of group logic is, as Ruesch and Bateson have demonstrated,[22] the property of the organizing function of a group, regardless of whether that group is a tribe, a corporation, a committee, or a family. And this movement is entirely a function of a particular group's pattern of persistence over time. The concept of evil relative to a group's history of "violent" action can, thus, only be understood through the experience of group membership and identification.

What we see when we take the time to consider violence for what it is as an existential experience of bodily expression is that violence bears only a neutral relationship to the concept of good and evil. Violence is, for good or evil, a type of liberation. It is an intense liberation of energy which, by virtue of the thermodynamics of bodies is felt, in its movement, as a strong impression on the sensitive skins of other bodies. Bodies must assert themselves; except in Warholian parody, there is no such thing as a dance or an art of the same. Organic life necessitates violence for its survival. It is only in the age of the machine that we can entertain the myth of an active consciousness—most likely, an implanted or artificial intelligence—that requires nothing of others. There is no thrownness to the logic and motility of a machine. Thus, the rhetoric of artificial intelligence is always, even when it surprises or amazes us, *parole parlée*. That is why technicians are called in to diagnose and prevent the danger. (For all its seeming symbolism, there was nothing poetic or even philosophically problematic about the so-called "Y2K problem.")

Viol is the everyday French word for "rape"—and it goes without saying that a rape is an act of force. But the *conceptual* relationship that is expressed in the iteration of *viol* or "rape" is not even a matter of clear connotative correspondence—especially when one considers the rhetorical power of the word "rape" in everyday discourse. In the contemporary discourse of communication ethics that has fully insinuated itself into all aspects of late-modern institutional life, the word "rape" cannot seem to escape a particular theatricality—namely, the theatricality of a vulnerable woman brutally overtaken by a dark male figure indifferent to her life, its meaning, its desires, its pleasures, or its existence. It is an overdrawn and overdetermined theatricality that functions to make the notion of such a thing as a "little rape" culturally incomprehensible. And it, rape, has become the transcendent symbolic referent in the passionate contemporary discourse regarding gendered "semiotic violence." The fate of discourse on the matter of sexism, however, cannot be spared the fate of discourse on the matter of racism—and if anything, the swollen imagery of "sexist semiotic violence" has produced a radical masculine Otherness that can never be reconciled with the implied system of civil differences in the emergent, utopian "law of communication." As Georges Bataille steadfastly maintains, "eroticism only includes a domain marked off by the violation of rules. It is always a matter of going beyond the limits allowed. . . . So it is a matter of passing from the licit to the forbidden. Man's [*sic*] sexual life developed out of the accursed, prohibited domain, not the licit domain."[23]

THE PARABOLICAL, THE DIABOLICAL, AND THE INELUCTABLE CROSS

It can be said that the kinetic energy of *parole* seeks its own "morality"—its own *habitus*, its own *ethos*. The dance (the *kinesis*) of energy is one and the same with the life and motility of bodies. We throw as we are thrown. Our speech is thrown from a silence that has no clear, identifiable place in discourse, that in fact will never know a place in discourse. The word "diabolical" also exemplifies a movement, a throwing and thrownness: a dance. The word "diabolic," from the Greek *diábolos*, a derivative of *dia-bállein* (which, even in Antiquity, most commonly connoted "slander, slanderer"), is more than just a cousin to the word "parabolic."

The linguistic space between them is quite small, especially when one considers the general semiotic indeterminacy (and, as well, interchangeability) of semantic prepositions. Prepositions, after all, function as stage directions for the theatre of semantic activity. The logic of stage directions entirely depends upon whether one is viewing the action from onstage—and then again, where from onstage—or in the wings or backstage or in the audience (and then again, *where*?) or from the grid and scaffolding above. The diabolical and the parabolical, the devil and *parole*, are separated only by the ambiguity of a stage direction for a production that can be seen by anyone at any time and from any angle.

Harold Bloom passionately claims that "Thrown" is the most powerful verb in the Gnostic vocabulary, "for it describes, now as well as two thousand years ago, our condition: we have been thrown in this world, this emptiness. Cast out, at once from God and from our true selves, or sparks, we live and die our sense of having been thrown, daily."[24] The language of human inquiry is rooted in the phenomenology of thrownness, movement, dance: the word "problem" refers to "a throwing, a putting forth"; the word "symbol" refers to a "throwing together," as when a compelling concept and its referent "move together" in discourse, thought, and the ballet of narrative. And "parable" refers to an allegorical or moral narrative, a mythic analogy whose verbal strategy moves in a poetic relationship with its moral content without ever touching it directly.

The word "diabolical" refers to a dancing-, moving-, or throwing-through, or perhaps a dancing-, moving-, or throwing-across. Hence, the "symbol" of the "devil" (namely, a "diabolical speaker") poses a "problem" for the life of a cultural body. The problem posed is a matter of energy, play, movement, motion. To move or play beside, beyond, or even contrary-to is parabolical. To move or play *across* or *through* is diabolical. A *dia*meter is a line that crosses through the center of a circle. A *dia*gonal is a line that crosses from one angle of a polygon to another. A *dia*logue is a "talking-across," a dance of words from one speaker to another. The *dia* in the word diabolical, then, emphasizes this notion of crossing, of going-through. In the notion of the diabolical, understood within the context of the existential communication theory entertained in this essay, the dancer becomes aware of conditions and boundaries. An impassioned dancer tests the meaning of these limits, knowing full well that in the execution of his or her inner will, some boundaries will be violated. (A frenzied or "mad" dancer, it may be said, dances without consciousness of limits. Such a dancer dances without inhibitions.) In *Thus Spoke Zarathustra*, Nietzsche intones: "Of all that is written I love only what a man has written with his blood. Write with blood and you will experience that blood is spirit."[25] To this he adds: "True, we love life not because we are used to living but because we are used to loving. There is always some madness in love. But there is always some reason in madness."[26]

Crossing lines, crossing swords, cross breeding, crossing our hearts (and then hoping to die), speaking cross words, but then crossing out our mistakes; bearing our cross, crossing the path, crossing the waters, crossing the stage, crossing against traffic, working at cross purposes, and, alas, getting crossed up. The diabolical dwells in the movement of crossing through. The diabolical is inescapably marked by the sign of the cross.

The parabolic dwells in the connection that is sought and, later, remembered, in the traces of movement that desire wishes to emulate. The parabolic dwells in dreams of flight, in the ethereal domain of light and energy. The fundamental difference between the parabolic and the diabolic, however, is not analytic; it is a matter of experience. The difference is discovered in life, in an existential *bios*—in my-Self, lived. Nietzsche further remarks:

> I would believe only in a god who could dance. And when I saw my devil I found him serious, thorough, profound, and solemn: it was the spirit of gravity—*through* him all things fall. Not by wrath does one kill but by laughter. Come, let us kill the spirit of gravity! I have learned to walk: ever since, I let myself run. I have learned to fly: ever since, I do not want to be pushed before moving *along*. Now I am light, now I fly, now I see myself beneath myself, now a god dances *through* me. Thus spoke Zarathustra.[27] [emphasis added]

When Nietzsche and—roughly a century later—Foucault proclaim that "man is something to be overcome"[28] (or, perhaps, crossed over) their language highlights a prepositional concern as much as an anthropological issue. If the dance of thought and spirit is to overcome the nervousness of prose and the order of things that modern rationality has chosen as its cultural benchmark, then such thought and spirit must literally go over. It must rainbow; it must arc. It must defy gravity.

As I mentioned in the introduction to this chapter, the literal origins of the modern English word *evil* mean much the same thing as "uppity." Joseph Ayto remarks that "it probably comes ultimately from *upelo-*, a derivative of the Indo-European base upo- 'under' (source of Greek *hupó* 'under,' Sanskrit upa 'at, to,' and English up and over), and so its underlying connotation is of 'exceeding due limits, extremism.'"[29] So, this notion of excess implies a relationship to a boundary condition; as such, it too invokes a diabolical crossing through and, as well, a parabolic crossing over. When Zarathustra speaks, "Behold, I teach you the overman. The overman is the meaning of the earth,"[30] Nietzsche is referring to a world of life *over* the modern conception of "man." One sentence later, Zarathustra commends his audience: "I beseech you my brothers, remain faithful to the earth, and do not believe those who speak of otherworldly hopes!"[31] It is in this simple elaboration of Zarathustra's fundamental pedagogical mission that we can see that the "*Über*," the "over-ness," of which Nietsche's Zarathustra speaks (*parole* yet again!—and it is not for nothing that Nietzsche reminds us over and over again that Zarathustra is speaking) does not entail anything more than what is—what exists for us in this life, what always-already is.

The *Über* is not a utopia. It is not a place out of time and space. It is not an afterlife. No, it is within life and embodiment. It is exotic—or as Baudrillard terms it, a "radical exoticism."[32] It is an exorbitance whose path has remained in the shadows of rationality for quite some time. John Sallis describes this moment of crossing for Nietzsche as "a twisting free from Platonism."[33] Sallis comments:

> A twisting free of Platonism into—what? Into a space lacking all the bounds, limits, measure previously installed by two-and-a-half millenia of Western thought and language; into a space—or, rather, an abyss—in which all bounds would be crossed, all limits crossed out, all measure exceeded. In telling the story, Nietzsche twists free into the exorbitant, the immeasurable, the boundless—in a word, *das Masslose*.[34]

Das Masslose, for Nietzsche, refers to a sort of spiritual excess, a Dionysian exuberance. It is a world of sacred experience or, rather, it is an experience of a sacred world, a world in which what one feels and knows is not subject to assessment, to measurement and place. This moment of discovery for Nietzsche was, literally, the moment when, through his heart and body, he thought for himself, for his existential sovereign being, for the first time.

It is my contention that the *Über* resides in the world that echoes and reverberates in the existential story (*l'histoire*) of *parole*. The world of life that lies outside of the rational self, that is both over and under because it is in parabolic movement, is the world symbolized by the figure of Dionysus. Dionysus is the god—in other words, the "power source"—of ecstasy (*ekstasis*). The characteristic instruments of ecstasy—*poiesis*, theatre, wine, music, eroticism—are not ecstasy themselves. Ecstasy is, instead, a particular sort of gnostic moment; it is a moment of being outside (i.e., "exotic"), a moment of feeling one's thrownness, feeling a deep sense of the earth's rhythms. Sallis again offers helpful commentary:

> In Dionysian ecstasy, in being outside oneself, one transgresses the limit that ordinarily would delimit one's self, one's individuality, one's subjectivity. . . [I]n ecstasy transgression cannot but disrupt the limit. . . . Let it be said, then, that Dionysian ecstasy is an exceeding of the limit that would delimit the self, an exceeding in the dual sense of transgression and disruption.[35]

This talk of transgression, of disruption, of exceeding limits, of excess implies that the *Über* meets all of the conditions of both violence and evil that the history of these words have come to entail. Zarathustra fully concurs: "By my honor, friend . . . all that of which you speak does not exist: there is no devil and no hell. Your soul will be dead even before your body: fear nothing further."[36]

THE DANCE OF ANGELS

In *Angels: A Modern Myth*,[37] Michel Serres stages an extended dialogue—or as Bateson might phrase it, a metalogue[38]—on the broad subject matter of "communication" between a man (Pantope) and a woman (Pia) in the terminal of de Gaulle Airport. Early on in the dialogue, Pia and Pantope broach the subject of angels. Now, the word "angel" means, literally (from the Greek), "messenger." As such, Pia carefully reasons that "At any given moment of the day the breeze plays on your cheek, and since it carries codes from everywhere, it's telling you about the state of the body of the world. If it is able to construct a universe in this way, it follows, conversely, that a universal reason blows in tiny particles, in legions of angels as numerous as the multinational crowds passing through our airports."[39] In the "communication ethics" utopia that Baudrillard takes to task, the universal reason to which Serres refers seems yet another ominous concern.

But on closer inspection, we can see that what Serres is talking about is a deeper sense of language—a Heideggerian *Ursprache*, if you will—that has come into view by virtue of a postmodern preoccupation with communication technology. It is no accident that during a historical period of unlimited electronic messaging—a period of constant and seemingly thoughtless digital electronic embodiment—we find also a growing preoccupation in popular discourse with the life of angels. And why not? We live in an ocean of messages. Few of them are worthy of repetition. Peirce's aphorism that the human being is itself a sign takes on even greater significance in the context of a world where so much of our dwindling energy resources are committed to the interlinking and internetting of our daytime consciousness. In other words, "Man" is not simply a sign, he/she is the ultimate sign. In the prattle—Heidegger's *Gerede*—of our daily discourse, the mystery of the body itself has increasingly become a primary currency in a desperate attempt to achieve communicative substance. In lieu of poetry, we offer our bodies instead. Therein lies the modern tragedy of "identity crisis"—in short, of misrecognition, of under appreciation—with regard to our failures to communicate.

And when our bodies reveal their ineluctable mundane, prosaic gravity, we should not be surprised that our fellow electronically-powered communicators seek a transcendent body—a choir of angels—to come and rescue, from all the noise, what remains of their lives. The everpresence of messaging has driven the soul out of verbal interaction. Baudrillard has likewise commented:

> Travel was once a means of being elsewhere, or being nowhere. Today it is the only way we have of feeling that we are somewhere. At home, surrounded by information, by screens, I am no longer anywhere, but rather everywhere in the world at once, in the midst of a universal banality—a banality that is the same in every country. To arrive in a new city, or in a new language, is suddenly to find oneself here and nowhere else. The body rediscovers how to look. Delivered from images, it rediscovers the imagination.[40]

Travel: the movement of bodies. Mobility. Motion. The parabolic flight of a jet airplane: the dance of life from here to there, the ascent and descent of all winged beings, bodies rocketed all over the face of the globe so as to have an experience.

Bloom writes, "For Milton, angels were a mirror into which all of us gaze, and behold neither ourselves nor an absolute otherness, but a middle region where self and other mingle."[41] He then later argues:

> To the extent that Christianity is essentially Pauline, it has no need and little use for virtuous angels. What Paul and Christianity needed were fallen angels, and their chief, Satan, in particular. . . . [I]n the Hebrew bible "Satan" is not a proper name. In the Book of Job, the reader encounters *ha-Satan*, "the Satan," which is a court title, akin to our "prosecuting attorney." As one of the *B'ne*

> *Elohim*, the "sons of God," the Satan is a divine being, or angel . . . or diplomatic representative of God. His title means "blocking agent": he is an adversary of human beings. In Greek, a blocking agent is a *diabolos*, and so the Satan became diabolical.[42]

The diabolical, then, represents the "fall" of our travels—the downbeat of the rhythm of life. Satan, the fallen angel, descends to earth and takes up residence in the figure of a serpent. Satan crossed the path of Eve and Adam. He crossed up their directives. In so doing, he invented their desire. By tempting their interests, he sent them traveling in a different direction, both inwardly and outwardly. The devil's speech praises risk, celebrates expenditure, denounces the order of things—especially order for order's sake.

The devil in speech calls us out. It makes us forget our objectives. The concatenation of useful activity, as Bataille puts it, dissolves into nothingness in the face of our prime existential reality. Bataille posits that "from very ancient times men had a tremulous awareness of death." He continues: "what we know about them enables us to say that they knew what animals do not know: that they would die."[43]

The devil in speech is an existential parable. It is one's delight in the paradoxical power of life, that is, in the will to live-through a mortal, terminal condition. (In this regard, Pia and Pantope are two "terminal cases" in a well-known, well-traveled terminal.) It is awakened by the presence of an Other's force of desire, the presence of will and urgency. It is in this moment that the energy of dark instincts eclipses all of the abstract assumptions on which we plan our days and on which we have, thus far, staked our social identities.

Bataille inquires: "If it is true the 'diabolical' means essentially the coincidence of death and eroticism, and if the devil is, in the end only our own madness, if we come to tears, if we shudder in sorrow—or if we are seized by fits of laughter—can we fail to perceive, linked to this nascent eroticism, the preoccupation with, the haunting fear of death?"[44] He ends Volume II of *The Accursed Share* with the observation that "Men committed to political struggle will never be able to yield to the truth of eroticism."[45] From this perspective we can also conclude that the political objectives implicit in the modern morality of communication (even in its most humane deployment) redeem us only from the thrill of a "useless" knowledge.

It is my contention that this "useless" knowledge is in fact what Foucault means by *savoir*, a knowing that is one and the same with the experience of meaning and the pure possibility of communication: that sacred moment when self and the other interlace, where familiar reason is, suddenly, grasped as the ultimate existential stranger to our being-in-the-world, where the foreignness of reason is enveloped by the thrownness—literally, the dance, the movement whose exoticism exceeds the domain of rational consciousness—of our being-at-all.

NOTES

1. Ayto, *Dictionary of Word Origins*, 492.
2. Claiborne, *Roots of English*, 119.
3. Claiborne, *Roots of English*, 119.
4. See Foucault, *Order of Things,* 115–20; 200–08.
5. Ayto, *Dictionary of Word Origins*, 210.
6. Ayto, *Dictionary of Word Origins*, 210.
7. Baudrillard, *Transparency of Evil.*
8. See Merleau-Ponty, *Phenomenology of Perception.* See also Richard Lanigan, *Speaking and Semiology.*
9. Green, *Greek and Latin Roots of English*, 156.
10. Baudrillard, *Transparency of Evil*, 82–83.
11. Baudrillard, *Transparency of Evil*, 105.
12. Baudrillard, *Transparency of Evil,* 46.
13. Baudrillard, *Transparency of Evil,* 46.
14. Baudrillard, *Transparency of Evil,* 47.
15. Baudrillard, *Transparency of Evil,* 129.
16. Baudrillard, *Transparency of Evil,* 128.
17. Baudrillard, *Transparency of Evil,* 130.
18. See Lanigan, *Phenomenology of Communication*, 15–17.
19. Greimas and Courtés, *Semiotics and Language*, 73.
20. Ayto, *Dictionary of Word Origins*, 560.
21. Claiborne, *Roots of English,* 257.
22. Ruesch and Bateson, *Communication.*
23. Bataille, *The Accursed Share*, 124.
24. Bloom, *Omens of Millenium,* 242.
25. Nietzsche, *Thus Spoke Zarathustra,* 40.
26. Nietzsche, *Thus Spoke Zarathustra,* 41.
27. Nietzsche, *Thus Spoke Zarathustra,* 41.
28. Nietzsche, *Thus Spoke Zarathustra,* 12.
29. Ayto, *Dictionary of Word Origins*, 210.
30. Nietzsche, *Thus Spoke Zarathustra,* 13.
31. Nietzsche, *Thus Spoke Zarathustra,* 13.
32. Baudrillard, *Transparency of Evil,* 146.
33. Sallis, *Crossings,* 2.
34. Sallis, *Crossings,* 2.
35. Sallis, *Crossings,* 55.
36. Nietzsche, *Thus Spoke Zarathustra,* 20.
37. Serres, *Angels: A Modern Myth.*
38. See Bateson, *Steps to an Ecology of Mind.*
39. Serres, *Angels: A Modern Myth,* 29.
40. Baudillard, *Transparency of Evil,* 151.
41. Bloom, *Omens of Millennium*, 39.
42. Bloom, *Omens of Millennium*, 67.
43. Bataille, *Tears of Eros,* 25.
44. Bataille, *Tears of Eros,* 23.
45. Bataille, *Accursed Share,* 191.

Chapter Seven

Identity, Intimacy, and Eroticism

Deception, Sin, and the Existential Bargain of Adolescent Embodiment

SIN, CRIME, AND HUMAN DEVELOPMENT

As the world changes, evil changes with it. Evil, after all, has no objective, empirical reality in and of itself. It is in its essence an idea, a categorical designation that marks the disjunction of the human community, in its often-fragile multiplicity, from that which is perceived as having the capability to undo it. It is something we talk about but, then again, it exists primarily as a function of talk; it dwells semiotically in the ether of what Lacan has termed the "symbolic order."[1] Yet, even so, it is an idea whose potency may well serve to energize all of that which has been and will continue to be "human"—in particular, the capacity to transcend that which cannot be tolerated in the "we" of human order, identity, and community. The darkness of that which cannot be tolerated is the engine for strategies of "taking care": taking care of oneself, one's community, one's world. The discovery of the possibility of evil, then, can be tied to an affirmative participation of one's being among a "we" of some sort. And, after Lacan, I would argue that the "we" is necessarily a product of a symbolic order—even more specifically that the "we" is a vital illusion (pointing backward and forward to the work of myth) shared by persons (for whatever reason) unsure of their own, autonomous vision.[2] In the event of communication, persons sense the boundaries and experience the transformations of the various symbolic orders that provide them comfort, security, as well as opportunities to play, to perform selfhood, to feel addressed and recognized. Likewise, it is in the event of communication that persons come to experience the narrative limits, ruptures, and discontinuities of the "we" that enables the experience as such.

Evil is instantiated in acts of crime. Where evil is the categorical disjunction, the enunciative surface of any moral imperative within a symbolic order (not simply an "either/or," but an "either/or else": *viz.*, an ultimatum), crime constitutes the performative element—literally (and phenomenologically) the *manifestation*—of evil within a symbolic order. Every symbolic order in some way or another pronounces: "We have got to draw a line somewhere." The line, once drawn, however, even if drawn clearly, is insufficient by itself to assess or even define a human performance as a crime. Criminality is a matter of judgment. It is, thus, a proper topic of communication, but it is also *as a performance* a form of communication in itself.

Now, I do not want the title of this essay to mislead. Crime and sin indeed compel this writing, but not in any particular mood, and certainly not as a matter of impertinence, anger or defiance. Moreover, this essay has no particular interest in justice as a philosophical topic, neither as problematic or theme. It is not my intention to assess the morality of a regime of behaviors or a historical period in which certain behaviors came to be assessed as morally problematic. Instead, I wish to consider crime and sin as *concepts* and, more than that, as matters of human expression. I have no interest in celebrating violence and its attendant terror (in any particular form)—either for their own sake or in support of some sort of noble or revolutionary cause. Nor am I interested here in embracing "resistance" and "paradigm subversion," dominant or otherwise, as ethics unto themselves. Instead, my source of fascination concerns the break with a given order, a break that is a wholly inevitable aspect of human experience both existentially and psychologically. The flesh that one lives exists as a duality. We do not see it when we are little children, even after our successful completion of the mirror stage. We begin to see it later, when we first experience disappointment and, more significantly, when we understand the ways in which we can be sources of disappointment in others. It is in this moment that we come to understand the importance of performance, and then later, as social narratives become increasingly legible to us, the importance of performing a *role*.

Etymologically, to disappoint is, literally, to be removed from an arrangement, to be cast out, if only for a moment, from a given order. For Freud, the Oedipal struggle begins with the boy or his father as potential understudies to one another—and twentieth century family-oriented psychotherapy thus arises from a premise of pluralism: the healthy family must create a role for the son, one that is to be distinguished from and complementary to the father. Along these lines, *all* children within the family need to discern the boundaries of Selfhood they are expected to live and rehearse. It is here that the concept that Lacan labels "the Name of the Father" exercises its function in the psychological world of the child; it is here that a symbolic order is introduced as a matter of consciousness and learning.[3] Without a role he or she can competently play, the child will *disappoint*. The child is unable to experience the sort of healthy narcissism that will enable her or him to explore potential relationships or experiment with the boundaries of the family drama. The child needs to know, through each stage of development, how to be a vital and competent part of its primary emotional "we."

When we disappoint as adults, we will likely return to an interiority of Selfhood that we find sufficiently secure. As children, our disappointment returns us to an interiority that offers us as yet no comparable level of security. A significant moment of disappointment can induce a shock of narrative and symbolic disengagement. It is here that a child can recover his *ek-sistence* and at least a semblance of her or his role in the "we" of the family drama through an encounter brought on by "acting out." The "acting out" serves no specific end other than inducing parental figures to perform their roles as parental figures and, then, to remind the child actor that the broader narrative context of his or her performance—though, in such a case, reactive, likely punitive—is still generally intact.

As we grow older, we do what we can to avoid disappointment. As we come to discover that not all of our responsibilities, obligations, commitments, and promises will be kept, we learn to manipulate our semiotic conditions to avoid the appearance of failure. Deception, rather than serving as a case of "acting out," seems to work in the opposite direction. It is a dissimulation of action. It is a semiotic performance that diverts attention in order to focus relational energy on matters of less anxiety. Now, the general task of this chapter is, despite its title, *not* to enter into an analysis of the general subject of deception and lying, certainly not of the sort that Sissela Bok undertook three decades ago in her widely-read text, *Lying: Moral Choices in Public and Private Life*.[4] My primary reservation with approaches of this sort in the context of my reflections here is that they consider only the sorts of ethical questions that arise as a matter of rational verbal exchange between, presumably, psychologically mature, competent persons in the context of freely chosen roles and relationships in democratic societies. As a consequence, one should not be at all surprised to discover that, as a general rule, these approaches tend to conclude that, for goodness sake, we should not lie to one another, that we should always endeavor to tell the truth, that lies erode trust, and that we are far better off personally and socially when we avoid deception in our personal and public lives.

My difficulty at this juncture concerns the very simple reality that the choice to knowingly deceive or express the "truth"—to express the world as we believe it to be—is a choice that we discover and embody from early childhood onward. *We do not need to be taught to lie.* We intuitively grasp that it is an inherent property of language from the moment we discover the power of gestures, symbols, and words. Independent of whether one's moral instruction forbids or excuses lying, we know how to do it and we can execute it without instruction. Various levels of deception are intrinsic to play. The fundamental phenomenal distinction between *being* and *seeming* is the quintessence of an infant's delight during a game of peek-a-boo. Piaget discusses the function of the ludic symbol inherent in our first games of "make-believe," games that we embody and enact well before we attain any meaningful level of verbal competence.[5]

So, the question of whether we should do it at all or rarely, or how we should feel about doing it, is secondary to the reality that we do it, we have always done it, we will continue to do it, our children will do it regardless of how we reproach them, and that it is a basic and ineluctable element of symbolic representation. Umberto Eco's summary of the field of semiotics in effect "gives the lie" to the longstanding moral fixation of a life contraposed to the sin of deception: "Thus *semiotics is the discipline studying everything which can be used in order to lie*. If something cannot be used to tell a lie, conversely it cannot be used to tell the truth; it cannot in fact be used 'to tell' at all."[6] The choice to interpret an act of deception as *a priori* "against" the project of human community—as a sin, in other words—has been, in my assessment, a strange propensity of Western moral consciousness, especially given that the human story finds its mythological roots in acts of crime and sin: the defiance of the creator god in paradise, the mysterious darkness of Angra Mainyu (Ahriman), the trickery and refusals of Prometheus. To proclaim deception as sin without the benefit of a phenomenology, without the experiment of radical reflection, is to side with the repressive for its own sake. It is why Nietzsche took us beyond good and evil.

My larger ambition as I work through these problematics is to assemble an outline for a theory of a particular aspect of human development: the transition of the child into adult embodiment and independent selfhood. It is in this context that I wish to consider the function of the lie: the act of deception, the willful and strategic withholding of what one knows as true, the architecture of the secret, the confidence game. Childhood is not the domain of mature, competent persons exercising free will—and all of the evidence accumulated through the course of the last century in developmental psychology makes a compelling case that it would be a disaster if it were to be treated that way. The parentally imposed "structure" that developmental psychology prescribes as essential to a child's growth and well-being functions as a necessary repression. And, so, the transition from childhood, through adolescence, into an emotionally stable ego identity, capable of independent and creative thought entails, at minimum, a "re-structuring." Inasmuch as "impulse-control" (a favored term of cognitive-behavioral psychotherapists describing a critical element of socially competent interaction) entails a certain measure of participation in self-governmentality at whatever age and level of development, the *habitus* of self emerges as "personality," in large part, on the condition of its restraint. The *habitus* of the child is simultaneous with the disciplinary order of her or his family. As such, one of the defining aspects of adolescence is found in the manner in which the emergent ego identity positions itself with respect to this disciplinary order.

In her or his pubescent embodiment, the adolescent represents, literally, a *derangement* within the family order. The adolescent body, ready or not, is taking on new habits. What is more, these new habits are not only alien to the order of childhood (which, in order to function, is necessarily a *possessive* order; that is, the child *belongs* to the family), but are alien to the adolescent consciousness as well. Becoming compliant with the expectations of a system or structure entails repeated experience; simply, the feeling of adequate conformity requires a minimum rehearsal of selfhood, which seems impossible when one's body is in the midst of its transformation into modalities of adulthood in size, shape, and comportment. For developmental psychology and for the medical community, all such transformations are fully within the statistical order of things. But for the growing child each transformation is a surprise. The changing voice, the appearance of pubic hair, facial hair, body hair, the flow and occasional deluge of hormones, the increasing size and fullness of reproductive organs, all of it, does not yet belong to them. To transcend these changes in any sort of language that makes sense to the young person will require not merely a claim of ownership ("This is my body/It belongs to me"), but a feeling, a certain confidence with regard to this new holding, a mutuality of embrace, a confidence of tenure. In this system of transformations, the adolescent belongs to no one and dwells in no order—not the family as she or he has lived through it, not to an Other.

THE EXISTENTIAL STRATEGY OF THE LIE AND THE EXPERIENCE OF ADOLESCENT DEVELOPMENT

Lying is frequently advantageous in specific instances; simply, that's why people do it and it is why they will, inevitably, continue doing it. Strategically and pragmatically (that is, leaving all matters of shame and virtue aside), lying is a conscious resistance to certain versions of systemic transformation. For the Self (at any age), it is a selective invocation of negentropy. When in common discourse a person claims, "I won't go there," or "don't go there," he or she is indicating that there are things that *can* be told that will, nevertheless, *not* be told. Such a choice invokes a strategy to restrict the flow of information. A person lies because the perceived consequences of speaking honestly are worse than they would be to mislead or deceive. To speak honestly in such an instance—that is, to authentically articulate one's primary thoughts, feelings, and/or images on a given matter—would require that the person address an experience he or she is not psychologically ready to address. It may be said that lying in such an instance is to preserve an aspect of psychological homeostasis. A fully "honest," fully confessed expression would signal a loss of personal control over one's perception of identity. For example, were I to tell the truth about why I am not showing up for work on a given day my colleagues and my boss might think less of me, particularly if I am taking the day off to sleep in, rest my hangover, and spend some money at the local casino. The weekend simply was not long enough, I might tell myself, fully convinced that I am entitled to spend this day as I please. Yet, however well I can convince myself of this "truth" I am also of the belief that it would be unpersuasive to the principal parties to whom it might be spoken.

So, the lie I use as a cover for my Self signifies a threshold of guilt. I use the word "cover" because it is of a piece with everyday discourse. But instead of the word "cover" perhaps the concept might better be served, at least for the moment, by the word "exterior." The exterior, in the case of the intentional deception, is a narrative mask, a disguise of both character and plot. The lie protects my secret. My secret is my business, I tell myself, and I know I am not the first and certainly will not be the last person to keep a secret. Like a spy operating in hostile territory, I must be doubly careful to keep my story and identity straight. I cannot say or do anything that I might impulsively want inasmuch as I have made a commitment to protect an ego identity that binds me to a particular narrative version of a relational order. When as a teenager I was asked by my parents if I smoked pot (or even cigarettes), I typically replied: "No, *I* would never do those things." A teenager is not free to assert the privilege of declaring an inquiry "none of your business." Democratic citizenship enables an American to "plead the fifth," but the family is not a democratic institution. As such, when a relational situation becomes dangerous to the habits one wishes to continue (and more fully embody), or vice versa, one creates a strategic relational distance between oneself and the source of inquisition. In this regard, adolescents commonly become psychological refugees in much the same way as political refugees seeking asylum in safer lands.

"Whatever is profound loves masks," Nietzsche asserts.[7] "It is not the worst things that cause the worst shame: there is not only guile behind a mask—there is so much graciousness in cunning."[8] He continues: "[A] concealed man who instinctively needs speech for silence and for burial in silence . . . *wants* and sees to it that a mask of him roams in his place through the hearts and heads of his friends. . . . Every profound spirit needs a mask: even more, around every profound spirit a mask is growing continually, owing to the . . . *shallow*, interpretation of every word, every step, every sign of life he gives."[9]

In Hermann Hesse's *Demian*, the protagonist Emil Sinclair, perhaps the perfect archetype for the process of adolescent transformation I am addressing in this essay, learns from his friend Max Demian of an alternate interpretation of the story of Cain and Abel,[10] Emil begins to grasp that Cain's crime might not have been a symbol of emotional failure and weakness, but may well have been a sign of strength. The Old Testament indeed offers jealousy and frustration as motives. But Demian chooses to reason not from the inner world of the crime, its imputed psychological architecture (which, as one might say, God only knows), but from the outer world of the mark he is given, or perhaps *earns*, as a consequence of his frenzied, impetuous, and (as yet) shameless act. The mark is an external sign. It becomes the mask of Cain, a source of potency were he or anyone so marked to accept it for what it *could* mean. It is the sign, the visible exterior, which is fully open to interpretation. And this epiphany is articulated by Hesse's protagonist Sinclair: "Yes, at that moment, I who was Cain and bore the mark, had imagined that this sign was not a mark of shame and because of my evil and my misfortune I stood higher than my father and the pious, the righteous."[11]

What may most fully be said at this juncture is that Demian's case is, at least, sufficiently persuasive to Sinclair to enable him to transcend the cloud of dark shame in which he had been dwelling prior to his friendship with Demian. It had been Sinclair's conviction that he was unique in his guilt. Demian's counsel succeeds in reversing the polarity of what it means to be designated as a *marked man*. The tattoo, the ritual scar, dark clothing, long or unkempt hair, or perhaps a shaved head—each is a mark of Cain, a badge of indifference to the common morality. They can serve as signs of strength. Signs of strength are useful in confrontation. Adolescence, whatever else it is and however else it can function as a passage in human development, is a period in which intimacy and confrontation intertwine to define the ego identity of the speaking subject. One learns to take hold of the Other not just by becoming Other, but by dreaming and breathing and socially rehearsing this Otherness. Winnicott, as much as Erikson, takes note of this duality, especially within the crucible of the family. He writes:

> We need to translate this childhood game ["King of the Castle"] into the unconscious motivation of adolescence and society. If the child is to become adult, then this move is achieved over the dead body of an adult. (I must take it for granted that the reader knows that I am referring to unconscious fantasy, the material that underlies playing.) I know of course that boys and girls may manage to go through this stage of growth with a continued setting of accord with actual parents, and without necessarily manifesting rebellion at home. But it is wise to remember that rebellion belongs to the freedom that you have given your child by bringing him or her up that he or she exists in his or her own right. In some instances it could be said "You sow'd a baby and you reaped a bomb." In fact this is always true, but it does not always look like it.[12]

Winnicott concludes: "A proportion of adolescence will become casualties or will attain to a kind of maturity . . . perhaps becoming parents like the parents themselves. This may do. But somewhere in the background is a life-and-death struggle. The situation lacks its full richness if there is a too easy and successful avoidance of the clash of arms."[13]

In this confrontation, the adolescent literally builds a cover story. That is, she or he attends to the inner as well as the outer dimensions of selfhood. A book's cover can never tell such a thing as "the whole story" or even adequately reflect its inner dynamics. The cover is always a mask, an exterior that suggests its own story, that is always entailed in a different game than the pages secured within its binding. The exterior affiliates a being, a person, even the mask itself with one or more groups; that which remains interior, that which is on the *other side* of the exterior seeks to differentiate its being from its web of group affiliations. We are disguised by the marks that distinguish us. The costume of the skin is not the life of the flesh. The adolescent fights for the revaluation of selfhood and identity that can only emerge from a sense of victory, even if it occurs within the fog of a war no one really wins. It is performed in consciousness as the confidence one gains from surviving the last encounter.

The capacity to perform socially is the first test of adolescent identity. It is not a test that one enters into lightly. Peter Blos, in his pioneering study of adolescent development, writes: "Adolescent individuation is accompanied by feelings of isolation, loneliness, and confusion. . . . [S]ome of the dearest megalomaniacal dreams of childhood . . . must now be relegated entirely to fantasy: their fulfillments can never again be considered seriously."[14] The potency of a fertile body is not experienced as a matter of joy and freedom. The adolescent is most likely to experience a gnawing sense of social impotence, a constant fear of rejection. "The adolescent's slow severance of the emotional ties to his family, his fearful or exhilarated entrance into the new life which beckons him, these experiences are among the profoundest in human existence."[15]

Erik Erikson maintains that the epigenetic stage of psychological development following the achievement of "identity" is "intimacy." Nonetheless it takes a long time and a depth of experience to achieve an experience of intimacy with a person outside of the orbit and symbolic order of one's family. Such intimacy—except between the members of the marital/parental system—is not achieved in the symbolic order of the family. Intimacy is something one experiences during the moment, within the *semiotic* order of her or his *identity*, when she or he is comfortable enough to let go of control. The conscious subjectivity of a satisfactorily "identified" Self lets go of ego signifiers, ego signifiers held onto as emotional trophies, in pursuit of sensations of affection and affirmation with another Self who is a partner to these sensations. Erikson maintains that intimacy is "really a counterpointing as well as a fusion of identities."[16] To an impatient ear this may well seem a riddle, especially given that "fusion" might imply the very loss of autonomous selfhood that would make any sort of meaningful "counterpointing" impossible. Erikson offers some important clarification: "True engagement with others is the result and the test of firm self-delineation."[17] He maintains that intimacy is "the capacity to commit [one]self to concrete affiliations and partnerships and to develop the ethical strength to abide by such commitments, even they may call for significant sacrifices and compromises. Body and ego must now be masters of the organ modes and of the nuclear conflicts, in order to face the fear of ego loss in situations which call for self-abandon: in the solidity of close affiliations, in orgasms and sexual unions, in close friendships and in physical combat, in experiences of inspiration by teachers and of intuition from the recesses of the self."[18]

It is clear from Erikson's language that the rehearsal of identity is not merely a performance of a role in social situations. As well, by "intimacy" Erikson certainly means more than just *personal*—as opposed to *im*personal—relationships. Nevertheless, there is a difficulty in coupling either of these critical terms to the psychological elements of lived experience. If, for example, intimacy implies an experience beyond our experiences in, presumably more commonplace, personal relationships, then what is intimacy? How does one know when one has experienced it? Is it a judgment one makes over time? I do not think the questions are trivial. Erikson considers "intimacy" to be a phase unto itself in the process of human development, and although the word is commonly employed in a variety of contemporary discursive contexts, it is insufficiently clear what the experience of intimacy entails. Commonly, one hears words like "closeness," "affection," "love," and "communion" to describe the feeling of intimacy, yet these signifiers are no less ambiguous in what they signify than what can be inferred from "intimacy."

What I take from Erikson to be most valuable with regard to any phenomenology of identity and intimacy is that an intimate relationship becomes the test, the *agon*, of one's identity. It is through one's identity that he or she enters into a relationship holding the promise of closeness, affection, affirmation, respect, perhaps communion, perhaps love. To transform an impersonal relationship into something personal, and then to transform with this Other Self, in her or his identity, into a sister, a brother, a lover is a profound joy. But the possibility of rejection at every stage tempts one to perhaps soften one's role—to concede power, to give permission, to blur one's boundaries of identity, to become someone other to enable a flame to arise from a spark, perhaps to do so only for the warmth and comfort. Erikson considers it a "fact" that "the condition of a true twoness is that one must first become oneself."[19]

There is a game to the experience of intimacy that can be played a variety of ways. A significant part of the game consists in the assessment one makes of her or his own identity. Who do I want to be going in? What am I willing to give? What am I willing to sacrifice? What guilt do I confess, if any? What aspect of my shame will be exposed? The desire to keep secrets, a desire that marks the lived experience of adolescence, is the strategy, preconscious and conscious, of the body entering into a new field of play. The symbolic order of the family does not belong to this field of play. Even if relationships are arranged by the family elders, the play that follows belongs only to the interpersonal dyad sharing the private dialogue of their coupling. It was not simply the arrival of classical civilization or Christianity or even modernity that succeeding in transforming the practice of intimate communication into a private pursuit. It begins in what I am inclined to phrase as the internalization of taboo; that is, the moment that the socially aware reflective consciousness imposed a limit on its own desires.

INTIMACY AND THE LIFEWORLD OF EROTICISM

Georges Bataille attempts what might be termed a genealogy of transgression in his analyses of eroticism and general economy. Bataille asserts: "It is not only the great variety of their subjects but also a certain illogicality that makes it difficult to discuss taboos. Two diametrically opposed views are always possible on any subject. There exists no prohibition that cannot be transgressed. Often the transgression is permitted, often it is even prescribed."[20] Michael Richardson offers a potent summary of Bataille's position: "The interplay between taboo and transgression served as the basis for a social structure whose foundation lay in individual consciousness, so that the same pattern was repeated both within the individual and within the society. Where, in the social sphere, transgression was most immediately present within the festival, in the personal sphere its domain was that of eroticism."[21]

For the adolescent whose sense of identity has become both recognized and comfortable, as well as sufficiently rehearsed, the transition into meaningful intimate relationships is, thus, more than simply transitioning to a different field of play. It is a transition into eroticism. Bataille's concept of the erotic seems to draw very close to Erikson's description of intimacy as the *agon* of a developing person's ego identity: "My purpose is to see in eroticism an aspect of man's inner life, of his religious life . . . I said that I regarded eroticism as the disequilibrium in which the being consciously calls his own existence into question. In one sense, the being loses himself deliberately, but then the subject is identified with the object losing his [or her] identity. If necessary I can say in eroticism: *I* am losing myself."[22]

I cannot say I remember my adolescence with deep fondness. It was mostly awkward and painfully anxiety-ridden. I would never want to repeat it. The problem of identity as a matter of lived experience, as a matter of embodiment, is a problem whose duration is not clearly marked. In my case, I felt strong doubts about my adulthood even at age thirty. No one knows for certain when her or his ego identity—again, what Erikson posits as the socially marked Self—is complete, or at least sufficiently complete to make an entrance into the game of eroticism. Erikson's reflections regarding the phenomenon he termed "identity crisis" over four decades ago was built upon theoretical speculation about a growing anxiety, an ambivalence and a diffidence, that he had begun to diagnose in post-war youth. An inability to make commitments, to assert oneself, is the upshot of identity crisis. It even corresponds with both the incidence and diagnosis of clinical depression, a phenomenon whose reported incidence has skyrocketed over the last quarter century. Without exploring the contributing elements as Erikson saw them at the time, what can be said in these times is that adolescence is taking considerably longer to complete. Throughout the globe, vastly larger numbers of young men and women are spending considerably longer in school, postponing marriage, postponing a deep and rich engagement with their life's work. At the same time, average life expectancy has expanded considerably, increasing on average by over 30 percent during this last century, and thus decreasing the urgency for the adolescent to begin a life of adult responsibility and commitment.[23]

As a consequence, the psychological potency of the symbolic order of the family has come to remain ambiguously active for a longer period of time. My argument in this context is that the performance of ego identity among young persons who still find themselves emotionally or economically responsive (or both) during this passage will continue to be diffident. The boundaries of selfhood, in both psychoanalytic theory and ego psychology, are independent of mature ego identity. Selfhood begins when the young child understands the difference between "me" and "not-me." The embodied experience of puberty serves as the existential and phenomenological grounding of a person's relational identity as an *erotic* identity. This passage is never simple and is fraught with tension and radical boundary questions. The passage from the communicative *ek-stasis* experienced by a "parent's child" into the *ek-stasis* experienced by a being, in these moments, principally "marked-by-others" (and without a rehearsed and inhabited adult subjectivity), is a passage *away* from the familiar temple of family order—and *toward* the uncertain sketch of an ideal ego insufficiently reflected in the narrative orbit of lived experience.

The story that the emerging ego identity will enter is, of course, not as yet written. What is more, the story of the self as well as the narrative role and function of the emerging ego identity is entirely a fiction. This is in no way to diminish the significance of self and identity as matters of psychological strength and communicative agency. In fact, to phrase it in this way is to understand the assumption of relational identity as a *will to power*. For

Nietzsche, a revaluation of values becomes a matter of freedom and the ascendancy of the human beyond good and evil. For the adolescent coping with the inescapable and irrevocable experiences of a post-pubescent, erotogenic body, a revaluation and re-imagining of shame becomes vital to his or her capacity to cope with this new set of realities. The assumption of authorship is outside the emotional memory of the symbolic order.

It is at this particular juncture that Hesse's story of the self-possessed, confident Max Demian and the equivocal, apprehensive Emil Sinclair becomes, again, quite helpful. Demian guides his friend, Sinclair, to a consciousness that his miserable feelings of failure regarding his handling of a neighborhood bully that resulted in blackmail and panic were not something "special"; it was not a failure of character or a sign of moral defect. It was simply something beyond his control, an incompetence in dealing with dark hearts for which no ingenuous child can be blamed. In Sinclair's words: "Something was very wrong with me . . . I had lived in a wholesome and clean world, had been a kind of Abel myself, and now I was stuck deeply in the 'other world,' had fallen and sunk very low—yet it hadn't basically been my fault! How was I to consider that?"[24] The transformation of the body—its growth into adult size, the hormonal changes, the final advancement and refinement of the cerebral cortex—places the consciousness and memory of childhood at a remove from the affairs of daily living. One moment we are innocent, and then suddenly it seems so far away. The angst that attends to expressing and seeking affirmation for one's identity in the context of a sacralized childhood innocence, perhaps sweetly remembered, begins to feel like the accursed share.

But the erotogenic growth and maturation of the human body and the transformed consciousness and relationships that transfigure our stance in the world—this too cannot be helped. That which was both forbidden and poorly apprehended is now an object of desire. Bataille remarks: "We use the word eroticism every time a human being behaves in a way strongly contrasted with everyday standards and behavior. Eroticism shows the other side of a façade of unimpeachable propriety. Behind the façade are revealed the feelings, parts of the body and habits we are normally ashamed of."[25] Demian expresses a similar perspective:

> [T]his God of both Old and New Testaments is certainly an extraordinary figure, but not what he purports to represent. He is all that is good, noble, fatherly, beautiful, elevated, sentimental—true! But the world consists of something else besides. And what is left over is ascribed to the devil, this entire slice of the world, this entire half is suppressed and hushed up. In exactly the same way they praise God as the father of all life but simply refuse to say a word about our sexual life on which it's all based, describing it whenever possible as sinful, the work of the devil. . . . I mean we ought to

> consider everything sacred, the entire world, not merely this artificially separated half.[26]

What Hesse, through the voice of Demian, describes is a world that cannot be inhabited by a child. But it is a world in which the adolescent must make his or her way, a world in which the confession and candor expected of children living and learning the symbolic order of the family cannot realistically be expected of this newly forged person, this new creature, monstrous still in certain eyes, whose urges and fantasies remain unspeakable as matters of truth.

INTIMACY, COMMUNICATION, COMMUNION

It might be said that, as an essential matter of philosophy, my argument is eventually reducible to the concept that authentic being-in-the-world requires the sin of eroticism and the crime of lying—if not sympathy for the devil, then sympathy for devilish doings—but that would miss a critical element of the discourse I have been cultivating. At the same time as I have been, after Nietzsche, reflecting on a concept of human development beyond good and evil, I have been attempting to comprehend and articulate a concept of relational embodiment that embraces the fiction of identity (both social and personal) as a key to intimate experience. Bernard Stiegler has remarked:

> The power of saying *we* requires that I "fiction" a past that is not mine, and this allows me to fiction a future that I hope will belong to us. . . . This future that I fiction—that is, which I desire and fantasize—I will without doubt never see: it will very probably never happen. . . . Desire is structurally related to infinity . . . *it is necessary that I fantasize my energy as unlimited.* This is merely a fiction, but *without this fiction there would be no desire*. What I love I love without limit, without condition: I cannot love it other than in a manner that is (phantasmatically) unlimited. That which I love and those whom I love, you, that is, us insofar as we are capable of forming a we—all this I love, and I love it (and I love you) *infinitely*. I love to the infinite. I love only to the infinite, as one says, "to the infinitive." Without which no *we* is possible. This is nothing but a fiction. There is no infinite love—no *we* as the origin of an *I*—that is not a phantasm. But I repeat: without this fiction . . . the *we* is impossible.[27]

The capacity of this fiction as a source of faith is rooted in the "impossibility" of my existence as social subjectivity. I both am and am not my "cover story." My recognizable exteriority, my "me," as George Herbert Mead would have it, signifies my presence to an other.[28] My utter lack of consciousness of what you "see" in "me" combined with the play of desires utterly without signification in my outward presence makes it impossible for the meaning of the relationship we share to be rationally comprehensible.

Our intimate relationships are not rationally comprehensible but they are nonetheless deeply meaningful. Our we, our interlaced and intertwined identity, transfigures the brute reality of protoplasm, bone, chemistry into a symbolic realm. We talk ourselves into or let ourselves be talked into a situation, a gestalt, and now, from this situation, enable—no, liberate—consciousness into what Lacan has termed the *Imaginary*.[29] "This is why," according to Bruce Fink, "Lacan said [in *The Seminar*, Book III] that 'meaning is imaginary.'"[30] Fink continues: "He did not imply thereby that meaning does not exist, or that it is simply something we dream up in our imagination. He implied that it is tied up with our self-*image*, with the image we have of who and what we are."[31]

This fiction, this "impossible," does not occur as a mere trick of mind. It is not a "pretend" *topos*. It is, as Stiegler emphasizes, an embodied space.[32] Bataille defines it as myth.[33] Merleau-Ponty defines it as *chiasm*, or flesh. It is the blood-pulsingly and emotionally electric space where *we* exist. It is our secret place, a place where we imagine ourselves together through each other, through the gathering of names, identities, cover stories, each fictioning the cover story of *us* that we each offer to those who care to ask. As in a dream, you are there, but what I know of you is imaginary. None of anything that I dream is really happening. It is not that it has not happened yet, it is instead that it has not happened at all. But at the same time what I feel is everything. Something is revealed, and even if I had the perfect words to describe it, I could not begin to explain it. None of this is real. Nothing will become real until I awaken and rediscover the outline of the possible: the world that will separate us, that will fill us each with images and symbols alien to our desires. In this world, as we live it and embody it, *we* are not. Perhaps we are not yet, but at so many moments *we* are not anywhere in the game. In moments that I steal from the day, from the order of the day, I *will* myself back into *us*. I take time from work and there you are you, and here *we* are again, still a dream, still an intimacy beyond words, laced through with unexpressed thoughts, feelings, ambiguous and unseen gestures, a relationship that defies logic, a relationship that seems all in my head.

Bataille coldly pronounces that "science is practiced by men in whom the desire to know is dead."[34] As I let my mind wander with this comment and its context, I am reminded of the sociological writing of Richard Sennett. Sennett worked closely with Erikson at Harvard, and has recalled Erikson commenting at the time of mass student unrest: "You pass through an identity crisis, you don't dwell in it."[35] Sennett has himself referred to the prolonged adolescent diffidence marking the agon of identity and intimacy as "a search for purity."[36] He notes that the "effect of this defensive pattern is to create in people a desire for a purification of the terms in which they see themselves in relation to others. The enterprise involved is an attempt to build an image or an identity that coheres, is unified, and filters out threats in social experience."[37] Sennett references a body of research pointing to a search for purified identity among high school and college students: "One study estimates that about three out of every five entering college students choose careers for themselves before having any experience or knowledge of their future pursuits. In talking to students who have so committed themselves, one feels the intense desire many of them have to move out on their own; yet something hidden in themselves, something they can't vocalize, chains them back. . . . [M]any young people in choosing a lifework also chain themselves voluntarily. Many don't want to wander; they want to be sure of what they are doing in advance of doing it."[38] And then, more than a quarter of a century later, Sennett similarly observes: "Today, in the new regime of time, that usage 'we' has become an act of self-protection. The desire for community is defensive."[39]

What Bataille terms as the "desire to know" is another incarnation of Nietzsche's will to power. The "desire to know" is, for Bataille, a step beyond the profane world of work. It describes terrain familiar to Heidegger's critique of technocratic and rationalist inquiry in *Was Heisst Denken?* and is echoed in Heidegger's assertion that modernist humankind "is in *flight from thinking*."[40] Bataille seeks an encounter with the "impossible," with that realm of being beyond what is at all conjecturable, conjectured, apprehended, apprehensible in human experience. He muses: "I walk with the help of feet. I philosophize with the help of fools."[41] The impossible, the infinite *we*, the dream that sweeps what might, in a different context, be called the energies of faith into an encounter with the unspeakable sacred—all of this can only be committed to life, to others, once the evolving person has an identity, a rational, exchangeable economic self to give away. Bataille continues his remarks: "I incarnated the ungraspable. If I lead being to the extreme limit of reflection, to its misunderstanding of itself, like the infinite starry expanse of the night, *I fall asleep*. And the *impossible* is there. (I am *it*.)."[42]

And *what is it*, then, one might ask, to which all of this energy, this infinite promise, this boundless and ecstatic energy is given? Is it a pointless giving? Are these the random acts of kindness that we hear about in popular culture? Suddenly I am given to smile! No, there is nothing necessarily "kind" about this giving. Bataille's rhetoric makes clear that he is talking about sacrifice, and that he means for the sacrifice to be a dark, moist, and licentious affair.

So, what is it then? I am taken back to the concept of the *we*. The child does not get to choose her or his family, her or his first and most fundamental *we*. Rather, in this *we*, the child seeks to be chosen, to be affirmed, to know that his or her childishness, clumsiness, callowness, incompetence, forgetfulness—all of it—will be forgiven, that he or she will still be special, that warm loving arms will be there to hold and comfort. The metaphor of "thrownness," so fundamental to the rhetoric of existential thought, is entirely incomprehensible to a child. There is no thrownness for a child! All of Genesis is sufficiently illustrated in the family album, in family stories, in the Eden and Lascaux of the family homestead. Mother and Father are mysterious and powerful beings who make things happen, who feed us, who give light and who can take it away. It is when paradise is lost for the child, when he or she ceases to be a child, when the mysterious powers of Mother and Father begin to recede, when our powers of speech and reckoning match up well with our authority figures, that a sense of thrownness and *ennui* begin to preoccupy the consciousness of the emerging person.

It is at this moment that we each become responsible for the love that human consciousness demands. The human sacrifice, our ecstatic expenditure, is given to the various *"we"s* that come to represent the greatest value. So which *we*, and more specifically, *who* is worthy of this promise? It is impossible to know. A dream makes just as much sense. In the context of the argument I have been weaving through these pages, the object of desire becomes a partner in intimacy through a choosing that is wholly existential. It is derived of situation, circumstance, and the aesthetic play of nonknowledge. How do I know that pizza is the right food for my dinner? I don't know. I was hungry. It was ordered. Someone ordered it. (Was it you?) It was served. There it was. So, I ate it. Was it right? I don't really care. I am no longer hungry. Bataille writes: "Beyond a certain point, foolishness is inescapable. My intelligence offers me the comfort of stupidity (a calm certainty). The idea is breathtaking. Still, it suffices to be indifferent: begin a friendship with odious chattering, with silences, with terror, with whims. A friendship that you cannot imagine. Nothing seems more foolish to me than the sovereign contempt for others to which my position condemns me."[43]

Why is it good that I am lost—good and lost—in my intimate dreams of you? It is good not because *you* are worth the sacrifice—and here I must confess: I know so little about you! Even after all this time, you are a mystery and a puzzlement. God only knows what you feel about me at this moment, at any moment. No, it is good because *we* are worth the sacrifice—or rather: *I* am worth the sacrifice when I feel the ecstatic secret of this *we.* Stiegler writes: "If every *I* is inscribed in the *we* that constitutes it, and that it constitutes, if the *I* and the *we* are *two faces of the same process of individuation* . . . this projection is never concretized except *by default*, in other words, by ceaselessly *deferring* this completion which if realized would be the end of the process of individuation. . . . The *end* is, then, since it can never be *realized*, ceaselessly *fictioned*."[44] Because we each take pleasure in who we imagine we are when we are with one another, whoever we are at any given moment, whatever my personal identity happens to be, it is worth spending, like the money in my wallet, as I inhabit the time and space of this unfolding dream.

CONCLUSION: THIS IMPOSSIBLE BEING THAT I AM, THAT WE ARE

This impossible being that I am is sure to disappoint. I have been doing it all my life. What allows me to carry on, assuming I carry on, on is a confidence in all that has become possible. The later writing of Foucault on the techniques of selfhood serves as a fascinating bookend to his early work on normalization, disciplinary society, and panoptic power. The care and cultivation of my Self enables new possibilities both for the development and rehearsal of my performance as a differentiated and individuated social agent and, as well, for my pleasure in engaging new horizons of experience, new fictions, different fictions, new and different imaginaries.

The impossible being that we are should be distinguished from the numerous possible manifestations of "we." There is the *we* of one's culture, one's country, one's language, one's ethnic and religious heritage. Then there are countless *"we"s* in the complex web of group affiliations and group identities. Most importantly, there is the *we* of our birth—our family order and our family name. Yes, it is true that we experience intense relations and an intimate form of caring from within the family order. In fact, what we experience is a model of intimacy, a deeply influential and indelible sense of how love and closeness and attentiveness can work. But it is not intimacy itself.

Intimacy implies agency. It is a *we* that each of us can only choose to enter—but it is even more than that. Intimacy is experienced in the interpersonal, or dyadic (that is, one-to-one) modality of communication. In intimacy, one face encounters and submits to the light and shadow of another face. The fullness of the encounter places all of our symbolic order at risk. For the post-pubescent person, that which is risked is already very new and quite fragile. More to the point, however long we live, it never becomes a matter of our own secure possession. Bataille addresses the experience of eroticism in these very terms: "The whole business of eroticism is to strike to the inmost core of the living being, so that the heart stands still. The transition from the normal state to that of erotic desire presupposes a partial dissolution of the person as he exists in the realm of discontinuity. . . . The whole business of eroticism is to destroy the self-contained character of the participators as they are in their normal lives."[45] Bataille then continues this train of thought: "Erotic activity, by dissolving the separate beings that participate in it, reveals their fundamental continuity, like the waves of a stormy sea."[46]

What I am describing is an aspect of falling. It is not a falling away of the sort that Heidegger sees as a turning away from *Dasein*. It is instead a sudden discovery of the groundlessness of our being-in-the-world—that once we both recognize and sense our thrownness, we fall inasmuch as we "remain in the throw."[47] As little children, we learn to stand, and then to walk, by falling much more often than we can remember.

It is not exceptional for children to cry when this happens, and one might arrive at the conclusion that it is because falling hurts the child physically. Nonetheless, a fascinating thing is that if toddlers are not aware that an adult is watching, they do not cry when they fall; they just pick themselves up and begin again. Letting go, in other words, is not the same thing as giving up or giving in. Intimacy is a "falling-for" toward a fiction of a "falling-together." Bataille comments: "In . . . this painful feeling of a lack, I have a premonition of my absence through which the presence of the other reveals itself, provided that the other is also examining the edge of his own nothingness. *Communication happens only between two beings at risk.*"[48]

It is here that we can catch a glimpse of what Bataille means when he asserts that "all communication partakes of suicide and crime."[49] To communicate, to express intimacy, is to transgress. It is not *pro*gress—no one, of course, knows what will happen and where we will fall. It is not an *e*gress or an *in*gress; simply, it is not reducible to mere motion or movement. It is *ourselves* that we abandon as we give way to a mutuality of *ek-stasis*. No, it is a crossing, a crossing over, a throwing across; literally, it is to become "dia-bolical"—to engage in transgression. Bataille again notes: "In this light, evil appears as a life source! Ruining the integrity of being in myself and in the other, I open myself to communion."[50]

In this transgression, in this fiction, in this conspiracy, we share a secret. Literally, we enter a confidence game. It is here that we gain confidence. It is here that we lose confidence. It is here that life begins—where we begin to consider everything sacred, the entire world, not merely this artificially separated half.

NOTES

1. Lacan, *The Four Fundamental Concepts of Psychoanalysis.*
2. Lacan, *The Four Fundamental Concepts of Psychoanalysis.*
3. Lacan, *The Seminarsof Jacques Lacan, Book III: The Psychoses.*
4. Bok, *Lying: Moral Choices in Public and Private Life.*
5. Piaget, *The Child's Conception of the* World, 95–100.
6. Eco, *A Theory of Semiotics*, 7.
7. Nietzsche, *Beyond Good and Evil*, 50.
8. Ibid., 50–51.
9. Ibid., 51.
10. Hesse, *Demian.*
11. Ibid., 32.

12. Winnicot, "Adolescent Process and the Need for Personal Confrontation," 752–53.
13. Ibid., 753.
14. Blos, *On Adolescence: A Psychoanalytic Interpretation*, 12.
15. Ibid., 12.
16. Erikson, *Identity: Youth and Crisis*, 135.
17. Ibid., 167.
18. Ibid., 263–64.
19. Erikson, *Identity and the Life Cycle*, 101.
20. Bataille, *Erotism: Death & Sensuality*, 63.
21. Richardson, *Georges Bataille*, 102.
22. Bataille, *Erotism: Death & Sensuality*, 31.
23. Centers for Disease Control, "Ten Great Public Health Achievements—United States."
24. Hesse, *Demian*, 31.
25. Bataille, *Erotism: Death & Sensuality*, 109.
26. Hesse, *Demian*, 62.
27. Stiegler, *Acting Out*, 47.
28. Mead, *Selected Writings*.
29. Lacan, *The Language of the Self*.
30. Fink, *A Clinical Introduction to Lacanian Psychoanalysis*, 24.
31. Ibid., 24.
32. Stiegler, *Acting Out*.
33. Bataille, *The Unfinished System of Nonknowledge*.
34. Ibid., 82.
35. Sennett, *Respect in a World of Inequality*, 30.
36. Sennett, *The Uses of Disorder*, 9.
37. Ibid., 9.
38. Ibid., 14.
39. Sennett, *The Corrosion of Character*, 138.
40. Heidegger, *What is called Thinking?*, 25.
41. Bataille, *The Unfinished System of Nonknowledge*, 84.
42. Ibid., 84.
43. Ibid., 83.
44. Stiegler, *Acting Out*, 4.
45. Bataille, *Erotism: Death & Sensuality*, 17.
46. Ibid., 22.
47. Heidegger, *Being and Time*, 179.
48. Bataille, *The Unfinished System of Nonknowledge*, 29.
49. Ibid., 30.
50. Ibid., 30.

Chapter Eight

An Archaeology of Gender Symbols and a Theory of Communication

INTRODUCTION: THE COMMUNICATIVE BODY

To lose oneself into nothingness. It is this dimension of being—of being-before-the-void—that best describes Georges Bataille's concept of communication. It is a radical concept of communication as eros, death, sensuality, and transgression. It is a remarkably vivid and vital concept, but it is an idea that has yet to find its vocabulary reflected in serious academic writing on the subject of communication. To think of communication expressed as anything but an abstract function of mind and culture (as, for example, an ecstatic transformation of the body) is to violate a taboo of *academic* communication—or so it would seem. As Bataille himself has remarked, "I repeat: if I sometimes speak as a man of science I only seem to do so. The scientist speaks from the outside, like an anatomist busy on a brain."[1] He later adds: "I have to pick my way along a lonely path, no tradition, no ritual to guide me, and nothing to hinder me, either. In this book of mine, I am describing an experience without reference to any special body of belief."[2]

As I assemble my thoughts, I shall take Bataille's experience as exemplary—and thematic. I am aware that the subject matter I have chosen does not quickly lend itself to a familiar discourse, academic or otherwise. As such, if what accumulates before us here is not, strictly speaking, an academic monograph, so much the better. For what I am attempting to do in this chapter is follow Bataille's concept of communication into an area generally not explored as a matter of theoretical seriousness. What I shall be contemplating is the body of eros: interpersonal erotic embodiment. More to the point, I shall be considering the body of eros as a concept (Foucault's *ars erotica*[3])—not as an abstract notion grounded in a mathematics of probability (Foucault's *scientia sexualis*[4]), but as a concrete possibility of meaning and experience. In doing so, I shall unite two other discourses on consciousness and experience that, at least on the surface, do not appear to have all that much in common: the archetypal collective unconsciousness of Carl Jung, and the archaeological and genealogical projects of Michel Foucault.

What is perhaps more unlikely, but which I cannot in good conscience ignore, is the role played by the communication theory of Georges Bataille in establishing a discursive matrix for the possibility of articulating a relationship between these two historically disparate systems on thought. It is well known that Bataille's work had a substantial influence on Foucault's concepts of transgression, expression (*énoncé*), and sexuality. As a matter of fact, Foucault's homage to Bataille, titled *"Préface à la transgression,"*[5] serves as a marvelous introduction to the philosophical positions of both men. Where Foucault's debt to Bataille is most clearly revealed is in his concept of space (heterotopia and the folds of language, in particular[6]), and the limits of human knowing. For both, the *body*, understood as the medium and repository of lived experience, emerges as an accumulation of surfaces, of conjunctions signifying the discontinuity between inner and outer, subject and object, self and other, same and different. This enunciative surface, which Foucault terms a "positivity," is both a threshold and a limit; it is a certain density of value that expresses a relationship between the speaking subject and power. "Neither hidden, nor visible, the enunciative level is at the limit of language,"[7] Foucault argues—in effect, explicating the density of a signification as bearing but a peculiar and indifferent relationship to its visibility and familiarity as a sign. The tension implied by this density of meaning and value for Bataille—as I have already suggested—is not a matter reducible to the conceptual analysis of traditional studies of language and psychology. Instead, he claims that this tension is a matter of humankind's primal awareness of death, and that this tension is recognized and expended in the interplay between transgression and taboo.

In addition to his debt to Alexandre Kojève's highly influential reading of Hegel, Bataille draws much of his insight from the works of scholars outside the ordinary reaches of philosophy, notably Georges Dumézil, Marcel Mauss, Sylvain Lévi, and, in particular, Mircea Eliade.[8] In effect, Bataille is as much an antholopologist and mythologist—and student of divinity—as he is a philosopher in the modern French Hegelian tradition. Bataille openly acknowledges that his thinking on communication, the transgressive, and the erotic, is a theoretical journey into the dark and fabulous realm of primary religious experience. In this regard, Bataille bears some substantial relevance to my reading of Carl Jung, whose later work and vision contributed in very important ways to the work of Eliade.[9] So the theory of communication articulated by Bataille is a theory that places the moment of unity, a moment in which we slip imperceptibly into the otherness and nothingness of an unfamilar and yet-to-be-explored body, as a moment outside of our primary condition of existence (*viz.*, discontinuity and death).

THE BODY AND ITS SURFACE

The surface of this body, or rather, its *surface tension*, consists of the combination of forces (seemingly opposed in their expressive truth) that join to signify the creation of an exquisite possibility of silence—of meaning experienced outside of discourse and invisible to rationality. Foucault has termed the emergence of this space of pleasure, will, and power as *heterotopia*,[10] "a floating piece of space, a place without a place, that exists by itself, that is closed in on itself and at the same time is given over to . . . infinity."[11] The surface of the communicative body is thus an enveloped density having an opening and an exit, but it is an opening and an exit that has no identifiable locus—no more visible to ordinary perception than the pores of our flesh. What Bataille underscores, and Foucault affirms, is that the opening is given in time, as a ritual, symbolic experience. It is given by the necessity grounded in all tragic reflection: we enter these moments, consciously or not, Bataille insists, because we all inescapably must experience our own death.

The opening is present because the closure—the dissolution of this density—is inevitable. One way of capturing this notion is to say that we may talk, but we just haven't the time to talk persistently, or even protractedly. Another, more concrete, possibility is to consider the surface tension of a balloon. Air (perhaps "spirit," understood in its elemental being) enters, usually for no good reason, and then it exits. Sometimes the exit is sudden. A small opening in the surface gives way to a large rush of air. A noise is heard after which the surface structure fragments into useless and unrecognizable traces. Sometimes the exit is gradual. But in either case, we know there is an exit. The event of the popped or withering balloon is a source of curiosity and sadness to children. As we grow older our curiosity diminishes, often disappearing, yet we are inclined to speak of communication, of the ostensive reality of such enveloping bodies, as though the balloon will fly on its string forever. Such has been the modern technocratic view of human order and relations. Given its irony it could be a source of amusement were it not so pervasive and, given the contemporary obsession with regard to the neurotic, rationalist association of order with power, so politically charged.

I offer this discourse on gender, space, and surface tension because, in a very strict sense, I find that I have no choice. Quite literally, I find myself with no satisfactory alternative with which to speak and with which to comment on such speech in contemporary discourses of social and human relations. Which is to say that meaning is, no doubt, "given" in the discourses of modern empiricism, discourses that are even now generously rendered and actively repeated, but meaning is not clearly revealed. It is the language of this discourse that now begs the attention of a philosopher of human relations. The burrowing of meaning in any relationship is but poetically represented—never literal, never in fact visible—by any given surface apprehensible to mind. As Heidegger has maintained, poetic meaning is never teased or tricked out. There is no map. (All models and paths are themselves poems.) And any chase quickly becomes comical.

Discourse tempts understanding. As it seduces, however, it cannot be seduced. It is rendered in a language that is only to be spoken and heard. What I shall posit is that the language of human relations, a language that must be carefully and deliberately spoken, is given in the discourse of gender. *Gender*, understood in its broad and bountiful etymological contiguity as a matter of invention, accumulation, context, and separation (invoking genius, genesis, genre, generation, generous, gentle, genuine, and progeny), is perhaps the critical unity of seeming oppositions in the surface tension of the body invented, entered, and experienced in human communication.

At a very early age we learn that we cannot communicate simply because we "have to"; later in life we learn that communication driven solely by habit mocks its fundamental intention. The nervous hesitation before speech, explicated in exquisite detail in the opening and closing paragraphs of Foucault's Inaugural Lecture at the *Collége de France*,[12] is a recognition of discontinuous individuality and the contingency of personal identity. In the hesitation before speech, before the body of communication is invented as a reverberation of our presence, we find ourselves asking, with Beckett, "Who is speaking?"[13] The doubt expressed herein bespeaks a search for identity through our viscera down to our core. Foucault offers us startling evidence of this notion in the case of Adélaïde Herculine (Abel) Barbin.[14] The modern, materialist archaeology of the body has insisted that this core, this final surface, be sexuality and sexual identity. The tragedy of this error is not simply given in the suffering and suicide of this unfortunate spirit (incarcerated in the material, biological body named "Barbin"), but in the absurd reduction of the body to the blueprint of its sexual surface—as though "this" surface, from infancy to childhood to puberty to the creases of old age, offers any material permanence or any fixity of meaning. As Richard Lanigan insightfully argues, the case of Adélaïde Herculine (Abel) Barbin illustrates, if we choose to look closely, the irreducible truth of the communicative body: "Barbin asserted, *I Lie: Some Body is Now Here. I Speak: Somebody is Nowhere.*"[15] The empirical givenness of my body is a powerful fiction. Yet the dynamic and, yes, empirical givenness of my speech will, invariably, invoke an embodiment.

SURFACE TENSION AND "MEANINGFUL" ENERGY

Human being *beyond* sexuality, what Foucault tentatively suggests as an *ars erotica*,[16] is the concept of embodiment in which our communication ruptures the everydayness of being within one's hungry and desperate flesh. The surface tension of the body exists as a moment of power, its symbolic significance radiates as an effect of its movement and activity. In his detailed commentary on Nietzsche's *Will to Power*, Gilles Deleuze contends: "Every relationship of forces constitutes a body—whether it is chemical, biological, social, or political. Any two forces, being unequal, constitute a body as soon as they enter into a relationship. This is why the body is always the fruit of chance . . . and appears as the most 'astonishing' thing, much more astonishing, in fact than consciousness and spirit."[17] If I may be indulged another passage, this one from Bataille, I believe that we might observe a foundation for a more precise exposition of how this tension gathers at the density of a surface, of how this body is occupied between a subject and the otherness that shall erase it, at the liminality of *le même et l'autre*.

> What you are stems from the activity which links the innumerable elements which constitute you to the intense communication of these elements among themselves. These are contagions of energy, of movement, of warmth, or transfers of elements, which constitute inevitably the life of your organized being. Life is never situated at a particular point: it passes rapidly from one point to another (or from multiple points to other points), like a current or like a sort of streaming of electricity. . . . [Y]our life is not limited to that ungraspable inner streaming; it streams to the outside as well and opens itself incessently to what flows out or surges forth towards it. The lasting vortex which constitutes you runs up against similar vortexes with which it forms a vast figure, animated by a measured agitation.[18]

On the basis of these two accounts of *embodiment*, both decidedly Nietzschean in metaphor and temperament, we can gain a clear sense that force and power have very little to do with the mechanics of governing systems or social institutions. These functions simply describe routine matters in which power is predictably gathered and released. In both accounts, power lies not at the surface, but just near what announces itself to be the surface. It describes the surface as a gathering or density of energy, in much the same manner as the tain of the mirror reflects the energy of light to the engaged retina or the camera lens refracts it to the emulsion applied to the surface of photographic film. As much as one may care to search the tain or the retina or the film for, say, the cathedral, the bird, or the outstretched hand, one finds only the propensity to accept a play of radiant energy in the chemical, the tissue, or the paper. Regardless of how powerfully this density is heard to speak, on the surface there is nothing but silence. But the energy, in fact, stops nowhere. It streams continuously, introducing one surface after another, animating one body after another.

ARCHETYPE AND ARCHIVE

Carl Jung posits that on either side of this liminal density, one finds an opposition of archetypes. Again, the body is something through which blood and other forms of energy flow and, following Nietzsche's account, in this body there must be resistance. There is resistance between disparate forces, between chance and fate, light and shadow, knowledge and ignorance. And for Jung, there is a primary opposition between feminine and masculine forms of energy. He terms this opposition the syzygy: *anima* (feminine energy) and *animus* (masculine energy). "In both its positive and negative aspects the *anima/animus* relationship is always full of 'animosity,' i.e., it is emotional, and hence collective."[19] Now, in the context of the theory of communication advocated thus far, the animosity that obtains invents the body that speaks. Given Jung's perspective, the surface tension conceived as a sexual energy of animosity is no ordinary "conflict." In fact, it cannot precisely be understood as a conflict at all.

There is a habit peculiar to the modern mind to conceive of "crisis" or, as we have it here, animosity, as a matter of contentious struggle—as opposition rather than as difference. Perhaps, as Bataille is inclined to suggest, the denial and romanticization of death—that is, rather than its recognition and affirmation—has contributed to this inarticulate experience of crisis as some sort of apocalypse. In any case, for Jung, *anima* and *animus* are engaged in a particular animosity that describes the space of a genital, genetic, genitive, generative (not to mention ingenious) body.

It is Jung's habit to articulate the activity of these symbolic forces through primary mythological figures, which would *seem* to suggest that one's intellectual engagement with this body is primarily a literary activity. It is my firm belief that this is a mistaken notion. The study of the body transcends the disciplines of structuralism and hermeneutics. As Lanigan maintains, the study of the body is not properly the domain of studies in literature, psychoanalysis, sociology, or information (that is, "communication" taken as an essentially quantitative or digital phenomenon). Communicology (which Lanigan explicates as a *semiotic* phenomenology) is the human science whose subject matter transcends the symbolic event of text, mind, event, and communication. Communicology necessarily asks again (after Beckett), "Who is speaking?" The modernist answers, "It is I," or "I, myself, am speaking," are no longer sufficient. (The postmodern problematic bespeaks an essential crisis in language: what pronoun, these days, can be said to make sense upon critical reflection?) Moreover, to say "It is my body that speaks" is to articulate a tautology. As Deleuze and Guattari have recently noted, "things are interactions, bodies are communications."[20] So, it is the body that speaks; it is communication—that is, the embodied relational connection—that speaks. It is, therefore, communication that communicates.

Jung's unique method of psychoanalysis necessitates a closer investigation of what might be entailed by the term "archetype." The expression of "type"—derived from the Proto-Indo-European (or P-I-E) *(s)teu—gives emphasis to the manner in which a type is struck by a blow. It is a sustained impression on the surface of an object. Here we are reminded of the coinage of money, the indentation of soft tissue (say, the flesh), the hitting of a typewriter key upon a sheet of clean white paper, the play of light upon the retina. In this "typing," we are impressed. We are, quite literally, touched. The prefix "arche-" is directly derived from the Greek *árkhö* meaning: first, beginning, rule, order.[21] So, an archetype serves as the symbolic rule for what, ironically, could be labeled as "first impressions."

In a manner parallel to the Jungian *archetype*, Foucault's concept of *archive* does not do its work at a "conscious" level of human intellectual activity—that is, it occurs at a level of mind imperceptible to the everydayness of everyday consciousness. It is imperceptible to the extent that it is, according to Lanigan, carefully coded as "an infrastructure for identity and adherence in rhetorical practices."[22] Foucault comments:

> Instead of seeing, on the great mythical book of history, lines of words that translate in visible characters thoughts that were formed in some other time and place, we have in the density of discursive practices, systems that establish statements as events (with their own conditions and domain of appearance) and things (with their own possibility and field of use). They are all these systems of statements (whether events or things) that I propose to call *archive*.[23]

Ayto notes that the "Greek *arkheion* was the official residence of a ruler, a 'public office,' and its plural *arkheia* was used for public records."[24] Although typically thought of as a place (usually a structure) where records are kept, the etymology of "archive" reveals that it is a space—a *topos*—where originary (i.e., *gen*uine) meaning is sustained both in speech and in expressive silence. Its practical definition refers us to the site where one is present before the speech (speaking, *parole parlante*) of an *ancient document*—the document that is transformed via "rarity, exteriority, and accumulation" into a monument.[25] An archive, thus, serves as a both a naming, or descriptive, function and an expressive, emphatic function, both of which reside in the domain of a reigning discursive power configuration. Lanigan asserts that "Foucault reminds us that the factual presence of language is a positivity, a datum. The blunt fact is that modernity offers us an 'ordinary language' which is no less than positivism in the disguise of symbolic presentation."[26]

What we can also see is that the Jungian "archetype" corresponds to the Foucaultian "archive" in much the same fashion as perception corresponds to expression in the existential and semiotic phenomenology of human speech (*parole*). Perception and expression are not merely coextensive operations of mind, they are integral significations of one and the same thing: the folding, unfolding and becoming of the *communicative body*.

Jung comments that "an archetype—as far as we state it empirically—is an image. An image, as the very term denotes, is a picture of something. An archetypal image is like the portrait of an unknown man in a gallery."[27] The Jungian archetype, moreover, is a divine image. It is a primary symbolic medium through which we sense a sign of difference. It gives an order to what and how we sense. An ordering of sense is, then, one and the same as to *have* sense; it is how we take possession of it. The content of what we perceive is revealed to us in terms of its archetypal impression. The primordial character of the archetype reveals a fundamental outline, an imprint, of how this difference will come to be embodied. If myth, to paraphrase Eliade, is a story about the work of god(s), then an archetype entails a story about the embodiment of god(s)—in other words, the receipt of sacred impressions into the *l'histoire* of primary lived experience.

The archetype, as I interpret it here, is the body's perception of difference as communication. It is the body coined (viz., touched and shaped) as sacred and, hence, powerful. The sacred sense of the body, however, cannot help but remain ambiguous. Like the identity of the man depicted in the portrait hanging in the gallery, or an indubitable familiarity in the face of someone we know with certainty that we have never met before, our inner sense of relatedness requires no knowledge of the, now, inaccessible biography of the "original" person.

The Foucaultian sense of "archive" entails a naming of the expressive domains of embodiment. Again, the archive is, especially given the context of an "archetypal" relation, the concept of both speech speaking (namely, Merleau-Ponty's *parole parlante*) and speech spoken (*parole parlée*). More specifically, it is the body-lived, living, in its milieu. In other words, if the archetype can be understood as *in-spiration*—namely, a sort of visitation and contact of the ambiguous-sacred—then the archive is *ex-piration*: a release of the ambiguous-sacred. One is significative of originary, primary life, the other as originary, primary death.

Between the two of them is memory. In other words, between perception and expression is lived-experience. Between—and, then, among—the speech that is spoken and the speech that is speaking is the communicative body. As Merleau-Ponty asserts: "The relations with others, intelligence, and language cannot be set out in a lineal and causal series: They belong to those cross-currents where someone lives."[28]

Now, the animosity that resides within the body and energizes its expressive function is not a conflict between perception and expression, between archetype and archive, between silence and speech. Nor is it a conflict between male and female, between masculine and feminine. And it is not a conflict in any ordinary sense of the term. Animosity articulates a tension between *anima* and *animus*. To grasp this in a fundamental way, we must get beyond the ever-present and stereotypic notions that distort our capacity to understand masculine and feminine. In other words, not only must we get beyond the world of modern commercial television, but centuries of sacralized artistic representation as well.

"*Anima*," from the P-I-E *anh, means "breath, soul, spirit." Etymologist Robert Claiborne reminds us that "many cultures link 'breath' and 'spirit,' believing that the spirit leaves the body with the last breath."[29] He continues: "The related *ANIMUS* = mind."[30] So, what we find here is that the modern "mind-spirit" ambiguity is bound up within a masculine-feminine animosity.

Just how helpful this may be shall depend upon how we are able to generate meaningful associations with these ambiguous elements. Upon developing another aspect of the relations between *anima* and *animus*, this time with *logos* and *eros*, Jung (1951: 21) offers a further elaboration: "Even in Christianity, the divine syzygy has not become obsolete, but occupies the highest place as Christ and his bride, the Church." A footnote in Jung's text traces this observation to the Second Epistle of Clement of Rome (c.96 AD): "For the Scripture says, God made man male and female; the male is Christ, the female is the Church."[31] To this notation Jung adds: "In pictorial representations, Mary often takes the place of the Church."[32]

This distinction I take to be most powerful. It situates the perception-expression function of archetype and archive within a framework that permits it to speak through the ambiguity of modern discourse on "male/masculine" and "female/feminine." And this distinction is also decidedly Foucaultian. The heroic figure of the crucible—*animus*, the archetype—is paired with the expressive function of its immediate, enveloping ecosystem. *Anima* is the figure of embodiment. Mary, the Church, embracing the Christ, holding "him" in her arms, placing his suffering and passion at the center of her devotion, reveals the symbolic function of unity. Or in terms more familiar to Foucault's *Archaeology*: it is not the hero who "speaks"; instead it is the hero's discourse—the mythic language in which the hero, like Achilles, is fully immersed—that speaks and is heard to speak. The echo of discourse cannot resonate without a symbolic object in search of invention and recognition.

Moreover, this distinction reveals something other, something not entirely visible upon first glance. The body of the church—a symbolic accumulation of discontinuous beings united in the purpose of defying the ever-present existential and biological loneliness of their being at all—necessitates no material marker of its expressive function. To wit, when a church is burned to the ground, what we witness is a structure engulfed in flames as its body stands to one side and shakes its head. But more than this, we also see a problematic conflation of "archive" and "architecture." It is not that the architecture of human relations (or even the "*archae*/texture" of documents and monuments) is insubstantial or irrelevant to our concerns. It is that any particular schema of architecture—whose primary medium of expression is found in the positivity and materiality of surfaces—is, in an important sense, unnecessary.

So, here, the architecture of the body has a material signature, but, significantly, its presence in communication is a matter of coincidence. "Co-incidence" can be viewed, with Foucault, as an essential element of order and knowledge. In other words, coincidence becomes an important synonym for the four similitudes articulated in the second chapter of *The Order of Things*: *convenientia*, *aemulatio*, analogy, and sympathy.[33] Things *occur*, and they occur "with"—that is, simultaneous with, in sequence with, in conjunction with, in coordination with, in balance with, in comparison with, in contrast with. So the architecture of the body and, hence, of communication itself is the pattern of traces that tell the story of a coincidence of forces that addressed one another at a certain time and place. The observable quality of the similitude is, then, what pronounces the body's meaning as it speaks. For Bataille, for Jung, for Dumézil, and for Eliade, this concept of meaning is known as myth (*mythos*, the Greek concept of "speech within" or embodied voice). As such, the architecture of a body is revealed as discourse and it is experienced as myth.

BETWEEN *ANIMA* AND *ANIMUS*

Architecture is never an examination of raw materials as much as it is a study of the strategy of joints and connections, of functions and supports. Between the forces addressing one another, between the one and its shadow, between the same and the different, between the self and the other—between *anima* and *animus*—there is a being (a knowledge and an identity) whose birth can only be traced to the conjunction of these forces. In the myth that inheres in a matrimonial pattern of associations, this being is represented in the metaphor of the "child." The figure of the child's body traces the genesis of an inspired animosity: he or she defines the moment wherein the sign of potentiality (a germ, a seed, a spore) is enveloped in an otherness and transforms into a sign of presence and activity (a tree of knowledge, a family tree, a branch of growth, growth of knowledge defined in terms of branches). All of this is nothing new. But what I shall propose is that the space situated between the *le même et l'autre* of *anima* and *animus* as symbolic archetypes of communication (as an embodied moment) is the "child," or "pro*geny*."

More than anything else, the figure of the child, this entity that literally *survives* "us," signifies a nothingness into which one steps. The child is a thing, a consequence of intimate meeting, that lives on as we die, that lives on with or without our names. As Bataille contends, we invest ourselves in human communication by sacrifice: we give ourselves away to communication. Each commitment of movement in the direction of the other is a sacrifice of the known. Though the *movement* is traceable, the *known* is not, for it cannot be thought or felt as such again. Even if there is no suckling infant, there is always something between us. The figure of the child, our relational progeny, is that which lives between us. This progeny, whatever it happens to be, is the deepest and innermost architecture—the *arche*-text—of the body, a domain that serves us as the medium of flow for memory and consciousness. In order to experience the ecstasies of body consciousness, that is, in order to understand feelings as dimensions of verbal knowledge (and vice versa), one must have a self to give away. Being must find itself in excess, in the transcendence of the everyday. There can be no identity remaindered in the moment. It may be recovered, but it will be recovered as some aspect of the same, not as itself.

Incorporated into this reasoning are Wittgenstein's dicta that one person alone cannot follow a rule and that one person alone cannot speak a language.[34] One person alone cannot give birth to another. (More to the point, there cannot be one "person" alone!) And the surface of the other that is at once the surface to which we have given birth defines the limit of our being—our being together (i.e., "as-gathered"), our being as concurrent, our being as persons, our being as ritual, our being as knowledge. But, as Wittgenstein may have hinted, there is nothing necessarily interesting about following a rule, or watching someone follow a rule, or knowing that persons are one and the same as users of language and hence are obliged to rules beyond their capacity for invention. What is more interesting is that rules reveal boundary conditions just as much as they ostensibly suggest schemas and orders of predictable probability and probable predictability.

Once we can move our thinking about communication beyond the technocratic empiricist fascination with the comportment of social aggregates—the fact that most people will tend to behave as most people tend to behave—we can take note of the rupture that inheres in the formation of any rule. For in the instance of what might appear to be a breach or fracture, *what we find is a surface and a space*. This discovery does not call upon any discourse of modern psychological (*viz*., causal) explanation; that is, it is of no matter whether the breach precedes the surface or vice versa. That the surface speaks as a motif of the breach and the breach a motif of the surface is sufficient discourse with regard to "motive." The conjunction of pause and space, breach and surface, produces a rule that is always already reconciled with the language of its own articulation, but the conjunction speaks to a moment during which the rules became silent, a moment that describes the language of discourse as, literally, out of control.

Any such rupture is the terminal point of a continuity. A stream of consciousness, a line of thought, each, eternal, limitless, deathless, and each defined, somewhat paradoxically, by a point of initiation. A point of contact, a point of departure, a digression, each, is an invitation into an uninhabited place, a place outside of time. And each is composed of the very stuff that constitutes the world from which it seeks escape. The rupture is the terminal point of any world. It is the point in the phenomenon of lived experience where thinking commences. It may be expressed, quite directly, as the ecstasy of an existential and phenomenological transformation.

It is not simply "there" that a counterfeit historical continuity or a simple relational presupposition was exposed as an error, a misunderstanding, a gap in logic, or an act of selfishness. Nor is it simply "there" that the continuity is heard to speak in a voice typically unheard in the routine play of its lines and projections. Again, this rupture, this opening in space and time, is not a consequence of a dialectic, nor is it a faith reconciled with the stubborn rhetoric of "fact." Rather, it is the point wherein one mythic unity subtly yields to the powers and seductions of another. It is the point where interpersonal communication can truly begin.

The privation of self, of *persona*, that obtains in the rupture, is a disposal, but it is not an execution. That is, *persona* rediscovers itself as thrown, but not thrown away. As the symbolic rhythm and rhyme of one myth shifts, changes, and is reinvented as another, the identity who now speaks accommodates and endures the name that is now its silent foundation and partner. The rupture and opening—the interstice—of one countenance, one aspect and another, one world, one domain and another is the space of a myth that accounts for the life of a child. It accounts for the life of the progeny whose existence is a forcefield of the mystery of all that cannot be reconciled between that which we are and that to which we are drawn.

THE CHILD PROBLEMATIC (OR THE "PROBLEM CHILD")

Now, all of this has become a matter of deep interest to me inasmuch as the figure of the child has emerged as the moral centerpiece of contemporary American life. The government of individual adult ethics has become a matter of concern primarily in relationship to the effect an individual's "behavioral choices" might have on the life of children. For most persons, this may seem a perfectly natural, if not logically preeminent, decision-making paradigm. My point, however, is that the figure of the child is no longer primarily understood as a participant in culture—that is, as a source of subjectivity having her or his own identity—but instead, as a ubiquitous symbol of adult conscience. The child, in other words, has become the moral default for modern rationality. The phrase, "children are our future," has an odd ring to it if examined in the light of a different anthropological mindset. For there is only a limited truth to this commonplace sentiment. The meaning of the statement hinges on our interpretation of what constitutes "our."

Even if we substitute the article "the" in the place of "our" the question still arises: *whose* future? At what point did the figure of the child become a millenial symbol? If not "us," then who are these children? Without attempting to grasp their names, or even (as parents are inclined) naming them as subjects, "we" somehow have become convinced that the moral consequence of our choices has been hypodermically injected into the flesh of these anonymous young persons.

There is a tremendous irony at work in this symbolic configuration. For here we have a moral system dependent on a belief in a causal relationship between various models of adult behavior and the perceptions of young people. Again, as with the commonplace ratio of children and the future, there is an element of truth in the relationship. But the relationship is hardly causal. Even behavioral psychology, a rational system based upon a positivistic model of human interpersonal and social relationship, would not support the assertion as causal. Behavioral psychology, for all of its limits as a schema of human explanation, does not attempt claims entailing anonymous subjects. But, nonetheless, there is a persistent and unmistakable strain of rhetoric that violates the scientific principles of causal correlation and the analysis of variables. Popular morality speaks of such vague abstractions as "heroes" and "role models" as though children process such ambiguous symbolic information in a manner quite similar to the way in which their bodies digest Vitamin C.

A more important point, perhaps, is that the term, "child," though alive with symbolic energy, has no meaning in the context of positive science. The term is, from the standpoint of modern empiricism, a deictic ghost. Does childhood include infancy and, if not, when does infancy end? When does childhood end? Does childhood include part of adolescence? When does adolescence begin? Are older children less vulnerable to the influence of behavior models than younger children? If so, can we recognize the difference as a matter of degree? If we cannot recognize the difference as a matter of degree, should we treat the difference as meaningful, or regard the difference at all?

Popular morality might be inclined to respond that I have muddied an important concept in a gratuitous effort to be precise. Is it not the case, one might ask, that adults influence young people? And if that is true, then why complicate matters with such sophistry?

I can only respond that morality, which for the purposes of this monograph I define as the lifeline of that which is sacred, begins and ends as a symbolic matter. And it would, therefore, follow that one can only be deceived by mixing arguments of causation (derived from a discourse of modern science) with the poiesis of archetypal judgment. Establishing a foundation for morality in modern rationality is a matter that can only guarantee confusion, as Foucault explicitly notes in the *Order of Things*,

> The modern one [ethical form], on the other hand, formulates no morality, since any imperative is lodged within thought and its movement towards the apprehension of the unthought; it is reflection, the act of consciousness, the elucidation of what is silent, language restored to what is mute, the illumination of the element of darkness that cuts man off from himself, the re*anima*tion of the inert—it is all this and this alone that constituted the content and form of the ethical. Modern thought has never, in fact been able to propose a morality. But the reason for this is not because it is pure speculation; on the contrary, modern thought from its inception and in its very density, is a certain mode of action. Let those who urge thought to leave its retreat and to formulate its choices talk on; and let those who seek, without any pledge and in the absence of virtue, to establish a morality do as they wish. For modern thought, no morality is possible.[35]

On this basis, the derivation of value premises from the effects of one's adult actions on the life of a symbolic phantom, the illusory "child" and its delusive plural, "children," is less a postponement of ethical responsibility as it is a dissimulation. It is a fragmentation of meaningful action into a moral nothingness. Nonetheless, it has remained a persuasive premise of contemporary moral rhetoric.

There is another important dimension of the symbolic currency of the "child," and that can be found in the discourse of popularized psychotherapy. To speak of one's "inner child" is to speak of something one wants to "get in touch with." And while such talk is often mocking and derisive, at neither the center nor the margins of this discourse can we find an opposing theory of personality. The talk of an inner child slips comfortably into the mindset of contemporary discourse as though there has always been an accomodation for it. The modern mind, in all of its permutations, embraces the concept of innocence and play both, I would venture, because of its edenic moral ascendancy and because of its mysterious disappearance from the *habitus* of contemporary adult life. As Witold Rybczyinski has observed, "The lack of carelessness in our recreation, the sense of obligation to get things right, and the emphasis on protocol and decorum do represent an enslavement of a kind. People used to 'play' tennis; now they 'work' on their backhand."[36] Rybczyinski is left to conclude: "We want leisure, but we are afraid of it, too."[37] For the unreflective mind, the concept of an inner child is yet another abstraction regarding the makeup of the human psyche, an abstraction that carries with it whatever weight a speaker is inclined to invest in it; an abstraction that makes as much or as little sense as any other piece of gossip such a mind hears spoken about itself. And this is so to the extent that the concept of the inner child is as seemingly unempirical as the concept of "mind." Moreover, the notion of "inner life" of any sort is tolerable to the workings of the modern mind to the extent that, at least on the surface, inner being bears no threat to the modern moral order of causal posterity. (When activity is invisible, it would seem, nothing is shamed.)

The concept of the inner child is, of course, a Jungian invention, and in many ways can be seen as the cornerstone of his analytic work. The intention of this concept is toward the development of the personality of the reflective mind. Quite simply, for the unreflective mind—the mind perplexed by all of the abstractions (superficially, of equal value) tendered to describe its inner work—there is no inner child. Yet the genesis of the surface that obtains between *anima* and *animus* is a subtle affair. For the unreflective mind, consciousness's address of the world invests no *pathos* in a relationship of I-Thou and, hence, cannot begin to explore the moment in which the surface of communication commences the development of its inspired life.

That the life of this delicate surface is often stillborn or aborted in the haste of economic relations goes without saying in the politics of modern human self-fulfillment. It is, anthropologically speaking, a "primitive desire" for there to be such exquisite care taken in the relations of self and other. Lanigan's insightful commentary on Lévy-Bruhl's "Law of Participation[38] makes this quite clear:

> He [Lévy-Bruhl] argues that some "underdeveloped peoples" . . . have mystic mentality that perceives a reality of beings related to objects that are not perceptible to the senses. Hence, the statement of the Law of Participation: "In varying forms and degrees they [the relations] all involve a 'participation' between persons or objects which form part of a collective representation." This law describes a human science in which "The prelogical mind does not objectify nature thus. It *lives* it rather, by feeling itself participate in it, and feeling these participations everywhere. . . ."[39]

The "prelogical mind" of which Lévy-Bruhl speaks is the mind liberated from the *habitus* of modernity which, again, has come to occupy the "natural attitude" of mind and whose ethical bearings are grounded in the strategic intelligence quotient of an inflated personal economic perfomance.

As both Jung and Lanigan would probably imply, Lévy-Bruhl's Law of Participation entails a significant personal and, hence, ethical choice. It entails an embrace of the other in the discovery of one's body, an engagement and conjunction with an energy that is unfamiliar to the architecture of everyday life. It entails the inhabiting of a new body that stands in between my *memory* and my *desire*, my *name* and my *subjectivity*. And it entails an active withdrawal from the cold, sterile body of a "logic" that seeks to substantiate the limits of knowledge and experience. It does not ask that I risk death. It asks that I embrace the reality of my death and the ongoing nature of death (in which I willingly transform the truth of myself into the nothingness that it is), as it also asks that I embody the life that I engender. It asks that I choose to participate with, to live with, the world in which my flesh is immersed.

In short, the Law of Participation is *pre*logical as it also *post*modern. The difficulty with much of the contemporary writing on culture and communication that seeks a postmodern premise and attitude is that it is still quite guarded, tickling the idea of a "post"-modernity but not acknowledging an end to anything. It bespeaks a world in which all structures of consciousness retain their integrity, but appear in profoundly different sorts of sentences—or, as Elias Canetti has phrased it, as "a powerful man who cautiously dreams of powerlessness."[40] The shift that is implied in a theory of communication grounded in Lévy-Bruhl's Law of Participation is not a shift from *logos* to something other, to some sort of preordained anti-Aristotelian antipode. In fact, it is simply a shift from the ethical dimension of *logos* to the mythical (*mythos*) dimension of *logos*. But with this shift the world, the body that *anima*tes my flesh, appears to me for the first time. In this world language gestures and words speak. Or as Lanigan discovers, "The paradigm of 'social reality' (lifeworld) is counterposed to 'reality' (theory world) therewith and conversely."[41]

The child, the progeny, whose life is magically convened in the animosity that occupies the interstice of *anima* and *animus*, lives in the realm of myth. The symbolic effect of its birth can be likened to a coin of a sacred realm; to wit, it is formed from an archetype. Its value cannot be exchanged for any sort of material substance. That is, it is not an economic commodity. Its value is that of a token, a token that permits entry, signaling a beginning, a commencement, the very sort of token that gains one admission to a carnival ride or a movie theatre. Life, then, is to be experienced by way of a coin of the realm, not in the realm of the coin.

The child's world is fiction. The child itself is always figurative or figurational, always more than is present: it is never the child who is spanked—it is the flesh of the being who has betrayed "the child" that is spanked. As children, we never really think of ourselves as mere children; we only know what we know. We think of ourselves as distant from certain sorts of knowledge (an event of mind that does not really change in adulthood), and the persistence of this distance over time can bring on accusations from our parents of "being childish." But the accusation is paradoxical; it is intended as pejorative while at the same time merely descriptive of a condition that the parent has imposed upon this small human from the beginning. The child nurtured by two well-meaning parents is both daydream and nightmare. They not only have hope for the child, their hope is invested deeply within the child. The child whose body is destined for greatness is like the constellation that appears in the heavens: a fiction defined by a group of points that, in the moist glow of night, offers a moment of foolish participation in an ancient fairy tale. At daybreak the constellation disappears and the "real" child emerges. This is the child who does not, as a matter of course, refer to itself as a child. This child, in fact, soon becomes a young person. And it is inevitable that the person this "child" grows into will be a betrayal of all of the starry-eyed dreams and rented fictions that enticed the investment of parental hope. Or as Jung so disturbingly remarks, "There is no human horror or fairground freak that has not lain in the womb of a loving mother."[42]

The child who is experienced, upon considered reflection, in adulthood is a vastly different child from the "child" that each of us once was. Jung's commentary on the circumstance of modern adulthood is most amusing: "Everyone who has finished his course of studies feels himself to be fully educated; in a word, he feels grown up. . . . People expect him to be efficient and good at his job and not to have doubts about himself and his capabilities. The professional man is irretrievably condemned to be competent."[43] (Again, at daybreak the constellation disappears!) So it is no accident that the everyday discourse of contemporary life has begun to speak the metaphor of the inner child and to fix its morality in the life of children. What Jung referred to as "the standardized, mass-produced, 'normal,' human being demanded by the machine age"[44] hungers for a fuller sense of its life. It is equally evident that the moment of one's arrival at adulthood hardly satisfies this condition. Jung's observations are indeed prophetic: "I suspect our contemporary pedagogical and psychological enthusiasm for the child of dishonorable intentions: we talk about the child, but we should mean the child in the adult. For in every adult there lurks a child—an eternal child, something that is always becoming, is never completed, and calls for unceasing care, attention, and education. That is the part of the human personality which wants to develop and become whole."[45]

A CHILD'S FAITH AND PUERILE BELIEFS: COMMUNICATION, ARCHETYPE, *PISTIS*, AND ETHICS

The moment of communication that is sought, however, is not some sort of moral imperative. Communication, following Bataille, describes the process—electrical, spiritual, alchemical, yet ordinary and everyday—of a transformation of inner meaning. In communication there is a death and rebirth of relations and, hence, of knowledge. Relations and meaning are understood by Bataille in a profoundly mythic, archetypal, and erotic sense. Yet at the same time, communication is an animal (i.e., "*anima*l") act. How can this paradox be explained? Both Jung and Bataille would concur that modern humanity has limited its own access to the animal through the retreat of knowledge from positive science to mythic symbolism. As Bataille remarks, "The animal opens before me a depth that attracts me and is familiar to me. In a sense, I know this depth: it is my own. It is also that which is farthest removed from me, that which deserves the name depth, which means precisely *that which is unfathomable to me.*"[46] Bataille's point is that communication is not understood if it is merely about relations of subject matter. It is not today's headlines that draw us together. Even the rhetorical tropes and figures that constitute the strategy and play of our discursive relations speak little, if anything about the moment of communication. Instead it is *you* and *your* unfathomable depth that draws *me* into *your* life and *your* world and draws *me* out of mine. It is *that* process that Bataille reserves for the moment of communication.

The other with whom one typically communicates is, of course, no "other" at all. She or he, in this critical context, is not a void, not an alterity, not a yawning abyss, not an archetype, and not a sign. She or he is flesh and blood. She or he is alive, as I am alive, deep inside of a life, surrounded by a world, breathing in this world, gradually issuing myself into this world, feeling myself slip through my own fingers. Everything that I know about this person is what draws me into her presence. If we are to define this moment in Bataille's terms, can we say that on drawing close, and then closer to her, has communication begun? If she asks me for the time of day and I tell her, and then we speak no more, have we communicated? Bataille replies, "'Communication' only takes place *between two people who risk themselves*, each lacerated and suspended, perched atop a common nothingness."[47] Now, how is this possible, one may ask. Isn't this again taking the experience of communication into the realm of religious ecstasy? (And, perhaps, isn't the existentialist language rather gothic in this context, even for Bataille?)

The limits of religious moments have been obfuscated beyond everyday understanding over the last millenium. It is not at all clear what is to blame, nor is it in fact important. One declares that he or she is a "born again" Christian in much the same way that he or she declares allegiance to a professional athletic franchise. It entails, simply, playing a game of identification. It is a categorical matter, and not a tremendously intellectual one at that—although were it to become deeply intellectual, that is all it would likely become. Emotions may give way, but the moment is not transformational. For nothing of value is at risk. I have no doubt that the terms Bataille sets as a condition for communication are terms that entail an engulfing transformation of self. If, in the exchange I described in the previous paragraph, there has been no difference in the course of consciousness, then there has been nothing of communication, I forget the moment, and resume the pace of my life. And in this calculus, Bataille's condition for the moment of communication is remarkably similar to Jung's concept of the development of personality. A yearning for fulfillment entails a risk, a sacrifice of self, and vice versa. Communication is a discontinuity; as such, it requires a rupture and a breaking away. It may or may not be consciously desired, but it is always a matter of necessity. Or in more Heideggerian terms, a moment of communication begins in unsettledness and is remembered as a moment having roots in anxiety. For Heidegger *and* for Bataille, communication needs to be distinguished from idle talk.

Bataille's language indeed does reflect a gothic rhetorical architecture. It is even more evident in the following passage: "If human beings had kept their own integrity and hadn't sinned, God on one hand and human beings on the other would have persevered in their respective isolation. A night of death wherein Creator and creatures bled together and lacerated each other and on all sides, were challenged at the extreme limits of shame: that is what was required for their communion."[48] In the course of this seemingly gory passage Bataille is making a very simple point. The community of humanity and its investment in an intuition of a meaning greater than that which is present to us in its everydayness begins in a moment of pain and unease.

Simply: one is driven to communicate by necessity, and this necessity is translated by Bataille as being "challenged at the extreme limits of shame." Bataille continues with the following assertion (emphasis in original): *"Thus 'communication', without which nothing exists for us, is guaranteed by crime. 'Communication' is love, and love taints those whom it unites."*[49] A few paragraphs later, Bataille concludes: "A fundamental principle is expressed as follows: 'Communication' cannot proceed from one full and intact individual to another. It requires individuals whose separate existence in themselves is risked, placed at the limit of death and nothingness; the moral summit is the moment of risk taking, it is a being suspended in the beyond of oneself, at the limit of nothingness."[50]

Again, the otherness whose world I enter upon the moment that I risk myself in communication is not a void. But it is also not the case that I enter the lived-body and psychological mind of another person. The space I enter is outside of my self, but I in fact learn nothing of what another person knows privately, intimately, sacredly. The other person presents to me an opportunity for my own knowledge and discovery and between the two of us there is formed a conceptual body—that is, "we," together, conceive a body. In Bataille's gothic metaphor, we bleed together. In what is in fact a less wildly figurative likening, it can be said that we breathe together. We, literally, *inspire* a body. A current is felt between us. Each of our experiences with this body is private and our own. And we can only speculate on what the "other" (this new terrain of consciousness, this new energy field outside of "us") is feeling.

In Jung's language, this body is the "mysterious conjunction" (*mysterium coniunctionis*) of *anima* and *animus*.[51] It is not so much that you have entered my world; it is instead that you have entered the world of an other. And I have myself entered this otherness inasmuch as, like you, I am in search of something. In my state of isolation I am lacerated—or as Jung would say, "wounded"—and I am ashamed. It is a "shame-ful" need for a fuller understanding of that which shames me that leads me out of myself. In Lévy-Bruhl's formulation, I seek the experience of communication to the extent that I seek to participate with my enveloping world and in doing so, perceive it for the first time. I seek this experience, in Nietzschean terms, so as to conduct a firsthand genealogy of morals. Or in Foucaultian terms, I gain an insight into the archival forms of power to which I am subject, as well as those in which my subjectivity can be heard to speak—which is to say that this experience entails, for me, an archaeology of my lived-body.

The body that is formed as I shed the scaly skin of my claims to self-knowledge (*qua* self-consciousness) and enter the otherness of the world in which I find myself is always my body. Regardless of whom I communicate with, it is *my* body—that is, it is my body if I choose to have it. The modern world is littered with half-formed and still-born bodies that have been abandoned by commonplace moralities and illusions of self-satisfaction. Modernity has never insisted that the human quest for wholeness be taken in earnest. Or as Jung has argued, "Can we, therefore, blame humanity, and all the well-meaning shepherds of the flock and worried fathers of families, if they erect protective barriers, hold up wonder-working images, and point out the roads that wind safely past the abyss?"[52] In the modern world, we are free to deify virtually anything, but we have chosen strategies of mystification and circumvention in our address of myth and sacred experience, along with rhetorical manipulation as the path of primary self-knowledge. An overwhelming concern for the narrative order and appearance of what can safely be articulated as "virtuous" character has emerged in contemporary life as the principal doctrine by which a subject exercises "care of the self." This doctrine has merited two equally satisfactory names: one is "ethics," the other is "public relations," and as with Frege's case of the Morning Star and the Evening Star (namely, Venus), they both refer to the same thing.

The concern that is so commonly exhibited for the appearance of virtue, regardless of whether the virtue is derived from, say, popular morality, Calvinist theology, Augustinian metaphysics, or classical Greece, is part and parcel of a discursive strategy. It operates as a decisive function of a narrative and rhetorical system of semiotic demonstration, namely, the species of *pistis* (misleadingly translated as "proof") that Aristotle called *ethos*. There is no compelling evidence that Aristotle encouraged a doctrine for the care of the self that could be conflated with image consciousness. As Heidegger puts it, the *Rhetoric* of Aristotle, particularly its doctrine on *pistis* (Book 2), "must be taken as the first systematic hermeneutic of the everydayness of Being with one another."[53] Instead, what we find at work in this narrative system that most fully accounts for the persistence of an "image-control strategy of meaning" is a myth that has been at work in other dimensions of modern economic relations.

In this myth, the symbol of evil is that which poses a threat to knowledge, its order, and its evolved scientific history. Criminals and criminal behaviors, for example, do not threaten this order. Irrespective of the danger their acts pose to humanity, their actions are completely within the symbolic pattern of the narrative. Criminality is completely affirmed by the order of things. As Bataille interprets the moral problematic of this narrative pattern, "what is *substantially* rejected in evil is a concern with the time to come."[54] The adaptation of one's public body (that is, as a condensation of public relations) to a canon of archetypal virtue and against an archetype of symbolic evil describes the pattern of unreflective human participation in this mythic scheme. The participation is unreflective inasmuch as it is derived from a concept of isolated individuation (that is, "my flesh marks the limit of my body") in which the good of practical *logos* is situated in a "concern with the time to come."

The article of faith that anchors the doctrine of virtue in the public body of a carefully managed portfolio of self-images becomes an equivocation of subjectivity and identity, and then subtly emerges as a matter of gender. This particular yet pervasive concept of *ethos* entails a strategy of presenting one's public body as heroic and, hence, as archetypal. To the extent one seeks judgment in terms of archetypal identity, one builds oneself toward identification with the archetype. In other words, this literally amounts to building one's body in an effort to become an archetype. James Hillman has observed that "to take Jesus as model leads to the *imitatio Christi* and the guilt of never measuring up."[55] Jung, in his exegesis of Nietzsche's *Zarathustra* takes it a step further: "Whenever one is caught in an archetype, one forgets oneself completely, one is in a heightened condition, just inflated; then one lives on and can see later that one has suffered from an inflation. Primitives know that."[56] Jung concludes: "Therefore, in certain tribes the successful warrior is not received in triumph as we would treat him, but is sent to a lonely place where he is fed on raw vegetables for two months in order to thin him down, and then when he is quite meek he is allowed to come back."[57]

THE CHILD AND ITS GENDER

The matter of gender is, for Jung, tied to the manner in which the archetype is embodied. There are two things at work here. The first is an argument quite familar to students of Foucault. It is an argument that finds its fullest articulation in *The Order of Things*, namely, that the disciplines whose works exemplify the practice and trajectory of modern thought have been long tied to an anthropological myth whose narrative is reducible to a masculine heroic epic, or as Foucault expresses it, "the precritical analysis of what man is in his essence becomes the analytic of everything that can, in general, be presented to man's experience."[58] In this regard, character virtues that one seeks to exhibit as facets of one's public self, regardless of whether they are displayed upon the flesh of a biological man or woman, are the character virtues "of what *man* is in *his essence*." The subject who speaks, and who speaks with a passion to be taken seriously and to make his reason known, is the body-subject who, as a self-contained system, seeks to advance his marker and sweeten his portfolio in the game of practical matters (*phronesis* as pragmatic *logos*). Quite simply, the power of rationalism, in all forms in which it has been practiced and developed, is an *animus* myth.

The second thing that exhibits the gender of the archetypal virtue that has been emulated in the practice of caring for oneself (conflated with the Aristotelian concept of *ethos*) is somewhat more obscure, but it is no less significant. It is a point that I demonstrated earlier in this monograph: the symbolism of an archetype is opposed to the environs of an archive as *animus* energy opposes *anima* energy. The relationship of one to the other opens up and demarcates a space. The relationship, being one of animosity, begets the surface and quickens the surface tension of a body. Although the archetypal symbols that have circulated throughout mythological history do represent varying gender powers (some male, some female, some hermaphrodite), the role of an archetype in its genealogical relationship to archival signs and functions is a masculine, dominant role. It parallels the relationship of "monument" to "document" which Foucault articulated in *Archaeology of Knowledge* and, along these lines, it can be said that Foucault's reinterpretation of the patterns and persistent narrative continuities of intellectual history has been an attempt to energize the narrative power of archival figures and tropes. Foucault's work, like that of Peirce's phaneroscopy and Husserl's phenomenology, is an attempt to investigate discursive existences beneath the surfaces of "history," and to do so not by dismissing or discarding the surfaces themselves, but by engaging the life and energy of all of the surfaces with which one is engaged.

Simply, Western intellectual history as it is typically narrated is full of deep influences and great moments—that is, great moments that never *quite* happened.[59] In much the same way that we cannot say with any degree of certainty how "children" are "caused" to behave like the adults they eventually become, we cannot say where Nietzsche's Zarathustra really came from or if Montaigne wrote with any active consciousness of Descartes or if and how Peirce influenced Husserl (and vice versa). Anchoring the discursive practice of intellectual history in primary figures is, in effect, admitting to something along the lines of a "great man/eloquent speeches/decisive moments" theory of events. However, the "commonsense" reasoning that drives this practice as some sort of pedagogical shortcut or analytical default is incapable of seeing through the flimsy premises that have barely managed to sustain this model of history. The work of prior epistemes emerges, thus, as *monument*—as merely a symbolic foundation for modern thought—and then rationality, in its forgetfulness, replicates its processes without consciousness of its archaeological and genealogical conditions. In so choosing its narrative strategy, rationality thus emerges as a formula for superficial explication—that is, as a surface-level grasp of the dynamics of surface tension.

At this juncture, the question now emerges as follows: In what way is *ethos* necessary for *pistis*? Or, in more ordinary terms: why has this particular strategy of self-care been so essential for what we have named "persuasion"? Is there an alternate mythic configuration that can generate in communication a *pistis* that is strategically indifferent to the modern strategy of *ethos*? Well, as every student of Aristotle knows, there are two modes of *pistis* other than *ethos* that a wise speaker has at her or his disposal: *pathos* and *logos*. It would be a mistake—a mistake that has been made a thousand times over—to see the task that lies before us as simply a re-ranking of these modes of persuasion. And the task that lies before us is not merely a matter of changing the heads on a totem pole (as though that is how primitives think).

Moreover, *ethos*, *pathos*, and *logos* are not constituent elements of *pistis* because they are reducible to intellectual strategy, but because they are principal elements of the space of human experience: *ethos* qua habit, habituation, habitat (from P-I-E swedh, "disposition or placement of self"); *pathos* as, literally, passion, suffering, feeling (or existential-phenomenological "necessity"); and *logos* in the character of word, sign, representation, speech/*parole*, speaking. They each fundamentally participate in the description of how a body comes into being. To recapitulate, when is a body brought into being?—when one chooses to communicate. When and how does one choose to communicate?—taking Bataille's interpretation as thematic, persons communicate when they begin to "live outside of themselves."

Now, if we can grasp the concept of communication in terms of entering and participating in the space of this subtle body, and if we can appreciate that *ethos*, *logos*, and *pathos* describe the phenomenological space of this body, we are left to ask: What is *pisits*? It is not "proof," although centuries of study in rhetoric and argument seem to suggest that it might be. It is also not gained by modern techniques of persuasion or interpersonal compliance-gaining. Jung writes: "*Pistis* means fidelity, confidence, trust, loyalty, wrongly translated by 'belief' or 'creed.'"[60] In fact, for Jung, *pistis* entails an inner knowing. It is not the same thing as a promise or even a social contract. In allegorical language, Jung can be understood as saying that *pistis* describes the manner in which we invest the gold of our inner dwelling.

And so, following Foucault, we can see that modern rationality has failed to grasp *pistis* in much the same way that it has failed to speak or enunciuate a grounded doctrine with respect to its regard for the human subject. Modernity as an intellectual project is a study of the strategies of acquiring and dispensing power. And it is plain to see that power, understood this way, admits of no axiological foundation. As a concept or as a strategy, it participates in no world beyond itself. It is defined in terms of the world of past-perfect and future-perfect: power, as a stategy, is gathered from the time we know and is only relevant "in the [presupposed] time to come." In short, modernity is a narrative of a particular manifestation of power, and this particular "power" is wholly dependent on stable appearances. So there is no wonder why *ethos* has come to serve such an equivocal interpretation of hermeneutical *pisits*.

On the other hand, we cannot conclude by simply heralding the virtue of an *anima* myth over what seems an exhausted orbit of *animus* myth. As Bataille comments, we enter our communion because we have been "challenged at the extreme limits of shame." So, if *ethos* has become a strategy in which we carefully mask our shame (our *anima*lity and our vulnerability) does it not make sense that we will find the liberation we seek by unmasking our shame, perhaps even celebrating our shame, if not flattering it? If our passions have been carefully hidden, then ought we not set them free? And if *pathos* is indeed the unspeakable element of *pistis*, do we err in speaking its name?

To think of *pathos* or "the passions" in this way is not only to reify the dominant pattern of archetypal myth, it is to participate in stereotype as well. In other words, it would rediscover the discourse of hysteria and the pre-Freudian pathologies of emotional infantilism, it would then celebrate them as a new *ethos* of speech, and hail them as a source of power—bringing, in effect, the essential logic of any person's personal struggles (literally, a *logos* of *"mein kampf"*) to the order of discursive ascendancy. Needless to say, modern society's participation in such a discourse has well become a matter of "been there, done that."

Passion, though often performed, performed carefully or carelessly, or even exhibited as a function of inflated self-consciousness, is an element of expression, of language, and communication, and it is a very real element of the phenomenology of interpersonal situations. But, in any case, *pathos*, like *ethos*, is a sign—as discourse itself, as myth, as narrative, as poetry, as argument, as *logos*, is also a sign; all of which are signs whose meaning is contingent upon lived experience. *Pistis* is not belief, Jung reminds us, and nowhere in Aristotle was it claimed that *pistis* is *logos*.

Pistis is the investment of the individuated subject in the body. Jung writes in his studies on alchemy, "Man [*sic*] stands forth as he really is and shows what was hidden under the mask of conventional adaptation: the shadow. . . . Wholeness is not so much perfection as it is completeness. Assimilation of the shadow gives a man body, so to speak. . . . In this way, man becomes for himself the difficult problem that he really is."[61] *Anima*, like Foucault's archive, is the symbolic shadow of modern knowledge or, rather, the symbolic shadow of the modern narrative of classical knowledge. The embrace of Jung's shadow or Foucault's archive does not call forth the long night and dark specters of a time before shame, before evil, or before consciousness. The language of *pistis*, which cannot be sufficiently explicated in any familiar (linear) discourse, is the ritual semiotic phenomenology of life lived in the twilight.

Anima myth is not a substitution for archetypal myth, which is also to say that gender is not a contest. Gender, in fact, is itself a myth. It is a myth of unity. The pre-Christian and pre-Homeric gods of creation in the *Rg Veda* and in the *Zendavesta* (and it is worth noting that Zarathustra was the prophet of Ohura Mazda, the creation god of the *Zendavesta*) were hermaphrodite entities, divine bodies having world creating and world expending powers, powers far greater than the simple magic of persuasive/coercive power that has been recklessly bargained for since the dawn of modern desire.

The body of the communicative progeny (i.e., of the phenomenological child) is also born with a duality of gender. This might well account for the innocence of (biological) childhood ecstasy. The child's *ek-stasis*, its being beyond and beside itself, bears no necessary relation to what Foucault termed a *scientia sexualis*. The biological child not only cannot truly *know* itself as a child, as childish, it also cannot understand itself as a *sexual* being—that is, unless it has been taught to "think" in this way. But such a "thinking" reveals itself as merely a behavioral response, impersonating the rule of a world it is too young to grasp. It stands to reason that "sexuality" is a *sign*, a sign not merely *of* the body but *for* the body. In the same sense that the moment of communication places one at the limit of death and nothingness, one's first (perhaps brusque) conscious encounter with sexuality entails a recognition of mortality, mortification, humility, and the sudden foreclosure of facile speech.

The world of the child—*both* the mythic *and* the biological/historical child—is one of continual passages and beginnings, openings and limits. However, the experience of sexuality as communication addresses the moment when one's life "finally" becomes an empirical matter—that is, the narrative is effaced or at least suspended, a chapter is closed, and the book must begin again. We have understood for quite some time that sexuality is not merely a reproductive matter, that it entails a peculiar desire to sequester, expose, and secrete the energy of one's own being into the life of an other, perhaps into the life of all aspects of otherness. This ingress is, literally, an act of violence. (As Bataille, once again, refers to this moment of communion: "A night of death wherein Creator and creatures bled together and lacerated each other and on all sides.")

Now, there are crucial differences between the sorts of violence that a body experiences in the course of a life. When a child is corrected for behaving selfishly, the intervening parent intentionally commits a violation of the child's body. Moreover, the establishment of any sort of personal boundary entails an act of force, a concurrent gesture of self-directed "yes" and other-directed "no." The etytmology of the word "violence" derives from the Latin noun *vís*, meaning "force, energy." There is nothing linguistically inherent in the word, or even the concept of violence to necessitate that it be grasped as essentially inhumane. The same may be said of terror and, as well, horror. Life entails struggles of all sorts. Our bodies emerge from a dance of forces, and our minds are enjoined by a discipline that is grounded in the expressed reality of the multiple signifiers of "no."

Although it is quite true that children are indeed capable of "violent" acts of all sorts, it is also a matter of general psychoanalytic regard that the biological/historical child cannot grasp the symbolism and communicative significance (i.e., relational and cultural codes encountered by experience and learned by reflection) of these acts. An important detail is that the figure of the child is savage (*sauvage*), not "vicious." "Vice" (from which the word "vicious" is but an adjectival modification) is an extension of an entrenched *habitus*, just as sadism is in so many ways nothing more than the full and perfected (*ergo*, "extreme") embodied performance of modern *ressentiment*. Recognition and pursuit of vice is, for the subject, a learned condition. It takes time for an experiment of self (*hexis*) to become an experience (*habitus*) of vice. It is not simply or even merely the innocence of childhood that is sacrificed in the fixation of a mortifying *habitus*—irrespective of how it is learned. The innocence of childhood is a concept, not a condition, and it is a concept that is grasped by way of re-cognition, not cognition. The innocence of childhood is something adults think about and romanticize, not something that children "know."

The body that is born and gestates in an act of communication is a body that enters into the life of gender, transcending the discourse and grammar of mere sexuality. Now, it is not my claim that the being of a child is separate from *any* sense of what modernity takes as sexuality. Indeed, the biological child embodies *eros*, if only by virtue of its innocence, much more fully than the adult, and the child is certainly conscious of her or his embodied gender with, no doubt, some sense of its future possibilities. Yet, as Foucault carefully argues, the expressive element of sexual being has also made it a social (and political) matter: the *scientia sexualis* is, in every respect, a game—a game whose consequence is a hierarchy of bodies, a virtual social register of *animus* archetypes.[62] And as Kelly Oliver, in her extraordinary analysis of masculine and feminine in the context of "the family," maintains: "Self-identity is not necessarily bought through the sacrifice . . . of others. Somewhere between the animal body mother and the no-body father is love . . . love is flesh and word. The rhythms of dynamic bodies and bodies interacting, the rhythms of affects circulating between bodies at the heart of sociality, becomes language and culture. Love is the support that makes identification and separation possible and gives birth to the subject."[63]

The trajectory of this moral reflection on violence and the experience of bodily anguish—or, for the Christian mind, "passion"—nonetheless, does not find its arc painted toward a vision of "silenced voices" or "exclusionary practices." Oliver also concurs: "Culture and society need not be seen as the result of the repression of our hostile instincts, instincts directed originally against mothers and fathers."[64] Ultimately, a phenomenology of the body entails much more than, simply, yet another call for liberation and the circumscription of bio-power techniques. Ultimately, a phenomenology of the body entails a careful reflection on the concepts of sacrifice and discipline.

And this is why, for me, the embodiment of what is most fundamentally tragic in modern rationality's concept of communication (and, as such, through our "investment *habitus*" in an archetypal narrative of *pistis*) can be found in the event of Adelaide Herculine (Abel) Barbin. Gender in modernity is about the power of knowledge to be found in the names of things. Gender, understood in symbolic terms, is about life, creation, and the power of discovery. Some body *is* nowhere. In a certain sense, it always is. No body is reducible to names and parts and skin and bone. Yet in the sacrificial movement beyond the nothingness of self-knowledge, any body and every body can be anywhere and everywhere.

NOTES

1. Bataille, *Erotism*, 31–32.
2. Bataille, *Erotism*, 34.
3. Foucault, *The History of Sexuality, Vol. 1*, 67–71.
4. Foucault, *The History of Sexuality, Vol. 1*, 67–71.
5. Foucault, "A Preface to Transgression," 29–52.
6. Foucault, "Of Other Spaces," 22–27.
7. Foucault, *Archaeology of Knowledge*, 112.
8. See Bataille, *Theory of Religion*, 117–27.
9. See Schwartz-Salant, "Introduction," 10. See also Eliade, *Myths, Dreams, and Mysteries*.
10. This language appears fairly early in Foucault's work. See *Order of Things*. We can find its fullest articulation in Foucault, "Of Other Spaces."
11. Foucault, "Of Other Spaces," 27.
12. Foucault, *Archaeology of Knowledge*.
13. Beckett, *Stories and Texts for Nothing*, 16. The power of this question becomes fully manifest in Foucault, "What Is an Author?"
14. Foucault, *Herculine Barbin*.
15. Lanigan, *Human Science of Communicology*, 113.

16. Dreyfus and Rabinow, *Michel Foucault.*
17. Deleuze, *Nietzsche and Philosophy,* 40.
18. Bataille, *Inner Experience*, 94.
19. Jung, *Psyche and Symbol*, 16.
20. Deleuze and Guattari, *What Is Philosophy,* 123.
21. Ayto, *Dictionary of Word Origins,* 33–34.
22. Lanigan, *Semiotic Phenomenology of Rhetoric,* 31.
23. Foucault, *Archaeology of Knowledge,* 128.
24. Ayto, *Dictionary of Word Origins,* 34.
25. See Foucault, *Archaeology of Knowledge*.
26. Lanigan, *Human Science of Communicology,* 83.
27. Jung, "Questions to Jung and His Answers," 15.
28. Merleau-Ponty, *Themes from the Lectures,* 21.
29. Claiborne, *The Roots of English,* 48.
30. Claiborne, *The Roots of English,* 48.
31. Clement of Rome, "The Second Epistle of Clement to the Corinthians."
32. Jung, *Psyche and Symbol*, 21.
33. Foucault, *Order of Things,* 17–29.
34. See Wittgenstein, *Philosophical Investigations.*
35. Foucault, *Order of Things*, 328.
36. Rybczyinski, *Waiting for the Weekend,* 18.
37. Rybczyinski, *Waiting for the Weekend,* 234.
38. See Lévy-Bruhl, *How Natives Think.*
39. Lanigan, *Human Science of Communicology*, 193. The quoted material is drawn from Levy-Bruhl, *How Natives Think*, 76; 130.
40. Canetti, *The Agony of Flies,* 193.
41. Lanigan, *Human Science of Communicology*, 195.
42. Jung, "The Development of Personality," 195.
43. Jung, "The Development of Personality," 193.
44. Jung, "The Development of Personality," 190.
45. Jung, "The Development of Personality," 193–94.
46. Bataille, *Theory of Religion*, 22.
47. Bataille, *On Nietzsche,* 20–21.
48. Bataille, *On Nietzsche,* 18.
49. Bataille, *On Nietzsche,* 18.
50. Bataille, *On Nietzsche,* 19.
51. Jung, *Mysterium Coniunctionis.*
52. Jung, "The Development of Personality," 210.
53. Heidegger, *Being and Time*, 178.
54. Bataille, *On Nietzsche,* 28.
55. Hillman, *Kinds of Power,* 104.
56. Jung, "Nietzsche's Zarathustra," 27.
57. Jung, "Nietzsche's Zarathustra," 27.
58. Foucault, *Order of Things,* 341.
59. A similar sort of argument is posed in Baudrillard, *The Gulf War Did Not Take Place.* Another excellent example can be found in Pencak, "The Civil War Did Not Take Place."
60. Jung, "Nietzsche's Zarathustra," 442.
61. Jung, *Jung on Alchemy*, 194.
62. See Carse, *Finite and Infinite Games.*
63. Oliver, *Family Values*, 232.
64. Oliver, *Family Values,* 232.

Chapter Nine

The Flesh of Human Communicative Embodiment and the Game of Intimacy

GLORIOUS EXPERIENCE AND RISK

It has been two decades since I smoked my last cigarette. Long before I quit I fully understood the extent to which I was putting my health and the quality of my life in serious jeopardy. I was more than sufficiently informed of these risks even before I started smoking at age seventeen. I also have no doubt that *the risk*, the stroll into darkness, the dangling of oneself over the abyss, was all part of the attraction. The association of smoking with black and white danger as well as with black and white glamour and noir sophistication became my semiotic hook into a world of people whose perspectives on life were, in my mind, wider and more intrepid than the prudent yet neurotic stance of the normal and everyday. I felt as though I shared with other smokers the treasured secret that *we did not need to be safe all of the time*.

My simple faith in the existence of that secret led me to a feeling of mysterious confidence with other smokers. As I imagined it, we were all willing to die, at least a little bit, in order to live more completely. To say that I am "romanticizing" the reality of a known carcinogen and, in so many other ways, a pathetic and unfortunate addiction in itself is, I think, missing the point. Even now, the discursive and embodied gesture of smoking reveals, perhaps, the essence of what it means for an anxious subject to overcode the meaning of her or his worried, despairing, apprehensive, often frenzied existence. It likely does not cross the threshold of romance, but it may lie at the heart of romanticization. It is impossible to countenance a day, even long, long before the conclusions of the 1964 Surgeon General's Report, during which sensible people looked at the habit of cigarette consumption and remarked to themselves: "that surely seems like a smart and healthy choice for a person to make." It seems as silly as imagining the likelihood of a consensus affirming that eating excessive amounts of candy to be good for a child's development.

The embrace of any taboo entails the psychology of an anxious subjectivity in search of selfhood. It is no different than tattooing or ritual scarring: what one undertakes does not advance the cause of one's organic embodiment, at least taken from a physiological or medical perspective. Ostensibly, it does a body no good at all, deadening, perhaps toxifying one's skin or sensitive, perhaps delicate tissue with fire or chemicals. It may well be said that the inner experience of decadence is a sacrifice *of* the body *for* the flesh—a sacrifice of longevity and organic strength for what Merleau-Ponty terms *chiasm*. Here, decadence enlivens the flesh. It enables a modality of communication and, hence, of social embodiment, that lights psychological vistas for the possibilities of agency and experience.

As such, smoking cigarettes even years after I had experienced a few episodes of coughing and shortness of breath placed me at tremendous risk for numerous respiratory and circulatory ailments but, at the very least, it put me in league with other smokers. Now, of this one broad social category, I did not seek communion with the whole. Cigarette smoking, like eating, is a mannered activity. We all eat, but the social event of eating does not make us all the same. Consuming food together, we observe, in the manners of the table, the style of selfhood that each of us brings to the occasion. How quickly do we finish what is cooked? Are we masticating each mouthful with a pattern that enables the appreciation of subtle flavors, and are our palates even sufficiently cultivated to recognize such differences? Are we embracing or avoiding contact with unfamiliar, perhaps daunting, specimens, shapes, flavors, and culinary combinations?

Smoking is, of course, similarly mannered—and, during the time in which I smoked, my reading of its codes was a function of my perception of the historical context in which smoking seemed to possess a semiotic passage to a world of cosmopolitan decadence. This passage is not a function of a single sign (i.e., the cigarette) but of an interstitial symbolic amalgam that enables the motility of imagination into the plasma of reverie. For me at age thirty-six, one full year before I successfully quit, each cigarette, now that I look back on it, was a hopeful embodiment of the social milieu and dramatic gesture of a European salon or a New York City café. Georges Bataille provides on-point commentary to the subject under discussion: "In one way or another, something is always missing from the communion sought by humans, driven by the feeling that solitude is impotence itself. We must risk our lives: this implies entering into a movement connecting ourselves to other humans who are similar to ourselves. This is absolutely necessary for the life of the flesh." Bataille frames this particular insight on human communion in terms of what he identifies as a "concern for glory." "In my view," he writes, "the concern for glory is conveyed in the form of energy spent toward no other end than the pursuit of glory."[1]

GLORY AND INTIMACY, SPEAKING AND FREEDOM

Glory, as I interpret it, is an in*tra*personal and, to some extent, narcissistic event of ecstasy. Yet my argument is that it is, in itself, anything but a pathology. It is my interpretation that it dwells in the most earthly sense of Nietzsche's "will to power." The concern for glory is fully consonant with what Foucault means by "care of the self." It is the recognition that there is pleasure in living, and that such pleasure is derived in terms of the reverie of the becoming-self. The symbolism of the becoming-self dwells within the embodied memory of the subject just as much as it presents itself as an inarticulate vision of that which awaits our arrival at the vanishing point of the horizon. We can find an earthly glory in a dish of ice cream consumed during a stolen moment of a hectic day just as much as we can experience another kind of glory, not earthly but *worldly*—a *triumph* in this case—in the accomplishment of a difficult task during that same day. There is a bit of worldly glory, again a triumph, in finding a twenty-dollar bill on the pavement of an empty street just as we can experience a more earthly glory in purchasing an article of clothing that makes us feel more attractive, perhaps sexy—and there is once more a worldly victory in discovering the item to be on sale. Bataille defines the concept of glory, this earthly glory, almost in so many words, as "the negation of the avaricious isolation of the individual."[2]

Bataille seeks to demonstrate "that the search for glory . . . is the means by which communication occurs between [human beings]."[3] He then offers an illustration with particular regard to smoking: "It seems certain to me that tobacco, even smoked in solitude, is a connection between [persons]."[4] In a similar sense, when we talk to ourselves, we depend upon the same language we use when we talk with others. Our selfhood is never achieved alone. Bataille then maintains that the "consumption of tobacco [i]s a purely glorious expenditure, having for its goal to procure for the smoker an atmosphere detached from the general mechanics of things."[5] He continues:

> When smoking, the human mind not only surrenders itself to a squandering that is indefensible according to sound reason: it is, above all, a squandering deprived of meaning, deprived of any knowledge of itself; such deprivations allow absence to reappear. . . . Insofar as we are absorbed in smoking we escape ourselves, we slip into a semiabsence, and if it is true that a concern for elegance is always connected to waste, smoking is elegance, is silence itself."[6]

Bataille's concept of "the communion," illustrated by his reflections on smoking, is central to a discussion of what is entailed by intimacy. The existential psychology of intimate communication does not reveal a phenomenology of "warm, human relations" as an end in itself. From infancy onward, we seek separateness, albeit cautiously, as much as we desire a stable and secure base of attachment.

Bataille's concern for ecstasy and glory is a strategy of sensing and feeling the whole person.[7] Communion is not an account of self-negating sacrifice. Even the Holy Communion of the Catholic Church entails, at its core, an act of self-enhancement. For its completion there is not simply Christ's *giving* of his being, his body and his blood, but "our" *taking*. Each person feasts. In church, the share is meager (obviously inadequate to sustain any sort of life) but it is mythically a reenactment of The Last Supper. The last supper, any last supper, is a glorious feast, even for the guilty and condemned. Culturally, it can be seen as an interstitial glory: the last supper for our profane being, the first supper for our being as sacred, the last supper for our being as social bodies, as subjects and objects, the first supper for our life as flesh. The concept of communion is at once the concept of a glorious intimacy—of a possibility for sensing the depth of our being with all others, all others living and dead, dead and years away from being borne into life. It seems to me that quite a bit of meaning is left to hang on this ostensibly negligible serving of wafer and wine, and it is no mystery to me that the modern Christian laity seems to have so little understanding of what it is that they *might* truly be invited to become.

Michel Foucault comments: "In Christianity, asceticism always refers to a certain renunciation of the self and of reality because most of the time your self is a part of that reality you have to renounce in order to get access to another level of reality. . . . In the philosophical tradition dominated by Stoicism, *askēsis* means not renunciation but the progressive consideration of self, or mastery over oneself, obtained not through the renunciation of reality but through the acquisition and assimilation of truth."[8] Foucault's comments pertain immediately to the project he undertook in the closing years of his life. And, yes, it entailed a "history" of human sexuality, but it was really much more than what those words seem to imply. It was a careful study of a hidden archive and a set of strategic possibilities for "better" living—or perhaps I should say: *more glorious* living.

It is no accident, then, that Foucault's study of sexuality overlaps his lectures and writings on *parrhesia*—in other words, the expressive moment in which truth is spoken to power. *Parrhesia*—which Foucault himself has translated into English as "fearless speech"[9]—entails a practice of freedom much more than it entails a *connaissance* of words and things. Foucault notes that "in Christianity, achieving salvation is also a caring for self. But in Christianity, salvation is attained by renunciation of self."[10] Because sexuality emerged from the beginning as an intractable problem for the psychology of shepherding entailed by the early Christian evangelists, it became a matter of fascination for Foucault, especially given his instincts as a Nietzschean philosopher. David Halperin is, I believe, enormously convincing in his argument for the manner in which Foucault *can* be considered (at least poetically) a "gay saint,"[11] but Foucault's overarching project *clearly transcends* the matter of sexuality as a set of embodied practices in and of themselves, not to mention his own status as a gay man. The problem of sexuality, regardless of whether one is in the mind of the church, the state, or the individual person, has never *really* and *fully* been about the problem of bodies as objects, their relative nakedness, their cleanliness, their orgasms, their pleasures—in other words, all of that stuff "scandalously" reported by Kinsey through the second half of the twentieth century. The question, instead, is one of Selfhood. For, Foucault, as well as for the church and the state, the problem of sexuality boils down to four separate yet fully interrelated matters: language, speech, discourse, and truth. Each of these matters emerges fairly early on in Foucault's philosophical journey, and together they are analytically considered (and charted) as critical elements in the quadrilateral of language he outlines in *The Order of Things.*[12]

Sexuality can be read as residing at the core of our embodiment not because it has ever succeeded in telling the truth of our embodied *savoir*, nor because the ecstasies of erotic pleasure, orgasmic, tantric, whatever, are holy truths in themselves. No, what the problematic of sexuality entails, instead, is the *communicological* thematic of intimacy. There is no doubt that the human hunger for intimacy is deeper and more complex than the human hunger for sexuality. The Western religious instinct to see this matter as a disjunctive, either-or choice has been a disaster for humanity on so many levels that there is no point of even articulating just one. That one desire might, from time to time, be stronger and more pervasive should not eclipse the significance of the other, especially when the two are so powerfully related. Nonetheless, our attachment longings begin in infancy, and they continue throughout our life, especially as the truths revealed during our mortal transformations compel us to find a means, yet again, to cling to one another.

INTIMACY AND SEXUALITY

The notions of intimacy and sexuality, of course, have quite a bit in common. They are both active elements of "love" and "loving," regardless of whether we are speaking from a Western or Eastern cultural perspective. Yet neither of these terms, intimacy nor sexuality, satisfies what is meant by the concept of love. In the case of intimacy, it can best be said that its variation from "love" is a matter of the difference between space and time. Intimacy, generally, is strategy of space while love is a psychological condition of temporality; it is inner and reflective. Intimacy entails a strategy of unveiling and disclosure, connection and relationship, nearness and intersubjective immediacy. For Bataille, "the sense of shame we feel in our nakedness is the beginning of communication and crystallizes the urge of love."[13] Taking off our clothes, unveiling, revealing, making visible our earthly condition to an Other, our animal capabilities and unmediated emotionality is, thus, a serious and ceremonious act, even when it is playful. Then, once we become intimately familiar with others, it is quite possible to hardly notice one another in stages of undress. It is not that the "shock" has worn off—whatever that might mean—it is that the game has changed and the act as a deployment of a strategy does not mean what it once did.

Love can be glorious, but it is not synonymous with Bataille's concept of glory. At a minimum, it can be said that "love" is a semantic entity of insufficient definition in the West. And, it seems quite reasonable to anticipate that any effort to introduce a table of specifications into either the academic, the theological, or the common discourse will be met with resistance; it is a culturally unachievable feat whatever its merits might be. As a consequence, what we mean when we say "love" is *precisely* this *imprecision.* The hesitation in sincerely expressing, "I love you," to an intimate is based upon the reality that an infinite field of possibilities are called into play when one says it.

Consequently, throughout the West to love is to love without conditions, whether implied or articulated. Again, what I am describing inheres in the lexical nature of the word itself. Now, the notion that lived-reality *"conditions"* all of our conscious intentionalities have little bearing on the modern Western act of declaring one's love. It can be reasonably inferred, thus, that the concept of love and loving is, in the West, built less upon a myth of romance and spiritual fulfillment than upon a myth of heroic sentiment. Understood in this sense, love becomes analogous to patriotism: we gallantly promise to do the *impossible* and the *inexpressible* for our beloved. And so, finally, when a situation demands more than we can ably perform or imagine, we are all too inclined to give up our freedom, to give up our dignity, to give up our dreams, and to give up our lives.

Many marriages all too commonly emerge out of a comparable reality: the partners choose an illusion of the impossible because they have exhausted what they think remains of the other possibilities. They have, in effect, run out of moves in the games they had been playing up to that point.[14] To put it even more cynically, such a decision to marry requires *romanticizing* the drought of interpersonal vision and imagination. Such a "heroic" sense of love and loving, it might be said, initiates a kind of suicide pact. We kill ourselves, just as we kill others: out of intense feelings that find no desirable prospects of choice, chance, and embodiment. As such, the heroic formula emerges as a disjunctive paradigm of choice: either victory or death; either glory or nothingness.

INTIMACY, STRATEGY, AND SELF

Intimacy is a strategy—which is to say, a process coupled with an intentionality; it is a process of psychological transition and embodied motility. Because the transition is experienced retrospectively and through sideways and backward glimpses of difference, the motility of our moving intersubjectively closer and deeper in our sense of connectedness can be talked about as occurring in stages. Though such stages cannot be said to exist as matters of intersubjective consciousness, they persist in memory as moments of experience and growth. It is common in both in the East and the West to speak of these moments as affairs of physical contact and of the verbal interpenetration of psychological gestalts. We speak of when we first held hands, our first kiss, our first night together; we fully recall extraordinary and unanticipated compliments as well as expressions of gratitude and commitment.

In narratives of past intimacies we can address both the moments and the *motifs* when "everything changed," when it became clear that there was no going back. Yet, the motility of such an increasingly detailed intertwining and interlacing is preconscious; it is always-already a function of a broader gesture of psychological attachment and personal recognition. As Merleau-Ponty remarks in *Phenomenology of Perception*, "there is in human existence a principle of indeterminacy."[15]

The motility of our movement through the flesh of intimacy underscores what may well stand as the first lesson of Merleau-Ponty's philosophy: that our being-in-the-world is inescapably one of ambiguity. As "knowing" beings, we are imperfect, insufficient, incomplete. Gary Madison helpfully observes that "existence is not a factual state of affairs, and 'man' [or 'woman'] is not a 'substance,' a sort of super-thing, an animal endowed with a soul. Existence is an *act*."[16] The *phatic communion* of intimacy places the equivocal act of our being in the context of an Other's expressive gesture. Together, our mutual recognition enables a feeling, a feeling about our relational and intersubjective experience that transforms the "equi-vocality" of our expression into a perceptual ambiguity having a certain character and emotional quality. If you tell me that I look beautiful, I may wonder "*how* beautiful?" or perhaps question what you mean by the word "beautiful," but I will probably feel good nonetheless. Thus, it can be said that the motility of interpersonal intimacy describes our desire to confirm, to verify, to bear out the meaning of my body's presence in your eyes.

My intimate engagements with Others—especially with *you*—are essential to my strategy of "self-care." You constitute the only meaning I have of my Self. On the broad question of what he has intended through his work, Foucault comments: "The main interest in life and work is to become someone else that you were not in the beginning. . . . What is true for writing and for a love relationship is true also for life. The game is worthwhile insofar as we don't know what will be the end."[17] So, it is essential to the experience and the enjoyment of interpersonal intimacy that I never quite know who you are. It is essential that you remain mysterious. It is in your mystery that I can appreciate and begin to size up the shadows of my own unconscious world.

What I have just described represents the central problematic of intimacy understood from an existential-psychological point of view. Intimacy represents our need for attachment and our desire to be recognized and affirmed, but it necessitates that we tolerate ambiguities in our perceptions and interpretations of what we experience, and it requires that we admit to the equivocations inherent in our own expressions and statements of who we are and what we mean. Our embodiment of any motility of intimacy becomes the crucible for addressing our deepest anxieties both toward ourselves and toward others—phenomenologically there is no difference.

Children are no less anxious than adults in this respect, but they are blessed with far fewer questions of identity. Group identity is a dominant theme for children in their individual manners of mastering experiences.[18] Whatever children *do* needs to be understood by them as fully sufficient to belong to any group with whom they seek attachment, making the development of friendships with other children very much a feature of comparing and supporting one another's competencies, as well as forgiving one another's limitations. If adult affirmation of group activities is not operative, it makes perfect sense for them to form groups—or gangs—on their own.

SELF, SELF-CARE, AND SEXUALITY

As we get older, matters of identity entail greater agency of self-regulation. We choose which groups will function as vehicles of our social and cultural identity, and we choose the extent to which and the manner in which our commitment will define our styles of social embodiment. Yet, making friends is harder when we grow older. Even if we are not philosophers or psychotherapists we have at least a subtle awareness of the ambiguity and equivocation embedded in our communicative relations with others. We know, at least generally, what feelings and emotions are not fully represented in what we speak, and it seems more than reasonable to suspect that others hold meaningful aspects of themselves in reserve as well.

This is why I began this discussion of intimacy and sexuality with a discourse on smoking. My participation in a ritual concern for glory placed me in communion with other smokers, especially those with quiet fantasies of becoming, perhaps, Parisian. It placed me at a distance appropriate to my level of satisfaction from those who hold the taboo of smoking in particular sorts of regard. It may even be said that my participation in this ritual of glory, however taboo, was a sort of "gang" behavior. It was my way of addressing an ongoing experience of social anxiety tied to unconscious and still-active feelings of inferiority and role confusion. My choice to smoke was a concern for glory in pursuit of what Foucault terms "self-care," and my choice to quit was an embodiment of self-caring understood from a transformed sense of worldly being.

Foucault argues: "We find it difficult to base rigorous morality and austere principles on the precept that we should give ourselves more care than anything else in the world. We are more inclined to see taking care of ourselves as an immorality, as a means of escape from all possible rules. . . . 'Know thyself' has obscured 'Take care of yourself' because our morality . . . insists that the self is that which one can reject."[19] As such, my own transformed sense of myself as a nonsmoker—a sense that was given in the eyes of a new and powerful intimate interpersonal relationship—required that I refuse the self of "old glory." Nonetheless, the capacity of consciousness to shed the system of embodiment constitutive of a surpassed self should not authorize a strategy of self-abnegation.

After the passage from a pagan thematic of self-development and pleasure into a Christian thematic of self-renunciation and asceticism, the concept of sexuality began to emerge as a locus of glory in and of itself. Rules of austerity and proscriptions of shameful practices had begun to emerge even by the time of the Stoic thinkers. It was not Christianity in itself that planted the first seeds of anxiety and fear into the manners of how we are ethically constituted through our social and intimate relations with others. But it was on the whole through this period of the first several centuries of the Christian order that a powerful paradox of sexuality as a cultural practice began to come into view.[20] The Christian interdictions that succeeded in subduing erotic selfhood also succeeded in making sexual relations wild and naughty—and glorious.

In general, sexuality, of course, could not be avoided, despite the preachments, proscriptions, and interdictions enunciated by the church and state. What changed was how it became featured in language and discourse. The embodiment of the act itself, especially that between a husband and a wife, found itself situated in a language of moral metaphor—that is, as idealized temporalities of dreams and symbols. Foucault sees this moral objective being played out over an expanse of time through a broad strategy of converting and shepherding people into a vision of themselves *as* religious images—the insistence upon the (mythic and, hence, presumed) celibacy of Jesus being no doubt important in sustaining an attitude of piety in the inarticulate performance of erotic acts among members of a flock.[21]

Because sex was deprived, during this period, of a *language* which could be learned and mastered, the Christian head of a household—in other words, the master of his own domain and the leader of his own genealogical flock—turned *inward*. Foucault maintains, "Problematization and apprehension go hand in hand; inquiry is joined to vigilance."[22] He further argues: "[I]n these modifications of preexisting themes one can see the development of an art of existence dominated by self-preoccupation. This art of the self no longer focuses so much in the excesses one can indulge in and that need to be mastered in order to exercise one's domination over others. It gives increasing emphasis to the frailty of the individual faced with the manifold ills that sexual activity can give rise to."[23]

John Rajchman argues that the intent of Foucault's analysis can most effectively be grasped

> in contrast to the displacements Christianity would introduce. In Christianity, what one would be asked to attain is no longer the proud virility of the master; it is an inner purity of being. . . . And it is thus that we find the dietary, medical, poetic, and erotic means the ancients devised to maintain a noble self-possession are replaced by the endless and arduous task of deciphering one's inner thoughts: the temptations, the seductions, the deceptions that the devil has put in our heads. Christianity thus would be the start of the internalization of eros. . . . Now, this internalization of a problematic of love, eros, sexuality, one's body, and the urge toward others in therapies of communion, friendship, society, and identity virtually guarantees a reflective process of obsessive rumination—that is, unless, one commits oneself, consciously or otherwise, to a discipline of spiritual guidance.[24]

So, in a movement of *logos* that culminates in the work of Augustine, the art of the self gives way, over the course of roughly half a millennium, to the order of the confessional. Here Rajchman is inclined to frame a classical problematic in the form of a modern epistemic question: "When did people start to assume that what is most questionable, or potentially most glorious or heroic about themselves as erotic beings, were not the occasions and distinctive pleasures of their activities but the 'truth' of the fantasies wishes and thoughts locked deep within the recesses of their minds or souls?"[25] Rajchman then sharpens his focus upon the epistemic origins of psychoanalysis: "How, in short, had people been brought to believe that a terrible truth about their sex resided in some inaccessible or blocked portion of their psyches . . . ?"[26]

Again, the problem of sex is a problematic of language. It is a problematic of language in that sexuality became the subject of discourses rather than an embodied modality of liberation—of experiential freedom, of self-mastery and transformation through relational intimacy, of joyful glory. The order of the confessional is a *dispositif* of guilt and shame. The movement toward greater intimacy in cherished interpersonal relationships—relationships that can rightly be called sacred—shares with intimate sexual communication the reality that the experience is ultimately a matter of boundaries. The notion of personal and relational boundaries has been a central feature of psychological thought, both clinically and academically, for much of the last century. Irrespective of whatever discourse on boundaries one wishes to invoke, Foucault's basic position seems quite inescapable: the perception of boundaries between one human being and another simultaneously invokes questions of power and knowledge.

PARRHESIA AND SELF-CARE

For Foucault, questions of power and knowledge must be pursued in ways that resist what he terms—in the first volume of *The History of Sexuality*—the "repressive hypothesis."[27] They are questions concerning knowledge, mastery, and discipline. His general philosophical position is Nietzschean, but it takes its lead, interestingly enough, from Socrates. It is here that the matter of *parrhesia*, to which I alluded earlier, takes on particular relevance. For Foucault, the target of the form of *parrhesia* of particular interest to him "is not to persuade the Assembly, but to convince someone that he must take care of himself and of others and this means he must *change his life*."[28] For Foucault, this aspect of *parrhesia* can and ought to be tied to the matter of friendship—thus becoming a duty of interpersonal intimacy.

The system of social relations that can be seen as producing bodies having certain interests and capabilities, as having a certain mannered approach to things and a preferred style of expressive embodiment is seen by Foucault as operating with the logic of a game. For a number of years I questioned this formulation, given that I could only see the logic of games as operating within a performative, economic, manipulative, perhaps inauthentic sphere of intentional consciousness.[29] When we are speaking truthfully and openly with one another, I maintained, we are operating outside of the strategy of social order. My mind immediately flashed to the circle of cigarette smokers of which I was a part, regularly exempting ourselves from the order of expected cultural practices—for instance, catching a cigarette between classes, stepping outside of the cocktail party to get some "fresh air" with other smokers, to experience some glory on our own terms. When we are speaking truthfully, I maintained, we are not "gaming" one another.

Foucault's perspective, on the other hand, is remarkably compelling, enabling a system of thought absolutely fundamental to a *communicology* of human relations. Foucault remarks: "The analyses I have been trying to make have to do essentially with the relationships of power. I understand by that something other than the states of domination. The relationships of power have an extremely wide extension in human relations. There is a whole network of relationships of power, which can operate between individuals, in the bosom of the family, in an educational relationship, in the political body, etc."[30] The notion of the game, in this context, operates as a matter of syntagmatic connection and paratactic implication. The rules of the game, simply, are mutually known discursive contexts and conditions. Despite the seemingly sacred connotations of "dialogue" and "intimacy" it must be emphasized that *in the absence of a game logic* and some sort of knowledge of the constitutive and regulative rules of play, *we* cannot have a conversation of any sort.

The outcome of the game, then, is immediately tied to the self-care of the player. What the player chances is the possibility of experiencing power, pleasure, glory, and triumph. What is at stake is the condition of the Self as body and as object. For Foucault, as for Nietzsche, what is at stake is *mastery.* In his lectures on *parrhesia,* Foucault finds a useful connection to the Platonic dialogues *Alcibiades* and *Laches.*[31] Both of these dialogues concern the question of *ethos.* Foucault notes: "[In the ancient world] One's *ethos* was seen by his dress, by his bearing, by his gait, by the poise with which he reacts to events, etc. . . . The [person] who has a good *ethos,* who can be admitted and held up as an example, he [or she] is a person who practices freedom in a certain manner."[32] In other words, she or he shows evidence of discipline, she or he embodies her or his world artistically; in other words, she or he exhibits *mastery.*

Foucault continues: "I don't think that one can say that the Greek who cares for himself should first of all care for others. . . . One must not have the care for others precede the care for self. The care for self takes moral precedence in the measure that the relationship to self takes ontological precedence."[33] Now mastery, with its deep connection to *parrhesia* and power, is to be defined relationally. Foucault, reflecting again on Greek culture, defines it as "nonslavery." He remarks: " . . . [this definition] is political in the measure that non-slavery with respect to others is a condition: a slave has no ethics."[34] Although this language might seem daunting and turgid, it is easily unpacked. Foucault is speaking of the Greeks symbolically. What he is arguing is that a person who has not mastered the art and discipline of selfhood and self-care is still a "slave," a servant to orders of power and psychological manipulation. Simply, such a person is psychologically set up to be "gamed." So, in saying that a person without sufficient social and psychological agency is without *ethics,* Foucault is, in effect, maintaining that such a person does not truly have a *Self.* In the twenty-first century, one's *ethos* is *still* seen by one's dress, by one's bearing, by one's gait, by gestural grace, by the poise with which one reacts to challenges and events. As such, a person without sufficient social and psychological agency is lacking in embodiment. The truth-teller, the *parrhesiast,* must speak masterfully; he or she must express the world *as* her or his body, and must have courage to open its earthly awareness, its fleshly consciousness, to the flesh of the other. And it should also go without saying that without a body it is very difficult to have sex.

IDENTITY, SEXUALITY, DIFFERENTIATION, AND PSYCHOLOGICAL BOUNDARIES

It is precisely at this juncture that I wish to speak of an incredibly strong and important connection of Foucault's historical and philosophical argument concerning the problem of agency and the discipline of power to the theory of human sexual psychology advanced by David Schnarch.[35] Schnarch's theory of sexuality, drawn extensively from the family systems theory of Murray Bowen,[36] can very much be seen as a philosophy of self-care and of psychological mastery of embodiment. Instead of the words discipline, mastery, *ethos*, and self-care, Schnarch prefers the term *differentiation*. Now it must be said at the outset that Schnarch is a professional psychotherapist, not an academic philosopher. His writing is carefully argued and intellectually adroit, but he is not interested in advancing or defending an epistemological perspective or research paradigm. Though his most recent works have been geared somewhat toward a less academic audience, his most significant achievement, *Constructing the Sexual Crucible,*[37] stands as a serious work of critical scholarship. It is widely considered to be the most important work on this subject matter published in the last half-century.

Unlike Foucault, whose interest in writing about sexuality is principally philosophical, historical, and political, Schnarch, as a psychotherapist, is directly invested in improving marriages, improving people's sexual lives and in treating sexual disorders. Like Foucault, Schnarch is concerned with the flood of discourses that have emerged over the course of the last century, most of which have subsumed the topic of sexuality under a medical model of human embodiment and which have, as well, continued the Christian pastoral of selfhood and embodiment, of the internalization of eros and the nervous anxiety of our practices of intimate yet incomprehensible erotic coupling. Schnarch is well aware that people are shamed and embarrassed by the empirical fact of their bodies and their sexuality. As such, I read his perspective on Bowen's concept of differentiation as being at the cornerstone of our experience of meaningful sexual relations.

So, we may ask, what exactly is differentiation for Schnarch and what is its relation to intimacy? Neither Schnarch nor Bowen are phenomenologists but they would wholeheartedly affirm Merleau-Ponty's observation that we are inextricably "tangled" in the world.[38] The Gordian Knot of our beginnings, psychologically speaking, is the family. Schnarch writes: "family values and history are encoded, like a rich metaphor, in the child's *eroticism*. . . . [E]roticism (as reflected in inclusions and exclusions in sexual repertoire) displays one's personal, marital, and familial history."[39] Our initial entanglement is emotional. Our expressive, prehensile, and movement capabilities, limited as they are through our early childhood, leave us physiologically and psychologically dependent upon our families of origin. Expressions of libido and expressions of need, virtually indistinguishable from one another until the young and evolving person has begun to establish levels of communicative competency, are the *lingua franca* of childhood reality.

It is not that we are born fused to our family's emotional network, but our emotional connections are nonetheless quite powerful and, importantly, as children, they are all that we have got. It is, thus, an infantile wish to relive this level of nested, emotional connectedness in adult intimate relationships. Interestingly, we affirm this preconscious desire in the discourse of popular culture. We tell each other that we want to be one another's "baby." Such expressions are not *necessarily* pathologically symptomatic inasmuch as the silent language of eroticism inescapably seems to entail a journey into the electric arms of a mysterious providence. What seems the whole of our *earthly* being, our *ur*-humanity released through our flesh as through the other's flesh, our animality *mastered* and yet unleashed—recentering and transfiguring everything that we thought possible in human encounter—entails a spiritual surrender. And I think there ought to be no shame in living as innocents before it as we discover this power in the face of our objects of desire. We cradle one another. We rock one another. The expressiveness of kissing naturally takes on qualities of nursing and oral play. Tickling and teasing, ostensibly such instinctive games of childhood, become adult speech acts testing and pushing the limits of one's self-definition.

The desire becomes infantile, according to Schnarch, when what we seek is a symbiotic fusion, particularly when we seek to be the other's "one and only."[40] What eventually happens in such cases is that the desires of the one become engulfed in the needs of the other. The risk of parenting one another as our intimacies embed our interpersonal relations in more tightly woven fabrics of connectedness is, then, offset by learning to recognize and acknowledge the importance of personal boundaries.

Boundaries, as I read them semiotically, are not discourse (*discours*) or language (*langue*) phenomena. They are, instead, functions of *parole*. More specifically, they are functions of what Foucault has termed *parrhesia*. There are no "unspoken" rules of intimacy. Simply, we "speak" ourselves into and out of interpersonal binds. Some of the binds are experienced as bonds that we wish to honor and sustain; some of them are traps and dilemmas, what Gregory Bateson came to term "double-binds." Some of the bonds are invisible to conscious experience. Whatever the case, it is *parole* that brings the relations into being. As such, *parrhesia,* more than anything, refers to the capacity to articulate oneself in such a way that one's body sets its own limits.

Again, Foucault carefully describes his concept of freedom as *nonslavery*—as psychological independence from emotional encroachments upon our field of expressive activity. As children we give up ground to others all the time. Our first concept of justice is one of fair play and, on that basis, we will willingly concede ground to further the agency of our selfhood within our families of origin. This is also to say that we learn the art of politics at a very young age. The family is, inescapably, a hegemonic system of psychological development. Our democratic impulses and our trust in games of self-definition are cultivated and encouraged in social relations with siblings, cousins, and relationships outside of the family. The extent to which one's sense of self can be embodied with confidence and security thus emerges as a function of the extent to which the flesh that one embodies in the bosom of one's family is sufficiently recognized and valued (and energized) in the play of social relations—and vice versa. Good-enough parents, as Winnicott would phrase it, pay meaningful attention to the self-formation arising from the play of their children.[41] A sufficiently secure and well-grounded parent can allow her- or himself to rethink a child's embodied selfhood on the basis of observing the child's relation with others.

The child ventures out, experiments with whomever he or she dreams of becoming, and then these fictions of inhabited being—upon affirmation by the hegemonic symbolic psychological order of the family—enable a field of possibilities for living one's life in the morning, the twilight, and the dark of tomorrow. We see this pattern repeated when young adults head off to college and experiment with so many aspects of their ritual embodiment, not the least of which actually entails selecting a major course of study for their life's work. As they define themselves sexually during this period, they have, as a whole, relatively little life experience outside of their families on which to establish a grounded definition of self for such intense, arousing, perhaps terrifying "intimate glories" as can be found in the exploration of their own primal, feral sexuality.

The capacity to manage their selfhood through the tangle of *both* intimate and intense friendships *and* emotionally responsive sexual contact does not happen overnight. Simply, it takes time. It takes time to embody an honest selfhood into a healthy living fiction of power and will. It takes time to embody a socially viable *ethos*. For the Greeks, as Foucault emphasized through his final works, learning to do so was an art guided by discipline, a disciplinary institute of apprentice and master, of student and teacher. Schnarch makes clear that the passage into relationships of sustained intimacy necessitates a differentiated and mature self. He draws upon Erikson to argue: "An individual is available for an intimate relationship only after he or she has achieved a core sense of identity."[42] Working directly from Bowen's family systems theory, he similarly maintains: "'Know thyself' is the first step for those aspiring to attain intimacy."[43] Know thyself, take care of yourself, take care of yourself as though you are the most important person in the world. The achievement of identity entails the overcoming of confusion regarding one's self in social relations, yet the test of identity emerges in the capacity of *Geist* to sustain itself—its integrity and its *savoir*—when the visible limit of its boundaries are called into question by the voice of the other and then lost in the play of light and shadow.

CONCLUSION: COMMUNION, ECSTASY, AND THE DREAM OF THE IMPOSSIBLE

This daunting psychological task, what Erikson terms the *crisis* of identity, emerges in adolescence.[44] Of course, it was in adolescence that I began smoking. Not knowing who I was, I let images of Sartre, Bogart, James Dean, Bob Dylan, and Keith Richards guide my social body forward. It was quite easy, really. Smoking, during the time at which I took up the habit, was a publicly permitted, culturally tolerated, medium of self-expression and personal pleasure. It was a symbolic form of communion that enabled conversation, perhaps even in itself a mild political statement, and that equipped insecure young persons like me with a ready-made social gesture and theatrical prop. Sexuality remains metonymically and metaphorically linked to cigarette smoking in the still-breathing archive of twentieth century discourse, although smoking is now far less visible than it was in my youth. Talk of sexuality is considerably less taboo, yet both still continue to share a common symbolism of danger.

Sexual communion, despite the blurring of social inhibitions and the pervasiveness of sexual images, texts, and subtexts in advertising and popular culture, is still a journey along an unlit path. It is a journey our bodies begin in adolescence even if consciousness, for whatever reason, resists. Even if consciousness is wide-awake during this period, Schnarch has cautioned: "When we believe that adolescence is the time of sexual peaking, we are indirectly espousing sex between strangers."[45] Our knowledge of what is happening when intimacy takes on sexual dimensions is tenuous; semiotic correspondence with past experience is as much a limiting function as it is a source of guidance. We cannot begin to understand our body's sexuality until we have experienced our body's sexuality. It certainly is not a knowledge we can gain, simply, by hanging out and watching others. Schnarch insists that sex, as we have come to value it, is not "a natural function—at least not intimate sex. Intimate sex is a natural potential that requires development for its fulfillment. No other species on Earth requires as much time to reach full sexual maturity."[46] This dimension of intimate communion is, if we let ourselves grow through it, a means to a greater contact with all that resides in the dark of our subjectivity.

Writing off, perhaps papering over, this shadow element of our earthly, and earthy, interconnection through the persistence of a language that embeds its shamefulness—and quietly reminds us of our guilt in choosing to peek behind the curtains—leaves us tongue-tied. Literally, "tongue"-*tied*:

communicatively knotted within ourselves and within our social and cultural bodies, anxious, embarrassed, and speechless. Once more, we talk ourselves into and out of interpersonal binds. *Parole* is not *discours* but our speaking nonetheless puts us, knowingly and unknowingly, into games that may well place everything about us at risk—for better or for worse, for richer or for poorer, in sickness and in health. The risk is not, in itself, a problem. Again, we don't need to be safe all the time. As well, the "binds" (or relationships) are certainly not in themselves problematic—especially inasmuch as we exit the womb aching for connection.

The important thing is that *parole* can never control the relationship. *Parole* gives evidence of *discours* as a token to a type, never becoming a "rule" of the game while the game is in play. *Parrhesia*, as a *techné* of *parole* and a *techné* of mastery, serves as an exercise of agency to the extent that it gives light to the simultaneity of *other games*. It is *parrhesia* that unfetters us, enabling us to weave and braid our Selves into the *chiasmus* of multiple communicative potentialities and imaginaries—and thus into being, yet again, as Selves. By itself, sexuality, as Foucault himself confessed in one of his interviews with Dreyfus and Rabinow, "is boring."[47] The guilt, even the ostensive vulgarity and decadence of sexuality—or any other earthly glory—dissolves into interest and curiosity once we mature into a feeling for its vital participation in the relationships, interactions, and liaisons that animate our most complex experiences of identity and intimacy.

Unspoken rules are the raw materials of double-binds. They have no existence in themselves, of course. Proscription is a verbal act—everything else is a matter of even greater ambiguity. The emotionally debilitating constraint of a double bind entails living through an event (often long in duration) in which the successful expression of one's body is, ironically, well within the person's grasp. The movement, the gesture, the language is "already known" in experience but entirely invisible to consciousness. It is an unspoken rule that inhibits one's freedom—articulated rules always specify how they can be broken. Giving voice and kinetic embodiment to that which had been unspoken alters the disposition of its hold upon us. At least phenomenologically, this is what I take to be the essential pragmatic of talk therapy.

What is experientially glorious about decadence of any sort, at least initially, is its break from the *habitus* of perceived security and safety. Though the two words do not share the same root, it is here that something "prodigious" emerges from "prodigality." The seduction into greater (perhaps even grave) danger becomes a function of whether the experiencer can sense the interconnection and simultaneity of other games beside the one he or she has begun to play. Vice becomes vicious when we have lost perspective on the confluence of narratives contributing to the currency of our identity—when we let ourselves believe that a gesture's significance is limited to a narrow field of games. A smoker addicted to tobacco, a drunk addicted to alcohol begins, it is true, with that first cigarette which produced a mysterious sensation of gratification, with that first night of drinking wherein his or her body was somehow more suffused with warmth and joy than nausea. A sustained memory of exotic pleasure, of glory however brought into being, makes a strong enough impression on consciousness that a newly born image for Self emerges as thematic.

Occluded from sensations and intuition of the possible (forgetting what Bataille terms "concern for the future"), momentarily blind to corporeal mortality and the wholeness—literally, the "health"—of one's being, an inarticulate hunger for such liberation all too often gives way to the sad logic of addiction, and the toxin is sufficiently positioned in consciousness to offer its own particular instruction to the body on what to do next. Nonetheless, ecstasy (*ek-stasis*) is neither reverie nor fantasy, just as it has never been a threshold of failing and corruption. The odyssey of one's Self seeking embodiment on its own terms is, for Bataille, a *spiritual* matter, a matter he is careful to distinguish from "mind" and "intellect," entailing sacrifice, risk, and vice. Noting a powerful isomorphism between communication and the life of humanity, Bataille maintains: "Humans can only 'communicate'—live—outside of themselves, and since they must 'communicate,' they must *want* this evil, this desecration. . . . Thus, all 'communication' *partakes of suicide and crime*. . . . In this light, evil appears as a *life source*! Ruining the integrity of being in myself and in the other, I open myself to communion. . . ."[48]

"Popular morality," Bataille argues, makes an allowance for our taking of risks "only *for a useful cause*."[49] This is the unspoken rule of unbearable anxieties. Our spiritual development, on the other hand—what is, for Bataille and Nietzsche a psychological "midnight ramble"—necessitates our stepping into a fleshly affair with the impossible. This interconnection is not the same as the heroic concept of love; it does not pledge us to perform that which lies beyond our competence and imagination. Instead, it seduces us, if we attend to its call, into a blood union with the impossible—that is, a sense of the impossible that can only come to life in the imagination, an imagination that has never quite belonged to any of us as individuals in the first place.

Reflecting on the spirit of Nietzsche as he started to spiral downward in health, Bataille remarks that he "said no to life while it was easy: but yes when it took the form of the impossible."[50] None of us gets out of this alive. "Health," both physiological and psychological, entails a choice to live as though the Self might truly matter, an existential investment in an impossible fiction whose glory opens up to us at the moment we fully grasp that we cannot escape our own death, a dream whose knotted *logos* is revealed in glimpses through the ecstasies situated in moments of communion. Bataille's gloss of what he takes as Nietzsche's poetic premise in *Zarathustra* also gives language to the reflection (not quite a thought as it first appeared) initially motivating this essay: "To hold, without elusion, life to the standard of the impossible demands a moment of divine friendship."[51] A moment of divine friendship—is this *love*? And what might be meant by "a moment"? As a Westerner, I now feel ill equipped to speak with any feeling of certainty. But what I can say is that it is a moment compelling enough to terminate my addiction to smoking.

NOTES

1. Bataille, *The Unfinished System,* 6.
2. Bataille, *The Unfinished System,* 6.
3. Bataille, *The Unfinished System,* 6.
4. Bataille, *The Unfinished System,* 6.
5. Bataille, *The Unfinished System,* 6.
6. Bataille, *The Unfinished System,* 6.
7. See Bataille, *Erotism*. See also *Inner Experience* and *On Nietzsche.*
8. Foucault, "Technologies of the Self," 35.
9. Foucault, *Fearless Speech.*
10. Foucault, "The Ethic of the Care of the Self as a Practice of Freedom," 5.
11. Halperin, *Saint Foucault.*
12. Foucault, *Order of Things*, 201. See Lanigan, *Human Science of Communicology*, 155–77.
13. Richardson, *Georges Bataille*, 38.
14. See Dym and Glenn, *Couples.* See also Malone and Malone, *The Art of Intimacy.*
15. Merleau-Ponty, *Phenomenology of Perception,* 169.
16. Madison, *Phenomenology of Merleau-Ponty,* 48.
17. Foucault, "Truth, Power, Self: An Interview with Michel Foucault," 9.
18. Erikson, *Childhood and Society*. See also *Identity and the Life Cycle*.
19. Foucault, "Technologies of the Self," 22.
20. Foucault, *Care of the Self.*
21. Foucault, *Use of Pleasure*. See also *Care of the Self.*
22. Foucault, *Care of the Self,* 239.
23. Foucault, *Care of the Self,* 238.
24. Rajchman, *Truth and Eros*, 91.
25. Rajchman, *Truth and Eros*, 89.
26. Rajchman, *Truth and Eros*, 89.
27. Foucault, *History of Sexuality*, Vol. 1.
28. Foucault, *Fearless Speech,* 106.
29. Macke, "Reading the Collaborative Language Systems Approach Phenomenologically."
30. Foucault, "The Ethic of the Care of the Self as a Practice of Freedom," 3.
31. Foucault, *Fearless Speech*. See also Foucault, "The Ethic of the Care of the Self as a Practice of Freedom."
32. Foucault, "The Ethic of the Care of the Self as a Practice of Freedom," 6.
33. Foucault, "The Ethic of the Care of the Self as a Practice of Freedom," 7.
34. Foucault, "The Ethic of the Care of the Self as a Practice of Freedom," 6.
35. Schnarch, *Constructing the Sexual Crucible.*
36. Kerr and Bowen, *Family Evaluation*. See also Bowen, *Family Therapy in Clinical Practice.*
37. Schnarch, *Constructing the Sexual Crucible.*
38. Merleau-Ponty, *Phenomenology of Perception,* 454.
39. Schnarch, *Constructing the Sexual Crucible,* 307.
40. Schnarch, *Constructing the Sexual Crucible,* 206.

41. Winnicott, *The Family and Individual Development*. See also *The Child, the Family, and the Outside World.*
42. Schnarch, *Constructing the Sexual Crucible.* 129.
43. Schnarch, *Constructing the Sexual Crucible.* 129.
44. Erikson, *Identity: Youth and Crisis.*
45. Schnarch, *Passionate Marriage,* 77.
46. Schnarch, *Passionate Marriage,* 79.
47. Dreyfus & Rabinow, *Michel Foucault,* 229.
48. Bataille, *The Unfinished System,* 30.
49. Bataille, *The Unfinished System,* 30.
50. Bataille, *The Unfinished System,* 22.
51. Bataille, *The Unfinished System,* 23.

Chapter Ten

The Dream and the Self

Consciousness, Identity, the Sign, and the Image

THE LINE OF CONSCIOUSNESS

Are you awake? The question is not as odd as it might seem. As I compose these sentences, I am not sure of the precise extent to which *I* am awake. In the act of writing, I enter into a different sort of consciousness from the one that is alive and active when I am speaking, and it is different, again, when I am swimming, at the theatre, talking to a stranger, talking to an old friend, reading a novel, reading a newspaper, reading a work of theory, watching a film, or watching television.

The line of consciousness is an elusive one. Simply, wakefulness and sleep are not the oppositions we ordinarily take them to be. Waking, or being awake, entails a practical awareness of the events occurring in what existential psychiatry has termed *Mitwelt*.[1] When I am not listening to certain elements of my surroundings, which is typically the case when I am writing, I might as well be asleep. As far as the human beings in my environment might be concerned, I may well be better off asleep—at least I might attend to them somewhat rested rather than aggravated. When my *Geist*[2] is elsewhere, I need to be roused to consciousness to take care of people and things that seem to plead for my attention. As Bachelard has maintained, reverie and the embodied scene of consciousness are not separated by any sort of "matter" in experience.[3] What enables their interplay is the experience of the "image."

The dominant discourse on this topic (a discourse which most of the modern world finds most comfortable and familiar) is one that seems to hypothesize some sort of limit condition between moments of perceptual consciousness in the realm of the oneiric and in waking life. There is a line between them—or, rather, our discourse has come to assume some sort of limit or boundary condition. There must be a line between them, yes? No? —How could discourse function without such a line? How such a boundary might be constituted and how we might know it as such remains a highly elusive epistemological matter.

Dreaming, reverie, and the oneiric are inseparable from the work of mind. It is only a habit of culture that persists in the maintenance of the presupposition that the linear progression of consciousness is a defining feature of waking life. It is by way of reverie, of the mind's wandering, that any and all signs can find themselves in connection—and connected in such a way that, upon their seemingly spontaneous manifestation as a statement or an image, they offer sudden (yet, still, somehow, seemingly impossible) visions of utter clarity and continuous occasions for consciousness to be amazed. The boundary condition of the oneiric is not language or logic but the presence of the other and the existential obligation to communicate. Putting my new visions in language with which someone else can think and, perhaps, dream necessitates a commitment to linear thought progression and language that delimits or governs the capacity of consciousness to drift or lose sight of the path to this active, waking, relational connection.

The dream is not a virus. It is not an intrusion upon a more fundamental or valuable mode of conscious activity. The sobriety and pragmatism of thought and speech between persons in dialogue, however, is itself not a fully stable set of boundaries and conditions. In intimacy we often dream together. Bachelard writes: "The reveries of two solitary souls prepare the sweetness of loving. A realist of passion will see nothing there but evanescent formulas. But just the same it is no less true that great passions are prepared by great reveries. The reality of love is mutilated when it is detached from all of its unrealness."[4] Nietzsche reminds us that the psychology of the oneiric consciousness can be collective as well: "The utter clarity of all dream-ideas, which presupposes an unconditional belief in their reality, reminds us once again of the state of earlier mankind in which hallucinations were extraordinarily frequent, and sometimes seized whole communities, whole nations simultaneously. Thus, in our sleep and dreams, we go through the work of earlier mankind once more."[5] Rationality represents "a stricter demand" (as Nietzsche phrases it) upon the work of consciousness, but "even now, our functions of reason and intelligence reach back instinctively to those primitive forms of deductions, and we live more or less half our lives in this state."[6] In the necessary rationalizations of work and power as well as in the pragmatics of human communication we are repeatedly signaled back from the drift of consciousness toward the play of images and the sanctuary of private reflection and fantasy. When we are so summoned and signaled, we are reminded of the everyday-ness of our drift through the interstices of perceptual consciousness. We can with some degree of confidence say in retrospect that such a shift has occurred. As the shift toward reverie is being experienced, however, it is not so easy to say.

As I reflect upon it, the psychological drift (or shift) from one scene of embodied consciousness to another is what I am inclined to call a "continental" matter. On one level, there are two obvious plays on words. My scholarly grounding in what Americans call "Continental" philosophy (and which those on the European continent are inclined to call, after translation, "the human sciences"[7]) makes clear to me that the behaviorist, materialist, pseudo-empiricist conventions of what all too often passes for psychological reflection is deeply insufficient to the task of addressing the problematic of wakefulness and reverie. As well, I am inviting a reflection, perhaps a reverie, on the theory of continental drift put forward in geology—a theory that has undergone significant revisions since it was first put forward in 1596, and which has, only within recent decades, secured a strong evidentiary foothold for its scientific articulation.[8] But it is a theory that, even from the start, has always offered the framework for a fascinating myth of relationship and entropy.

But on yet another level, my claim entails the notion that the shift (or drift) of dreaming and reverie from "ordinary" waking consciousness involves the "embodiment problematic" of *continence*. The concept of continence, linguistically and etymologically, entails the notions of containing, continuity, content, and countenance. In its most familiar contemporary usage (as "continent") it refers to a bounded land mass whose separations from other territories are either geological or based upon matters of historical and cultural distinctness.

As well, it has come to refer, generally, to notions of self-restraint and self-control. For children, as well as for the infirm and aged, continence specifically addresses the matter of bowel and bladder control. Children who come to embody intense anxieties about their toilet training will, invariably, experience multiple dimensions and symbolisms of shame and will live and adapt in such a way that this shame is not regularly triggered—entailing such psychological defense mechanisms as hyper-vigilance or compulsive neatness. It is, as well, a matter of well-established clinical understanding that bedwetting strongly correlates with antisocial behavior and damaged self-esteem in children.[9]

But the concept of continence, of course, can address all sorts of boundary problems and control issues. One can even see the notion of "containment" illustrated in the materialist and territorial urges of Western rationality, in the modernist myth of individuated selfhood and, as well, in Cartesian dualism. All of these matters—rationality, selfhood, and dualism—are matters of intense concern about borders and boundary maintenance. And. as I think about the mysterious border separating or seeming to separate waking consciousness from dreaming and reverie, I think about the drift and flow and shifting of perceptual realities. It can happen so suddenly. Of course, with sleep, the shift is accompanied by a neurochemical event, an event that cannot be rationally willed. Nevertheless, in any case the drift of perception in consciousness occurs first. Our boundaries of ego and reflectivity dissolve. Our images and concepts of identity lose their narrative continuity.

In Book VII of the *Nichomachean Ethics*, Aristotle identified continence (*enkrateia*) as performing a critical role in living within and through the premise of the Golden Mean. In effect, he equates continence with "mastery," which he then contrasts with incontinence (*akrasia*).[10] Incontinence emerges, through this reasoning, as roughly equivalent with having a weakness for hedonistic pleasure, what in contemporary clinical terms would be termed impulsivity, or instant gratification—having a need to immediately reduce the anxiety feelings of a challenging situation.[11]

In this light, continence becomes virtually synonymous with the notion of historical continuity and narrative integrity for the waking cogito. In George Herbert Mead's sense, the imaginative "I" emerges from the foundation of a socially grounded and symbolically recognizable "me."[12] Yet Mead's thinking—original, incisive, and remarkably phenomenological given the context in which he was working—is nonetheless tied to a rationalist notion of selfhood, cognition, and consciousness.[13] Even though Mead's contributions to the then infant field of psychology were published during the ascendancy of the psychoanalytic movement, Mead published writings reflect no interest in dreams, no interest in psychosexual development, and no interest in an embodied *un*conscious mind.

Perhaps it may best be said that my objective in this essay is to problematize, or at least make less stable, the "me-image" that situates the continent, masterful, reasonable, and practical "I" that has emerged, up through modernity, as the proper wellspring of imagination and creativity. (Here, Dionysus has surfaced as the well-mannered alter ego of Apollo. Perhaps it is time for these two characters to spend some time apart. Perhaps this decoupling should enable other affairs, other hookups, other marriages, other alters [or altars], perhaps multiple partners.)

THE DRIFT OF CONTINENCE

The continental drift from the oneiric experience of perceptual consciousness to the social ground of everyday meaning is an ongoing event and can be—analogous to the dimensions of a continental shelf—a slippery slope. The world in which I awaken is a world in which things and people are meaningful in terms of their history. As my eyes open, I remember them. In fact, in the familiar room that comes into focus as I awaken, there is, in this oncoming drift of consciousness, nothing but history. To awaken in an unfamiliar space requires some orientation or reorientation, a gathering of notions in time to place my body in space. I need to figure out where I am and at least be able to work through a basic plot of how I got there. The waking world itself is not constituted principally, or even primarily, as a world of objective *l'histoire*. As with my dream world, it emerges (to paraphrase Heraclitus) from an *idios kosmos*[14]—literally, a cosmos of my own. But the dream lives and lives well without a rational regard (or etiquette) for the history of this cosmos. And the waking world, through its ongoing social negotiations in the bodies of all who perceive and negotiate its traffic, continually campaigns to hold a place for itself as a function of objective history. It strives to be lawful, even taking the time to rationalize and reconstruct laws that no longer serve its movement. Good ideas, like hotel guests or parolees, register with us and with others.

Words, as we so deeply depend upon them in waking life, take on an entirely different function in dreams. In his reflection on Binswanger's *Dream and Existence*, Foucault notes that "the word implies a world of expression which precedes it, sustains it."[15] In dreams, the spoken word is indifferent to our expectations of diction and syntax, of syntagmatic form and paradigmatic suitability. Foucault remarks: "dream interpretation, naturally, becomes a method designed to discover the meanings of words in a language whose grammar one does not understand. . . . "[16] Dream words are not to be taken literally. They function in dreams as they function in impressionist and post-impressionist paintings: they are a part of the scene, no more and no less significant than the small painted figure who appears on first glance to be a man, and who also appears to be wearing a hat.

The tension between words and images have become something of a semiotic and psychological perplexity in the technological episteme of the photograph and the ready-made still image. McLuhan's theory of technology and human experience, most clearly articulated in the four laws of media,[17] makes a compelling case for the hypothesis that the unfolding photographic and cinematic (as well as televisual) grammar of image-experience has fundamentally and irreversibly altered the thinking and perceptual patterns of an entire planet. The logocentric, literacy-centered modality of adult mastery and maturity has, for better or for worse, given way to a new *techné* of the image. The world of noetic experience will now and forever be audio-visual. The telephone, which served to collapse vast acoustic distances separating people from one another, has now become a camera, a stereo system, a typewriter, and a computer. The writing instrument on which I composed these thoughts is also a computational device, an archive of my own scholarly output, a newswire, a stereo system, a mail system, a storage bin for favorite photographs, an exponentially growing research library, a television, and a shopping center. It shows me elegant photographs of idyllic natural scenes when my writing activity stalls for too long a period of time. As I contemplate the experience of oneiric consciousness, I can easily get lost in any aspect of this *techné*. It can easily be said that I composed these words from the realm of dreams. Borges maintains that "writing is nothing more than a guided dream."[18] We are no longer writing with ink on tablets of paper or on typewriters or even on "word processors." We write with the multiple, multiplying consciousness of the Internet. We write both with and against the winds and storms of a collective intellect that in its fragmentation, its persistence, and its ubiquity has become a dream that we may not ever be able to wake up from. In his last days, the surrealist/beat novelist William S. Burroughs concluded: "Thinking is not enough."[19] Perhaps the continental drift has overwhelmed our capacity to reason through the outline of where our own thoughts begin and end, as well as where our thoughts end and our dreams begin.

THE PROBLEM OF THE IMAGE

One undeniable consequence of this shift in the continence of literacy is that our experience of "the image" has been pictorialized. The word "image" has no necessary etymological connection to still frames of color and light. From the Latin *imago*, the word essentially refers to a "likeness" of something. A likeness is simply a similitude. It is not a copy or a replica. Two things can be likened because they occur together, because they move at comparable speeds, because they occupy the same space, because they make comparable or perhaps harmonious sounds, because they are of comparable chemical make-up, because they are comparable or companionable in color, because they evoke comparable effects or feelings, or because they compete with one another, or even *oppose* one another. We have, nonetheless, come to associate talk of images, however, with *photographic resemblance*. And what is most curious about this emerging discursive habit of reducing images to "pictures" is that in the general syntax of this expression, the concept of the image seems to be a visual representation that is *still*—motionless.

My point here is that there are no still images in consciousness. All of thought, whether it is that of the Cartesian cogito or that of oneiric rhapsody, is in motion. Even were I to think of the proverbial "pink elephant," that elephant would be a part of a living scene. Were the elephant alive (as opposed to, say, a pink statue of an elephant), the elephant in conscious reflection would be doing more or less what I have come to take elephants to do in an existential situation that is, itself, a scene of motion. As such, the contemporary habit of discourse regarding the status of *the image* is remarkably out of touch with our embodied and existentially grounded experience of *images*. The dream image and the waking-consciousness image do not differ in their continence with respect to their motility, their performance, their intensity, and their possibilities. How they differ is in their palpability.

The image of waking consciousness does not occur at an existential remove from the time and space in which my body functions to sustain its existence. As such, the experience of paranoia in waking consciousness will occur through my body in waking life just as it occurs when I am dreaming or delusional. My capacity to adapt to such intense feelings, then becomes entirely a matter of performance and, hence, communication. If such paranoia proves worrisome or tiresome to persons with whom I share my experience of these images, or if my paranoid actions only serve to reinforce and strengthen my overall level of anxiety, for whatever reasons, it, rather than the threat as I perceive it, becomes the defining matter for my "me-image." As Merleau-Ponty maintains throughout *The Phenomenology of Perception*, the imagining and perceiving cogito "has" no image of its corporeality.[20] Simply, I have a body but I cannot see it except from a limited aspect. As was the case with Narcissus, my efforts to sustain my gaze at any element of my body-image (as far as it can be sensed), or to fixate on my body-image as such, jeopardize my capacity to engage my interpersonal and intersubjective field of perception. I may not immediately perish, but my power of social engagement will wither.

Yet even though I may be quick to concede that I indeed "have" no body-image that is anything other than partial and retrospective, I am not so quick to concede that I am without an image of projective social and psychological identity. To follow Mead's profoundly compelling logic once again, it is because of my recognizable communicative *identity* that "I" *am* at all.[21] Freud summarized this teleological function of projective existence as an "ego ideal."[22] Lacan affirms this general concept and further specifies an affective and performative distinction between an "ego-ideal" and an "ideal ego."[23] The "ideal-ego," it might be said, is the image of embodied excellence that the ego strives to emulate. It is an extension of Lacan's theory of the mirror stage.[24] It is decidedly *developmental* in its general epistemological and practical function and it addresses the psychological order of what Lacan terms "the Imaginary"—that is, the experiential domain in which desire and fantasy enable a condition of psychological agency having the potentiality to become a communicative event. For Lacan, the ego-ideal describes the function of "the Symbolic order" in which probability and judgment combine to assess the value of communicative possibilities as well as a proper affect for past events. It is, for Lacan, a much more detailed rendering of what Freud came to call the function of "conscience" in the superego. The ego ideal, for Lacan, is what enables a person to feel that his or her career or social relationships or romantic life or athletic training have been "failures." Likewise it is what enables a person to believe that a decision to do something, anything, will end badly. Existentially, of course, no one "knows" how anything is going to come out. All that we have to guide us in our assessment of what we should do at any given point in our lives are images.

BECOMING WHAT WE PERCEIVE, BECOMING WHAT WE ARE

The Nietzschean call for us to "become what we are"[25] blends exquisitely with Merleau-Ponty's incitement for us to affirm that we have "always and already" become what we perceive[26] once we begin to sense that the oneiric image and the waking image are fundamentally intertwined. It might be tempting to suggest, at the outset, that waking life is a property of what Lacan terms the Symbolic while the oneiric belongs to the Imaginary. But that impulse is far too facile and would very much miss the point of what my reflections are attempting to say. We are mistaken when we speak of the *imago* and the imaginary as primarily or principally visual. There are sensuous, sensorial rhythms and patterns in waking life which, if we let ourselves move with them, invite us to participate in images and imagery that enable capacities and conditions for touch and which, in turn, invite the world to touch us back.

In a delicate sense, McLuhan captures this subtle notion in his well-known aphorism: "We become what we behold. We shape our tools and . . . our tools shape us."[27] We make cameras that in turn make still images of thick and kinetic perceptual experience that in turn can render our experiences of thick, kinetic, perceptual experiences into frozen, photographic reductions. The contemporary conventions of marriage entail the hiring or appointment of someone to serve as the wedding photographer. A ritual of communion and commitment functions as series of photo opportunities. This is a situation of perceptual drift and image transformation and it is, now, entirely normal. Given the strength of argument that sustains McLuhan's "Laws of Media," there is nothing particularly odd or even troublesome in this turn of events (at least insofar as weddings go). What has made our thinking about the experience of "image" so perplexing, however—especially over the course of the last century of technological progress—is that the still image, the frozen photographic reduction of the thick, kinetic perceptual experience (an enhancement of oral memory by way of the camera) has come to reverse our cultural understanding (which was itself enhanced through the explorations of depth psychology) of how images enable and sustain the meaningfulness of our intersubjective and communicative being.

In the *Phenomenology of Perception* Merleau-Ponty contends that, for example, individual instances of color are, in themselves, inexpressible—beyond description. Instead, colors become my own when I am constituted with them. Merleau-Ponty writes: "The sensation of blue is not the knowledge or the positing of a certain identifiable *quale* throughout all of the experiences of it which I have, as the geometer's circle is the same in Paris and Tokyo."[28] He continues later in that very same extended paragraph: "And yet I do so only when I am invited by it, my attitude is never sufficient to make me really see blue or touch a hard surface. The sensible gives back to me what I lent to it, but this is only what I took from it in the first place."[29] Again, the color becomes my own when I coincide with it. "I abandon myself to it and plunge into this mystery, it 'thinks itself within me.'"[30]

The function of an image, phenomenologically considered and at least momentarily decoupled from a consciousness retooled by way of its own instruments of depiction, is to bring us, both back and forward, into the intersubjective composition of an event. Nocturnal dreams, in this regard, are "pure" event and "pure" image. In *The Poetics of Reverie*, Bachelard comments: "The night dream does not belong to us. It is not our possession."[31] In his discourse on Binswanger's *Dream and Existence*, Foucault notes that "between the sleeping mind and the waking mind, the dreaming mind enjoys an experience which borrows from nowhere its light and its genius."[32] That which is perceived is neither intended nor subtended. Importantly, from a phenomenological standpoint this world of perception is clearly protended; that is, as *eidos*, this world is a rich tissue of connection to multiple shapes and dimensions of all other *eidos* within reach.

THE PROBLEM OF THE DREAM

But, both beginning and ending in and through my body, that which is present to dreaming consciousness must be both intended and subtended from some source, some agency, must it not? It is here, at this very juncture in the history of consciousness, that the theory of dreams and dream images began to engage a fascinating and at times philosophically awkward dialogue with theology and moral philosophy. Foucault draws reference to this moment in the theory of dreams by citing Book X of Plato's *Republic*:

> [I]n our dreams . . . the reasonable and humane part of us is asleep and its control relaxed, and our bestial nature, full of food and drink, wakes and has its fling and tries to secure its own kind of satisfaction. As you know, there's nothing too bad for it and it's completely lost to all sense and shame. It does not shrink at the thought of intercourse with a mother or any one else, man beast, or god, or from murder or sacrilege. There is in fact no folly or shamelessness it will not commit.[33]

Foucault sees this essential logic as a reaffirmation of Heraclitus, in which he maintains: "We share a world when we are awake; each sleeper is in a world of his own."[34] Hence, the pleasure of the dream experience belongs to the world of the incontinent and, following Heraclitus, the dream and its content are all a part of our own nature, our own natural tendency, our own *idios kosmos*.

So, here the dream is an excursion into the nether world of our own worst inclinations, and God (or the gods), in the form of reason, give us a capacity to wake up to Truth. In *Water and Dreams,* Bachelard considers the figure of Narcissus and his seduction before the shimmering image he is presented of a possible Self, a Self projected to him from the other side of this world.[35] Bachelard's thinking enables a fascinating and original departure for a theory of conscious experience. It is not just another moral interpretation of this myth, and it succeeds in helping us reconsider the matter of continence, the matter of liquidity, and the liquidity of matter—or at least how the objects of perception matter to us. It is clear that on the other side of the surface, the touch and temperature of everything will be different. Unlike Jung, Bachelard has little to no interest in the dream as a form of therapy. His interest is entirely epistemological and phenomenological. He seeks to rescue the dream from the realm of hermeneutics and moral interpretation and enable its participation in all aspects of the human sciences: as *parole, discours, langue, and langage*.

In many ways, what Foucault set out to accomplish, at least methodologically in both his archaeology and his genealogy seems remarkably compatible with what Bachelard was seeking through his poetics and psychoanalyses. Where Foucault was looking at the rhetoric and discourse embedded in the discrete institutional relationships that lay just outside the margins of orthodox cultural practices, Bachelard was looking at the tropes and figures of rich poetic writing on the inner world and inner experience of so-called empirical reality. It may well be said that for Bachelard, the language of inquiry had become far *too* continent. It was contained within the bounds of matter looked at just so far—right up to the edge of discourse and no further. The power of poetic expression was one such place that no right-thinking scientist had at that point considered for depth explanations of how the world is experienced and becomes meaningful. The oneiric was another.[36] For Foucault, the prose of social and medical life given in the discursive practices of the human sciences, as they had been constituted from antiquity onward, would open up to new vistas of possibility and freedom once they could be read and imagined in *other tropic configurations*.[37] At the very moment one was able to read the implied master tropes of classical and modern scientific discourse as fully interchangeable with one another, the language of empiricism broke open, freeing thought to look beyond, perhaps dissolve the categories that had given the disciplines of inquiry and governmentality their order and metaphysical certitude.

In effect, Foucault frees the thought and practice of modern science from the grand narrative of its waking consciousness. His methods seek to free the codes and constructs of life, labor, and language from their history. Edward

Casey (1991, p. 109) points out that Bachelard "frees images from memory—insofar as they are unframed and open."[38] Rather than seeing them and their work as caste in the image of an Oedipal conflict with the paternalistic hold of the sciences of "man"—the "name-of-the-father" in Lacan's terms—one might consider the image of Prometheus in place of Oedipus. Bachelard, himself, proposes an Orpheus complex in the place of an Oedipus complex. Casey (p. 110) notes: "In the new complex, what matters most is not rivalrous influence but 'active vibrant repose,' 'an always possible childhood,' and that 'lyrical state' which consists in 'letting images succeed images' and which is best realized in *poetry*."[39] Casey cites, directly from Bachelard himself, the last two sentences of the book he considers to be pivotal in the development of Bachelard's thought: "Poetry, thus liberated from habitual involvements, becomes again a model of rhythmatized life and thought. It [is] thus the most appropriate means for . . . returning to the mind the mastery of the dialectics of duration."[40]

IMAGE AND IDENTITY

Edith Wyschogrod has commented: "The world built up by vision is not pregiven but constructed by memory and by the creation of categories and relations."[41] If memory is continuity, then the *image*—once taken out its current discursive habitat as a sign, an icon of resemblance, a still pictorial gloss—is *counter*-memory. It is on the basis of this hypothesis that I consider the significance of "adolescence transition" as both a problematic and a thematic for the discussion of dreams, images, and continence with particular reference to what, psychologically speaking, we have come to call "self" and "identity." Erik Erikson claims to have derived his concept of identity most fully from Freud and William James.[42] From James, he appropriated the centrality of character in social experience and from Freud he saw value in further explicating the social dimension of the "ego-ideal" function in the superego. For Erikson, "ego identity" (the "ego" part of which was set aside after his writing on this subject become increasingly prominent by the late 1940s) was always tied to a matter of social agency. More or less, it began to serve as a communicative pragmatic in response to the hypothetical question: who are you *outside* of your family? As modern, increasingly urban societies had begun to dissipate the intense emotional and psychological strongholds of family insularity on monolithically religious cultures through the nineteenth and twentieth centuries, this became a more practical matter for the assessment of human agency.

And it goes without saying that the question of identity is entirely a matter of continence. Stepping outside of the boundary of how one has been raised, especially in an increasingly "low-context" culture,[43] a culture that has become electronically and economically interconnected in startlingly intense ways (and in such a short period of time), is a powerful psychological moment for a person during her or his adolescence. "Keeping everything together" or "getting one's act together" is one of the most difficult tasks for the person having entered the waking consciousness of puberty. At puberty, one's image of an embodied self is startled. It had never been stable to being with, although, for the child, days do pass much more slowly when he or she is younger in age. The advanced maturity of the cerebral cortex during adolescence, especially at the middle teens, coincides with the onset of numerous anatomical changes.[44] Time typically seems rushed. Inner continuity and social sameness are difficult to manage, even for growing children in families, and for the adolescent the development of an ego identity—which is a stage of social and oneiric consciousness that is *both* imaginary *and* symbolic—is the pivotal psychological instrument for the management of ego in the *habitus* of social arrangements that are growing ever more complex.

Erikson's reflections on the experience of identity formation make clear that he is not merely thinking through the later stage Oedipal struggles that attend to young persons' ego strength in relationship to the analytical gaze of their parents; he is thinking about "the community's response to the young individual's need to be 'recognized' by those around [her or] him; for it is of great relevance to the young individual's identity formation that [she or] he be responded to, and be given function and status as a person whose gradual growth and transformation make sense to those who begin to make sense to [her or] him."[45] Erikson then summarizes the general existential parameters of this embodied crucible in a very helpful way:

> It has not been sufficiently recognized in psychoanalysis that such recognition provides an early indispensable support to the ego in the specific tasks of adolescing, which are: to maintain the most important ego defenses against the vastly growing intensity of impulses (now invested in a matured genital apparatus and a powerful muscle system); to learn to consolidate the most important "conflict-free" achievements in line with work opportunities; and to resynthesize all childhood identifications in some unique way, and yet in concordance with the roles offered by some wider section of society—be that section the neighborhood block, an anticipated occupational field, an association of kindred minds, or perhaps . . . the "mighty dead."[46]

Anyone familiar with Erikson's well-known "eight stages of human development" is aware of the importance of initiative and industry on the final accomplishment of a nondiffuse and then, subsequently, nonconfused ego. The stage of identity formation, thus, is a psychological achievement beyond that of ego affirmation and ego defense. It requires a creative freedom and a creative act—an act of image, dream, the imaginary, and imagination—to avert the "identity crisis" on which Erikson has written at length[47] and which seems to lay in wait for the psychologically incontinent.

When Erikson speaks of a *resynthesis* of "all childhood identifications *in some unique way*,"[48] he suddenly draws attention to the mythic and oneiric function of the image upon which a socially recognizable ego identity is embodied. Phenomenologically, an identity functions both as a "name" and as a style of embodiment. It expresses a desire and communicates a function. It arises from an interpretation of the adolescent *Umwelt*. For the teenager in the modern world, clothing functions like armor in the school and social setting. It functions like body armor until the style of embodied ego enables the ego to feel, intersubjectively, a significant reduction of anxiety in its discursive matrix. When the adolescent finds herself or himself at home in this new, extra-familial discursive matrix, an identity has been lived. When the identity has been lived sufficiently for a performative self-consciousness to begin to emerge as a style of being, he or she can reengage his or her presence before the "mirrors" of their consciousness and then dream about what all of this—childhood, adulthood, freedom, responsibility—can mean.

Now, the concept of emotional and individual development can be troubling to psychology. James Hillman has been particularly critical: "Psychoanalysis has swallowed whole the myth of individual development away from the family. . . . Psychology has even invented secondary embellishments to make its myth of individual independence more compelling. . . . [It] has discovered an entire demonology within the family: irremediable envy of sibling rivalry . . . castration threats . . . cannibalism by sons, devouring mothers and schizogenetic mothers, as well as omnipotent, amoral, polymorphously perverse children."[49] My choice, therefore, to speak of development is ultimately about phenomenological freedom, organismic health, and matters of biological and anatomical reality.

Hillman's critique is familiar enough. And it is well worth our concern as we think through the dream of our personal being in later years. There is and ought to be no particular moral or bourgeois hermeneutics of what it means to develop out of the polymorphous perversities and innocences of being young and without full adult agency and competency. But we live in a world in which the incest taboo, its intercultural enforcement, and the rules of civic communication are strict enough that the cultivation of an extra-familial identity requires an imaginative rupture from the symbolic orders of life, labor, and language. In my grandfather's time, his multilingual illiteracy and technical simplicity were not, for him, a deep source of shame. He immigrated from Lithuania after the turn of the century and was able, with my grandmother (also illiterate), to raise a family and participate in some sort of Lithuanian American dream. (A century later, the rhythm of life has, it seems, come to require a more psychologically and semiotically nimble immigrant.)

The dream image of identity is always in motion. Even in psychological waters without tide or current, we have to at least tread water to remain afloat. Even in a simpler age (however we might imagine such experience—with all the mental cinematic edits and effects that we now use to get us to such places), in places where we might imagine ourselves living among the Aztecs or Egyptians or sailing to the New World, our tools exhibit a much closer companionship to our bodies. As it always has, our world still sculpts us into shapes that can as easily be as breathtaking as they can, and will, be tragic. Our own imagination and artistry at forming ourselves may be nothing in comparison to what the oncoming floods and meteors have in store for us, but it remains the wellspring of all of the currents and currency that we have within us.

In his translator's introduction to Foucault's famous essay on Binswanger, Forrest Williams makes clear: "In the order of inquiry the dream, not the perception comes first."[50] This is to say that the image is always already there, not for us, but within and among us as we take measure of the world and ourselves within it. In its way the dream image is embedded in the perceiving consciousness of the "awake" subject. Hillman remains one of those thinkers inclined to employ the word "myth" where I am stressing the word "image."[51] My thinking through the years has taken quite a bit of instruction from this tradition in general (and Hillman in particular), but I find myself strongly inclined to resist the temptation of "myth." Perhaps it is just a matter of clarity in connotation, but "myth" has come to bear too strong a relationship to narration and narrativity—suggesting, perhaps, that the anthropologists and linguists have "the answers" in their archives.

No doubt there is great healing power in myth. Feeling its rhythms, poetry, and elegance, we can be reminded of the possibility of a constancy running beneath the chaos. Mythic analysis of nocturnal dreams can certainly help sort through them. But the experience of dream images and the discovery that waking life is not nearly so continent as we have long presumed it to be, both in our philosophy and our psychology, is a matter of unsettling and dehiscence rather than questions for which answers can be found. At several key points in his essay on Binswanger, Foucault cites Cicero's dictum: *Nihil est magnum somnianti.*[52] ("Nothing is great to a dreamer.") From this, it also would follow that nothing in dreams can be "off limits." Nothing is great, nothing small. As with Foucault's method of inquiry, the dream is beyond structuralism and hermeneutics.

AND NOW, TO WAKE UP

Bachelard asserts that the "psyche is animated by a veritable hunger for images. It craves images. Meanwhile, psychoanalysis looks for the reality beneath the image but fails to perform the inverse search: to look beneath the reality for the absolute image."[53] What any of us *are* as people is not the result of an inevitable classification built into the logic of any sort of world external to us. For Foucault, "[t]he imaginary world has its own laws, its specific structures, and the image is somewhat more than the immediate fulfillment of meaning. It has its own density, and the laws which govern it are not solely significant propositions, just as the laws of the world are not simply decrees of the will, even a divine will."[54] Foucault continues: "the dream is not a modality of the imagination, the dream is the first condition of its possibility."[55] There is an "imaginary" that is trapped in the image, and it is the course of the dream to release it. The synthesis of this thinking thus leads Foucault to assert: "The imagination is in essence iconoclastic. Metaphor is the metaphysics of the image, in the sense that metaphysics is the destruction of physics. The true poet denies [her or] himself the accomplishment of desire in the image. . . . The value of a poetic imagination is to be measured by the inner destructive power of the image."[56]

The ambiguous, oneiric image of adolescent development (that is, the image of Selfhood and ego identity) as I have been dreaming about it up through this moment comes into being, thus, as a crucial gesture—an identifying gesture that marks the birth of an erotic Ideal Ego in the mature flesh of the emergent person. To return to Nietzsche's and Merleau-Ponty's axioms, it is through the dream image that we can find the freedom to become what and who we are and, simultaneously, to become what we behold. The difficulty for intellectual work, as well as the difficulty for life itself, is that narrative discontinuity runs counter to everything we have ever learned about making sense. In an age of human relations management (which really is far from the worst thing that can be said for the time in which we live) the problem of psychopathology or insanity or madness or folly is ultimately one of communicative disjointedness.

Yet, since the commencement of the post World War II era, the era of our times, the era of the American "baby boom," the era of televisual rock and roll affluence, teenage expression and adolescent pleasure has come to emerge as the symbolic center of what Lyotard years ago referred to as a libidinal economy.[57] Youthful *ressentiment* not only has its own fully operative discourse systems but an emergent worldwide aesthetic as well. Voices and subcultures of resistance no longer threaten the order of things or the rules of communication. They have become fully commodified and anticipated by the world economic order. What had seemed to emerge in the twentieth century as troubling dream images of repressed Oedipal, anti-paternalistic urges no longer appears to be coming from the underworld, "from nowhere," as alien or strange. Rock and roll is the music we now hear on elevators. It is the music playing on sound systems as we do our shopping.

But it is also quite apparent that even through the images and seductions and embodiments of these times that we have also *not* become what we are. Psychotropic medications of all sorts have become standard in the lives of the most educated and cultured among us. Clinical diagnoses for anxiety, depression, or other mood disorders are no longer stigmas that the otherwise continent and virtuous citizens among us (including ourselves) hide in shame.[58] As I read Merleau-Ponty's discourse on expression, perception, the flesh, and the visible, I am persuaded that the transformative human science of "becoming what we are" entails rigorously and systematically learning *how* to become what we behold. (In contemporary psychiatric practice, "becoming what we are" entails an increasing likelihood of neurochemically adapting ourselves to become what we behold.[59]) Simply, the dream images of our desires and longings are never what they seem. And in a hyper-capitalistic and electronically mediated society suffused with images continuously summoning our selfhood, the dream images of our desires and longings seem destined to withhold themselves from embodiment.

Erikson's articulation of the psychodynamics of modern "identity crisis" makes clear that identity is never fully achieved.[60] His theory is that the experience of a pragmatically secure identity through the passage from adolescence into young adulthood is necessary to enter into intimate relationships.[61] Intimate relations, of course, change us. A case study can be found in every person's first extrafamilial love relationship. None of our identities are equipped to survive it intact. They are sundered, reassembled, and put back into play only after we—each of us—can feel and see our image in the rhythms of meaningful interaction once again.

To reiterate Bachelard's comment from above: "the night dream does not belong to us."[62] Neither does my identity belong to me. My identity is something I seek in the faces of others. During my adolescence, it was something I hoped, like Narcissus, to find in the mirror. I still do, of course. I still go looking, but I no longer wish for anything in particular and I no longer expect magic. I no longer hope to be swept away by the power of what can be imagined from what I give, what is given, and what remains to be taken away. Bachelard continues: "With regard to us, [the dream] . . . is an abductor, the most disconcerting of abductors: it abducts our being from us."[63] In other words the surprise of the dream is that, in its action and in its theatre, it succeeds in making off with things and aspects that we had come to believe—often with great certitude—that were fully attached to us.

Like Nietzsche's Zarathustra, the dream laughs and dances and carries us away, setting us down again in odd yet oddly familiar places, leaving us to chase after all that we thought was our own. Bachelard comments: "Nights, nights have no history. They are not linked to one another. . . . The night has no future."[64] The order of things, as Foucault captured it almost half a century ago, has not already made a place for what we dream ourselves into. If we listen carefully, the dream will serve to continually remind us that all new experience begins outside of history. The dream image of my identity is what I take pleasure and rich experience from becoming. I never get there, but, if I take the pains to listen, I may be seduced into believing (if not knowing) that it is really me who is calling. Or is it "I" who is calling? Maybe it is "you." Maybe it is a long distance call.

All new experience begins outside of history. All new experience, thus, cannot be *imagined* beforehand. Foucault maintains that "imagination adds nothing new to what I already know. Yet it would be incorrect to say that it brings nothing and teaches me nothing."[65] My position is that imagination, the imaginary, makes my new experience "live-able." It is my dream image of myself as an identity. It is my image of my Self *identified*, identifiable, living with others. Foucault summarizes: "[I]magining is to take aim at oneself in the moment of dreaming; it is to dream oneself dreaming."[66]

Our style of being in the world, our gesture of Self-with-others, is in this sense an image of how we might wish to be taken. To be taken, to be abducted: stolen like Persephone in the night of our daily affairs and guided into a whole new set of relations, a whole new set of relations and a whole new identity. These are the blessings of love and sleep. This is what becomes of us if we truly let ourselves dream. Bachelard muses: "A word is a bud attempting to become a twig. How can one not dream while writing? It is the pen which dreams. The blank page gives the right to dream."[67] Thinking is not enough. The words of this chapter, as I read back through them, are no longer recognizable to me as the molecular elements of thought that must have occurred to me in specific moments of rumination as I attempted to puzzle through the questions that must have circulated in reflective consciousness as I began this writing weeks ago. Right now it's all a blur. At various points I was distracted and no doubt drifted into reverie, but where those points are or were are entirely unrecognizable to me now. How can one not dream while writing? It was my computer that dreamed, and I was dreaming with it.

NOTES

1. See Spiegelberg, *Phenomenology in Psychology and Psychiatry*, 220–23.
2. Throughout this chapter I will use the German word, "*Geist*" instead of the English semantic equivalent words "spirit" or "mind"—or, for that matter, "ghost."
3. Bachelard, *The Poetics of Reverie*.
4. Bachelard, *The Poetics of Reverie*, 8.
5. Nietzsche, *Human, All Too Human*, 20.
6. Nietzsche, *Human, All Too Human*, 21–22.
7. See Foucault, *Order of Things*, 353–55.
8. See Oreskes, *The Rejection of Continental Drift*.
9. The well-known McDonald Triad, now an established premise for the study of personality disorders in the DSM IV, consists of the three primary warning-signs in children and young

adults indicating a tendency to become not merely violently anti-social, but perhaps a serial murderer. One leg of this triad consists of bedwetting beyond the age when children normally grow out of such behavior. See McDonald, "The Threat to Kill."

10. Aristotle, *Nichomachean Ethics*. See especially Book VII, sections 1–10.

11. One might well be reminded, in this context, of the notorious episode of the American situation comedy, *Seinfeld*, during which the four central characters place bets to see who can undergo the longest period of time without masturbation. The phrase "master of my domain" was comically used as a metaphor for this species of self- and self-image regulation.

12. Mead, *Selected Writings*.

13. See Aboulafia, "Introduction."

14. See Jessica Ann Mayock, *Borderlands of Psyche*, 152.

15. Foucault, "Dream, Imagination, and Existence," 35.

16. Foucault, "Dream, Imagination, and Existence," 35.

17. McLuhan, *Understanding Media.*

18. Borges, *Doctor Brodie's Report,* 11.

19. Burroughs, *Last Words*, xx.

20. Merleau-Ponty, *Phenomenology of Perception.*

21. Mead, *Selected Writings*.

22. Freud, *New Introductory Lectures on Psychoanalysis*.

23. Lacan, *The Four Fundamental Concepts of Psychoanalysis*, 144.

24. Lacan, "The Mirror Stage as Formative of the Function of the I."

25. Nietzsche, *The Gay Science*, 219.

26. Merleau-Ponty, *Phenomenology of Perception,* 207–26.

27. McLuhan, *Understanding Media,* 8.

28. Merleau-Ponty, *Phenomenology of Perception*, 214.

29. Merleau-Ponty, *Phenomenology of Perception*, 214.

30. Merleau-Ponty, *Phenomenology of Perception*, 214.

31. Bachelard, *The Poetics of Reverie*, 145.

32. Foucault, "Dream, Imagination, and Existence," 44.

33. Plato, *Republic*, 344–45.

34. Foucault is referring to a Heraclitean fragment (Fragment No. 15) in *Herakleitos and Diogenes*, 13.

35. Bachelard, *Water and Dreams,* 21–26.

36. See Chimisso, *Gaston Bachelard.*

37. See White, "Foucault Decoded: Notes from Underground." See also White, *The Content of the Form*, and *Tropics of Discourse*.

38. Casey, *Spirit and Soul*, 109.

39. Casey, *Spirit and Soul,* 110.

40. Casey, *Spirit and Soul,* 110.

41. Wyschogrod, *Crossover Queries*, 113.

42. Erikson, *Identity: Youth and Crisis,* 19–21.

43. See Hall, *Beyond Culture.*

44. See Moshman, *Adolescent Rationality and Development.*

45. Erikson, *Identity and the Life Cycle*, 120.

46. Erikson, *Identity and the Life Cycle*, 120.

47. Erikson, *Identity: Youth and Crisis*.

48. Erikson, *Identity and the Life Cycle*, 120.

49. Hillman, *A Blue Fire*, 197

50. Williams, "Translator's Preface," p. 22

51. Hillman, *The Dream and the Underworld.*

52. Foucault, "Dream, Imagination, and Existence," 43.

53. Bachelard, *Earth and Reveries of Will*, 15

54. Foucault, "Dream, Imagination, and Existence," 35.

55. Foucault, "Dream, Imagination, and Existence," 21.

56. Foucault, "Dream, Imagination, and Existence," 72.

57. Lyotard, *Libidinal Economy.*

58. See Kramer, *Listening to Prozac.*
59. See Moncrieff, *The Myth of the Chemical Cure.*
60. See Ermann, "Identity in Change," 209–10.
61. Erikson, *Identity: Youth and Crisis.*
62. Bachelard, *The Poetics of Reverie*, 145.
63. Bachelard, *The Poetics of Reverie*, 145.
64. Bachelard, *The Poetics of Reverie,* 145.
65. Foucault, "Dream, Imagination, and Existence," 68.
66. Foucault, "Dream, Imagination, and Existence," 68.
67. Bachelard, *The Poetics of Reverie*, 17.

Chapter Eleven

Conclusion

The Dawning of Communicology

When John Dewey took the reins as chair of the Department of Philosophy at the University of Chicago, there were, at that time, few expectations of what an American Department of Philosophy should look like. Some departments focused on classical thought. Some included theology as a curricular theme. Some emphasized logic and scientific method. The work of German Idealists, Kant and Hegel in particular, had only been translated into English for a few decades; as such there were very few American scholars working in what was soon to become the modern European tradition. Rather than conforming to any sort of template of what his department should resemble, Dewey guided his colleagues toward the work of the human sciences as they availed themselves of the philosophy and metatheory that had begun to evolve in the wake of thinkers like Hegel, Marx, Nietzsche, Kierkegaard, Darwin, Royce, Peirce, James, Weber, Brentano, Wundt, and Freud. The insights into the processes of learning, experience, and pedagogy had given birth to a newly formed field of "education," which Dewey enthusiastically had hoped to explore and help define. As well, with George Herbert Mead, Dewey sought to explore the limits and possibilities of the as-yet-unformed and undefined field of "psychology." Basically, as a turn-of-the-century pragmatic intellectual Dewey decided to put philosophy and philosophical concepts to work.

A fundamental premise of pragmatism is that good ideas are not to be held hostage to any extraneous considerations—along with, of course, not being held hostage to tradition or orthodoxy. The academic field of psychology, especially as it has emerged in the United States, exchanged pragmatism for orthodoxy well over a half-century ago. The ambitions of Dewey and

Mead to understand the function of mind as an extension of grounded (embodied) experience have essentially fallen away from mainstream discourse in psychological theory.[1] Pragmatism, despite the remarkable achievements of Dewey, James, Peirce, and Mead, had become an unreliable occurrence through most of the twentieth century, particularly in the human sciences.

A number of remarkably good works have attempted to recover the voice of pragmatic thought during the last quarter century,[2] but taken together they have not fully succeeded in resituating the energy of Dewey's Chicago ensemble—or the intellectual dynamics of the pragmatic movement as exemplified by Dewey—into the work of contemporary human science scholars in such a way that one might observe, say, a clearly discernable—and mainstream—pragmatist psychology or sociology. The technologically oriented mode of intellectual, academic and scientific orthodoxy has become powerful in ways that pragmatism and phenomenology have not. And, even worse, by and large the persons most likely to enthusiastically refer to themselves as "pragmatists," both within academia and without, are those who understand little of the intellectual tradition marked by the achievements of Peirce, Dewey, and James—conflating the nonfoundational epistemology of human experience with self-serving (typically profit-motivated) common-sensical utilitarianism.

My essential point is that participating in the development of new theory should not feel like radical and reckless experimentation with an established and thriving status quo. Disciplinary discourse becomes orthodoxy when the structures of knowledge begin to define themselves through a continuous pattern of discoveries and findings. Modes of probing and experimentation emerge, over time, as methods of inquiry. The words that surface in experimentation and theoretical speculation become the language of a discursive field. The language of a discursive field becomes terminological to enable ever-wider patterns of intellectual exchange and scientific communication, as well as modes of pedagogy for the education of the next generations of scientists and thinkers.

Foucault's *Order of Things* weaves a fascinating story about systematic occlusions in perceptual fields logically and lexically embedded in discursive formations, and how those discursive formations have led, from epistemic period to epistemic period, to assumptions of knowledge structures in scientific enterprises that were nothing more than narrative or rhetorical projections—but which nevertheless functioned to establish a range of permissible discourse among scientists and practitioners. Foucault's argument is powerful and impressive because of the manner in which it manages to not only tie the always-volatile problematic of representation to the work of the empirical sciences but to trace the problematic of discourse, representation, knowledge-assumptions (and scientific "truth"), and the expected modalities of scientific expression, back through centuries of epistemological work.

In citing the case of John Dewey at Chicago during the first decades of the twentieth century, I am taking note of an epistemological problematic and discursive event that occurred over a much more concentrated period of intellectual history than anything envisioned by Foucault in *Order of Things*—and one which, as Kurt Danziger has carefully argued,[3] is in many ways currently ongoing. In the case of Dewey, what we are witnessing is a turn-of-the-century event of theory construction across a range of largely untilled academic fields with remarkably few terminological markers. Nonetheless, the institutional and rhetorical pushback to Dewey and the pragmatist movement is well worth noting. In 1929, Robert Maynard Hutchins was installed as president of the University of Chicago. According to historian Jay Martin, by the early 1930s, Hutchins began to "tear down the school of philosophy that Dewey had created."[4] In 1930, Hutchins "forced the philosophy department to accept . . . philosopher Mortimer Adler, even though the department voted against his appointment. At this, Dewey's two former colleagues, James Tufts and George Herbert Mead, both resigned their professorships in philosophy. Then Hutchins attacked Dewey's philosophy itself in his book *The Higher Education in America*."[5] Martin further notes that in 1937, Dewey (who had left Chicago for Columbia in 1904) "heard that in a lecture his former student Mortimer Adler, now an ally of Hutchins, had named Dewey 'Public Enemy Number One.'"[6] The discursive contest over Dewey and his approach to philosophy and the human sciences at Chicago very much played out as a conflict between orthodoxy and tradition on one side versus experience, exploration, and discovery on the other. Hutchins and Adler became vocal proponents of a "Great Books" approach to higher education, an approach that set out to correct disciplinary problems in higher education, which Hutchins characterized as "slackness and disorder in university curricula"[7]—all of which he associated with pragmatism.

I have no doubt that the intellectual arguments marshaled against the pragmatist movement are of the same general form that one will find leveled against any threat to conventional practices in institutional settings, even if those conventional practices are without any sort of epistemological grounding. And it is in this context that I wish to comment on the case of communicology as a human science as I bring my reflections on embodiment and communicative experience to a close.

The field that now is most readily identified on American college and university campuses as "communication studies" is less than a half-century old. It replaces curricular and research programs in speech, rhetoric, and persuasion that had only begun to accumulate on American campuses around the turn of the century. One would therefore think that there would not be a sufficient historical, much less epistemological, foundation for orthodoxy in programs of communications studies—or even for American programs in speech and rhetoric for that matter. (Aside from classical thought, rhetoric has been a very much contested area over the past several centuries, particularly with regard to elocutionism on one hand and the rise of modern epistemologies on the other.) Nonetheless, *conventionality* in academic discourse regarding the subject of communication began to present itself within the first decades of its appearance as a critical topic of study and research in departments of speech and rhetoric in the post-WWII years.[8] Terms of study began to suggest themselves by the early 1970s and then a general curriculum began to gel, especially among university departments offering graduate degrees. By the time I began graduate study in 1978, categories of study had become fairly sedimented: interpersonal, group dynamics, organizational, and broadcasting/mass communication interest groups were structured into the national and regional organizations.

But the area where conventionality and intellectual orthodoxy had become most fully pronounced (and problematic) was in the area that had become summarily labeled "communication theory"—a category that had insinuated itself as a separate course of study in departmental curricula as well as among the subdivisions of the national and regional organizations. In the formulation of a "theory of communication" there was, simply, no effort expended to inquire about what communicative experience *is*, or what the limits of communicative experience might be. When undergraduate students were initially introduced to the content of this new field, they were typically informed that "communication" was distinct from the subject matter of rhetoric or speech because communication was a *process*, and that the process was dynamic and ongoing and, importantly, entailed feedback from the receiver as well as the initial message from the sender.

The only "model" of communication appearing in undergraduate textbooks even up through the last decade of the twentieth century was that of Claude Shannon and Warren Weaver which, although they included the word "communication" in the title of their initial publication, was only intended to offer a theory of information flow.[9] In the model itself, however, there is nothing that serves to explicate anything remotely resembling a theory of communicative experience. The model describes a rational and mechanical process of codes, messages, noise (or interference), and feedback. In this regard, the word "communication" becomes merely a cipher to signify a process of information transfer between sources of intelligence (or intention) understood as separate entities. In this context, the "sender" need not be a body and need not be human. Given that Shannon and Weaver were mathematicians, engineers, and cyberneticists, one should not be surprised that the seeming psychological element of their model is so thoroughly mathematized that it is barely recognizable in any other dimension but that of coded logic. As such, the grounding metaphor for understanding the discourse of communication theory for undergraduate students was that of an interactional, information-exchange process with emotionality, attachment, and the narrative dimensions of relationship strategically bracketed.

The world of "communication theory" as represented by the various attempts to adjust the Shannon and Weaver model to the rhetoric and subject matter of undergraduate textbooks in public speaking, interpersonal, group, organizational, and mass communication[10] is a world in which the phenomenological structuralism of Jakobson would have become difficult to comprehend and the Nietzschean existentialism of Bataille might well have seemed ridiculous. My interest in transforming the concept of communication, both as a *topos* of intellectual work (and dialogue) and as a domain of human experience, is *not* about, simply, updating the language of my academic field to better reflect the increasing sophistication of human science theory or to reflect the epistemic transition to postmodern thought (whatever that might mean) and the increased reliance on Continental philosophy in the articulation of research thematics and problematics. My interest is not merely discursive, even if the discourse concern is richly disciplinary and has the capacity to sophisticate and deepen the theoretical, methodological, and pedagogical dialogues occurring within either communication studies or communicology for decades to come.

My interest in developing a concept of human communicative experience is a matter of philosophical and epistemological necessity. For far too long, theorists in the human sciences, whether they consider themselves philosophers or not, have engaged in a dialogue about consciousness, rationality, language, discourse, meaning, interaction, and sociality as though the human being emerged as a communicative being somewhere during late childhood and adolescence. For far too long, theorists in the human sciences have operated under an assumption that no psychoanalyst or psychotherapist would tolerate for even a moment in the course of her or his work: the assumption that the experiences of infancy, childhood, and family can somehow be bracketed from the manner in which we engage one another in social interaction.

From Husserl onward, the so-called "Cartesian" problem of body and mind has engaged the method of phenomenological reflection and the demands of radical interpretation to somehow synthesize that which remains partitioned (at least intellectually) in Western consciousness. Yet, as long as the analytical project focuses on a concept of "the body" as a discrete thing, as a separate entity in *either* space or time, all the phenomenological reflection will be able to accomplish is a softening of some of the terms of rational inquiry, perhaps resulting in the reformulation of a problematic if the theorist is sufficiently tenacious. We have, of course, been fortunate that the tenacity of Heidegger and Merleau-Ponty was able to lead them and their students well beyond a concept of embodiment (or *ek-sistence*) as a thing-in-the-world. But, even for phenomenologists and aspiring phenomenologists the path has been difficult. Simply, the difficulty is getting beyond the concept of the *Cogito* as an active, temporal consciousness situated in a world. It confuses the question of agency. If I understand my perceptual experience to be that of an intelligent camera, having a memory of past perceptions and an informed, rational perspective on future perceptions, I am inclined to grasp that which I perceive as *ex camera*—that is, as properties of a world "out there," not in my mind, not in my consciousness. (Perhaps that is why we are inclined to want to *take pictures* of what we see, inasmuch as we become convinced we could never hold onto, never sufficiently grasp that to which we are drawn in acts of perception.)

But the *Cogito* can only work from this limited concept of embodied agency if it valorizes "impulse" and "impulsivity" as modalities of pragmatic observation. In this instance, *now*, suddenly, I can see the things that clutter the room in which I write these sentences with the same sort of candid glimpses of sight that can serve to either amuse or panic a restless child in an unfamiliar or uncomfortable setting. (With this precipitous observation, I might feel, suddenly, motivated to straighten up my office; although I think I shall wait to act, I am now quite aware that I seem to create an enormous mess when I work.) Even though impulsive observation has never emerged as a preferred mode of seeing, it is common enough in modern experience to both disturb the *habitus* of reflective inquiry and to orient consciousness to new and different *topoi* of thinking. (Commercial advertisements would never have succeeded as modes of propaganda and influence if impulsive observation were not already a practiced and habituated mode of modern perception.) Nonetheless, the impulsivity of perception enables one to partition the moments of cognition, one from the other, to such an extent that the "I think" of this moment seems to belong to its own destiny and its own place of origin. To wit: I am aware of my Self and I am aware of my general framework of perception and thought from yesterday (and, to some extent, the day before), but today and now, at this moment, *now*, "I am." In many ways, this view of mind comports well with an information-theoretic concept of meaning, expression, and social interaction. In this framework, it is not discourse or language or culture or even power that is speaking, it is "I," instantiated, *now*, in this moment of the *Cogito*, as though "I" invented language, as though I am not dispersed within a system of textual relations, as though I am not a subject, subjected to my own *l'histoire.*

The search for a grounded view of the *Cogito* serves, in many ways, as a brief description of psychoanalytic inquiry over the course of the last century. And when we follow the flow of psychoanalytic thought from Freud, Klein, and Lacan to the object-relations theorists to the theorists and researchers writing on the subject matter of attachment, development, maturity, individuation, and differentiation, we can see the ways in which perception and the embodied *habitus* of perceptual activity each serve as possible narrative frameworks of cognitive envelopment. If, as Foucault has maintained, we are each a product of a system of *dispositifs*, the most powerful of these apparatuses is the family.[11]

It is within the crucible of the family that childhood is experienced and it is within the crucible of the family that the terms of adolescent development—terms that invariably emerge from crisis—set the course of the rational dispositions and conventions describing the "grown up" minds that cognitive psychology and analytic philosophy have come to take as their subject matter. The quiet assumption that we leave our childhood and our infancy behind us when we enter into adult games of reason, power, and social connection is, for me, one of the most puzzling errors that a human scientist could make. Nonetheless, it pervades any sort of thinking that finds itself comfortable with a system of linear connections and exchanges, like that implied by Shannon and Weaver's mathematical model, as descriptive of the everyday psychology of human interaction.

Simply, the human experience of communication begins in attachment. We do not enter the world as rational beings, somehow "electing" to enter into the loving and soothing arms of our nurturers. We enter the world innately predisposed for human connection, and the modalities of our initial, primal bonding, from feeding, to attunement, to all of the other subtle elements of touch and discovery, are anything but rational.[12] As we progress from infancy through childhood, the connection that we maintain to others in our lives is emotional—which is to say that our primal experience of human communication is emotional and, thus, grounded in memories and anticipations of fear and pleasure. We do not enter the world as "cognitive" beings and there is no watershed moment of consciousness whereby we become rational subjects strategically thinking our way through groups and intimacies. Taylor Carmen effectively captures this theme: "The intentional constitution of the body is not the product of a cognitive process whose steps we might trace back to the founding acts of a pure I. Rather, the body in its perceptual capacity just is the I in its most primordial aspect."[13]

The psychological need to bond with others as we move through the various stages of cognitive and social development is built upon a set of hypotheses that, essentially, mirrors the process of attachment from infancy and childhood. Peter Blos, upon whose work I relied in chapter seven, makes the case that the adolescent undergoes, essentially, a second process of attachment and individuation in the struggle to find her or his new bearings in the world. He writes: "It has become convincingly clear from clinical investigations of the adolescent process that both the task of disengagement from primary objects and the abandonment of infantile ego states necessitate a return to early phases of development."[14] Although we might articulate instrumental reasons for the relationships we develop and sustain with others in adolescence and adulthood, we do not truly escape the volatile holds of jealousy, envy, idealization, guilt, shame, and competition that drive our emotions in childhood. Any notion that such cultural and technological phenomena as literacy, education, social order/population management, and urbanization might have enabled consciousness to somehow transcend these sorts of "primitive" drives is mistaken from the start. As Blos concludes: "The adolescent's slow severance of the emotional ties to his family, his fearful or exhilarated entrance into the new life which beckons him, these experiences are among the profoundest in human existence."[15]

James Lock, thinking with Blos's concept of adolescent and early adult development, offers a useful definition of the concept of "acting out," a form of expressive behavior in which each of us has partaken and which so few of us ever seem to grow out of. Lock writes: "Acting out is a result of a fundamental rift between language and emotion when language fails as a form of communication—language has 'miscarried.' What is delivered in its place is acting out."[16] Acting out, in all of its intense emotionality, in all of its regression and infantilism, in all of its hormonal energy, is as much a form of communication as the intellectual exchanges of scholars—even more so, I would argue, inasmuch as the "passage" of adolescence, although physiologically demarcated by spermarche and menarche at the beginning, does not seem to have any sort of boundary marker letting us know when we are, at long last, mature adults. (I have had grey hair since my late twenties—for three decades, in fact. I keep waiting and hoping to find out that I am finally all grown up.) And, as Bernard Stiegler maintains (in his book titled, appropriately, *Acting Out*[17]), these tangled paroxysms of emotion and gesture and language and speech are quickly becoming the rule rather than the exception in our era, particularly with regard to increasingly desperate public and political efforts at communication.

In any case, irrespective of what sorts of expressive episodes can be anticipated from the diminishing fortunes of late modernity, what I am examining and exploring regarding the emotional (and then, eventually, hormonal) drives toward attachment is, ultimately, in service of my effort to describe an existential theory of human communicative experience. If I were to be asked the question "what is communicology?" my answer would be that communicology is the human science best able to address the manner and motif in which persons connect and attach to one another.

I have absolutely no doubt that Claude Shannon and Warren Weaver were brilliant scientists. A model they constructed to track the flow of coded bits of information through a system of cybernetic connections, however, was appropriated by a field of study they knew very little about (and, likely, was one in which they had very little interest) and was made to carry a very heavy burden. Their model was burdened with depicting the manner in which an abstracted conceptualization of the human interacted and "shared" its "meaning" with other abstracted conceptualizations of the human. Simply, how would one employ the theory, both implied and modeled, in the linear schemes taught to university students for decades to describe and explain the emotionality of childhood attachment?—or adolescent acting out?—or adult acting out? Or are these examples not proper cases of human communication?

The abstracted conceptualization of the human implied in the persistent image of linear, systematic exchange is in many ways a surrealist imagining, an *impossibility*—not merely an *odd* impossibility (like, say, a newborn-infant brain surgeon or a tennis-playing pat of butter) but an everyday impossibility, such as that depicted in Magritte's repeated instantiations of the bowler-hatted man, with all of his contradictions and secrets discretely tucked way in his overcoat, hat, and blank expression. It is a depiction of the human who never shits, who never wet the bed, who never masturbates, who has never had a violent urge, whose erotic fantasies are all "family-friendly," and who has a clear sense of the line separating reality from illusion. Foucault's appreciation for the surrealist movement is no mere coincidence. Like the notion of "man" who is destined to "be erased, like a face drawn in sand at the edge of the sea,"[18] the hypostatization of the human that undergoes radical interrogation in the work of Foucault is a reflected but nevertheless constricted notion that has sought a line of validation in the human sciences from Descartes up through Kant, positivism, and modern technocratic empiricism. Unlike many intellectuals of his generation, Foucault was not inclined to tuck the secret of his own sexuality inside the topcoat and bowler hat of the elite French academy. And so, motivating the works of Foucault we can see the absurd (or surreal) circumstances of the embodied human in the standard thematics of reason and *anthrōpos,* thus rupturing all of their presumed lines of empirical validity: madness, medicine, the mobile and arbitrary categories of mental illness, crime, transgression, discipline, power, control, education, punishment (amidst its all of its sadism and failures), and sexuality.

It is important, when discussing concepts central to phenomenology like intersubjectivity and embodiment, to keep our terms grounded in *vécu*—what in English has been translated as "lived experience." For several decades, there has been, particularly in the area of cultural studies, a heightened interest in *writing* about the human body. Much of this thinking and commentary, however, has been unable to escape the grip of Cartesianism, if not rationalism or positivism. The body is talked about as though it exists and is experienced as a discrete thing—as though it is not entirely contingent on perception, language, discourse, time, and the participation of others in the experience and meaning of expression and movement. Yes, the body is a site of contest and domination but, as Merleau-Ponty eloquently argues, it is so much more complex than that. (In fact, its *Dasein* is one and the same with it complexity.) For Merleau-Ponty and, I would argue, for communicology, the body *is* perception and expression—and, thus, communication itself. When the body is addressed as a "medium" for expression and perception, it invites thought to consider the body yet again as a *ding an sich*, as a thing phenomenally separate *from* thought, spirit, and consciousness—thus enabling thought, spirit and consciousness to drift toward intellectualist illusions, such as perfect languages, ideal forms, and universal consciousness.

It in this context that the communicology that I envision will need to address some of the more "crypto-normative" assumptions of theory and epistemology that will likely continue for some time in the academic arena that situates research and pedagogy in speech, rhetoric, and communication studies. An outline for these assumptions can be found in a text of remarkable ambition, published in 1999, by John Durham Peters and titled *Speaking into the Air: A History of the Idea of Communication.*[19] Peters' text constitutes the first and, in many ways, only comprehensive study of the word "communication" as it has journeyed through Western history. In many ways, his text reads like a historical philosopher's narrative of the way in which "communication" has appeared in the vocabulary of several centuries of thinkers whose works have had a noticeable impact on the social and human sciences. The text, to be sure, has garnered no small amount of praise, especially among scholars in the field of communication studies. And it poses a unique challenge to scholars who have entered into various aspects of a research enterprise within the "communication" field without taking the time to think through the operative terms of their chosen disciplinary discourse.

Nonetheless, Peters' work is a close study of the concept of communication that, alas, bears very little relationship to grounded communicative experience. Whether he would admit it or not, much of his text addresses the concept of communication as a transcendental mental/spiritual event. In the third chapter of the text, he addresses the body and *eros*, but he only does so in the context of Kierkegaard, Hegel, and Socrates (as symbolized in Plato's *Phaedrus*), as a modality of thinking and reflection and mutuality, but not in the context of Heidegger or Merleau-Ponty. Which is to say that he writes about the body abstractly, seeing it, of course, as a critical medium of experience, but not in the inherent ambiguity of its being at all—in the ambiguity of its proprioception, perception, and expressive existence, of its intertwined sensations, feelings, emotion, and reflective consciousness, of its desires, urgencies, moods, and motifs of arousal.

Philosophical terms like "grounding," "embodiment," "intersubjectivity," and even "being-in-the-world" can be used in a number of frameworks. They are terms that became part of the established vocabulary of phenomenological investigation for most of the twentieth century. As such, they are studied and used by philosophers and human science theorists regardless of whether the philosopher or human science theorist is sympathetic with or practicing a phenomenological method. They are terms that can be used with disdain. They can be used ironically. They can be used as though the speaker or writer is, psychologically, wearing latex gloves prior to integrating them into her or his thought. One of the reasons I am always wary of writers who comment on the significance of "the body" is that the body cannot *escape* significance in our era. Neuroscientists, psychiatrists, pharmacologists, medical doctors of all sorts (including plastic surgeons), cultural theorists, everyone connected with the cosmetics, fitness, and fashion industry, as well as everyone flooding to the internet to look at pictures and streaming video (no small amount of which is pornographic) of strangers and celebrities and of one another, have come to view the body with greater fascination than at any time in the last millennium. So, when Peters criticizes attempts to understand communication as a means to pure communion, writing that it "invites us into a world of unions without politics, understanding without language, and souls without bodies, only to make politics, language and bodies reappear as obstacles rather than blessings,"[20] not only do not I not know what sort of theories of communication he is talking about, I also do not know what view of embodiment he is working from. Yes, the body is mortal. Yes, the body needs regular, if not constant, attention and must be fed and allowed to rest and recuperate. But the same things can be said of my car. It, too, won't last forever. It too needs to be refueled and looked after. Talking eloquently or passionately of the body, even a "high-maintenance" and deeply-complex body, can still serve to disguise a Cartesian concept of discerning, perceptual activity as that of an intelligent camera grafted onto a living carcass of skin, organs, and bone. The problem of understanding, here, is not that "the body is so much more than any old piece of equipment," it is that the body, simply, is not a *thing*. We are each, from the moment of our conception and birth, a set of relations. A dance instructor, for example, may see my body as a thing unto itself, having height, weight, muscles, and other quantitative dimensions that serve to define it, but *I* cannot experience my body this way (I cannot even *see* its outline without a mirror) and, as Merleau-Ponty illustrates through numerous cases from medical history throughout *Phenomenology of Perception*, I enter into madness to the very extent I become convinced that I *can* experience my body this way.

Peters takes a strong interest in Hegel's *Phenomenology of Spirit* based on his belief that Hegel is the first great theorist of intersubjectivity.[21] The problem for Peters, if he is sincere in his concern for the body, is that "intersubjectivity" is a term that has no strong existential meaning for Hegel (and is as much about the "communion of souls" as anything Peters criticizes in the first one hundred pages of his writing) and it is a term that has come to enjoy widespread usage among analytic philosophers and cognitive scientists—thinkers, in other words, for whom the well-known "brain-in-a-vat" thought experiment remains a vexing puzzle (rather than a graduate school version of comic-book solipsism). The concept of intersubjectivity is transformed by the existential conditions of the phenomenological method. Now, the existential condition is not "language"; the focus on language as the principal problematic is what separates "hermeneutics" (even as critical-interpretive inquiry) from phenomenology. Instead, the existential condition is embodied. It is entailed by a thematic and problematic of *vécu.* As a problem of lived experience, it demands that thought be given to a question of what can only be defined as behavior (*comportement*), which is, to some degree, ironic, considering that it was the failure of "behavioral psychology" and "behaviorism" that motivated both Husserl and Merleau-Ponty through their initial forays into phenomenology. The question concerning *comportement* concerns the very matters of human experience for which scientific or analytical inquiry has thus far been unable to provide satisfactory explanations or even sufficiently meaningful descriptions.

As I have attempted to argue throughout this book, the *vécu*, the lived experience of human communication is, again, *fundamentally* an embodied event of bonding, coupling, connecting, and holding. As I have argued elsewhere: "Simply, the human being over and above its other mammalian traits is an attached creature. To the extent it gains its biological survival through means other than caring contact by adult members of its species, it ceases to be human to that very degree. Not just infants, but children up through their teens are tremendously dependent beings."[22] The body is not a thing and intersubjectivity is not a philosophical abstraction. The matter of attachment is as deeply and richly psychological as much as it is physiological. It is the grounding of our perceptual activity. As such, when Merleau-Ponty describes *flesh*—namely, the chiasm, the intertwining—he is describing the *topos* of communicative experience; he is describing the communicative body.

Often our moments of interaction are defined by talk. In these situations, it may seem as though communication is a verbal matter. We formulate sentences and speak them to one another. We take turns, or at least attempt to take turns, although sometimes we talk over one another and other times we can barely keep our signals straight. In these situations, it may seem as though communication is about sending and receiving messages. Sometimes these messages seem to plant seeds in our minds. Sometimes we undoubtedly learn new things from listening and paying attention. In these cases it truly seems as though communication occurs because we are able to speak clearly, because we obey rules of civility, and because we employ logic.

Sometimes we must talk to strangers. Perhaps we may do so in order to navigate our way through a new environment. Perhaps we do so for "reasons" of basic curiosity. Sometimes we must speak to groups of varying sizes whose members are largely unfamiliar to us. When we have an opportunity to think about what we are going to say, we can use the moment to try to affect people and circumstances in ways that comport with our desires and dreams.

For quite a few people, this is what communication is about. Communication is about expressing ourselves sincerely and effectively. Communication is about making intelligent points, winning converts, influencing people, and, hopefully, making some friends along the way. (It is this on general plane of ethical responsibility and concern for the other that the concept of *eros* is brought into play by Peters as a broad contextualization of what communication can mean in civic life and human affairs.[23]) In this framework, communication is simultaneously about community and about citizenship. But, in this romantic panorama of life and civic responsibility, we can see nothing unique about the notion of "communication" or about the concept of communicative experience that was not articulated in textbooks on rhetoric and public speaking for the last two centuries—or, for that matter, in the themes of the citizen orator as expressed by Cicero, Quintilian, Aristotle, or Isocrates. As well, the notions of dialogue and dissemination, whether in opposition or apposition—which emerge as critical, dueling thematics for Peters—have been a feature of writing about rhetoric and persuasion for quite some time.

Yes, communication entails the dynamics of talk and dialogue and disagreement and persuasion, but the *relationship* that *defines* the participants *in their interaction* is what truly distinguishes the study of communication from the study of rhetoric. It is the relationship that entails the elements of the narrative that brought us together in the first place. And irrespective of what gets said, what ideas become subject to change, and who gets the last word, it is the status/*stasis* of the relationship both before and after the exchange that ought to become the primary subject matter of the communicologist. It is in the relationship that we can find the connection, the game matrix, the narrative and its mythic horizon, the role possibilities, and the dramatic stakes that serve to illustrate the semiotic and emotional *vécu*—which is to say: the phenomenological psychology of communicative experience.

Questions of "governmentality" (both of self and of others) are central to problems of human community and citizenship. Nonetheless, psychoanalytically speaking, most of what constitutes our social behavior throughout our childhood is built upon an etiquette of impulse control that is, in its principal dynamic, largely repressive. This is to say that our initial efforts at self-government and citizenship in the domestic world of the home and neighborhood and within the *dispositifs* of school and structured social situations consist of keeping our compulsions and urges at bay. We "discipline" ourselves as best we can (and as much as we are willing) to work with the group and to speak within the tone and register of the group situation. This also includes refraining from moving or gesturing in distracting ways as well as refraining from various boorish or antisocial behaviors: sneezing too loudly, coughing without a handkerchief, picking our noses, burping, farting, and so forth. We could say it is "reason" that drives our governmentality of self toward the production of a positive *ethos* of effective group membership, but it is more accurate to credit "common sense" (or *sensus communis*) as the more probable explanation.

Again, we repress our compulsions and urges to help meet or set the terms of a relationship. We do this as children to feel loved, affirmed, and validated within our families. We do this as grownups to live and work in psychological systems and networks of connectedness that give us pleasure and that keep us happy and productive. Although the relationship serves as the psychological game-matrix for expressing approval and showing affection toward the persons who inhabit our orbits of life and work, our motivations, as I argue in Chapters Six and Seven, are not always noble. We often tell lies. We lie: all of us, not some of us. We commonly do so. We lie to make one another—and ourselves—feel better. We use words in ways that are deceptive and we make up stories that never happened or, at least, never quite happened. Of course, we endeavor to tell the truth as often as we can and, indeed, we routinely succeed in doing so. But we also lie—not because it is diabolical but because it human, all too human to prevaricate, to go astray. We lie for the purpose of emotion, not dissemination, not dialectic or dialogue, but *feeling*. We lie to keep our relationships where we want them or, perhaps, where we believe, where we *imagine* they ought to be. We lie to enter into the interstices of escape. The erotic component of *sensus communis,* as embodied in intense moments of sexual desire, is not about the holiness of our finitude as we live through it. It is not that, in this case (as with love), the particular has become higher than the universal. It is that in the psychology of arousal, in the moment that the flesh of the other and the flesh of my body are one and the same, in the moment that we each become vanishing points in the consumption of our desires, my ecstasy (*ek-stasis*) and my euphoria take me *out* of the relationship that enabled this moment and place me back *into* a relationship that likely will feel very much similar to the relationship I just exited, but may in fact never be the same. Which is to say that sexuality and its attendant euphorias are forms of escape. They entail relational and personal transformations, but they are, as well, vital forms of escape: escape from the *habitus* of work and economic identity, escape from narratives of social and civic virtue, of our clearly stated and avowed obligations, and of public performances of piety and nobility.

The embodied human consciousness often speaks glowingly of its own mind and spiritual (*Geistliche*) ambitions. The embodied human also is hormonal, with pheromones, vapors, and fragrances stirring urges to connect with one other that are often sudden and unanticipated. It can experience dimensions of arousal far beyond its ability to think clearly and responsibly. And so the common sense of relational tact is simultaneously an implicit strategy of ego, momentary loss of identity, and *ek-stasis*. An embodied *sensus communis* becomes in many ways a lived *habitus* of communicative discretion. Sometimes we talk to one another. Sometimes we irritate one another. Sometimes we pleasure one another. Sometimes these forms of communicative *activity* overlap in communicative *experience*. When these forms of expression conjoin we are not, as Peters suggests, "speaking into the air." We are instead speaking into one another's worlds and through one another's bodies. It is a process that begins in infancy, it begins in our families of origin, and it is a process that continues as we seek to create experiential networks and, yes, families that will embrace us in our mortality.

The dawning of communicology has been motivated not so much by a felt need to protect an academic field from modes of inquiry but by not standing in the way of inquiry into the event of communicative experience. Communicology, as with all of the existentially and phenomenologically grounded human sciences of the modern era, has been and, of course, will most likely be unable to meaningfully interrupt the intrusion of technocratic empiricism (or technology itself) into the *habitus* of human life. Technocratic empiricism is a mode of disciplinarity that very much seems to have a mind of its own, and its modes of inquiry tend to follow rather than lead the seemingly endless proliferation of chemicals and gadgetry into myriad domains of the human ecosphere. In so many ways, the great achievement of Peters' *Speaking into the Air* is his detailed exegesis of the manner in which twentieth-century scholarship in "communication" somehow, someway, managed to avoid taking a serious look at the terms of its own field of study. Which is to say that the field of study has already been far too protected in its terms of disciplinary work.

Communicology, as I see it, is about following the evidence of embodiment (as expression and perception) wherever it leads. The technocratically-empirical fields of medical, pharmacological, and academic psychology have endeavored and, no doubt will continue to endeavor to find and follow the evidence of carnal expression and perception by way of chemistry, tomography, and electronic imaging where it serves their paradigmatic interests in locating the problems of human understanding and meaning in the physical, anatomical being of "the body." To follow the evidence of the human—that is, *all* of the evidence, all of the *signs*: the oneiric, the erotic, the diabolical, the transgressive, the demented, the infantile, the helpless and disabled—is to let it speak and let it be heard. It, therefore, demands that we step back from the anatomical subject and let the person, the *persona*, live in her or his psychological and cultural world. It demands that we grasp that the world of the person is a world in which time and space are not separate entities subject to different metrics and assessments but are lived simultaneously and without clear markers and measured horizons. Equivocal assumptions of "intersubjectivity" will continue to serve as a pretext for sustaining a theoretical orthodoxy of *Geist*, of mind as an elegant, uncluttered theatre of noesis and semiotic coordination—an orthodoxy that has, astonishingly, perpetuated the relevance of the Shannon and Weaver model (and metaphor) of information transfer as a schematic of communicative experience well beyond its expected shelf-life.

The task of communicology, as I see it, is to continue with the same independence of spirit and consciousness as that exhibited by Dewey's ensemble at the turn of the century, and in turn hopefully step into the horizon of Merleau-Ponty's vision of "the philosopher" that he so poetically voiced in his inaugural address at the *Collège de France*. John Wild and James Edie, in their preface to the translated publication of this address half a century ago, comment that the "humanistic disciplines" in their era "have little sense of a human world with distinctive structures of its own, or of a disciplined method for its exploration. Hence we find them exposed to the constant encroachment of alien methods and concepts taken from the various sciences and suffering from an inability to communicate, from the relativism that follows in its train, and from a general loss of nerve."[24] And so, to carefully paraphrase Merleau-Ponty, communicology must possess "*inseparably* the taste for evidence and the feeling for ambiguity."[25] If a human science "limits itself to accepting ambiguity, it is called equivocation."[26] Communicologists, "in order to experience more fully the ties of truth which bind [them] to the world and history,"[27] should find "neither the depth of [themselves] nor absolute knowledge, but a renewed image of the world and of [themselves] placed within it among others."[28] In short, the communicologist must become the human scientist "who wakes up and speaks."[29]

NOTES

1. Danziger, *Naming the Mind.*
2. See Rorty, *Consequences of Pragmatism*; Menand, *Pragmatism: A Reader*; Dickstein, *The Revival of Pragmatism*; Hickman, *Pragmatism as Post-Postmodernism*; Hickman, *Reading Dewey*; and Langsdorf and Smith, *Recovering Pragmatism's Voice.*
3. Danziger, *Naming the Mind*; Danziger, *Marking the Mind*; and Danziger, *Constructing the Subject.* See also Mills, *Control.*
4. Martin, *Education of John Dewey*, 453.
5. Martin, *Education of John Dewey*, 453.
6. Martin, *Education of John Dewey*, 456.
7. Martin, *Education of John Dewey*, 453.
8. Lanigan discusses the choice of "conventionality" as a mode of disciplinarity, institutional organization, and "professional mass communication" within the academic field of communication in *Phenomenology of Communication*, 246–60.
9. Shannon and Weaver, *The Mathematical Theory of Communication.*
10. Rather than listing textbook after textbook, I will only posit that in my classroom teaching experience, begun in 1980, the only disciplinary undergraduate textbooks in which I encountered a model of communication *other* than the linear, sequential, process model of information flow (whether directly attributed to Shannon and Weaver or not) have been published within the last decade—and, even then, these cases are the exception rather than the rule.

A post-Cartesian concept of communicative experience simply has yet to find its way into the orders of discourse fundamental to the development of budding communication students.

11. See Bronfenbrenner, "Ecology of the Family."
12. See Solan, "Jointness."
13. Carmen, "The Body in Husserl and Merleau-Ponty," 224.
14. Blos, "The Second Individuation Process of Adolescence," 184–85.
15. Blos, *On Adolescence*, 12.
16. Lock, "Acting Out and the Narrative Function," 554.
17. See Stiegler, *Acting Out.*
18. Foucault, *Order of Things*, 387.
19. Peters, *Speaking into the Air*.
20. Peters, *Speaking into the Air*, 30–31.
21. Peters, *Speaking into the Air*, 109–16.
22. Macke, "Intrapersonal Communicology," 51.
23. Peters, *Speaking into the Air*, 36–65.
24. Wild and Edie, "Translator's Preface," xxii.
25. Merleau-Ponty, *In Praise of Philosophy*, 4.
26. Merleau-Ponty, *In Praise of Philosophy*, 4–5.
27. Merleau-Ponty, *In Praise of Philosophy*, 63.
28. Merleau-Ponty, *In Praise of Philosophy*, 63.
29. Merleau-Ponty, *In Praise of Philosophy*, 63.

References

Abecassis, Jack. "The Fragility of Philosophy: Passions, Ancient and Modern." *MLN: Modern Language Notes* 110, no. 4 (Comparative Literature Issue) (1995): 918–42.

Aboulafia, Mitchell. "Introduction." In *Philosophy, Social Theory, and the Thought of George Herbert Mead.* Edited by Mitchell Aboulafia. Albany: State University of New York Press, 1991.

Alexander, Thomas. *John Dewey's Theory of Art, Experience, and Nature: The Horizons of Feeling*. Albany: State University of New York Press, 1987.

Aristotle. *Nichomachean Ethics*. Translated by Roger Crisp. New York: Cambridge University Press, 2000. (Original work published between 335–323 BC.)

Askew, E. W. "Water." In *Present Knowledge in Nutrition*, 7th Edition. Edited by Ekhard E. Ziegler and L. J. Filer, Jr. Washington, D.C.: International Life Sciences Institute Press, 1996, 98–108.

Ayto, John. *Dictionary of Word Origins*. New York: Arcade, 1990.

Bachelard, Gaston. *The Poetics of Reverie: Childhood, Language, and the Cosmos*. Translated by Daniel Russell. Boston: Beacon Press, 1969.

———. *The Poetics of Space*. Translated by Maria Jolas. Boston: Beacon Press, 1994.

———. *Water and Dreams: An Essay on the Imagination of Matter.* Translated by Edith R. Farrell. Dallas: The Pegasus Foundation, 1983.

———. *Earth and Reveries of Will: An Essay on the Imagination of Matter*. Translated by Kenneth Haltman. Dallas: The Dallas Institute Publications, 2002.

Ball, Phillip. *Life's Matrix: A Biogra phy of Water.* Berkeley: University of California Press, 2001.

Barnhart, Robert K., Editor. *The Concise Dictionary of Etymology*. New York: HarperCollins, 1995.

Bataille, Georges. *Erotism: Death & Sensuality.* Translated by Mary Dalwood. San Francisco, CA: City Lights, 1962. (Original work published in 1957).

———. *Inner Experience.* Translated by Leslie Anne Boldt. Albany: State University of New York Press, 1988. (Original work published in 1954.)

———. *Tears of Eros*. Translated by Peter Connor. San Francisco: City Lights Books, 1989.

———. *Theory of Religion.* Translated by Robert Hurley. New York: Zone Books, 1989. (Original work published in 1973.)

———. *On Nietzsche*. Translated by Bruce Boone. New York: Paragon House, 1992. (Original work published in 1945.)

———. *The Accursed Share, Volumes II and III.* Translated by Robert Hurley. New York: Zone Books, 1993.

———. *The Unfinished System of Nonknowledge*. Edited by Stuart Kendall. Translated by Michelle Kendall and Stuart Kendall. Minneapolis: University of Minnesota Press, 2001.
Bateson, G. *Steps to an Ecology of Mind.* New York: Ballantine Books, 1972.
Baudrillard, Jean. *Simulations*. Translated byPhil Beitchman and Paul Foss. New York: Semiotexte(e), 1983.
———. *The Gulf War Did Not Take Place.* Translated by Paul Patton. Bloomington: Indiana University Press, 1995. (Original work published in 1991.)
———. *The Transparency of Evil*. Translated by James Benedict. New York: Verso, 1993.
Bauman, Zygmunt. *Liquid Modernity.* New York: Polity, 2000.
———. *Liquid Love: On the Frailty of Human Bonds.* New York: Polity, 2003.
———. *Liquid Life.* New York: Polity, 2005.
Beckett, Samuel. *Waiting for Godot*. New York: Grove Press, 1954.
———. *Stories and Texts for Nothing.* Translated by the author. London: Calder and Boyars, 1974. (Original work published in 1955.)
Benjamin, Walter. *The Arcades Project.* Edited by Rolf Tiedemann. Translated by Howard Eiland and Kevin McLaughlin. Cambridge, MA: Belknap/Harvard University Press, 2002.
Benjamin, Walter. *The Writer of Modern Life: Essays on Charles Baudelaire.* Edited by Michael W. Jennings and translated by Howard Eiland and Edmund Jephcott. Cambridge, MA: Belknap/Harvard University Press, 2006.
Bion, Wilfred R. *Learning from Experience.* Lanham, MD: Rowman & Littlefield. 1962.
Bloom, Harold. *Omens of Millennium: The Gnosis of Angels, Dreams, and Resurrections.* New York: Riverhead, 1996.
Blos, Peter. *On Adolescence: A Psychoanalytic Interpretation.* New York: Free Press, 1962.
———. "The Second Individuation Process of Adolescence," *The Psychoanalytic Study of the Child* 22, no. 2 (1967), 162–86.
Bok, Sissela. *Lying: Moral Choices in Public and Private Life.* New York: Vintage, 1978.
Borges, Jorge Luis. *Doctor Brodie's Report.* Translated by Norman Thomas Di Giovanni. New York: E. P. Dutton, 1972.
Bowen, Murray. *Family Therapy in Clinical Practice.* New York: Jason Aronson, 1985.
Bowlby, John. *The Making and Breaking of Affectional Bonds.* London: Tavistock, 1979.
Bowlby, John. *A Secure Base.* New York: Basic Books, 1988.
Bronfenbrenner, Urie. "Ecology of the Family as a Context for Human Development: Research Perspectives." *Developmental Psychology* 22, no. 6 (1986): 723–42.
Buber, Martin. *I and Thou.* Translated by Walter Kaufmann. New York: Scribner's, 1970.
Bubner, Rüdiger. *Modern German Philosophy.* Translated by Eric Matthews. New York: Cambridge University Press, 1981.
Burroughs, William S. *Last Words: The Final Journals of William S. Burroughs*. New York: Grove Press, 2001.
Cairns, Dorian. *The Philosophy of Edmund Husserl.* Edited by Lester Embree. New York, Springer, 2012.
Canetti, Elias. *The Agony of Flies: Notes and Notations*. Translation by H. F. Broch de Rothermann. New York: Noonday Press, 1994. (Original work published in 1992.)
Caplan, Eric. *Mind Games: American Culture and the Birth of Psychotherapy*. Berkeley: University of California Press, 1998.
Carmen, Taylor. "The Body in Husserl and Merleau-Ponty." *Philosophical Topics* 27, no. 2 (1999): 205–26.
Carse, James P. *Finite and Infinite Games: A Vision of Life as Play and Possibility.* New York: Ballantine, 1986.
Casey, Edward S. *Spirit and Soul: Essays in Philosophical Psychology.* Dallas: Spring Publications, 1991.
Cassirer, Ernst. *The Logic of the Cultural Sciences.* Translated by S. G. Lofts. New Haven, CT: Yale University Press, 2000.
Centers for Disease Control. "1900-1999: Ten Great Public Health Achievements—United States." *Journal of the American Medical Association* 281, 16 (1999): 1481–84.
Chimisso, Cristina. *Gaston Bachelard: Critic of Science and the Imagination.* New York: Routledge, 2001.

Chumlea, W. Cameron, and Shumei S. Guo, Christine M. Zeller, Nicholas V. Reo, and Roger M. Siervogel. "Total Body Water Data for White Adults 18 to 64 Years of Age: The Fels Longitudinal Study." *Kidney International* 56 (July 1999): 244–52.

Cicero. *On the Orator, Books I-II*. Translated by E. W. Sutton and H. Rackham. Cambridge, MA: Harvard University Press, 1942.

Claiborne, Robert. *The Roots of English*. New York: Anchor Books, 1989.

Clement of Rome. "The Second Epistle of Clement to the Corinthians." *The Apostolic Fathers*. Translation by Kirsopp Lake. Cambridge, MA: Harvard University Press, 1912-1913. (Original work written circa 96 AD.)

Damasio, Antonio. *The Feeling of What Happens: Body and Emotion in the Making of Con sciousness*. New York: Harvest Books, 2000.

Damasio, Antonio. *Looking for Spinoza: Joy, Sorrow, and the Feeling Brain*. New York: Harvest Books, 2003.

Damasio, Antonio. *Descartes' Error: Emotion, Reason, and the Human Brain*. New York: Penguin, 2005.

Danziger, Kurt. *Constructing the Subject: Historical Origins of Psychological Research*. New York: Cambridge University Press, 1990.

Danziger, Kurt. *Naming the Mind: How Psychology Found its Language*. Thousand Oaks, CA: Sage, 1997.

Danziger, Kurt. "Comment." *International Journal Of Psychology* 41, no. 4 (2006): 271.

Danziger, Kurt. *Marking the Mind: A History of Memory*. New York: Cambridge University Press, 2008.

Deleuze, Gilles. *Nietzsche and Philosophy*. Translated by Hugh Tomlinson. New York: Columbia University Press, 1983. (Original work published in 1962.)

Deleuze, Gilles and Félix Guattari. *What Is Philosophy?* Translated by Hugh Tomlinson and Graham Burchell. New York: Columbia University Press, 1994. (Original work published in 1991.)

Descartes, Rene. "The Dioptrics (1637)." In *Philosophical Writings*. Edited and Translated by Elizabeth Anscombe and Peter Thomas Geach. New York: MacMillan, 1971.

Descombes, Vincent. *Modern French Philosophy*. Translated by Lorna Scott-Fox and J. M. Harding. Cambridge: Cambridge University Press, 1980. (Original work published in 1979.)

Dickstein, Morris. *The Revival of Pragmatism: New Essays on Social Thought, Law, and Culture*. Durham: Duke University Press, 1998.

Dillon, Martin C. "Merleau-Ponty and the Reversibility Thesis." In *Merleau-Ponty: Critical Essays*. Edited by Henry Pietersma. Washington, D.C.: CARP, University Press of America, 1989.

Dillon, Martin C. *Merleau-Ponty's Ontology*, 2nd Edition. Evanston, IL: Northwestern University Press, 1997.

———. *Semiological Reductionism: A Critique of the Deconstructionist Movement in Postmodern Thought*. Albany: State University of New York Press, 1995.

Dor, Joel. *Introduction to the Reading of Lacan: The Unconscious Structured Like a Language*. Edited and Translated by Judith Feher Gurewich and Susan Fairfield. New York: The Other Press, 1998.

Dreyfus, Hubert L. *Being-in-the-World: A Commentary on Heidegger's* Being and Time, *Division I*. Cambridge, MA: MIT Press, 1991.

Dreyfus, Hubert L., and Paul Rabinow. *Michel Foucault: Beyond Structuralism and Hermeneutics*, 2nd Edition. Chicago: University of Chicago Press, 1982.

Dym, Barry, and Michael L. Glenn. *Couples: Exploring and Understanding the Cycles of Intimate Relationships*. New York: Harper Collins, 1993.

Eco, Umberto. *A Theory of Semiotics*. Bloomington: Indiana University Press, 1976.

Eicher-Catt, Deborah, and Isaac E. Catt, Editors. *Communicology: The New Science of Embodied Discourse*. Madison, NJ: Fairleigh Dickenson University Press, 2010.

Elade, Mircea. *Myths, Dreams, and Mysteries*. Translation by Philip Mairet. New York: Harper, 1960).

Elliott, J. E. "What Was Cultural Studies? Learning the Uses of Error." *Studies in the Literary Imagination* 31, no. 1, Spring (1998): 59–86.

Erikson, Erik. *Identity and the Life Cycle.* New York: W.W. Norton & Co., 1959.
———. *Childhood and Society.* New York: W.W. Norton & Co., 1950.
———. *Identity: Youth and Crisis.* New York: W.W. Norton & Co., 1968.
Ermann, Michael. "Identity in Change." *International Forum of Psychoanalysis* 13 (2004): 209–10.
Evans, Fred, and Leonard Lawlor, Editors. *Chiasms: Merleau-Ponty's Notion of Flesh.* Albany: State University of New York Press, 2000.
Fink, Bruce. *A Clinical Introduction to Lacanian Psychoanalysis: Theory and Technique.* Cambridge, MA: Harvard University Press, 1997.
Fonagy, Peter. *Attachment Theory and Psychoanalysis.* New York: The Other Press, 2001.
Fóti, Véronique. *Vision's Invisibles: Philosophical Explorations.* Albany: State University of New York Press, 2003.
Foucault, Michel. *The Order of Things: An Archaeology of the Human Sciences.* Anonymous translation. New York: Vintage, 1970. (Original work published in 1966.)
———. *The Archaeology of Knowledge and the Discourse on Language.* Translated by A. M. Sheridan Smith. New York: Pantheon, 1972. (Original work published in 1969.)
———. "Gaston Bachelard, le philsophe et son ombre: piéger sa proper culture," *Le Figaro* (30 September 1972): 16.
———. "A Preface to Transgression." In *Language, Counter-memory, Practice.* Translated by Donald Bouchard and Sherry Simon. Edited by Donald Bouchard. Ithaca, NY: Cornell University Press, 1977. (Original work published in 1963.)
———. "What Is an Author?" In *Language, Counter-memory, Practice.* Translated by Donald Bouchard and Sherry Simon. Edited by Donald Bouchard. Ithaca, NY: Cornell University Press, 1977. (Original work published in 1969.)
———. *The History of Sexuality, Vol. 1: An Introduction.* Translated by Robert Hurley. New York: Vintage, 1978. (Original work published in 1976.)
———. *Power/Knowledge: Selected Interviews and Other Writings, 1972–1977.* Edited by Colin Gordon. Translated by Colin Gordon, Leo Marshall, John Mepham, and Kate Soper. New York: Pantheon, 1980.
———. *Herculine Barbin: Being the Recently Discovered Memoirs of a Nineteenth-Century French Hermaphrodite.* Translated by Richard McDougall. New York: Pantheon, 1980. (Original work published in 1978.)
———. *The Use of Pleasure: The History of Sexuality, Vol. 2.* Translated by Robert Hurley. New York: Vintage, 1985. (Original work published in 1984.)
———. "Dream, Imagination, and Existence." Translated by Forrest Williams. In Foucault and Ludwig Binswanger, *Dream and Existence: A Special Issue.* Translated by Forrest Williams and Jacob Needleman. Edited by Keith Hoeller. *Review of Existential Psychology & Psychiatry* 19, no. 1 (1984-1985): 29–78.
———. *The Care of the Self: The History of Sexuality, Vol. 3.* Translated by Robert Hurley. New York: Vintage, 1986. (Original work published in 1984.)
———. "Of Other Spaces." Translated by Jay Miskowiec. *Diacritics* 16 (1986): 24. (Original work published in 1967.)
———. "My Body, this Paper, this Fire (1972)." Trans. Geoff Bennington. In Foucault, M. *Aesthetics, Method, and Epistemology: Essential Works of Foucault 1954–1984.* Ed. J. Faubion. New York: The New Press, 1998.
———. "Introduction." In Georges Canguilhem, *The Normal and the Pathological.* Translated by Carolyn Fawcett. New York: Zone Books, 1978.
———. *Discipline and Punish: The Birth of the Prison.* Translated by Alan Sheridan. New York: Vintage, 1979.
———. "The Ethic of the Care of the Self as a Practice of Freedom." In James Bernauer and David Rasmussen, Editors, *The Final Foucault.* Cambridge, MA: MIT Press, 1987.
———. *Maurice Blanchot: The Thought from the Outside.* Translated by Jeffrey Mehlman and Brian Massumi. New York: Zone Books, 1987. (Original work published in 1966.)
———. "Truth, Power, Self: An Interview with Michel Foucault." In Luther H. Martin, Huck Gutman, and Patrick H. Hutton, Editors, *Technologies of the Self: A Seminar with Michel Foucault.* Amherst: University of Massachusetts Press, 1988.

———. "Technologies of the Self." In Luther H. Martin, Huck Gutman, and Patrick H. Hutton, Editors, *Technologies of the Self: A Seminar with Michel Foucault.* Amherst: University of Massachusetts Press, 1988.

———. *Fearless Speech.* Edited by Joseph Pearson. New York: Semiotext(e), 2001.

———. *The Hermeneutics of the Subject: Lectures at the College de France 1981-82.* Edited by Frédéric Gros Lagrange and translated by Graham Burchell. New York: Palgrave Macmillan, 2005.

———. *The History of Madness.* Edited by Jean Khalfa and translated by Jonathon Murphy and Jean Khalfa. New York: Routledge, 2006.

———. *Psychiatric Power: Lectures at the College de France, 1973-1974.* Edited by Jacques Lagrange and translated by Graham Burchell. New York: Palgrave Macmillan, 2006.

Freud, Sigmund. *New Introductory Lectures on Psycho-Analysis (The Standard Edition).* Edited by James Strachey. New York, W. W. Norton & Company. 1990. Originally published in in 1933.

Green, Tamara M. *The Greek and Latin Roots of English.* New York: Ardsley House, 1990.

Greimas, Algirdas Julien, and Joseph Courtés. *Semiotics and Language: An Analytical Dictionary.* Translated by Larry Crist, Daniel Patte and others. Bloomington: Indiana University Press, 1982.

Habermas, Jürgen. *Legitimation Crisis.* Translated by Thomas McCarthy. Boston: Beacon Press, 1975.

Hacking, Ian. "Minding the Brain." *The New York Re view of Books* 51 (June 24, 2004): 35–36.

Hadot, Pierre. "Forms of Life and Forms of Discourse in Ancient Philosophy." Translated by Arnold I. Davidson and Paula Wissing. *Critical Inquiry* 16, Spring (1990): 483–505.

Hall, Edward T. *Beyond Culture.* New York: Anchor Books, 1976.

Halperin, David. *Saint Foucault: Towards a Gay Hagiography.* New York: Oxford University Press, 1995.

Heidegger, Martin. *Being and Time.* Translated by John MacQuarrie & Edward Robinson. New York: Harper & Row, 1962.

Heidegger, Martin. *Was Heisst Denken?* Tübingen: Max Niemeyer Verlag, 1954. English translation by J. Glenn Gray as *What Is Called Thinking?* New York: Harper and Row, 1968. (Page citations are to the English translation.)

Hepworth, Mike, Bryan S. Turner, and Mike Featherstone. *The Body: Social Process and Cultural Theory.* Thousand Oaks, CA: Sage Publications, 1991.

Heraclitus. "Fragment No. 15." In *Herakleitos and Diogenes.* Translated by Guy Davenport. San Francisco: Grey Fox Press, 1979.

Hesse, Hermann. *Demian: The Story of Emil Sinclair's Youth.* Translated by Michael Roloff and Michael Lebeck. New York: Harper & Row, 1965. (Original work published in 1925.)

Hesse, Hermann. *Siddartha.* Translated by Susan Bernofsky. New York: Random House, 2006. (Originally published in German in 1922.)

Hickman, Larry A., ed., *Reading Dewey: Interpretations for a Postmodern Generation.* Bloomington: Indiana University Press, 1998.

Hickman, Larry A. *Pragmatism as Post-Postmodernism: Lessons from John Dewey.* New York: Fordham University Press, 2007.

Hillman, James. *The Dream And The Underworld.* New York: Harper and Row, 1979.

Hillman, James. *A Blue Fire: Selected Writings.* New York: Harper & Row, 1989.

Hillman, James. *Kinds of Power.* New York: Doubleday, 1995.

Holenstein, Elmar. *Roman Jakobson's Approach to Language: Phenomenological Structuralism.* Translated by Catherine Schelbert and Tarscisius Schelbert. Bloomington: Indiana University Press, 1976.

Husserl, Edmund. "The World of the Living Present and the Constitution of the Surrounding World that is the Outside of the Flesh." Translated by Bettina Bergo and revised by Leonard Lawler. In *Husserl at the Limits of Phenomenology.* Edited by Leonard Lawler and Bettina Bergo. Evanston, IL: Northwestern University Press, 2002.

Illich, Ivan. *Gender.* New York: Marion Boyers, 1983.

Illouz, Eva. *Saving the Modern Soul: Therapy, Emotions, and the Culture of Self-Help.* Berkeley: University of California Press, 2008.

Jacoby, Russell. *The End Of Utopia: Politics And Culture In An Age Of Apathy.* New York: Basic Books, 2000.

Jakobson, Roman. "Linguistics and Communication Theory." In *On Language*. Edited by Linda R. Waugh and Monique Monville-Burston. Cambridge, MA: Harvard University Press, 1990. Original work published in 1960.

Jakobson, Roman. *On Language*. Edited by Linda R. Waugh and Monique Monville-Burston. Cambridge, MA: Harvard University Press, 1990.

James, William. *The Principles of Psychology, Vol. 1.* New York: Dover Publications, 1950. Original work published in 1890.

Johnson, Galen. "Ontology and Painting: Eye and Mind." In *The Merleau-Ponty Aesthetics Reader.* Edited by Galen Johnson. Evanston, IL: Northwestern University Press, 1993.

Jung, Carl. "The Development of Personality." In *The Essential Jung.* Translated by R. F. C. Hull. Princeton: Bollingen, 1983. Original work composed in German and published in 1934.

———. "Nietzsche's Zarathustra: Notes of the Seminar Given in 1934–1939." In *Jung's Seminar on Nietzsche's Zarathustra.* Edited by James L. Jarrett. Princeton, N.J.: Bollingen, 1988).

———. *Jung on Alchemy*. Edited by Nathan Schwartz-Salant. Translated by R. F. C. Hull. Princeton, N.J. : Bollingen, 1995. (Original work written in German and published in 1946.)

———. *Psyche and Symbol.* Edited by Violet S. de Laszlo. Translated by R. F. C. Hull. Princeton, N.J.: Bollingen, 1991. (Original written in German and published in 1951.)

———. *Mysterium Coniunctionis: An Inquiry into the Separation and Synthesis of Psychic Opposites in Alchemy.* Translated by R. F. C. Hull. Princeton, N.J.: Bollingen, 1970. (Original written in German and published in 1955–1956.)

———. "Questions to Jung and His Answers." Transcript of an interview in Howard Littleton Philp, *Jung and the Problem of Evil.* London: Rockliff, 1958.

Justman, Stewart. *The Psychological Mystique.* Evanston, IL: Northwestern University Press, 1998.

Kandel, Eric. *Psychiatry, Psychoanalysis, and the New Biology Of Mind.* New York: American Psychiatric Publishing, 2005.

Kandel, Eric. *In Search of Memory: The Emergence of a New Science of Mind.* New York: W. W. Norton and Co., 2006.

Kerr, Michael E. and Murray Bowen, *Family Evaluation: An Approach Based on Bowen Theory.* New York: Norton, 1988.

Kerr, Michael E. "Chronic Anxiety and Defining a Self." *The Atlantic Monthly* 262 (September 1988): 35–58.

Kramer, Peter D. *Listening to Prozac: The Landmark Book About Antidepressants and the Remaking of the Self.* Revised Edition. New York: Penguin, 1997.

Kristeva, Julia. *In the Beginning Was Love: Psychoanalysis and Faith.* Translated by Arthur Goldhammer. New York: Columbia University Press, 1988.

———. *Black Sun: Depression and Melancholia.* Translated by Leon S. Roudiez. New York: Columbia University Press, 1989).

———. *Melanie Klein.* Translated by Ross Guberman. New York: Columbia University Press, 2004.

Lacan, Jacques. "The Mirror Stage as Formative of the Function of the I." *Écrits*: *A Selection.* Translated by Alan Sheridan. New York: W. W. Norton and Co., 1977.

———. *The Four Fundamental Concepts of Psychoanalysis.* Translated by Jacques-Alain Miller. New York: W.W. Norton & Co., 1978.

———. *The Language of the Self: The Function of Language in Psychoanalysis.* Translated by Anthony Wilden. Baltimore: Johns Hopkins University Press, 1968.

———. *The Seminar of Jacques Lacan, Book III: The Psychoses*. Translated by Russell Grigg. New York: W.W. Norton & Co., 1993.

Lakoff, George and Mark Johnson, *Philosophy in the Flesh: The Embodied Mind and Its Challenge to Western Thought.* New York: Basic Books, 1998.

Langsdorf, Lenore, and Andrew R. Smith, eds. *Recovering Pragmatism's Voice: The Classical Tradition, Rorty, and the Philosophy of Communication.* Albany: State University of New York Press, 1995.

Lanigan, Richard L. *Speaking and Semiology: Maurice Merleau-Ponty's Phenomenological Theory of Existential Communication.* The Hague: Mouton, 1972.

———. *Semiotic Phenomenology of Rhetoric: Eidetic Practice in Henry Grattan's Discourse on Tolerance.* Lanham, MD: University Press of America, 1984.

———. *Phenomenology of Communication: Merleau-Ponty's Thematics in Communicology and Semiology.* Pittsburgh: Duquesne University Press, 1988.

———. *The Human Science of Communicology: A Phenomenology of Discourse in Foucault and Merleau-Ponty.* Pittsburgh: Duquesne University Press, 1992.

———. "The Self in Semiotic Phenomenology: Consciousness as the Conjunction of Expression and Perception in Communicology." *The American Journal of Semiotics* 15 and 16, nos. 1–4 (2000): 91–111.

Lawlor, Leonard. "Becoming and Auto-Affection, Part 2: Who Are We?"*Graduate Faculty Philosophy Journal*30, no. 2 (2009): 219–37.

Ledoux, Joseph. *Synaptic Self: How Our Brains Become Who We Are.* New York: Penguin Books, 2003.

Levin, David Michael. *The Body's Recollection of Being: Phenomenological Psychology and the Deconstruction of Nihilism.* New York: Routledge and Kegan Paul, 1985.

Lévy-Bruhl, Lucien. *How Natives Think.* Translated by Lilian A. Clare. Princeton, N.J.: Princeton University Press, 1985. Original worked in French, published in 1910.

Lock, James. "Acting Out and the Narrative Function: Reconsidering Peter Blos's Concept of the Second Individuation Process," *American Journal of Psychotherapy* 48, no. 4, Fall (1995), 548–57.

Low, Douglas. *Merleau-Ponty's Last Vision: A Proposal for the Completion of*The Visible and the Invisible. Evanston, IL: Northwestern University Press, 2000.

MacDonald, John M. "The Threat to Kill." *American Journal of Psychiatry* 120 (1963): 125–30.

Macey, David. *The Lives of Michel Foucault.* New York: Pantheon, 1993.

Macke, Frank J. "Communication Left Speechless: A Critical Examination of the Evolution of Speech Communication as an Academic Discipline." *Communication Education* 40 (1991), 125–43.

———. "Quintilian's *Institutio Oratoria* and Postmodern Pedagogy." *The American Journal of Semiotics* 17, no. 1, Spring (2001): 192–93.

———. "Reading the Collaborative Language Systems Approach Phenomenologically." *The Journal of Systemic Therapies* 23, no. 1, Spring (2004): 53–66.

———. "Intrapersonal Communicology: Reflection, Reflexivity, and Relational Consciousness in Embodied Subjectivity." In *Communicology: The New Science of Embodied Discourse*, Edited by Deborah Eicher-Catt and Isaac Catt. Madison, NJ: Fairleigh Dickinson University Press, 2010.

McLuhan, Marshall. *Understanding Media: The Extensions of Man.* New York: McGraw-Hill, 1964.

Madison, Gary Brent. *The Phenomenology of Merleau-Ponty: A Search for the Limits of Consciousness.* Athens: Ohio University Press, 1981.

Mahler, Margaret S., Fred Pine, and Anni Bergman. *The Psychological Birth of the Human Infant: Symbiosis and Individuation.* New York: Basic Books, 1975.

Malinowski, B. "The Problem of Meaning in Primitive Languages." Published as a supplementary essay in C. K. Ogden and I. A. Richards, *The Meaning of Meaning* (pp. 296–336). New York: Harcourt Brace Jovanovich, 1989. Original work published in 1923.

Malone, Thomas Patrick, and Patrick Thomas Malone. *The Art of Intimacy.* New York: Simon & Schuster, 1987.

Mark, Tami L., Katharine R. Levit, Rosanna M. Coffey and others. *National Expenditures for Mental Health Services and Substance Abuse Treatment 1993-2003.* U.S. Department of Health and Human Services, Substance Abuse and Mental Health Services Administration, DHHS Publication No. SMA 07-4227, 2007.

Martin, Jay. *The Education of John Dewey: A Biography*. New York: Columbia University Press, 2002.
Mayock, Jessica Ann. "Borderlands of Psyche and Logos in Heraclitus: A Psychoanalytic Reading." PhD Diss., Stony Brook University, 2008.
Mead, George Herbert. *Selected Writings*. Edited by Andrew Reck. Chicago: University of Chicago Press, 1964.
Melchior-Bonnet, Sabine. *The Mirror: A History*. Translated by Katherine. H. Jewett. New York: Routledge, 2002.
Menand, Louis. *Pragmatism: A Reader*. New York: Vintage, 1997.
Merleau-Ponty, Maurice. *The Phenomenology of Perception*. Translated by Colin Smith. New York: Routledge, 1962.
———. *In Praise of Philosophy*. Translated by John Wild and James M. Edie. Evanston, IL: Northwestern University Press, 1963.
———. *The Structure of Behavior* . Trans Alden L. Fisher. Pittsburgh: Duquesne University Press, 1963.
———. "Eye and Mind." Translated by Carleton Dallery. In *The Primacy of Perception*. Edited by James M. Edie. Evanston, IL: Northwestern University Press, 1964.
———. *Signs*. Translated by Richard McCleary. Evanston, IL: Northwestern University Press, 1964.
———. *The Visible and the Invisible*. Edited by Claude Lefort. Translated by Alphonso Lingis. Evanston, IL: Northwestern University Press, 1968.
———. *Themes from the Lectures at the Collège de France, 1952-1960*. Translated by John O'Neill. Evanston, IL: Northwestern University Press, 1970.
———. *The Prose of the World*. Edited by Claude Lefort. Translated by John O'Neill. Evanston, IL: Northwestern University Press, 1973.
———. *Nature: Course Notes from the Collège de France*. Edited by Dominique Séglard. Translated by Robert Vallier. Evanston, IL: Northwestern University Press, 2003.
———. *The Phenomenology of Perception*. Translated by Donald A Landes. New York: Routledge, 2012.
Mills, John A. *Control: A History of Behavioral Psychology*. New York: New York University Press, 2000.
Moncrieff, Joanna. *The Myth of the Chemical Cure: A Critique of Psychiatric Drug Treatment*. New York: Palgrave Macmillan, 2008.
Moshman, David. *Adolescent Rationality and Development: Cognition, Morality, and Identity*, 3rd Edition. New York: Taylor and Francis, Psychology Press, 2011.
Nietzsche, Friedrich. *Thus Spoke Zarathustra: A Book for All and None*. Translated by Walter Kaufmann. New York: Penguin, 1954.
———. *Beyond Good and Evil: Prelude to a Philosophy of the Future*. Translated by Walter Kaufmann. New York: Vintage, 1966.
———. *The Gay Science: With a Prelude in Rhymes and an Appendix of Songs*. Translated by Walter Kaufmann. New York: Vintage, 1974.
———. *Human, All Too Human: A Book for Free Spirits*. Translated by Marion Faber and Stephen Lehmann. Lincoln: University of Nebraska Press, 1984.
———. *The Twilight of the Idols and The Anti-Christ: or How to Philosophize with a Hammer*. Translated by R. J. Hollingdale. New York: Penguin Classics, 1990. Original work published in 1889.
NIMH (National Institute of Mental Health). *Depression: A Treatable Illness*. Bethesda, MD: National Institutes of Health Publication, March, 2003.
Noë, Alva. *Out of Our Heads: Why You Are Not Your Brain and Other Lessons From The Biology of Consciousness*. New York: Hill and Wang; First Edition edition (February 2, 2010).
Noë, Alva. "Art and the Limits of Neuroscience." *New York Times*, 4 December 2011: The Stone (Opinion).
Nussbaum, Martha. *The Therapy of Desire: Theory and Practice in Hellenistic Ethics*. Princeton, NJ: Princeton University Press, 1994.

Oliver, Kelly. *Family Values: Subjects Between Nature and Culture*. New York: Routledge, 1995.
Onions, C. T., Editor. *Oxford Dictionary of English Etymology*. New York: Oxford University Press, 1966.
Oreskes, Naomi. *The Rejection of Continental Drift: Theory and Method in American Earth Science*. New York: Oxford University Press, 1999.
Pencak, William. "The Civil War Did Not Take Place: Presidential Address, 30 September 2000." *The American Journal of Semiotics* 17, no. 2, Summer (2001), 7–29.
Peters, John Durham. *Speaking into the Air: A History of the Idea of Communication*. Chicago: University of Chicago Press, 1999.
Piaget, Jean. *The Child's Conception of the World*. Translated by Joan and Andrew Tomlinson. Savage, MD: Littlefield Adams, 1951.
Plant, Bob. "Perhaps: Jacques Derrida and Pyrrhonian Scepticism." *Angelaki: Journal of the Theoretical Humanities* 11, no. 3, December (2006): 137.
Plato. *The Republic*. Translated by Desmond Lee. Baltimore, MD: Penguin, 1963.
Rajchman, John. *Truth and Eros: Foucault, Lacan, and the Question of Ethics*. New York: Routledge, 1991.
Richardson, Michael. *Georges Bataille*. New York: Routledge, 1994.
Reisman, John M. *A History of Clinical Psychology*, 2nd Edition. Bristol, PA: Hemisphere Publishing, 1991.
Roberts, David. *Nothing but History: Reconstruction and Extremity after Metaphysics*. Berkeley: University of California Press, 1995.
Roberts, Julian. *Logic of Reflection: German Philosophy in the Twentieth Century*. New Haven, CT: Yale University Press, 1992.
Rorty, Richard. *Consequences of Pragmatism: Essays 1972-1980*. Minneapolis: University of Minnesota Press, 1982.
Ruesch, Jurgen and Gregory Bateson. *Communication: The Social Matrix of Psychiatry*. New York: W. W. Norton, 1951.
Rybczyinski, Witold. *Waiting for the Weekend*. New York: Penguin, 1991.
Safran, Jeremy D. *Psychoanalysis and Psychoanalytic Therapies*. New York: American Psychological Association, 2012.
Safran, Jeremy D. and J. Christopher Muran. *Negotiating the Therapeutic Alliance: A Relational Treatment Guide*. New York: The Guilford Press, 2003.
Sallis, John. *Crossings: Nietzsche and the Space of Tragedy*. Chicago: University of Chicago Press, 1991.
Salzani, Carlo. "The Atrophy of Experience: Walter Benjamin and Boredom," *Critical Studies* 31, 2009: 131.
Sartre, Jean-Paul. *Situations*. Translated by Benita Eisler. New York: George Braziller, 1965.
Schmidt, Alfred. *History and Structure: An Essay on Hegelian-Marxist and Structuralist Theories of History*. Translation by Jeffrey Herf. Cambridge, MA: MIT Press, 1981.
Schnarch, David. *Constructing the Sexual Crucible: An Integration of Sexual and Marital Therapy*. New York: Norton, 1991.
Schnarch, David. *Passionate Marriage: Keeping Love and Intimacy Alive in Committed Relationships*. New York: Owl Books, 1997.
Schrag, Calvin. *Communicative Praxis and the Space of Subjectivity*. Bloomington: Indiana University Press, 1986.
Schwartz, Stephen Adam. "Everyman an *Übermensch*: The Culture of Cultural Studies." *SubStance* 21, no 1 (2000), 104–38.
Schwartz-Salant, Nathan. "Introduction." In Carl Jung, *Jung on Alchemy*. Edited by Nathan Schwartz-Salant. Princeton: Princeton University Press, 1995.
Sennett, Richard. *The Uses of Disorder: Personal Identity and City Life*. New York: W.W. Norton & Co., 1970.
Sennett, Richard. *The Corrosion of Character: The Personal Consequences of Work in the New Capitalism*. New York: W.W. Norton & Co., 1998.
Sennett, Richard. *Respect in a World of Inequality*. New York: W.W. Norton & Co., 2003.

Serres, Michel. *Angels: A Modern Myth.* Translated by Francis Cowper. New York: Flammarion, 1995.
Sextus Empiricus. *Outlines of Pyrrhonism.* Translated by R. G. Bury. Cambridge: Harvard University Press/Loeb Classical Library, 1993. (Initially published in English in 1933. Originally written circa 200 AD.)
Shannon, Claude E. and Warren Weaver. *The Mathematical Theory of Communication.* Urbana: The University of Illinois Press, 1949.
Shilling, Chris. *The Body and Social Theory*, 2nd Edition. Thousand Oaks, CA: Sage 2003.
Simmel, Georg. *The Sociology of Georg Simmel.* Edited and Translated by Kurt H. Wolff. New York: Free Press, 1950.
Simms, Eva-Maria. "Milk and Flesh: A Phenomenological Reflection on Infancy and Coexistence." *Journal of Phenomenological Psychology* 32, no. 1(2001): 22-40.
Simms, Eva-Maria. *The Child in the World: Embodiment, Time, and Language in Early Childhood.* Detroit, MI: Wayne State University Press, 2008.
Smith, Christian. *What Is a Person? Rethinking Humanity, Social Life, and the Moral Good From the Person Up.* Chicago: University Of Chicago Press, 2010.
Solan, Ronnie. "'Jointness' as Integration of Merging and Separateness in Object Relations and Narcissism." *The Psychoanalytic Study of the Child* 46 (1991): 337–52.
Spiegelberg, *Phenomenology in Psychology and Psychiatry: A Historical Introduction.* Evanston, IL: Northwestern University Press, 1972.
Sroufe, L. Alan. *Emotional Development: The Organization of Emotional Life in the Early Years.* New York: Cambridge University Press, 1996.
Stiegler, Bernard. *Acting Out.* Translated by David Barison, Daniel Ross, and Patrick Crogan. Stanford, CA: Stanford University Press, 2009.
Storey, John. "There's No Success Like Failure: Cultural Studies; Political Romance or Discipline?" *Journal of Communication Inquiry* 21, no. 2, Fall (1997): 98–109.
Turner, Bryan. *The Body and Society: Explorations in Social Theory,* 2nd Edition. Thousand Oaks, CA: Sage, 1996.
Turner, Victor. *Dramas, Fields, and Metaphors: Symbolic Action in Human Society.* Ithaca, NY: Cornell University Press, 1975.
Van den berg, J. H. *The Changing Nature of Man.* New York: Norton, 1961.
Vanatta, Seth. "Radical Empiricism and Husserlian Metaphysics." *The Pluralist* 2, no. 3, Fall (2007): 17–36.
Varela, Francisco J., Evan Thompson, and Eleanor Rosch. *The Embodied Mind: Cognitive Science and Human Experience.* Cambridge, MA: MIT Press, 1991.
Watzlawick, Paul, Janet Helmick Beavin, and Don D. Jackson. *Pragmatics of Human Communication: A Study of Interactional Patterns, Pathologies, and Paradoxes.* New York: Norton, 1967.
White, Hayden. "Foucault Decoded: Notes from Underground." *History and Theory* 12, no. 1 (1973): 23–54.
White, Hayden. *Tropics of Discourse: Essays in Cultural Criticism.* Baltimore: Johns Hopkins University Press, 1978.
White, Hayden. *The Content of the Form: Narrative Discourse and Historical Representation.* Baltimore: Johns Hopkins University Press, 1990.
Wild, John, and James M. Edie. "Translator's Preface." In Maurice Merleau-Ponty, *In Praise of Philosophy.* Translated by John Wild and James M. Edie. Evanston, IL: Northwestern University Press, 1963.
Williams, Forrest. "Translator's Preface." In Michel Foucault and Ludwig Binswanger, Dr*eam and Existence: A Special Issue.* Translated by Forrest Williams and Jacob Needleman. Edited by Keith Hoeller. *Review of Existential Psychology & Psychiatry* 19, no. 1 (1984–1985): 19-28.
———. "Adolescent Process and the Need for Personal Confrontation." *Pediatrics* 44, no. 5 (1969): 752–56.
———. *The Family and Individual Development.* London: Tavistock, 1965.
———. *The Child, the Family, and the Outside World,* 2nd Edition. Boston: Addison Wesley Publishing Company, 1992.

Wittgenstein, Ludwig. *Philosophical Investigations*. Translated by G. E. M. Anscombe. Edited by G. E. M. Ansombe and Rush Rhees (New York: Macmillan, 1953). Original work published in 1945.

Wyschogrod, Edith. *Crossover Queries: Dwelling with Negatives, Embodying Philosophy's Others.* New York: Fordham University Press, 2006.

Index

abduction, 78
Abel, 124–125
The Accursed Share (Bataille), 117
acting out, 214
acts, evil as, 105
Adam, 117
addiction, 183–184, 184
addressee, 75
addresser, 75
Adler, Mortimer, 209
adolescence, 26–27; cerebral cortex during, 198; duration of, 128–129; identity crisis emerging in, 182; Other in, 125–126; as sexual peak, 182
adolescent development, 123–128, 201, 213–214
adolescents: body of, 126; derangement represented by, 123; eroticism transitioned into by, 128; identity, 126, 128–131, 197–199; intimacy of, 126–128; love responsibility of, 134–135; as psychological refugees, 124; selfhood revaluation of, 126; shame revalued by, 129–130; struggle of, 125–126; transformations surprising, 123
adulthood, child as experienced in, 155
adults, 19, 121, 122–123, 125–126, 181–182
agency: as competence matter, 16; embodiment and, 179; faith in, 20–21; family influencing, 49; intimacy implying, 135–136
air, 141
alchemy, 97–98
Alcibiades (Plato), 178
alcohol, 183
algebra, 106
Also Sprach Zarathustra (Nietzsche), 26, 104, 159, 184
ambiguity, 222
angels, dance of, 115–118
Angels: A Modern Myth (Serres), 115
anima. See feminine energy
animal, communication as act of, 155–156
animosity, 27, 144, 147, 160
animus. See masculine energy
anthropology, 50–51, 86–87
anxiety, as ennui, 42
Archaeology (Foucault), 147
Archaeology of Knowledge (Foucault), 160
archetype, 144–148, 155–159
architecture, 148
archive, 144–148
Aristotle, 5, 158–159, 190
ars erotica. See human being beyond sexuality
artificial intelligence, 111
ataraxia. See unperturbedness
atrophy of experience, 40
attachment, 75–77, 213–214
Augenblick. See moment

automobiles, 21–22
Ayto, John, 103, 145
Ayto, Joseph, 110, 114

Bachelard, Gaston, 25, 77, 81–82, 87–94, 97, 98, 187, 188, 195, 196–197, 200–201, 202–203, 203
Barbin, Herculine, 86, 100–101, 142, 165
Barnhart, Robert K., 42
Bataille, Georges, 22, 27, 28, 89, 112, 117, 128, 130, 132, 134, 135, 136, 139–141, 141, 143, 149, 155–157, 159, 162, 168–169, 169–170, 172, 184, 211
Bateson, Gregory, 24, 41–42, 43, 44, 111, 180
bathroom, 62
Baudelaire, Charles, 40
Baudrillard, Jean, 37, 105, 107–108, 109, 116
Bauman, Zygmunt, 99
Beavin, Janet Helmick, 101n29
Beckett, Samuel, 39, 142
becoming, 194–195
bedwetting, 189, 203n9
Beings, 87, 98, 99, 135–136
beliefs, puerile, 155–159
Benjamin, Walter, 38, 39, 40
Binswanger, Ludwig, 191, 195, 200
Bion, Wilfred R., 14
biopower, 72–73
birth, 77, 96
Blanchot, Maurice, 11
blink, 94–95
blood, 113
Bloom, Harold, 112–113, 116
Blos, Peter, 126, 213–214
bodies, 215–218; of adolescents, 126; animosity in, 147; archetype building, 159; brains as part of, 83; as communication, 26, 89; communicative, 43–44, 139–142, 146, 146–147; comparative assessments of, 63; concept of, 83–84; as contingent, 84; cultural turn toward, 85–86; definition of, 82, 83–84; desire influencing, 63; as discrete, 211–212; as empirical fact, 65; as flesh, 45; image, 63–68; intersubjectivity and, 72–75; Law of Participation influencing, 153–154; Merleau-Ponty's concept of, 61; in Merleau-Ponty's work, 55–57; as nowhere, 100–101; as organic autonomy, 25; Other and, 65–68; persons inspiring, 157–158; phenomenology of, 165; phenomenology of consciousness grounded in, 4; as positivity, 140; problematic, 72–75, 81–82, 211; Self and, 5, 65–68; sexuality and, 163; sign of, 66; student, 62–63; surface of, 140; thematic, 81–82; thickness of, 84–85; as thing, 83–84; as thought, 100; transformation of, 130–131; water of, 96. *See also* embodiment
The Body and Social Theory (Shilling), 101n2
The Body and Society (Turner, B.), 101n2
Bok, Sissela, 121
borders, 189–190
Borges, Jorge Luis, 192
Bowen, Murray, 49, 179, 182
brains, 18, 83
breach, 149–150
Buber, Martin, 8, 11
Burroughs, William S., 192

Cabot, Richard, 31
Cain, 124–125
cameras, 194
Canetti, Elias, 154
Canguilhem, Georges, 87, 88
Caplan, Eric, 31–32
car, in mirror, 64
care of self. *See* self-care
Carmen, Taylor, 213
Cartesian, 24–25, 53–54, 57, 57–58, 60
Casey, Edward, 196–197
Cassirer, Ernst, 12, 37
Catholic Church, 170
cerebral cortex, 198
Cezanne, Paul, 92
change, 26–27
chiasm. *See* flesh
childhood, 122–123, 151, 163, 213
children, 19; adulthood, as experienced in, 155; adult transition of, 122–123, 125–126; *anima* and, 148–150; *animus* and, 148–150; bedwetting and, 189;

continence of, 189; disappointment of, 120–121; faith of, 155–159; falling of, 136; family owning, 50; fiction as world of, 154–155; as future, 151; gender of, 159–165; group identity for, 174; identity questions of, 174; inner, 152–153; innocence of, 164; morality and, 150–152; mother and, 52n48, 75–77; myth lived in by, 154; nothingness signified by, 149; parents and, 154–155, 180; problematic, 150–155; puerile beliefs and, 155–159; as savage, 164; throwness for, 134; as vicious, 164; violence and, 163–165; in we, 133–135
Chomsky, Noam, 105
Christianity, 147–148, 170–171, 175–176
church, 147–148
Cicero, 200
cigarettes, 167–169, 183
citizenship, 219, 219–220
civic responsibility, 219
Claiborne, Robert, 103, 110, 147
Clement of Rome, 147–148
client, therapist playing games with, 33
clinical depression, 129
Cogito, 211–212
cognitive science, limit of, 78
coincidence, 148
cold weather, 95
colleges, psychotherapy in, 32
color, 194–195
combinations, 76–77
comment, as lived experience product, 33
communications: as animal act, 155–156; bodies as, 26, 89; communication of, 144–145; definition of, 2, 89, 155–157; etymology of, 2, 17; ghost of, 107; information's difference with, 89; law of, 107–109, 110, 112; as love, 157; modalities of, 41–42, 43–44; model of, 210–211, 214–215, 221–222, 222n10; moment of, 156–157; narrative forms of, 2–3; person as unable to use, 101n29; as process, 210; reflection on, 1–2; studies, 209–210; theory, 210–211; threshold of, 18–24; as transgression, 136; utopia, 105
Communication: The Social Matrix of Psychiatry (Bateson and Ruesch), 41–42
communicative agency, 48–51
communicative body, 43–44, 139–142, 146, 146–147
communicative ecology, 41
communicative embodiment, as medium, 96–98
communicative experiences, 2, 3–4, 18–28, 44–48. *See also* fiction
communicative intimacy, 28
communicative relationship, unperturbedness of, 43
communicator, competent, 16
communicology, 1–3, 28, 40–42, 144, 177, 214, 221–222
communion, 85, 131–135, 182–184; flesh influenced by, 168–169; fleshly, 77–79; phatic, 68, 71, 77, 78; sacred, 13; as sacrifice, 170
communitas, 7–11
community, 157, 219
comparative assessments, 63
competence, agency as matter of, 16
competent communicator, 16
concern for glory, 168–169, 174–175
confidence (*pistis*), 155–159, 161–163
consciousness: body grounding, 4; contact limit of, 75; as context's limit, 75; as embodied, 220–221; images in, 192–193; intersubjectivity and, 48; line of, 187–190; neural theory of, 18; phenomenology of, 4; reason as, 8–9; soul as, 74; term as discipline of, 8; theory of, 18
Constructing the Sexual Crucible (Schnarch), 179
consuming beings, 99
contact, 25, 65–68, 69n37, 71, 75–78, 78. *See also* human erotic contact
containment, 189–190
context, 74–75, 75, 77–78, 79
continence, 189–193
continental drift, 189–193
contradictions, as resolvable, 11
conventionality, 222n8
Cool Hand Luke, 24
Copernican view of world, 60

courage, intimacy entailing, 79
Courtés, Joseph, 68, 77, 89, 109
covenants, relationships as, 4–5
crimes, 22, 119–123
criminality, 159
cross, 112–115
cultural communication, 44
cultural studies, 55, 61, 72
cultural turn, toward body, 85–86
culture, 18, 44, 57–61

Damasio, Anthony, 83
Damasio, Antonio, 99–100
dance, 77, 115–118
dancer, 113
Danziger, Kurt, 32, 209
death, 154, 157, 184
decadence, 168, 183–184
deception, 121–122
dehiscences, 38–39, 39, 44–45, 79
Deleuze, Gilles, 89, 143, 145
Demian (Hesse), 27, 124–125, 130–131
deontic modalities, 109
Department of Health and Human Services, U.S., 31
Department of Philosophy, 207–208, 209
depression, 78, 129
depth, as life, 67
derangement, adolescent representing, 123
Descartes, René, 18, 54, 56, 57–61, 59, 60, 83
Descombes, Vincent, 55, 59–60
desire, 63, 77, 133–135
devil, 26, 103–104, 116–117
Dewey, John, 4, 207–208, 209
diabolic, 103
diabolical, 112–115, 116–117
diábolos. *See* slander
dialogue, 29n21
Didi, 67
difference, 105, 108–109, 146
differentiation, 179–182
Dillon, Martin, 54, 56–57, 74–75, 75, 93
Dilthey, Wilhelm, 73
Dionysus, 115
The Dioptrics (Descartes), 56, 57
disappointment, 120–121
disciplinary apparatus (*dispositif*), 6, 22
discursive formations, 208
dispositif. *See* disciplinary apparatus
distance, 18–19, 23
doctrine of flesh, 28
document, 11–15
Dor, Joël, 66–67
double-binds, 180, 183
Dream and Existence (Binswanger), 191, 195
dreaming, 28, 189–193, 203
dreams, 98–101, 182–184, 188–189, 191, 195–197. *See also* images
Dreyfus, Hubert L., 72–73, 183
driving, 21–22
dryness, 95
dualism, 53–54, 57–58, 189

eating, 168
Eco, Umberto, 122
ecstasy, 26–27, 38–39, 99, 115, 150, 163, 182–184
Edie, James, 222
education, 207
ego ideals, 13, 193–194
ego identity, 197
eight stages of human development, 198–199
electronic messaging, 115–116
elements, 84–87, 87
Eliade, Mircea, 140
The Embodied Mind (Varela, Thompson, and Rosch), 101n2
embodiment, 3–7, 82–87, 98–99, 99–101, 143–144; agency and, 179; communicology following, 221–222; emergence of, 81–82; ennui and, 38–40; of human consciousness, 220–221; image withholding, 202; speech invoking, 142
"Emil Sinclair," 124–125, 130
emotion (*pathos*), 90, 161, 162
emotional connectedness, relational connectedness as, 5
emotional states, 33–34
empiricism, 9, 18, 29n12, 53–54, 221–222
Empiricus, Sextus, 35–36, 38
encounter, life as, 11
end (*telos*), 10
energy, 143–144. *See also* feminine energy; masculine energy

Enlightenment, 19
ennui, 38–40, 42
entertainment, therapy of, 40
enunciative sign, surface conflated with, 56–57
envelopment, 9–10
Epicurus, 35
episode, 10
equipollence, 36–37, 41
equivocation, 221–222
Erikson, Erik, 18, 28, 125, 126–127, 128, 129, 182, 197, 198–199, 202
eros. *See* love
eroticism, 112, 117, 128–131
ethical crimes, 22
ethics (*ethos*), 18–24, 155–159, 161, 178, 179, 182
Eve, 117
evil, 26, 103–104, 104–106, 109–112, 114, 119–120, 159
existential beginning, 77
existential embodiment, 84–87
experience, 9–11; of adolescent development, 123–128; atrophy of, 40; of flesh, 27; in Merleau-Ponty's work, 55–57; narrative structure providing means for, 4; reason rupturing, 8–9; risk and, 167–169. *See also* lived experience
expression, 75, 84–85, 146
expressive transgression, 72
exterior, 124, 126
extrafamilial love relationships, 202
"Eye and Mind" (Merleau-Ponty), 24–25, 53–59, 66, 92

face, in mirror, 62
faith, 20–21, 155–159
family, 6, 44–51, 180–181, 213
father, 120–121
fear, of intimacy, 50
fearless speech (*parrhesia*), 170–171, 177–179
feelings, as voice, 47
feminine energy (*anima*), 27, 144, 147, 148–150, 162, 163
fiction, 2–3, 11–15, 131–135, 154–155
Fink, Bruce, 132
first impressions, 145
flag, as upside down, 65
flesh (*chiasm*), 25–26, 54, 218; as abstract, 93–94; as alchemy, 97–98; as Being element, 87; body as, 45; communion influencing, 168–169; contact and, 75–77; course of, 98–101; decadence enlivening, 168; definition of, 82; doctrine of, 28; dream and, 98–101; as element, 87; experience of, 27; as expression, 84–85; as intersubjective plasma, 26, 82; intersubjectivity and, 90; as liquidity, 94; Merleau-Ponty on, 59; mind as sublimation of, 42; mirror and, 62–65; philosophy of, 50–51, 76, 85–86, 86–87, 100; of self, 24–25; as shame source, 50; as skin, 28, 85; as solid, 98; subjectivity as witness and apprentice of, 96–97; thought as sublimation of, 42; transformation influencing, 92–93
fleshly communion, 77–79
flight, 106, 107
flow, 96, 100–101
fluidity, 91, 91–92, 93–94. *See also* liquidity
force, 110–111
forgetfulness, 60, 61
Fóti, Véronique, 85
Foucault, Michel, 6, 11, 12, 27, 28, 32, 33, 34–35, 35, 38, 39, 40, 46, 49, 50, 56, 57, 71, 72, 73, 77, 85–86, 86, 87–94, 100, 114, 117–118, 135, 140, 141, 143, 145, 147, 148, 152, 159, 160, 163, 169, 170–171, 173, 174–175, 175–176, 177–179, 180, 183, 191, 195, 195–196, 196–197, 200, 201, 202–203, 208–209, 213, 215
freedom, 16–17, 23, 50, 169–171, 180
Freud, Sigmund, 86, 105, 120, 193, 197, 212–213
friends, 174
friendship, 45, 184
future, 9–10, 28, 151

game, 177–179
Geist. *See* mind
Geistliche therapeutic experience, 31–33
gender, 27–28, 142, 159–165
ghost, 64, 106, 107
gift, 78

giving, as sacrifice, 133
glory, 168–171, 172, 174–175, 175–176, 183–184
God, 130–131, 157
gods of creation, 163
Gogo, 67
government, 45–46
governmentality, 219–220
grandfather, 199
Greek culture, 178–179, 182
Greimas, Algirdas Julien, 68, 77, 89, 109
group, 44, 44–48, 111, 174, 219–220
Guattari, Félix, 89, 145
guests, 108
guilt, 50, 124

Habermas, Jürgen, 46
Hacking, Ian, 99–100
Halperin, David, 171
hands, laying of, 78
haunting, 20, 41, 107
healing, 35
Hegel, Georg Wilhelm Friedrich, 59–60, 217–218
Heidegger, Martin, 24, 40–41, 50, 59–60, 74, 133, 142, 158–159
Heraclitus, 195–196
hermaphrodite, 100–101
hermeneutics of desire, 77
Hermeneutics of Subjectivity (Foucault), 40
"Hermeneutics of the Subject" (Foucault), 34–35
Hesse, Herman, 27, 124–125, 130
heterotopia, 141
The Higher Education in America (Hutchins), 209
Hillman, James, 159, 199, 200
history, 160–161
History of Sexuality (Foucault), 28
The History of Sexuality (Foucault), 177
Hölderlin, Friedrich, 40–41
holding, dance and, 77
Holy Communion, 170
honor, 111
horizon of future, 10
human being, 4, 5, 77
human being beyond sexuality (*ars erotica*), 143–144
human development, 119–123, 198–199
human erotic contact, holding of, 90
humanism, 60
humanistic disciplines, 222
humanity, community of, 157
human sciences, 17
humidity, 94
humors, 94, 97–98
Husserl, Edmund, 45, 58, 59–60, 60, 73, 218
Hutchins, Robert Maynard, 209

ideal-ego, 193
identity: achievement of, 202–203; adolescent, 126, 128–131, 197–199; children's questions of, 174; crisis, 115, 182, 202; differentiation and, 179–182; dreaming influencing, 28; ego, 197; fiction of, 131–135; formation, 197–199; group, 174; image and, 197–200; intimacy testing, 127–128, 128; as intimate experience key, 131–135; love influencing, 164–165; in motion, 200; psychological boundaries and, 179–182; reverie influencing, 28; sexuality and, 179–182
Illouz, Eva, 32
image perception, phenomenology importance of, 56–57
images: of adolescent development, 201; archetype as, 146; body, 63–68; in consciousness, 192–193; definition of, 192; embodiment withholding of, 202; function of, 195; identity and, 197–200; imaginary in, 201; problem of, 192–194; psyche as hungry for, 200–201; still, 194; words' tension with, 191–192
Imaginary, 132, 201
imagining, 203
impossibility, 215
impossible being, 135–136
impulsivity, 212
incontinence, 190
individuated Self, 99
infants, 75–77
influence, 98
information, 89, 123–124
inner child, 152–153

innocence, of children, 164
insanity, 58
institution, 43–44, 44
interactions, things as, 89
inter-group communication. *See* cultural communication
interiority of self, 19
interpersonal communication, 44, 94–96
interpersonal communicative experiences, 44–48
interpersonal contact. *See* contact
intersubjective plasma, flesh as, 26, 82
intersubjectivity, 48, 72–75, 86, 90, 97, 217–218, 221–222
intimacy, 131–135; of adolescents, 126–128; agency implied by, 135–136; capacity for, 48; as contact matter, 78; courage entailed by, 79; as death sentence, 92; definition of, 127; as dehiscence, 44–45, 79; as desire imagining, 79; eroticism lifeworld and, 128–131; in family, 46–47; fear of, 50; game, 127–128; as gift, 78; glory and, 169–171; identity tested by, 127–128, 128; interpersonal communication and, 94–96; love concept satisfied by, 171–172; moisture of, 94–96; problematic of, 174; self and, 173–174; self-care essentiality of, 173; sexuality and, 171–173; strategy and, 173–174; as transformation commitment, 92–93; in water, 93
intolerable deeds, 104–105
intrapersonal communication, 41–42, 44

Jackson, Don D., 101n29
Jakobson, Roman, 25, 37, 67–68, 71, 75–76, 77, 211
James, William, 100, 197
Jesus Christ, 175
Johnson, Galen, 54
Johnson, Mark, 101n2
Jung, Carl, 27, 140, 144–145, 146, 147–148, 155, 156, 158, 159, 161, 162–163
Justman, Stewart, 34

killing, 105
kinetic energy, 112
Kinsey, Alfred, 171
Klein, Melanie, 212–213
knowledge, 37, 117–118, 163
Kojève, Alexandre, 59, 87–88
Kristeva, Julian, 6

Lacan, Jacques, 41, 59–60, 66–67, 119, 120–121, 132, 193, 194, 212–213
Laches (Plato), 178
language, 18; as domain unto itself, 55; as flat, 41; moral problem of, 105–106; person speaking, 149; as positivism, 145–146; problematic of, 176; as surface phenomenon, 56–57; temporality and, 41
Lanigan, Richard, 3–4, 37, 62–63, 75, 78, 85, 100, 142, 144, 145, 145–146, 153, 154, 222n8
last supper, 170
Lawler, Leonard, 78
law of communication, 107–109, 110, 112
Law of Participation, 153–154
legitimation crisis, 46
Levin, David Michael, 50
Lévy-Bruhl, Lucien, 153–154, 158
liberation, violence as, 111
libidinal economy, 201
lies, 121–122, 123–128, 220
lifeworld, 3–4, 128–131
linguistic turn, 73
liquidity, 91, 91–93, 94–95, 96, 98, 100–101
literacy, 19
lived experience (*vécu*), 14–15, 33, 215–216, 218, 219
lives, 11, 13, 39–40, 65–66, 67, 99
Lock, James, 214
Locke, John, 7
"*L'Oeil et l'esprit*" (Merleau-Ponty). *See* "Eye and Mind"
logic (*logos*), 73, 79, 90, 111, 161, 162, 177–179
The Logic of the Cultural Sciences (Cassirer), 37
logos. *See* logic
love (*eros*), 14, 89–90, 113, 134–135, 139–140, 157, 164–165, 171–172
Low, Douglas, 55, 76
lying, 121–122, 123–128, 220

Lying: Moral Choices in Public and Private Life (Bok), 121
Lyotard, Jean-François, 201

Macey, David, 88
machine, ghost separated from, 64
Madison, Gary, 60, 100, 173
magic, 34
Mahler, Margaret, 76
major depressive disorder, 78
Malinowski, B., 68, 77, 78
man, as sign, 115
many-to-many communication. *See* cultural communication
mark, as sign, 125
marriages, 172–173
Martin, Jay, 209
masculine energy (*animus*), 27, 144, 147, 148–150, 159–160, 162
masks, 124, 126
das Masslose. *See* spiritual excess
masters, 34
mastery, 34, 178, 190
masturbation, 204n11
"Max Demian," 124–125, 130–131
McDonald Triad, 203n9
McLuhan, Marshall, 191, 194
Mead, George Herbert, 5, 131, 190, 193, 207–208, 209
meaningful energy, 143–144
mechanic, 64
medical care. *See therapeuein*
meditation, on modalities, 60–61
memory, 27–28, 107
mental states, 33–34
Merleau-Ponty, Maurice, 3–5, 9–10, 24–25, 25–26, 27, 28, 37, 42, 43, 47–48, 50, 50–51, 53–61, 64, 67, 68, 71, 72–75, 73–74, 76, 81–82, 84–87, 87–94, 97–98, 98, 100, 106, 107–108, 132, 146–147, 168, 173, 179, 193, 194, 194–195, 201, 215–216, 217, 218, 222
messages, 115–116
"The Metropolis and Mental Life" (Simmel), 39–40
metropolitan life, 39–40
Mill, John Stuart, 73
Milton, John, 116
mind (*Geist*), 20, 82–84; as animus, 147; communicology of, 40–42; dream of, 98–101; as flesh sublimation, 42; patriotic, 65; prelogical, 153; Western, 105, 105–106
mirror, 53–54, 56, 57, 61, 62–65, 66
mistake, 79
modalities, 41–42, 43–44, 60–61, 109
modernity, 31–33, 162, 165
moisture, of intimacy, 94–96
moments (*Augenblick*), 94–95, 99, 156–157, 184
monument, 11–15
morality, 112, 150–152
mother, child and, 52n48, 75–77
motility of psyche, 47–48
movement, of group logic, 111
mysterious conjunction, 158
myth, 76–77, 148, 154, 159, 163, 200

Name of Father, 120–121
Narcissus, 66, 193, 196
narrative, 5, 6, 7–15, 20
narrative consciousness, 28
narrative of self, 3–7
narrative projections, saturation of, 15–17
narrative structure, experience means provided by, 4
National Communication Association, 1–2
nature, 60, 88
neural theory of consciousness, 18
neuroscience, 18
neurosis, 42
new ontology, 55, 55–56
Nichomachean Ethics (Aristotle), 190
Nietzsche, Friedrich, 23, 26, 74, 104, 113, 113–114, 122, 124, 143, 159, 169, 184, 188, 194, 201
Noë, Alva, 18
nonslavery, 178, 180
nothingness, 22, 149
Nussbaum, Martha, 24, 29n21, 35, 47

objective spirit, thought situated in, 73
object perception, 9
Oedipal struggle, 120
Oedipus complex, 197
Oliver, Kelly, 164–165
ontology, new, 55, 55–56

The Order of Things (Foucault), 148, 152, 159–160, 171, 208–209
Orpheus complex, 197
Other, 18–21, 65–68, 108–109, 125–126, 156
Otherness, as difference, 105
overman, 114
over-ness (*Über*), 114–115

Palo Alto Group, 2
"Pantope," 115
parable, 26
parabola, speech of, 106–108
parabolical, 112–115
parents, children and, 154–155, 180
parole. *See* speech
parole parlante. *See* speech speaking
parole parlée. *See* speech spoken
parrhesia. *See* fearless speech
partitions, 18, 19–20
passion. *See* emotion
past, 9–10
pathos. *See* emotion
patriotic mind, 65
Peirce, Charles Sanders, 78
perception, 55–57, 67, 75, 95–96, 146, 194–195, 212
performance, 105, 120
persona, 150
personality, 5
personhood, instability of, 11–12
persons: body inspired by, 157–158; communication inability of, 101n29; definition of, 11–12; language spoken by, 149; in mirror, 57; as projection, 14; as Prospero, 14; relationships defining, 13; rules followed by, 149
persuasion, 161–162
Peters, John Durham, 216, 216–218, 219, 221
phatic communion, 68, 71, 77, 78
phatic function, 67–68, 75–76, 77, 78
phenomenology, 4, 7–11, 56–57, 165
Phenomenology of Communication (Lanigan), 222n8
phenomenology of consciousness, 4
The Phenomenology of Perception (Merleau-Ponty), 58, 59, 74, 84, 85, 107–108, 173, 193, 194–195, 217
Phenomenology of Spirit (Hegel), 217–218
philosophy, 33–37, 50–51, 76, 85–86, 86–87, 100, 207–208, 209
Philosophy in the Flesh (Lakoff, and Johnson, Mark), 101n2
"Pia," 115
Piaget, Jean, 122
pistis. *See* confidence
Plant, Bob, 36
Plato, 34, 178, 195–196
Platonism, 114
pleasure, 40, 49–50
poetic humors, 97–98
The Poetics of Reverie (Bachelard), 195
poison, gift as, 78
Porché, François, 40
positivism, language as, 145–146
positivity, 140
post-Cartesianism, post-modernism as affirmation of, 61
post-confessional mind, 20
postmodern cultural theory, 72–75
post-modernism, as post-Cartesianism affirmation, 61
power, will to, 23, 129–130, 133–135, 169
Pragmatics of Human Communication (Watzlawick, Beavin, and Jackson), 101n29
pragmatism, 207–208, 209
pragmatists, 208
precept, as signification agent, 57
"Préface à la transgression" (Foucault), 140
prelogical mind, 153
prepositions, 112
present, 9–10
projections, person as, 14
promise, terms satisfied by, 8
proof. *See* confidence
The Prose of the World (Merleau-Ponty), 59
Prospero, 14
psyche, 47–48, 51n1, 200–201
psychiatric power, 33
psychoanalysis, 33, 86–87
psychological boundaries, 179–182
psychological refugees, adolescents as, 124
psychological relationships, self in, 15–16
psychologism, 73

psychology, 51n1, 73, 207–208
psychotherapy, 31–33
puberty, 198
public relations, 158
puerile beliefs, 155–159
Pyrrhonian skepticism, 35–39, 51n20
Pyrrho of Elis, 35

Rabinow, Paul, 72–73, 183
racism, 108–109
Rajchman, John, 176
rape (*viol*), 111–112
rationalism, as masculine energy myth, 159–160
rationality, 161, 189
reason, 8–9
recognition, of body image, 66–67
reflections, 56, 65–68
reflective surface, as sign, 57
Reformation, 20
rejection, 126, 127
relational connectedness, as emotional connectedness, 5
relational connections, 6
relationality, 3–7
relational meaning, experience of, 9–11
relationships, 4–6, 7–8, 11, 13, 15–16, 131–132, 160, 202, 220
religious moments, 156
repression, 23
repressive hypothesis, 72, 177
The Republic (Plato), 195–196
Respect in a World of Inequality (Sennett), 79
Reusch, Jurgen, 24
reverie, 28
Rg Veda, 163
rhetoric, 29n21
Rhetoric (Aristotle), 5, 158–159
Richardson, Michael, 128
risk, experience and, 167–169
river, 100–101
Roberts, Julian, 73
role, 11, 120
Rosch, Eleanor, 101n2
Ruesch, Jurgen, 41–42, 43, 44, 111
rules, 6, 149, 149–150, 183
ruptures, 95–96, 149–150

sacred communion, 13
sacrifice, 133, 134–135, 170
Sallis, John, 114, 115
Salzani, Carlo, 39–40, 40
Sartre, Jean-Paul, 55, 59–60, 74, 87, 88
Satan, 116–117
savoir. *See* useless knowledge
Schnarch, David, 48, 92, 93, 179–180, 182
Schrag, Calvin, 90
sciences, 17, 73, 78
Second Epistle, 147–148
seeing, of Cartesian body, 57
Seinfeld, 204n11
self-care, 40, 50, 135, 169, 173, 174–179
self-control, 19
selfhoods, 4–5, 15–17, 20, 34, 126, 189
self-mastery, 34
self-perception, constancy in, 63–65
self-renunciation, 49, 49–50
Selves: appearance of, 12; body and, 5, 65–68; disappearance of, 12; emergence of, 4–5; flesh of, 24–25; habituation of, 64; haunting of, 41; human being possessing, 5; image of, 15–16; individuated, 99; instability of, 15–16; interiority of, 19; intimacy and, 173–174; narrative of, 3–7; performance of, 15–16; in psychological relationships, 15–16; self-care and, 174–176; sexuality and, 174–176; as signs, 25; stability of, 5; strategy and, 173–174; terms of, 18–21
semantic prepositions, 112
Semiological Reductionism (Dillon), 56–57
Semiotics and Language (Greimas and Courtés), 68
semiotic violence, 109–112
Sennett, Richard, 79
Serres, Michel, 115
sexuality, 86, 163–165, 171–173, 174–176, 179–183, 220
shame, 129–131
Shannon, Claude, 210–211, 213, 214–215, 221–222
Shilling, Chris, 101n2
signification, precept as agent of, 57
signs, 25, 55–57, 66, 95, 115, 125, 163
Signs (Merleau-Ponty), 54
Simmel, Georg, 39–40, 45

Simms, Eva, 19, 20, 21
Simms, Eva-Maria, 77
Simon, Paul, 76
sin, 119–123
skeptic, 42
skepticism, Pyrrhonian, 35–39
skin, flesh as, 28, 85
slander (*diábolos*), 103
sleep, wakefulness as opposition to, 187
Smith, Adam, 79
Smith, Christian, 11–12
smoking, 167–169, 169, 174, 177, 182, 183–184, 184
social contract, 7
social relations, game logic of, 177–179
social sciences, limitations of, 1–3
Socrates, 177
solipsism, 54, 58–59
son, 120
soul, 74
space of intersubjectivity, 90
speaking, freedom and, 169–171
Speaking and Semiology (Lanigan), 3–4
Speaking into the Air: A History of the Idea of Communication (Peters), 216, 216–218, 221
speech (*parole*), 26, 103–104, 106–108, 109–112, 116–117, 142, 182–183. *See also* fearless speech
Speech Communication Association, 1–2
speech speaking (*parole parlante*), 106, 107–108, 146–147
speech spoken (*parole parlée*), 106, 107–108, 109, 111, 146–147
Spinoza, Baruch, 83
spiritual excess (*das Masslose*), 114
spleen, 40
statements, communicative power of, 57
stereotype, 162
Stiegler, Bernard, 2, 131, 134, 214
still images, 194
story arc, 4
strategy, 173–174
stream of thought, 100
structure, 6, 7–11
The Structure of Behavior (Merleau-Ponty), 60
struggle, 120, 125–126
students, 62–63
subjectivity, as flesh's witness and apprentice, 96–97
surface, 56–57, 140, 143–144, 149–150
surface tension, 141–142, 143–144, 161
symbolic order, 119
sympathy, 79
systemic differences, 43–44
systemic transformation, institution as house of, 43–44

taboos, 22–23, 128, 168
talk, 218–219
technocratic empiricism, 9, 18, 29n12, 221–222
telos. *See* end
temporality, 9–10, 41
terminus, 11–15
terms, 6–11, 18–21, 82–83
terror, 108–109
terrorism, 91, 109–112
text, 74–75, 75
theory, 18, 208, 210–211
therapeuein (medical care), 35
therapist, client playing games with, 33
therapy, 33–37, 40, 47–48
The Therapy of Desire (Nussbaum), 24, 35
thickness, 84–85, 88–94
things, 83–84, 89, 217
thinking, 42, 56
Thompson, Evan, 101n2
thought, 42, 57–61, 73, 100, 152
three Hs, 59–60
threshold of communication, as ethics reconceptualization, 18–24
thrown, 112–113
thrownness, 134
Thus Spoke Zarathustra (Nietzsche), 113, 113–114
tobacco, 169
toddlers, 136
traffic, 21–22
tragedies, 65–66, 66
tragedy, 6–7
transformations, 92–93, 123, 130–131
transgression, 18–24, 72, 128, 136
The Transparency of Evil (Baudrillard), 105
travel, 116
tribes, 159

truth, 20, 86
Tufts, James, 209
Turner, Bryan, 101n2
Turner, Victor, 8–9
Twilight of the Idols (Nietzsche), 23

Über. See over-ness
undergraduate students, 62–63
universities, psychotherapy in, 32
University of Chicago, 207–208, 209
unperturbedness (*ataraxia*), 35–36, 38, 43, 47–48
unspoken rules, 183
untold narrative, 20
useless knowledge (*savoir*), 117–118
utopia, 105

vanishing point, 7–11
vapors, 94
Varela, Francisco J., 101n2
vécu. See lived experience
vice, 164, 183
victory, 111
viol. See rape
violence, 105, 109–112, 110, 163–165
virtue, 158–159
The Visible and the Invisible (Merleau-Ponty), 54, 55, 58, 59, 60, 65, 81, 84–85, 85, 88, 100
vision, 54, 58, 66, 94–95
voice, feelings as, 47

Waiting for Godot (Beckett), 39, 67
wakefulness, sleep as opposition to, 187
war on terror, 91
warrior, 159
Was Heisst Denken? (Heidegger), 40–41, 133
water, 92–93, 96, 98
Water and Dreams (Bachelard), 196
Watzlawick, Paul, 2, 101n29
we, 133–135, 135
Weaver, Warren, 210–211, 213, 214–215, 221–222
Western mind, 105, 105–106
Wild, John, 222
Williams, Forrest, 200
will to power, 23, 129–130, 133–135, 169
Will to Power (Nietzsche), 143
Winnicott, Donald, 125–126, 180
Wittgenstein, Ludwig, 149
words, 7–11, 191, 191–192
world, 60, 75
writing, 56, 203
Wyschogrod, Edith, 197

young adults, sexuality explored by, 181–182

"Zarathustra," 114, 115
Zendavesta, 163

CPSIA information can be obtained at www.ICGtesting.com
Printed in the USA
BVOW05*1327151214

379045BV00002B/2/P

9 781611 475487